© 1974 R. Charles Bryfogle

All rights reserved

Printed in Canada

Published simultaneously in U.S.A.

This publication, or parts thereof, may not be reproduced in any form by photographic, electrostatic, mechanical, or any other method, for any use, including information storage and retrieval, without written permission from the publisher.

ISBN 0-88874-003-4

Printed and bound in Canada by
T. H. Best Printing Company Limited, Don Mills, Ontario

To Bernard Silberman, who introduced me to the city and whose regimen taught me the meaning of scholarship.

Table of Contents

The complex framework outlined below was devised as a tool for easy selection by the reader. Although some works defy categorization, most fit into either the "general works" category under each heading, sub heading, or under more specialized headings.

The placing of a work in particular was determined by its primary content. As will be noted in a perusal of the reviews, many works may cover a wide field, but center upon one particular thrust. This emphasis determined location, irrespective of title.

It is the assumption of the compiler that the user will desire easily understandable divisions to assist in the selection of references for particular needs. Where works spread over more than one distinct category, secondary reference is indicated in the appropriate sections.

This more detailed categorization was established as the framework so as to avoid the necessity of a subject index, a rather cumbersome device for a listing of so many books.

PART ONE

    INTRODUCTION

1		BASIC WORKS IN THE STUDY OF URBANIZATION	page 1
	1.1	Basic Interdisciplinary Works	1
	1.2	Basic Discipline-Oriented References	7
	1.3	Bibliographies, Indexes and Abstracts	11
2		URBAN HISTORY	12
	2.1	General Works	12
	2.2	Ancient Cities	18
	2.3	Classical (Greek and Roman) Cities	20
	2.4	Medieval Cities	22
	2.45	Byzantium and The Muslim World 600-1600 A.D.	23
	2.5	Renaissance and Baroque Cities	24
	2.6	Nineteenth Century and Industrial Cities	25
	2.7	Cities In Pre-European Asia and Africa	28
	2.8	Cities In Pre-Columbian America	28

3		PLANNING I: URBANIZATION AS PLANNING page	29
	3.1	General Works	29
	3.2	Regional Planning	45
	3.21	Urbanization in Asia, Africa, and Latin America	48
	3.22	Urbanization in The Communist World	51
	3.3	Urban Sprawl and Suburbia	51
	3.4	Major Metropolitan Areas	52
	3.5	Urban Futures	60
	3.6	Urban Theorists	66
	3.7	Specific Techniques of Field Study	68
	3.71	Urban Models	69
	3.8	Urban Renewal and Renovation	69
4		PLANNING II: CITIES AS ARCHITECTURE	71
	4.1	General Works	71
	4.2	Historical Architecture	75
	4.3	Architects of The City	77
	4.4	Housing	77
	4.5	Vernacular Architecture	78
	4.6	Urban Design	79
5		URBAN TRANSPORTATION	80
	5.1	General Works	80
	5.2	Specific Studies or Technical Works	83
6		THE CITY AS A HUMAN PROCESS	85
	6.1	General Works	85
	6.11	General Texts in Sociology	91
	6.2	Specific Studies on Urban Man	92
	6.21	Urban Societies in Asia, Africa, and Latin America	96
	6.22	Urban Societies in The Communist World	97
	6.3	Social Psychology and Environmental Design	97
	6.4	Urban Political Systems	99
	6.41	Urban Law	105
	6.5	Urban Anthropology	105
	6.6	Urban Economics	106
7		URBAN GEOGRAPHY: THE MORPHOLOGY OF THE CITY	109
	7.1	General Works	109
	7.2	Historical Geography	113
	7.3	Industrial Geography	113
8		URBAN ENVIRONMENT AND URBAN ECOLOGY	115
	8.1	General Works	115
	8.2	Specific Studies	118
9		URBAN DEMOGRAPHICS: POPULATION	119
	9.1	General Works	119
	9.2	Historical Demographics	120
	9.3	Technical Demographics	121

10		CYBERNETICS AND URBAN SOCIETY	page 122
	10.1	General Works	122
	10.2	Specific Studies on Technology in Urban Systems	125
11		MISCELLANEOUS	128
	11.1	Illustrative Materials	128
	11.2	Compendia, Statistical Materials	129
12		PERIODICALS AND JOURNALS	130
	12.1	General Use and Technical Professional Sources	131
13		RELATED LITERATURE AND RESOURCES	132
	13.1	In The Natural Sciences	132
	13.2	In Science Fiction	133
	13.3	In Philosophical and Utopian Literature	136
	13.4	In The Arts and Humanities	138
14		MODULAR MATERIALS	140
	14.1	Major Modular Series	140
	14.2	Minor Modular Series	143

PART TWO

		INTRODUCTION	145
15		UNBOUND PRINT MATERIALS AND MAPS	147
	15.1	Reprints and Pamphlets	147
	15.2	Maps and Visual Aids	165
	15.3	Sources of Unbound Print Materials and Local Resources	166
16		AUDIO-VISUAL MATERIALS	168
	16.1	An Introductory Comment	168
	16.2	A Note About Films on Urbanization	168
	16.3	Slides and Filmstrips	169
	16.4	Filmloops	210
	16.5	Videotapes	212
	16.6	Records and Audiotapes	214
	16.7	Overhead Transparencies	217
17		SIMULATIONS AND MULTI-MEDIA KITS	221
	17.1	Books on Simulations	221
	17.2	Simulation and Multi-Media Kits	222
	Addenda	PART ONE	231
	Addenda	PART TWO	281

APPENDICES

1	Book Source Guide	294
2	Book Publishers and Distributors List	301
3	Non-Bound Print and Audio-Visual Publishers and Distributors List	307
4	Author-Title Index	309

Preface

Civilization began with the city and is maintained within cities. And yet, the city has received little more than cursory investigation throughout most of the history of civilization. Until the 19th Century, only two periods are noticeable for their attentions to cities. The city-states of classical Greece and the Italian Renaissance attracted not only intellectual examination, but were also magnets for strong loyalties. Aristocrats and commoners shared a feeling for their city which is visible today. Other epochs, from Mesopotamia through the Middle Ages in Europe, are noticeably lacking in evidence of a strong identity with cities. In fact, the opposite, an anti-urban or non-urban mood comes across in much of what little is commented upon about cities. Most often, the city is not remarked upon at all. It is seemingly neglected, apparently having too little an emotional or visible impact to warrant mention, much less observation, study or analysis.

In Europe the city became the focus of regrowth during the later Middle Ages and later (1200-1750 A.D.). But it was not until well into the middle phase of the industrial revolution that concern and analysis of the urban condition sprang forth. As the industrial city spread outward to engulf vast populations and hitherto rural space, the city, its character and condition, became increasingly important. In fact, as can be seen by dating the literature available, most of the works written are no older than man's use of the atom and computer. The city, as a subject of massive concern, or even awareness, is no more than a decade or two old. Little wonder that so much has been written that is so contradictory. Of course, a few older or out of print books will be noted, but these are relatively few in number. The vast preponderance of works on the city are recent. Being a new area of concern, there is no agreed-upon limit as to what constitutes "urban" studies--unless the entire spectrum of human knowledge and awareness is included. In consequence, books included in this bibliography cover the full spectrum of human endeavor. The user of this bibliography is therefore encouraged to examine all of the material included, and not just the "traditional" areas of study.

But what is "urban?" An examination of the term, as it is used today, shows marked variations in use. For the purpose of this work, "urban" will be defined as

1. of, in constituting, or comprising a city or town.
2. characteristic of the city as distinguished from the country; citified. Opposed to *rural*.*

---

*From *Webster's New World Dictionary Of The American Language*. College Edition. Cleveland and New York: The World Publishing Company, 1962. p. 1602. Similar definitions are to be found in the *Shorter Oxford English Dictionary* (1934) and the *American Heritage Dictionary Of The English Language* (1969).

The term "urban" has also come to be used as a definition of particular social problems which actually cut across the meanings of terms, encompassing far more than the city, its problems or environment. The most notable example is in the United States where the term has become synonymous with the conditions and problems of the minority peoples who make their home in the city. No where in this bibliography will "urban" be used with this connotation. In fact, books reviewed have been exclusively selected and rated on the basis of content relating to the city. Those relating to the American concern of minority conditions alone have been excluded as being outside the scope of urbanization because they deal with problems which exist irrespective of locale, be it urban or rural.

The minority problem is interpreted by the editor as being a cultural, social, economic, and political situation, rather than one which is directly a result of the urban process. Like many other human tragedies, this one has been spotlighted on the urban stage, but urban problems are not the sum total of minority problems, or vice versa. Unfortunately, society often finds it easiest to cope by oversimplifying a series of vastly complex situations. The editor does not wish to contribute to this fallacy.

Excluded from this selection of more than 1200 books are titles that are so specialized or technical that their usefulness is limited to that of professional reference. At the other end of the spectrum, works that are "patently" substandard efforts to sell pulp on the city have also been left out. Reports and other non-bound or audio-visual materials are reviewed in Part Two of this work. This bibliography is an attempt to provide the user with a comprehensive selection of books on the city--books chosen on the basis of their usefulness to the general reader, be he adult or student. As will be noted in perusal of the annotated selections, many of the works listed have been set aside as being sufficiently specialized, technical, or sophisticated to limit their use for other than the professional planner or academician. Two other bibliographies can be consulted for listings of professional sources (reviewed in section 1.3).

Organization and Annotation of References: In Part One, four categories of books are listed under 14 headings. In Part Two, materials are listed under three headings without a rating category. Each heading, in turn, is subdivided into whatever number of sections is necessary to sufficiently separate the works listed into identifiable groupings. In any case, most sections contain one or more works which have sufficient bibliographical listings to provide the user with as much further depth as might be required.

The selected references come from a wide range of sources. While many were noted by the author in the normal course of activities associated with urban studies curriculum and consultative work, a good number were gleaned from sources such as bibliographies included in books reviewed and journals, notably the American Institute of Planners Journal and the American Society of Planning Officials newsletter, both of which provide extensive listings on new books. Not a few were recommended by colleagues. Finally, a number of books were submitted for review following correspondence with publishers in Canada, the U.S., and Europe. Understandably, this list is not complete and, in fact, the task of review continues.

Selection was initially by title. As such, a good number of books were requested for review that have terms in their titles which suggest an urban studies orientation. Many did not have urban content and are, without prejudice, noted accordingly. As will also be noted, quite a few proved to be repetitive or superficial and are superseded by other works of more substantial content.

Materials written in a foreign language have largely been excluded. Therefore, although the focus of urban experience, problems, and prospects has been worldwide, a North American or English emphasis has resulted, but only as a consequence of a selection of books available in English.

The bibliographic information is for the specific work reviewed. In particular, the date of publication reflects the edition reviewed. Of course, this can change with the new editions becoming available and older ones going out of print.

The review of each work has included critical comment on content and usefulness. The annotation attempts to provide the user with a feeling for the content rather than an exhaustive listing of articles or chapter headings. In any case, a mere listing of content would still not provide the reader with substantive information on the item's level of suitability. Therefore, the compiler has risked possible criticism by including critical evaluations on the works reviewed. This was undertaken in an effort to provide the reader with a feel for the books or materials available while striving for objectivity. Hopefully, it has been achieved. It is assumed that the reader can, from the capsule provided, select titles that might be of value to the needs at hand. It is further assumed that the reader will only use this listing for what it is--a collection of titles relating to urbanization, a compilation with sufficient information to allow the reader to carry out personal research or selection, and, in doing so, personal evaluation of the works available.

The titles reviewed are divided into four categories. Those with the rating of (1) are recommended as being of value for use in a personal library. These works, of particular note, fulfill several requirements--being comprehensive, up to date, and interesting to read. Other works, of value for study and research, are listed under the category of (2). As will be noted, many of these works provide the substantive background for all of the sections listed. With few exceptions, most of these works are more suitable for location in a university, school, or public library rather than upon home shelves. It should be pointed out, however, that individuals wishing to explore an area in depth might well find many of these books to be valuable additions to their personal libraries.

Works that are too sophisticated, technical, or specialized for other than the professional or academician, are designated by the number (3). Please note that this categorization does not detract from the scholastic or academic value of the work listed.

Books listed with a rating of (4) are commented on briefly, namely that the title is out of print, dated in its content, not relevant (although the title might sugsest that it is), not sufficiently urban in its content (under 25% of the text), or is superseded by other books of far more substantial content.

Included as well is the binding available for each work reviewed. "HB" is used to indicate a hard board or conventional cloth cover. "PB" indicates those works which have a flexible, pliable cover. Most of these will, of course, be the conventional paper covers.

In most cases, the books reviewed drop comfortably into the category where they are listed. When books overlap into several sections, the annotation has been made with secondary referrals. This choice was made to avoid a subject index which, with 1500 books, would be cumbersome and of limited value. It is hoped that the categorization system used will fulfill this need for the reader.

No attempt has been made to list Standard Book Numbers or Library of Congress numbers: it is assumed that the reader will rely upon libraries and booksellers for additional information. Prices have also been excluded, in most cases, since this information is available in *Books In Print*, a reference available in any university, school, or public library. With the price changes occurring frequently, an accurate price is impossible to list.

The non-bound print and audio-visual materials in Part Two are not categorized by subject, but by producer. Prices are included for these materials because of the vast range of prices. The reasons for these differences are commented upon in the Introduction to Part Two.

This edition could not have been completed in its present form without the assistance of several individuals and professional organizations. The British Columbia Teachers' Federation, and more directly, W. V. Allester, Director of Professional Development, provided the facilities for collection and preparation of most of this material between 1968 and 1973. Assistance was also rendered in the printing of earlier, shorter portions of this bibliography in 1968, 1970 and 1971. Critical evaluation of these printings enabled the compiler to revise and improve the structure of presentation and annotation used in this edition. The B. C. Social Studies Teachers' Association also provided significant assistance through their financial assistance in 1970 and 1971.

Two colleagues have proven to be invaluable in their support over the past seven years. C. W. Dick and H. L. Walker have both given me valuable advice and comment on the development and growth of the materials review which led to this bibliography.

Part One

1
Basic Works in the Study of Urbanization

This section of the bibliography was inserted to call attention to a little more than 50 works of particular note. Of these, three titles can be singled out as being among the most influential works in urbanization on this century. They are:

>   Doxiadis: *Ekistics*
>   Lynch: *The Image Of The City*
>   Mumford: *The City In History*

The others are divided into three categories: basic interdisciplinary works, single discipline oriented references, and the other two major bibliographies. The interdisciplinary works provide a broad perspective of what the city is, has been, or could be. The discipline oriented references provide some of the most significant contributions available in their particular fields relating to the city. Several are unique works in urban analysis, urban futures, urban history, and urban group dynamics.

The bibliographies listed are the two extensive works available in book form. Where The Council of Planning Librarians in the U.S. (P.O. Box 229, Monticello, Illinois 61856) publishes many short specialized bibliographies, this pair deals with a broader spectrum of urbanization between each of their respective covers. Both are extensive sources for the professional and specialist, both are goldmines in supplementary sources of information, particularly printed reports and documents.

1.1 BASIC INTERDISCIPLINARY WORKS

Arango, Jorge. *The Urbanization Of The Earth*. Boston: Beacon Press, 1970.
    This is an interesting little book which presents a personal thesis on the nature and origins of urbanization in today's world and includes a possible approach to planning on a world wide scale. Although it has a fair amount of jargon, this work is of decided value as it presents a perspective of the city as a functioning organism.
                                                                    HB (2)

The City In Print

Banfield, Edward C. *The Unheavenly City: The Nature and Future of Our Urban Crisis.* Boston: Little, Brown and Co., 1970.
    Written by an expert in urban government, this book is crucial. It presents a point of view that most of our problems are long standing and insoluble. Banfield's references are of current concerns which have usually been around for a long time. He presents first and then another hypothesis, taking a fresh look at many of our socio-political problems. Among them are race (culture), unemployment (unemployables), welfare and education. The final chapters discuss several solutions, but none are politically feasable. Although this leaves the reader with frustrations, the book provides a deeper awareness of urban issues and conditions.
    PB (2)

Breese, Gerald. *Urbanization In Newly Developing Countries.* Englewood Cliffs: Prentice Hall, 1966.
    A companion to the reference volume by Breese, *The City In Newly Developing Countries* (3.21), this work is immensely valuable for the study of non-western urbanization. It refers to Anglo-European urbanization only as a model for that to be found outside the western world. Although it is heavy with footnotes, the text is quite informative, with in-depth coverage of world wide patterns of urban form and function. Essentially a geographical study, there are extensive sections dealing with urban dwellers (social patterns of the non-western city), developmental patterns, and future trends.
    HB/PB (1)

Chermayeff, Serge and Alexander Tzonis. *Shape of Community: Realization of Human Potential.* Harmondsworth: Penguin, 1971.
    A unique philosophical work which studies human nature and man's position in society--his own creation. Today's technology is viewed as both the creator of chaos and the future hope of mankind. Investigations into the human psyche and urban environment, including man's requirements for physical space (both in quantity and quality), transportation and containers (housing and other buildings), are well balanced in this study of the needs of urban design. The book format includes wide margins containing notes and vignettes, and an interesting appendix with glossary.
    PB (2)

Cullen, Gordon. *Townscape.* New York: Reinhold, 1961. See Lynch, Kevin. *The Image of The City.*

_____. *The Concise Townscape.* London: Architectural Press, 1971.
    Basically a paperback edition of the 1961 edition, but at one-third the cost. A highly useful work.
    PB (2)

Curl, James Stevens. *European Cities And Society: The Influence Of Political Climate On Town Design.* London: Leonard Hill, 1970.
    A supurb reference, comparable in value to Mumford. The approach of this book is sophisticated, but highly readable, covering the political and philosophical factors of urban design from Sumeria through the present city. Many good illustrations are included.
    HB/PB (2)

Basic Works In The Study Of Urbanization

Doxiadis, Constantinos A. *Ekistics: An Introduction To The Science Of Human Settlements*. London: Hutchinson, 1968.
    This work is an absolute must if you wish to deal adequately with the city. More than a little deep, it is nonetheless a successful attempt to combine various related disciplines and all dimensions, including time and space, into the study of the city.

    Divided into four sections, the first is possibly the most useful as it deals with the theory and practice of human settlements. The remaining sections provide vast amounts of information and more detailed study of the concepts initially presented. The profuse and excellent illustrations combined with the concise concepts of the human and the organic nature of cities make this book essential in order to clearly understand the totality of urban life. It is one of the four or five basic works in this century dealing with urbanization.
                                                                                            HB (2)

Dunstan, Maryjane and Patricia W. Garlan. *Worlds In The Making: Probes For Students Of The Future*. Englewood Cliffs: Prentice Hall, 1970.
    An excellent humanities oriented work with units on (1) "grokking" the problem, (2) coping with change, (3) exploring spaceship earth, (4) viewing the machine--enemy or ally, (5) evolution and revolution, and (6) discovering human nature. Vignettes by Heinlein, Toffler, Fuller, Ellison, Heller, Clarke, Doxiadis, Mumford, and Watts are included in this compendia of material on the future. Well structured to titillate the imagination.
                                                                                       HB/PB (1)

Esfandiary, F. M. *Optimism One*. New York: W. W. Norton, 1970.
    An essential reference, this work deals with man in today's urban world. Mr. Esfandiary's personal views warrant study because they are striking, provocative, and optimistic as to the present age and man's place in an increasingly complex world. Reading this work will cause one to question and to take issue with either Mr. Esfandiary's many theses or with the ideas of the 'experts' he comments upon.
                                                                                          HB (1)

Greer, Scott. *The Emerging City: Myth And Reality*. New York: The Free Press, 1972.
    This work is essentially a philosophical study of the forces which are currently affecting and molding the direction(s) and future(s) of urban problems. It is based upon evaluations that use the techniques of a large number of disciplines.
                                                                                     HB/PB (2)

Gruen, Victor. *The Heart Of Our Cities*. New York: Simon and Schuster, 1964.
    This volume complements and supplements Mumford. The nature of the city, with its current blights, dangers, and possible solutions, is discussed. It presents a balance to material presented in Mumford. The author acknowledges that he is beginning where Mumford stopped. Written by one of the most prominent planners in North America, this work is quite readable.
                                                                                     HB/PB (1)

The City In Print

Gutkind, E. A. *International History Of City Development*. 6 vols. New York: The Free Press, 1964-1969.
- I. *Urban Development In Central Europe.*
- II. *Urban Development In The Alpine And Scandinavian Countries.*
- III. *Urban Development In Southern Europe: Spain And Portugal.*
- IV. *Urban Development In Southern Europe: Italy And Greece.*
- V. *Urban Development In Western Europe: France And Belgium.*
- VI. *Urban Development In Western Europe: The Netherlands And Great Britain.*

This series is the best reference on the history and development of cities in each area from the earliest beginnings to the Nineteenth Century. The series was to eventually include the entire world. The present set actually consists of 8 volumes, but because the last two were compiled from the late author's notes, they are listed separately. Each of the volumes deals with a geographical region, studying the land, historical background, the rural settlements, and concludes with an extensive city survey. The text is clear and easy to follow with vast numbers of superb illustrations. For comprehending the form and function of the city outside of North America, this series is excellent. As a reference, these titles are the essential encyclopedia in urbanization.

HB (2)

Gutkind, E. A. *Urban Development In East Central Europe: Poland, Czechoslovakia, And Hungary.* Edited by G. Gutkind. Vol. VII of *The International History Of City Development.* New York: The Free Press, 1972.

This significant addition to a singluarly useful series is listed separately becuase it was composed from notes left by the late author and has considerable contributions by urban specialists in Poland, Czechoslovakia, and Hungary. As with the earlier six volumes, it is well illustrated, although not as profusely as the other volumes.

HB (2)

_____. *Urban Development In Eastern Europe: Bulgaria, Romania, And The U.S.S.R.* Edited by G. Gutkind. Vol. VIII of *The International History Of City Development.* New York: The Free Press, 1972.

The thrust of this volume is markedly different from the first six. With three distinct segments, the first was written by a Bulgarian academic who deals with urbanization in Bulgaria. This sparsely illustrated essay covers the feudal period (7th through the 14th Centuries), the Ottoman conquest (1396-1878), the Kingdom (1878-1944), and the Communist takeover. This segment is highly doctrinaire, with a more than liberal sprinkling of party thought spread through the information that is provided. It is also a storehouse of unavailable information.

The second section, dealing with Romania, was written as a joint project by a number of Romanian academicians. Moderately illustrated, it presents a well balanced picture of urban development in Romania from the 7th to the 20th Century.

The last section, comprising two thirds of the text, was written by E. A. Gutkind. Dealing with the U.S.S.R., this unit goes beyond the European analyses, as reviewed to date, into an area that has had distinctly different experiences with cities. The author begins with a masterful interpretation of the nature of man and the environment we call cities. The U.S.S.R. segment, moderately illustrated, presents a thread which runs from the neolithic settlements through the Eighteenth Century and concludes with a chapter on Kiev, Moscow, Leningrad, Bukhara, Samarkand, and Tashkent.

This unique reference cannot be recommended too highly.

HB (2)

Higbee, Edward. *A Question Of Priorities: New Strategies For Our Urbanized World.* New York: Morrow, 1970.
    A highly readable exploration of specific situations which are tied together in search of a feasible approach to the making of more livable cities. The exclusive use of American examples does not detract from the value of the work as a theoretical gadfly.

PB (2)

Jacobs, Jane. *The Economy Of Cities.* New York: Random House, 1969.
    This work presents a markedly different evaluation from that of Mumford of the origins, basic function, and development of cities through to the present day. A sophisticated work, it is significant in its impact on urban theory.

HB/PB (2)

Johnson-Marshall, Percy. *Rebuilding Cities.* Chicago: Aldine, 1966.
    This work is a valuable supplement to the study of urban history. Essentially a collection of diagrams, charts, and photographs built around a concise framework of text, this book presents a visual survey of the historical city, the city of today, and the alternatives for the restructuring of the modern city. Although the examples used are predominantly English, this work has a universal value.

HB (2)

Lynch, Kevin. *The Image Of The City.* Cambridge: The M. I. T. Press, 1960.

HB/PB (2)

    Also, Hosken, Fran P. *The Language Of Cities.* 2nd ed. Cambridge: Schenkman, 1972.

PB (2)

    Cullen, Gordon. *Townscape.* New York: Reinhold, 1961.

HB (2)

    These three basic works study the city and help readers to visualize the city for themselves. Rather than discuss problems or prospects, these books develop images, perspectives, and perceptions.

The City In Print

1.2 BASIC DISCIPLINE-ORIENTED REFERENCES

Lynch, the first of these to be published, develops perception in urban design. The city is analyzed both in its parts and as a whole. Perception through space and time is also dealt with in depth. This essential reference is one of the 4 or 5 basic works in this century dealing with urbanization.

Although developing imagery and perception, Hosken departs from Lynch's factual approach by studying the city with a visual analysis of urban form and design. Her work assists the viewer in 'seeing' and in discovering 'how we see and what we see.' Photographs are quite good and are representative of urban form throughout the world. The balance between illustration and commentary is also quite good.

Also dealing with imagery, but in an entirely different way, Cullen leads the viewer through the city in a study of urban design and form through micro-study of its detail. He aptly supplements Lynch by visually presenting individual perceptions which make up one's total awareness of a city. This, however, consists of only one-half of the text. The second half deals with town studies and proposals for England. It is for the first part that this book is so highly recommended.

The three books are valuable as aids to the development of an awareness of the nature of cities. The three together, supplementing one another, present quite a comprehensive study.

Minar, David and Scott Greer. *The Concept Of Community: Readings With Interpretations*. Chicago: Aldine, 1969.
    This is a collection of readings on the entire spectrum of the community, studying it through a variety of concepts and scales, and as a locus of political and social institutions. The readings are short and, on the whole, heavy, but essential for reference.

HB/PB (2)

Mumford, Lewis. *The City In History*. New York: Harcourt, Brace and World, 1961.
    The foremost interpretation of urban culture, both historical and current, this work is, unfortunately, heavy reading, but it is still absolutely essential. Mumford is the one author who can lead the reader to a feeling for the city. Where other authors provide information, Mumford gives awareness of and appreciation for the city. Recent publications have complemented Mumford as an historical reference, but for general use, it is still the best in its field. It is one of the most significant works of the century on the urbanization.

HB/PB (2)

---
*A word combining the sense of architecture and ecology, denoting a totality of human experience.

Basic Works In The Study Of Urbanization

Saarinen, E. *The City: Its Growth, Its Decay, Its Future*. Cambridge: The M. I. T. Press, 1966.
    This study looks at the city, first and foremost, as organic in form and function. The approach is quite different in tone and intent from Mumford's. Here the city is studied from decline to rehabilitation, with urban problems discussed in relation to their ecological components. Saarinen's thesis ties man to nature, giving him both biological and societal roles. It is of decided value, being a superb introduction to the nature of the city.
HB/PB (2)

Soleri, Paolo. *Arcology*: The City In The Image Of Man*. Cambridge: The M. I. T. Press, 1969.
    This is a remarkable book, but expensive. The first third deals with Soleri's concept of arcology, the human environment and man's prospects. This section is frankly of limited value to the general reader. However, Part Two, covering two thirds of the book, has 30 examples of Soleri's megastructures.* For this section alone, the work is well worth the cost. As examples of megastructures, Soleri's drawings are striking. As examples of possible future prospects in urban form, this work is an absolute must.
HB (2)

Soleri, Paolo. *The Sketchbook Of Paolo Soleri*. Cambridge: The M. I. T. Press, 1971.
    This volume, extracted from two of Soleri's ongoing sketchbooks (totaling six by 1970), covers the period 1959-1964 during which many of his ideas on the concept of arcologies matured. Of use where the reader is interested in further understanding the thought processes which resulted in the arcology concept.
PB (2)

Thomlinson, Ralph. *Urban Structure: The Social And Spatial Character Of Cities*. New York: Random House, 1969.
    This work is an analysis in which the author utilizes an urban ecological framework to tie together material from other disciplines, and thus is quite different from most works on the city. Interesting and containing much useful imformation, this work deals with space, the nature and origin of cities, urban development and growth, city structure, and includes a full discussion of urban alternatives and possible futures. A full bibliography is included.
HB (2)

---

*A term describing immense man-made structures capable of housing from thousands to millions, at least self-contained, if not self-sufficient.

The City In Print

Urban Studies Project. *The Teacher And The City*. Toronto: Methuen, 1971.
    This book was developed from three years of dialogue between eight teachers and dozens of urban specialists. Basically a teacher text, this work looks at the nature and scope of urban studies education at the secondary level. Detail is provided on scope and sequence, suggested lessons and auxiliary activities, alternate learning situations, and local resources.

Although this reviewer was one of the authors, it is felt that the book must be recommended to the educator as being both comprehensive and open ended, basically standing as a work which suggests "1001 ways to approach the study of urbanization."

                                                                                                    PB (2)

Abrams, Charles. *The Language Of Cities: A Glossary Of Terms*. New York: Viking, 1971.
    Although the language in this work ranges from standard usage to obtuse technical terminology, complete definitions and explanations are provided.
                                                                                                     HB (2)

Bernal, J. D. *Science In History*. 3rd ed. 4 vols. Harmondsworth: Penguin, 1965.
    I. *The Emergence Of Science*.
    II. *The Birth Of Modern Science And Industry*.
   III. *Science In Our Time*.
    IV. *The Social Sciences Past And Present*.

Volumes one and four are highly useful references. The first is of immense value in setting the scientific state for earlier epochs in urban history, dealing with science in the earliest urban periods through the middle ages. Relationships are quite easily drawn between technology and urban communities. Included are useful charts and illustrations.

Volume four looks at the development of the social sciences into the Twentieth Century. This is of reference value by providing in-depth analysis of science and its influence, responsibility to, and involvement in urban social conditions and problems.

                                                                                                    PB (2)

Berry, Brian J. L. and Frank E. Horton, ed. *Geographical Perspectives On Urban Systems With Integrated Readings*. Englewood Cliffs: Prentice Hall, 1970.
    An exceedingly worthwhile and sophicated re-examination of the current status of geography, this work is limited to use by urban geographers. The text is too detailed and complicated for general reference, but its value to the specialist is quite high. Chapters deal with city size, urban growth, types of cities, urban hierarchies, metropolis definition, social space and urban ecology.
                                                                                                     HB (2)

Blumenfeld, Hans. *The Modern Metropolis: Its Origins, Growth, Characteristics And Planning*. Edited by Paul D. Spreiregen. Montreal: Harvest House, 1967.
    This is an essential collection of worthwhile and readable essays on the full spectrum of urbanization. These essays, by a leading Canadian planner, present a distinctive approach to current urban conditions and problems--an approach which is both Canadian and universal.
                                                                            HB/PB (2)

Basic Works In The Study Of Urbanization

Fava, Sylvia Fleis, ed. *Urbanism In World Perspective*. New York: Thomas Crowell, 1968.
    Starting from a philosophical framework in urban sociology, this work is a well balanced collection which brings together a wide range of selections dealing with urbanism throughout the world. Of the 57 selections included, over half concern conditions and problems outside North America.
    PB (2)

Gould, J. *A Dictionary Of The Social Sciences*. New York: The Free Press, 1964.
    This work is unique in that it provides, under one cover, an extremely broad collection of definitions useful in the study of the city.
    HB (2)

Hauser, Arnold. *The Social History Of Art*. 4 vols. New York: Vintage, 1951.
    This four volume set is excellent. The effect of art modes upon urban life from the earliest to the present times is vividly present throughout this work.
    PB (2)

Meadows, Donella H., et. al. *The Limits To Growth: A Report For The Club Of Rome's Project On The Predicament Of Mankind*. New York: Universe (HB/PB), and Bergenfield (N.J.): New American Library (PB only), 1972.
    This significant work ties together the Club Of Rome's extensive research into the potentials of disaster in the coming decades. Of all the works reviewed on the future, this one is the most significant in light of its impact on intellectual thought and response. As a prophecy of doom, this group's work is most important, again in the light its impact. Caution should be suggested, however, as hypotheses of impending disaster are based on generalizations and assumptions which are not verified. Even so, the impact of this work on man and cities cannot be overstated.
    HB/PB (2)

Moholy-Nagy, Sibyl. *Matrix Of Man: An Illustrated Histry Of Urban Development*. New York: Preager, 1968.
    This reference supplements other illustrated histories, with views of urban form in the present, with the influences of the past, as well as the potentials for the future, all clearly illustrated. Of greatest significance is the fact that this work's emphasis complements, yet does not duplicate, other works on urban history.
    HB (2)

Murphy, Raymond E. *The American City: An Urban Geography*. New York: McGraw-Hill, 1966*.
    This is one of the basic reference works on urbanization and has had a marked effect on the analysis of North American cities. It deals with all aspects of the city, both practical and theoretical. Although oriented toward a single discipline (geography), it is still quite comprehensive.
    HB (2)

    **Exercises In Urban Geography*. New York: McGraw-Hill, 1968.
Also available is this disposable lab manual which supplements the text of *The American City*. Highly useful as a compendia of geography laboratory techniques.
    PB (2)

The City In Print

Parkin, H. ed. *The Social Animal: An Anthology For General And Liberal Studies*. London: Routledge and Kegan Paul, 1969.
    This is a highly unusual and provocative collection of 17 significant sections including:

    Robert Ardrey   "The Three Faces Of Janus"
    Lewis Mumford   "Rise And Fall Of Megalopolis"
    George Orwell   "The Road To Wigan Pier"
    Aldous Huxley   "Over Organization"
    A. S. Neill   "Summerhill"
    Samuel Butler   "Some Erewhonian Trials and Malcontents"

    These selections were brought together to "develop in the reader a critical awareness of his own nature and the quality of his environment." This goal is well achieved.

PB (1)

Robson, William A. and D. E. Regan eds. *Great Cities Of The World: Their Government, Politics And Planning*. 3rd ed. 2 vols. London: George Allen and Unwin, and Beverly Hills: Sage Publications (U.S. only), 1972.
    This set covers a wide range of cities, with nine in Europe, five in North America, three in Latin America, five in Asia, and four in Africa. Each city is analyzed in depth, presenting considerable information on government structure, but also information on more general urban characteristics.

HB (2)

Rosenfeld, Albert. *The Second Genesis: The Coming Control Of Life*. Englewood Cliffs: Prentice Hall, 1969.
    This is a unique and wide ranging work. The future is unfolded in terms of present developments and prevalent trends in electronic, biological and chemical influence on humans. Life extension, genetic engineering, programmed births, behavioral modification and control, and cyborg techniques are only a few of the topics covered in depth in this fascinating book. Well documented and interesting reading, it was written for the general reader, and provides a wealth of information.

HB (2)

Schneider, Wolf. *Babylon Is Everywhere: The City As Man's Fate*. London: Hodder and Stoughton, n.d., OP.
    An essential book, this is as comprehensive as Mumford, but much more easily absorbed. This work, primarily an urban history, begins with Ur and follows the city into the 1960's. Although it is more inclusive of modern urban centers than is Mumford, it is not as detailed. It should be searched for.

HB (1)

Scientific American, ed. *Cities*. New York: Knopf, 1967.
    This reader is a basic study of the urban process. Chapters by recognized and influential contributors in the field are included, as are individual studies of particular cities and the future of the city in general.
    HB/PB (1)

Smith, David C. *Changing Values: The Human Impact Of Urbanization*. Bellhaven House, 1971.
    This work contains studies on privacy, aesthetics, mobility, individuality, and responsibility. Well illustrated, this work uses concise case studies for each area concerned. Although a school text, it is one of the best general works on social values yet reviewed.
    HB (1)

Yeates, Maurice H. and Barry J. Garner. *The North American City*. New York: Harper and Row, 1971.
    This work focuses on the functional and organizational processes of the North American city. The content includes studies of urban areas as regions, urban geography, and urban planning.

A sophisticated work oriented toward geography, it is a well balanced reference which views the city as a system and not just the sum of its many functions.
    HB (2)

1.3 BIBLIOGRAPHIES, INDEXES, AND ABSTRACTS

Bestor, George C. and Holway R. Jones. *City Planning Bibliography: A Basic Bibliography Of Sources And Trends*. 3rd ed. New York: American Society of Civil Engineers, 1972.
    Seventy five per cent of the over 1800 entries are annotated. The body of the work contains a large number of book listings and their annotations, as well as a good number of non-bound print materials. There is a complete listing of organizations associated with the city, together with their publications and purposes. Also included is an extensive list of periodicals, and a complete list of publishers' addresses.
    PB (2)

Branch, Melville C. *Comprehensive Urban Planning: A Selected Bibliography With Related Materials*. Beverly Hills: Sage Publications, 1970.
    There are 1500 references included in this collection of professional and sophisticated sources. Books are listed as well as other publications such as articles, papers, reports, and pamphlets. The works are grouped under classifications of greatest use to the scholar or professional. Short descriptive annotations and content comments include in many cases a listing of chapter headings. An essential reference, this work has a good balance of periodical and "non-book" print materials.
    PB (2)

2
Urban History

Books in this section represent studies and interpretations of human history with a focus on the development of urban institutions. Titles reviewed are exclusively those which deal with urban history or those with titles suggesting that they deal with urban history. Of these, Lewis Mumford's *The City in History* (section 1.1) is the most important work in urban history, although his theses are not universally accepted.

This section is divided into works which deal with one or more epochs of urban history and those which relate predominantly to one period. It should also be noted that *The City In History* contains comprehensive units on each period. Included also is a series which covers a whole range of topics. *The Planning And Cities Series* (section 2.1) should be noted as being unique in its scope and in the richness of its illustrations.

These works can be of value in providing insights into the forces which have shaped the modern city and the way of life of its inhabitants.

2.1 GENERAL WORKS

Bellan, Ruben C. *The Evolving City*. New York: Pitman, 1971.
    This extremely detailed work is recommended for reference rather than general use. An urban history with a difference, the book is divided into three major sections: epochs of urban history, the evolution of municipal government functions, and the city in the national economy. Although sparsely illustrated, this work contains much interesting material.

    PB (2)

Burke, Gerald. *Towns In The Making*. London: Edward Arnold, 1971.
    An interesting book, one of the better general urban histories available With good balance, urban history is dealt with from its beginnings to the new towns of Britain. A good number of illustrations, but too few to offset the text, which is heavy going. An excellent reference.

    HB (2)

Callow, Alexander B., Jr. ed. *American Urban History: An Interpretive Reader With Commentaries*. New York: Oxford University Press, 1969.
    This work contains 53 readings: some summations of ideas presented in

Urban History

>other books reviewed, some new and interesting, and some dated. Useful as a source book and reference.
>
>> PB (2)

Cassell London Series.
>Baker, Timothy. *Medieval London.*
>Holmes, Martin. *Elizabethan London.*
>Margetson, Stella. *Regency London.*
>Merrifield, Ralph. *Roman London.*
>
>London: Cassell and New York: Praeger (U.S. only), 1969-1971.
> These four titles are detailed narratives of the growth of this major urban center. Sparsely illustrated, but rich in textual content, the books provide worthwhile information on these four periods. Not urban studies as such, but still highly useful as references. Two other titles have been recently published, but not yet reviewed: *Georgian London* and *Victorian London.*
>
>> HB (2)

Childe, V. Gordon. *Man Makes Himself.* New York: Mentor, 1963.
> A basic, readable study of man's pre-history and early civilizations. The chapters on the urban revolution are of immense value for their presentation of a feeling for the period. Although first published in 1951, most of the information is still valid.
>
>> PB (1)

Clark, S. D. *The Developing Canadian Community.* 2nd ed. Toronto: University of Toronto Press, 1968.
> Not urban history.
>
>> (4)

Cottrell, Leonard. *Lost Cities.* London: Pan, 1957.
> An account of the great cities of the ancient world--including Babylon, Ninevah, Ur, Pompeii, Chichen-Itza, and Macchu-Picchu. In his usual colorful style, Cottrell presents a highly readable narrative.
>
>> PB (2)

Couperie, Pierre. *Paris Through The Ages: An Illustrated Historical Atlas Of Urbanism And Architecture.* New York: Braziller, 1968.
> A superb reference with excellent visuals. The format is set around 48 maps of Paris from its pre-Roman beginnings to the present, with concise histories and photos facing on the opposite pages. Of immense value.
>
>> HB (2)

Daniel, Glyn. *The First Civilizations: The Archaeology Of Their Origins.* Harmondsworth: Penguin, 1971.
> A worldwide survey of the beginnings of civilization--Sumeria, Egypt, China, and Central America. An up-to-date, worthwhile reference.
>
>> PB (2)

The City In Print

De Camp, L. Sprague. *The Ancient Engineers*. Cambridge: The M. I. T. Press, 1962.
    An historical survey of an important aspect of urbanization: engineering and its technology, its development and relationships to architectural styles. Quite useful and readable.

                                                                                                  PB (2)

Derry, T. K. and T. I. Williams. *A Short History Of Technology: From The Earliest Times To A.D. 1900*. Oxford: At The Clarendon Press, 1960.
    A chronological and topical survey of the major technological innovations which enabled urban man to develop toward and through the early stages of the Industrial Revolution. Highly readable, with brief yet complete coverage of the significant technological innovations from an historical point of view. An essential reference.

                                                                       HB/PB (2)

Druks, Herbert and Silvio R. Lacetti. *Cities In Civilization: The City In Western Civilization*. Vol. I. New York: Robert Speller, 1971.
    A history with a difference, this work emphasizes people and their personal views of their world and their cities. Basically, the book is a diary of cities as seen through the eyes of contemporaries. The period dealt with is 100 B.C. through the 17th Century. A highly useful reference.

                                                                          HB (2)

Dyos, H. J. ed. *The Study Of Urban History*. London: Edward Arnold, 1968.
    Superior works exist.

                                                                             (4)

Fenton, Edwin and John M. Good. *The Humanities In Three Cities: An Inquiry Approach* New York: Holt, Rinehart and Winston, 1969.
    A humanities approach to the study of Athens, Florence, and New York. Utilizing literature and philosophical readings, this book provides much insight into and information on attitudes and values. In each instance, readings are supplemented with annotations. Questions are included for discussion and evaluation. An excellent supplement. Each chapter is available in PB.

                                                                          HB (2)

Ghurye, G. S. *Cities And Civilization*. New York: Humanities Press, 1962.
    A study with emphasis on historical urbanization in Asia, using Bombay as the detailed example. Earlier chapters look to the development of Western urban centers in this century. The city as a capital is studied from reference to ancient Egypt, China, and India. The city as a metropolis is also studied from a world-wide point of view. This book is printed in India on low quality paper that will not stand heavy use. A valuable work, more suited for reference than for the general reader.

                                                                          HB (2)

Glaab, Charles N. and A. Theodore Brown. *A History Of Urban America*. New York: Macmillan, 1967.

Urban History

>A worthwhile, detailed work, dealing with American urban history. Covers the United States from the 17th Century to 1960. Reference only.
>
>HB/PB (2)

Green, Constance McLaughlin. *The Rise Of Urban America*. New York: Harper and Row, 1967.
>A study of urban history in the U.S.. Highly readable, this work looks at urban history from a broad perspective, including economic, social, and political factors. Unique in its approach to U.S. urban history. A worthwhile reference.
>
>HB/PB (2)

_____. *American Cities In The Growth Of The Nation*. New York: Harper, 1965.
>A supplement to the other Green book reviewed. Where *The Rise Of Urban America* deals with U.S. urban history chronologically, this work focuses on the development of 18 U.S. cities.
>
>PB (2)

Hilberseimer, L. *The Nature Of Cities: Origins, Growth And Decline: Pattern And Form: Planning Problems*. Chicago: Paul Theobald. 1955.
>Superior works exist.
>
>(4)

Historical Cities Series. New York: Wiley.
>Nine volumes using a common format to present an in-depth study of a major world city at one place in time. Each title is reviewed separately under the appropriate period.
>
>>Africa, T. W. *Rome Of The Caesars*. (2.3)
>>Brucker, G. A. *Renaissance Florence*. (2.5)
>>Lubove, R. *Twentieth Century Pittsburgh*. (2.6)
>>Mandelbaum, S. J. *Boss Tweed's New York*. (2.6)
>>Miller, D. A. *Imperial Constantinople*. (2.45)
>>Monter, W. *Calvin's Geneva*. (2.5)
>>Ranum, O. *Paris In The Age Of Absolutism*. (2.5)
>>Robertson, D. W. *Chaucer's London*. (2.4)
>>Strauss, G. *Nuremberg In The 16th Century*. (2.5)

Jackson, Kenneth T. and Stanley K. Schultz, eds. *Cities In American History*. New York: Knopf, 1972.
>
>(3)

Korn, A. *History Builds The Town*. London: Lund Humphries, 1953.
>An historical work which encompasses much through the use of a large number of photographs and notes on historical background and urban patterns today. A large part of the section on modern towns deals with developments in England, the U.S.A., and the U.S.S.R.. An ideal reference.
>
>HB (2)

The City In Print

Lobel, M. D. ed. *Historic Towns: Maps And Plans Of Towns And Cities In The British Isles, With Historical Commentaries From Earliest Times To 1800.* Vol. I. Baltimore: The Johns Hopkins Press, n.d.

(3)

Planning And Cities Series. New York: Braziller, 1968-1971.
    Twelve volumes varying from general to reference use. Each title is dealt with separately. Each volume is about 125 pages in length, half as illustrations and half as text.

HB/PB

Argan, Guilio C. *The Renaissance City.*
    An excellent collection of illustrations warrant the purchase of this book. The text deals with the alteration of cities (Rome, Venice, etc.), new towns (Palma Nova), and the analysis of the cultural factors which resulted in the Renaissance City.

(1)

Choay, Francoise. *The Modern City: Planning In The 19th Century.*
    This text is more technical than others in the series. Illustrations are quite suitable for the subject, although the maps and diagrams included are of limited value. Also includes some photographs. Reference use only.

(2)

Evenson, Norma. *Le Corbusier: The Machine And The Grand Design.*
    An essential reference with superb illustrations of the ideas of this most significant 20th Century urban designer.

(2)

Fraser, Douglas. *Village Planning In The Primitive World.*
    Deals with eight peoples of Asia, Africa, and North America (Haida and Cheyenne). Exceptionally useful illustrations. An extremely valuable reference for 'pre-historic' urban development.

(2)

Hardoy, Jorge. *Urban Planning In Pre-Columbian America.*
    Quite good. Suitable for reference.

(2)

Lampl, Paul. *Cities And Planning In The Ancient Near East.*
    The best work yet reviewed on the ancient world. The text is short and well tied to the excellent illustrations. An essential general item.

(1)

Saalman, Howard. *Medieval Cities.*
    Illustrated with woodcuts and other contemporary illustrations rather than reconstructions. This limits the books usefulness for the general reader, although the textual content is quite good. A reference only.

(2)

Urban History

    Saalman, Howard. *Haussmann: Paris Transformed.*
       A superb reference of predominent value for the 87 illustrations of Paris from 1870 to the early 1900's. An interesting commentary provides useful information on this, the first example of planning in a major city in modern times.

                                                                                                 (2)

    Wiebenson, Dora. *Tony Garnier: The Cite Industrielle.*
       The topic is well handled, but its specialized nature makes this work suitable for reference use only.

                                                                                                (2)

    Titles Not Yet Published Or Reviewed:

       De La Croix, Horst. *Military Considerations In City Planning.*
       Maksimovich, Branko. *Socialist Planning In The Cities Of Eastern Europe.*

Rowland, Kurt. *The Shape of Towns.* London: Ginn, 1966
    The major part of this study of town design deals with the historical city from the Middle Ages through the 19th Century. The last third discusses modern town planning and the future city, and is of value for study of the modern city. Suitable for the general reader. As well as a useful teacher reference it is also available for the classroom.

                                                                                             HB (1)

Segal, J. B. *Edessa: The Blessed City.* Oxford: Clarendon Press, 1970.
    Not urban history.

                                                                                                (4)

Sjoberg, Gideon. *The Pre-Industrial City.* New York: The Free Press, 1960.
    Excellent for reference and introduction of terms, this item is a must for the beginner in urban studies. The work covers the structure, growth, and spread of cities, their demography, society, customs, economic structure, and religious bases. A comprehensive, world-wide view.

                                                                                            PB (1)

Strauss, Leo. *The City And Man.* (See 13.3)

Toynbee, Arnold. *Cities On The Move.* New York: Oxford University Press, 1970.
    A brief, highly readable study of the city from its origins through its future potentials. This work studies epochs of urban growth through their evolving complexities of function. Studied are the city state of the classical world, the ancient imperial capital city, and the transitions brought about by European developments during the last 500 years. The megalopolis follows this historical overview, with the concluding chapter looking at the "coming world city." A unique book on urban history and an essential reference for both the specialist and the general reader.

                                                                                           HB (2)

The City In Print

Troedsson, Carl Birger. *Architecture, Urbanism And Socio-Political Developments In Our Western Civilization.* Goteberg: Akademiforlaget, 1964.
    A highly technical and detailed historical/philosophical study of Western urban man. Truly significant, this work is comparable in value to Mumford and Pirenne, and is a basic reference for the urban history specialist. Although extremely sophisticated, it is included here with annotations because it is also an essential reference for those wanting a broad background in the field.

                                                                                                                                HB (2)

Tunnard, Christopher and H. Read. *American Skyline: The Growth And Form Of Our Cities And Towns.* New York: Mentor, 1956.
    An historical survey of the American city from colonial times to 1950.

                                                                                                                                PB (2)

_____. *The Modern American City.* Princeton: Van Nostrand, 1968.
    A Highly readable and well written study of the raison d'etre and development of the American city. Both sections, the historical overview and the selected readings, provide what is probably the best survey of the American city in history yet seen.

                                                                                                                               PB (2)

Wakstein, Allen M. ed. *The Urbanization Of America: An Historical Anthology.* Boston: Houghton Mifflin, 1970.

                                                                                                                                  (3)

Weber, Max. *The City.* The Free Press, 1958.
    A general discussion of the urban setting, this book has since been outdated by Mumford and others. These later works are of more use to the general reader. However, this is not to deny the book's usefulness to the specialist.

                                                                                                                               PB (2)

Zucker, Paul. *Town And Square From The Agora To The Village Green.* Cambridge: The M. I. T. Press, 1959.
    An interesting study approaching the topic of urban history through the study of site and function of the square. This is a well illustrated work, useful for reference.

                                                                                                                               PB (2)

2.2 ANCIENT CITIES

Adams, Robert McC. *The Evolution Of Urban Society: Early Mesopotamia And Prehispanic Mexico.* Chicago: Aldine-Atherton, 1966.
    A comparative analysis of two isolated city-state societies.

                                                                                                                                  (3)

Urban History

Aldred, Cyril. *Egypt To The End Of The Old Kingdom*. New York: McGraw-Hill, 1965.
    From the beginning of human settlements (5000 B.C.) to 2160 B.C.. A good reference, with photos, reconstructions and diagrams.
    HB/PB (2)

Braidwood, Robert J. and Gordon R. Wiley, eds. *Courses Toward Urban Life: Archeological Consideration Of Some Cultural Alternates*. Chicago: Aldine, 1962.
    (3)

Childe, V. Gordon. *What Happened In History*. Harmondsworth: Penguin, 1965.
    A general work on the ancient world with a superb study of the first three civilizations in western Asia. A good introductory item on the ancient city.
    PB (2)

Fraser, Douglas. *Village Planning In The Primitive World*. (See 2.1)

Kramer, Samuel Noah and the Editors of TIME-LIFE Books. *Cradle Of Civilization*. New York: TIME-LIFE Books, 1967.
    A study of ancient Mesopotamia, with several beautifully illustrated chapters on Sumer and Babylon. An excellent reference.
    HB (2)

Lampl, Paul. *Cities And Planning In The Ancient Near East*. (See 2.1)

Mallowan, M. E. L. *Early Mesopotamia And Iran*. New York: McGraw-Hill, 1961.
    A survey of ancient Sumeria, this book contains many beautiful illustrations--clear drawings of reconstructions and photos of artifacts and sites. A valuable reference.
    HB/PB (2)

Mellaart, James. *Earliest Civilizations Of The Near East*. New York: McGraw-Hill, 1965.
    From 10,000 B.C. to the late fifth millenium B.C. (4000 B.C.). A useful reference with good photos and reproductions.
    HB/PB (2)

Piggott, S. *Pre-Historic India*. London: Cassell, 1962.
    A must, this is a basic, readable account of the development of civilization in the Indus River Valley. It is needed to fill a vacuum left by most studies made of ancient civilizations.
    OP (2)

Watson, William. *Early Civilization In China*. New York: McGraw-Hill, 1966.
    From 4000 to 221 B.C.. A study of the culture, with no urban content.
    (4)

Wheeler, Sir Mortimer. *Civilizations Of The Indus Valley And Beyond*. New York: McGraw-Hill, 1966.
    Similar to the Mallowan item above, this book is quite good. Areas

dealt with include Mohenjo-Daro, Harrapa, and Lothal, with other areas looked at in brief. Good illustrations.

HB/PB (2)

Wooley, Sir Leonard. *Digging Up The Past*. Harmondsworth: Penguin, 1965.
    This work has interest and value as a highly readable account of the methods used in uncovering ancient towns and of how information is gleaned from the unearthed ruins.

PB (2)

_____. *Ur Of The Chaldees: A Record Of Seven Years Of Excavation*. New York: W. W. Norton, 1965.
    Not urban history.

(4)

2.3 CLASSICAL (GREEK AND ROMAN) CITIES

Acta Congressus Madvigiani. *Urbanism And Town Planning: The Classic Pattern Of Modern Western Civilization*. Copenhagen: Eijnar Munesgaard, 1958. Vol. I of the Proceedings of the Second International Congress of Classical Studies.
    This collection of several papers on town planning has two particularly good ones on Greek and Roman town planning. The material is heavy going, but well worth the reading. A good reference.

PB (2)

Africa, Thomas W. *Rome Of The Caesars*. New York: Wiley, 1965.
    A title in the Wiley Historical Cities Series. A worthwhile perspective of this ancient imperial center. Primarily in journalistic/biographical style, this work is a good reference.

PB (2)

Bernard, Paul. *Ai Khanum On The Oxus: A Hellenistic City In Central Asia*. London: Oxford University Press, 1967.

(3)

Burn, A. R. *The Warring States Of Greece*. New York: McGraw-Hill, 1968.
    A beautiful little book, but with no urban content.

(4)

Claster, Jill N. ed. *Athenian Democracy: Triumph Or Travesty*. New York: Holt, Rinehart and Winston, 1967.
    One of the European Problem Studies Series. Worthwhile for study of the beginnings, development, and demise of this urban institution in its birthplace. A good reference.

PB (2)

Castagnoli, Ferdinando. *Orthogonal Town Building In Antiquity*. Cambridge: The M. I. T. Press, 1971.
    Chapters on the Greek city, Miletus, Italic cities, Greek cities of the 4th Century B.C., the Hellenistic city, and Roman cities. A heavy text,

limiting usefulness of this item to reference. For urban history, this item is a must, contributing concise and well illustrated examples of urban design with interesting conclusions as to the factors which led to these designs. Good.

    HB (2)

Doxiadis, C. A. *Architectural Space In Ancient Greece*. Cambridge: The M. I. T. Press, 1972.
    For the reader wanting hundreds of photos, site layouts, and reconstructions on classical cities, this work is a gem. Its detail makes it more suitable for reference than for general use.

    HB (2)

Fustel de Coulanges, Numa Denis. *The Ancient City*. New York: Doubleday, 1955.
    A classic. A superb, highly detailed study of Greek civilization and culture from the point of view of Greek and Roman values. Immeasurably valuable insights into the Greek mind and through this, the culture and bases of Greek and early Roman cities. This work explains much of the confusion between the realities of the classical world and myths about it in our civilization.

    PB (2)

Glotz, Gustave. *The Greek City And Its Institutions*. London: Routledge and Kegan Paul and New York: Barnes and Noble (U.S. only), 1969 (Reprint of 1929 ed.).
    A complete study of the Greek city, from oligarchy through democracy to its decline with the conquest of Philip of Macedonia. Presenting a different picture than the Fustel de Coulanges work, this study should be of interest as a reference.

    HB (2)

Jones, A. H. M. *The Cities Of The Eastern Roman Provinces*. 2nd ed. Oxford: Clarendon Press, 1971 (Reprint of a 1937 ed.).
    This work deals with urbanization in the Eastern Mediterranean in the Greek, Roman, and early Byzantine periods. Quite detailed—373 pages of text with 200 pages of notes. An excellent reference. Expensive.

    HB (2)

Merrifield, Ralph. *Roman London*. (See 2.1)

Rivet, A. L. F. *Town And Country In Roman Britain*. 2nd ed. London: Hutchinson University Library, 1964.

    (3)

Scullard, H. H. *The Etruscan Cities And Rome*. Ithaca (N.Y.): Cornell University Press and London: Thames and Hudson (Canada only), 1967.

    (3)

Warmington, B. H. *Carthage*. Harmondsworth: Penguin, 1960.
    A useful study of this civilization with a section on the city of Carthage. A good reference.

    PB (2)

Wycherley, R. E. *How The Greeks Built Cities*. London: Macmillan, 1949.
    A good study of the Greek city with good illustrations including architecture and city plans. Of limited general use, but of great value for research.

                                                                                                           PB (2)

2.4 MEDIEVAL CITIES

Baker, Timothy. *Medieval London*. (See 2.1)

Benton, J. F. *Town Origins: The Evidence From Medieval England*. Boston: D. C. Heath, 1968.
    This reader includes brief theoretical essays by Pirenne and Mumford regarding the medieval development of cities. This section is followed by excerpts from contemporary treatises such as town charters, the Anglo-Saxon Chronicle, and the Doomsday Book. A useful reference for historical research.

                                                                                                            PB (2)

Coulborn, R. *Feudalism In History*. Princeton University Press, 1956.
    Superior works exist.

                                                                                                            OP (4)

Gies, Joseph and Frances. *Life In A Medieval City*. New York: Thomas Crowell, 1969.
                                                                                                                  (3)

Holmes, Urban Tigner, Jr. *Daily Living In The Twelfth Century: Based On The Observations Of Alexander Neckam In London And Paris*. Madison: University of Wisconsin Press, 1970 (Reprint of a 1952 ed.).
    Using the medieval manner of description, the author presents what reads like a non-fiction novel, but is in fact a study based on detailed examination of primary texts and archaeological evidence. The result is a work of value for its content and readability.

                                                                                                            PB (2)

Jacobs, David. *Constantinople: City On The Golden Horn*. New York: Harper and Row, 1969.
    A Horizon book. Not urban studies.

                                                                                                                  (4)

Mundy, John H. *The Medieval Town*. Princeton: Van Nostrand, 1967.
    This basic reader, with the usual Anvil division between text and documentation, presents a good historical overview which is easy reading and of definite value.

                                                                                                          PB (1)

Pirenne, Henri. *Medieval Cities*. Cambridge: Princeton University Press, 1956.
    This work, the most indicative of Pirenne's urban thesis, is essential because of the author's influence on subsequent historical thought regarding

the medieval period. Although it has been rejected by the humanistic oriented historians, Pirenne's thesis has been the foundation for economic oriented historians and sociologists.

HB/PB (2)

Robertson, D. W., Jr. *Chaucer's London*. New York: Wiley, 1968.
This work presents an account of London during the late 1300's. Using a biographical style of presentation, the author provides a well-rounded view of the city and its people. A useful reference.

HB/PB (2)

Rorig, Fritz. *The Medieval Town*. London: Batsford and Berkeley: The University of California Press (U.S. only), 1967.

(3)

Russell, Josiah Cox. *Medieval Regions And Their Cities*. Bloomington: Indiana University Press, 1972.
A unique work which studies the structure of urban regions in the Middle Ages. Relying heavily on geographical methodology, this work transcends the usual historical geography in that it lays out theses which present some new and well developed interpretations of urbanization during the Middle Ages. A wide coverage, including Northern Europe, Iberia, the Middle East, and India. Recommended for reference.

HB (2)

Saalman, Howard. *Medieval Cities*. (See 2.1)

Stephenson, Carl. *Borough And Town: A Study Of Urban Origins In England*. Cambridge: The Mediaeval Academy of America, 1933.

(3)

Troedsson, Carl Birger. *The Growth Of The Western City During The Middle Ages*. Goteberg: Gumperts Forlag, 1959.
Of value as a reference, this book includes a good section on the early medieval town (10th and 11th Centuries).

HB (2)

Waley, Daniel. *The Italian City Republics*. New York: McGraw-Hill, 1969.
Covering all aspects of the subject, with emphasis on population, government, and structure, this is a superb, beatifully illustrated study of the city state in Italy from the 10th to the 16th Century. An ideal reference.

HB/PB (2)

2.45 BYZANTIUM AND THE MUSLIM WORLD (600 - 1600 A.D.)

Lapidus, Ira Marvin. *Muslim Cities In The Late Middle Ages*. Cambridge: Harvard University Press, 1967.
This is a masterful piece of scholarship and a highly intriguing source

book on the Muslim city. Ordinarily, a work of such complexity and sophistication would be recommended only for the specialist, but in this case, the book's unique qualities make it an essential general reference.

HB (2)

Miller, Dean A. *Imperial Constantinople*. New York: Wiley, 1969.
    This title presents an in-depth analysis of the city as an imperial capital, focusing on both its leaders and culture. It unfolds with a compelling account of a city which was at once both western and eastern.

HB/PB (2)

Sherrard, Philip and The Editors of TIME-LIFE Books. *Byzantium*. New York: TIME-LIFE Books, 1966.
    Strong sections on Constantinople, lavishly illustrated, provide a good in-depth study of this significant world city. An excellent reference.

HB (2)

2.5 RENAISSANCE AND BAROQUE CITIES

Argan, Guilio C. *The Renaissance City*. (See 2.1)

Bridenbaugh, Carl. *Cities In The Wilderness: The First Century Of Urban Life In America, 1625-1742* (1938, 1966), and *Cities In Revolt: Urban Life In America, 1743-1776* (1955). New York: Oxford University Press, 1971 (both vols.). Previously published by Alfred A. Knopf in 1955.
    These works, recommended for reference rather than general use, are very heavy going, but contain much of value for detailed study.

PB (2)

Brucker, Gene A. *Renaissance Florence*. New York: Wiley, 1969.
    From the time of Dante to Machiavelli (1380-1450), the city of Florence is portrayed at its most creative period. An in-depth analysis of a dynamic community, many of the elements of urban life are dealt with which are unique to this work. A superb, well-rounded presentation on Florence the city, and Florence as a way of life.

HB/PB (2)

Clark, Peter and Paul Slack, eds. *Crisis And Order In English Towns, 1500-1700: Essays In Urban History*. Toronto: University of Toronto Press, 1972.

(3)

Holmes, Martin. *Elizabethan London*. (See 2.1)

Margetson, Stella. *Regency London*. (See 2.1)

Monter, William. *Calvin's Geneva*. New York: Wiley, 1967.
    Similar to the Brucker title in the same series (Wiley's Historical Cities Series), this work presents a detailed study of 16th Century Geneva.

HB/PB (2)

Urban History

Ranum, Orest. *Paris In The Age Of Absolutism*. New York: Wiley, 1968.
    This work, as part of the Wiley Historical Cities Series, is a literary/journalistic approach to viewing Paris at this very important place in time. A worthwhile reference.
HB/PB (2)

Reps, John W. *Town Planning In Frontier America*. Princeton: Princeton University Press, 1970 (paperback ed. of a 1965 work).
    An abridgement and popularization of the material gathered in the more extensive work, *The Making Of Urban America* (1965), by the same author. Covering the period 1565 (St. Augustine) to the mid 19th Century, this volume provides information on urban planning in Spanish, French, and English America. An exhaustively complete reference for the needs of the general reader.
HB/PB (2)

Strauss, Gerald. *Nuremberg In The 16th Century*. New York: Wiley, 1966.
    Similar to the Ranum title reviewed above.
HB/PB (2)

2.6 NINETEENTH CENTURY AND INDUSTRIAL CITIES

Ames, Herbert Brown. *The City Below The Hill: The Slums Of Montreal, 1897*. Toronto: University of Toronto Press, n.d..
(3)

Ashworth, William. *The Genesis Of Modern British Town Planning*. London: Routledge and Kegan Paul and New York: Humanities Press (U.S. only), 1954.
    A study of economic and social planning in the 19th and early 20th Centuries, this work is exclusively English in its orientation, but still of value as a comparative reference.
HB (2)

Benevolo, Leonardo. *The Origins Of Modern Town Planning*. Cambridge: The M. I. T. Press, 1971.
    A translation of a 1963 work which studies the effects of the disappearance of the medieval open-field system and the emergence of industrialization on urban design. A well illustrated and interesting presentation, with a balance between utopias and practical developments in Vienna, Florence, and Paris (Haussmann). A superb reference.
HB/PB (2)

Briggs, Asa. *Victorian Cities*. Harmondsworth: Penguin (PB), 1963 and New York: Harper and Row (U.S. only) (HB), 1970.
    A highly useful reference which deals with the Nineteenth Century in great depth, handling general characteristics as well as specific studies of Manchester, Leeds, Birmingham, London, and Melbourne (Australia).
HB/PB (2)

The City In Print

Choay, Francoise. *The Modern City: Planning In The 19th Century*. (See 2.1)

Collins, G.R. *Camillo Sitte And The Birth Of Modern City Planning*. (See Sitte item listed below.)

De Volpi, Charles P. *Ottawa: A Pictorial Record, 1807-1882*. Montreal: DEV-SCO Publications (order from Longman's Canada), 1964.
    A collection of 122 lithographs supported by a bilingual commentary, these superb illustrations are of great value for the study of the urban history of Ottawa.
HB (2)

_____. *Toronto: A Pictorial Record, 1813-1882*. Montreal: DEV-SCO Publications (order from Longman's Canada), 1961.
    Similar in content and value to the title commented upon above.
HB (2)

Evenson, Norma. *Le Corbusier: The Machine And The Grand Design*. (See 2.1)

Hammond, J. L. and Barbara. *The Town Labourer: The New Civilization 1760-1832*. Garden City: Doubleday, 1968.
    Not urban history.
(4)

Kyte, E. C. ed. *Toronto: A Selection From John Ross Robertson's "Landmarks Of Toronto."* Toronto: Macmillan, 1954.
    Not urban history.
(4)

Lubove, Roy. *Twentieth Century Pittsburgh: Government, Business, And Environmental Change*. New York: Wiley, 1969.
    Although this title deals with environmental change into the 1960's, the major focus of the work is toward the early Twentieth Century. A study of urban reform from the late 19th Century to the present, this work focuses on the actions of city leaders and others in bringing about the phenomenal changes which so greatly altered the urban landscape of this formerly bleak American industrial center.
HB/PB (2)

Mandelbaum, Seymour J. *Boss Tweed's New York*. New York: Wiley, 1965.
    This work, another of the Wiley Historical Cities Series, is primarily a journalistic/literary approach toward establishing a mood for this city in the 19th Century. Quite a worthwhile reference.
PB (2)

Masters, D. C. *The Rise Of Toronto: 1850-1890*. Toronto: University of Toronto Press, 1947.
    Not urban history.
(4)

Urban History

Saalman, Howard. *Haussmann: Paris Transformed.* (See 2.1)

Schlesinger, Arthur M. *The Rise Of The City, 1878-1898.* Chicago: Quadrangle, 1971. Reprint of this 1933 work.

(4)

Scott, Mel. *American City Planning Since 1890.* Berkeley: University of California Press, 1969.
    A vast compendium of information dealing with 80 years of thinking in regard to urban form and structure. A massive book of 750 pages which presents a comprehensive view of the emergence of city planning through periods of innocence and unlimited growth, to this day when planning has become imperative. A heavy book suitable as a reference, this work is essential for urban historians in North America.

HB/PB (2)

Sitte, Camillo. *City Planning According To Artistic Principles.* New York: Columbia University Press, 1965, HB (2), and Collins, G. R. and C. C. Collins. *Camillo Sitte And The Birth Of Modern City Planning.* New York: Random House, 1965, PB (2).
    These two books are companion titles. The first is a translation of the major work of this significant European planner of the last century. This work is a detailed analysis of the ideal of each aspect of a city's structure. Although the text is a bit heavy, the many illustrations are superb examples of 19th Century planning.

The second title is an analysis of Sitte's achievements and impact. More suitable for the specialist than the general reader, this work will be of immense value to the historian interested in developing the antecedents of modern planning philosophy in Europe and North America.

Speizman, Milton D. ed. *Urban America In The Twentieth Century.* New York: Thomas Crowell, 1968.
    Superior works exist.

(4)

Strauss, A. L. ed. *The American City: A Sourcebook Of Urban Imagery.* Chicago: Aldine, 1968.
    A symbolic, literary look at the 19th Century American city, presenting contrasting images through extractions from contemporary publications and dealing with the city from several points of view. Interesting reading.

HB (2)

Wade, Richard C. *The Urban Frontier: The Rise Of Western Cities, 1790-1830.* Cambridge: Harvard University Press (PB), and Chicago: University of Chicago Press (HB), 1967.
    A detailed study of the development of cities in the American Northwest Territory.

(3)

The City In Print

Weber, Adna. *Growth Of Cities In The Nineteenth Century: A Study In Statistics.*
    Ithaca: Cornell University Press, 1963.
        Superior works exist. (4)

Whitehall, Walter Muir. *Boston: A Topographical History.* 2nd ed., enlarged.
    Cambridge: The Belknap Press of Harvard University Press, 1968.
        Well illustrated, this work presents an intriguing glimpse into the history and people of Boston from the late 1700s through the present day, with emphasis on the 19th Century. Well written, this book is fascinating reading.

HB (2)

Wiebenson, Dora. *Tony Garnier: The Cite Industrielle.* (See 2.1)

2.7 CITIES IN PRE-EUROPEAN ASIA AND AFRICA

None reviewed to date.

2.8 CITIES IN PRE-COLUMBIAN AMERICA

Bushnell, G. H. S. *The First Americans: The Pre-Columbian Civilizations.* New York: McGraw-Hill, 1968.
        Although this work contains no reconstructions, it is still superbly illustrated. Interesting reading and admirably suited as a reference.

PB (2)

Hardoy, Jorge. *Urban Planning In Pre-Columbian America.* (See 2.1)

3
Planning I: Urbanization as Planning

This unit comprises close to one third of this bibliography. The items found in the following eleven sections deal, in the broadest sense, with the contemporary city. Most of the titles reviewed have historical or social elements, but their emphasis is on the city as a whole, viewed from more than one discipline. Works that are discipline oriented (e.g., urban economics, political science, anthropology) are reviewed elsewhere in this bibliography.

Although most of the sections are self-explanatory, several do bear mention. 3.21 and 3.22 deal with non-western urbanization or urbanization in the communist world. They have counterparts in 6.21 and 6.22, where items are reviewed on the social or cultural elements of the city in the non-western or the communist world. 3.4 includes works on specific cities, irrespective of the discipline or perspective used as a framework for their analyses. Historical or single discipline titles are therefore included. 3.5 consists of general works on the future, most of which are comprehensive reviews of the future. Items that deal with technology and its future are to be found in section 10.

3.1 GENERAL WORKS

Anderson, Nels. *Urbanism And Urbanization*. Leiden: E. J. Brill, 1964.
    Good readings on urbanization, both theoretical and practical, on a world-wide basis. This item is a detailed reference. The chapter on urban government by W. A. Robson is exceptionally good.
HB (2)

Arbital, Samuel L. *Cities And Metropolitan Areas In Today's World*. Mankato (Minnesota): Creative Educational Society, 1968.
    The main advantage of this inexpensive school text is that between its covers is found an entire range of urban conditions and problems. The past, future, and present conditions of a number of American cities are dealt with, as well as basic urban analysis. This work has a decided emphasis toward the urban conditions in the United States.
HB (2)

Bair, Frederick H. Jr. *Planning Cities: Selected Writings On Principles And Practice*. Edited by Virginia Curtis. Chicago: American Society of Planning Officials, 1970.
    A planning reader and reference work on specific problems, this work

presents practical advice about planning problems and possible means of solution for the various levels of jurisdiction. Both nuts and bolts' problem solving and policy setting are dealt with in this highly useful reference.

    HB (2)

Bartholomew, Harland. *Land Uses In American Cities*. Cambridge: Harvard University Press, 1955.
    Although a basic work at one time, this book is now dated.

    (4)

Berry, Brian J. L. and Jack Meltzer, eds. *Goals For Urban America*. Englewood Cliffs: Prentice Hall, 1967.
    Superior works exist.

    (4)

Blake, Peter. *God's Own Junkyard*. New York: Holt, Rinehart, and Winston, 1963.
    There are some excellent before and after shots in this pictorial essay on the blight and beauty of cities. This is a very useful and inexpensive reference for the observer of today's city.

    HB/PB (2)

Bollens, John C. and Henry J. Schmandt. *The Metropolis: Its People, Politics And Economic Life*. 2nd ed. New York: Harper and Row, 1970.
    A comprehensive, world-wide study of the city, this work has much to recommend it. The nature of metropolitan areas, social structures, economics, government, and service metworks are discussed. Specific problems and dilemmas are dealt with, as well as possible practical solutions. There are detailed studies included on London, Ibadan, Tokyo, and Sao Paolo. The urban condition in the United States is used as the basic frame of reference.

    HB (2)

Branson, Margaret and Evarts Erickson. *Urban America*. Glenview (Illinois): Scott Foresman, 1970.
    A school text on the city in the United States. This work begins with an overview of the city, and continues with urban history in the U.S., the automobile in the city, suburbia, urban migrations, urban ecology, urban renewal, and future alternatives. Each section includes abridgements from other works. Although prepared as a school text, it is a well balanced work and is good for general use.

    PB (1)

Canty, Donald. *The New City*. New York: Praeger, 1969.
    A study which analyses the urban crisis in the U.S., without including the racial problems, this title is divided between a concise text and unique illustrations. A visual study of urban man, his effect upon the city and its effect on him. This work is a worthwhile reference.

    HB (2)

Cary, Lee J. ed. *Community Development As A Process*. Columbia: University of Missouri Press, 1970.

    (3)

Planning I: Urbanization As Planning

Chermayeff, Serge and C. Alexander. *Community And Privacy: Toward A New Architecture Of Humanism.* Garden City: Doubleday, 1963.
    This general study of the city is well illustrated, quite readable, and supplemented with interesting quotes as introductions to each chapter. Sections are brief and engaging. One-half of the work deals with housing types, specifically from the viewpoint of human and social needs. This section is of particular value because it is the only work yet reviewed that is concerned with this aspect of human settlement.
    PB (1)

Cherry, G. E. *Town Planning In Its Social Context.* London: Leonard Hill, 1970.
    (3)

Christensen, David. *Urban Development.* New York: Holt, Rinehart and Winston, 1964.
    This school text attempts to cover the entire spectrum of the city, but it is short and superficial, filled with jargon, and rather popularized.
    PB (2)

Churchill, Henry S. *The City Is The People.* New York: W. W. Norton, 1962.
    This useful reprint looks at the city from quite a human viewpoint. One value of this item is its readability, making it suitable for general use. Primarily an historical survey, this work serves well as a study of the achievements and failures of urban development in the U.S.. Well illustrated.
    PB (2)

Congressional Quarterly. *Editorial Research Reports On The Urban Environment.* Washington: Congressional Quarterly, 1969.
    Superior items exist.
    (4)

Cullingsworth, J. B. *Town And Country Planning In England And Wales.* 3rd ed. Toronto: University of Toronto Press, 1971.
    (3)

Dentler, Robert A. ed. *American Community Problems.* New York: McGraw-Hill, 1968.
    Not urban studies.
    (4)

Downs, Anthony. *Urban Problems And Prospects.* Chicago: Markham, 1970.
    This book takes a look at the unevenly paced rate of change in eleven key urban institutions. Means of coping with the pressures of current tensions and conflicts are viewed through the prospect of major changes in existing institutions.

    A view is also presented which suggests that effective solutions can only result from challenging conventional wisdom and solutions. No attempt is made to present an "all encompassing theory." Accepting the reality of an exceedingly complex urban world and a rapid rate of change, the author presents a straightforward look at basic conditions without the use of jargon or technical terms.

Among the topics dealt with are urban growth, the American ghetto, housing, transportation, urban data systems, and urban education. A considerable amount of information is to be found in this highly recommended reference.

HB/PB (2)

Duhl, Leonard J., M.D., ed. *The Urban Condition: People And Policy In The Metropolis*. New York: Basic Books, 1963
   A reader with a difference, these selections include articles by planners, psychiatrists, biologists, and other disciplines not usually associated with planning. Cultural needs, transportation, engineering problems, a population's mental health, and other topics are well handled. A useful item.

HB/PB (2)

Eldridge, H. Wentworth, ed. *Taming Megalopolis: What Is And What Could Be*, and *How To Manage An Urbanized World*. Garden City: Doubleday, 1967.
   These two volumes form a compendia of articles by many of today's leading figures on urban conditions. Although many of the articles are too technical for general use, a large number are exceedingly useful. The many specific studies provided make for an excellent reference.

HB/PB (2)

Erber, Ernest. *Urban Planning In Transition*. New York: Grossman, 1970.

(3)

Ewald, William R. Jr., ed. *Environment For Man: The Next Fifty Years*. Bloomington: Indiana University Press, 1967.
   This reader has a number of provocative selections, including essays by Rene Dubos and Moshe Safdie. The topics encompass man's adaptation to his environment, the city as a state of mind, technology and the environment, and the future. The selections represent a variety of disciplines and make for a useful reference.

HB/PB (2)

Ewing, David W. *The Human Side Of Planning*. See Goodman, Robert. *After The Planners*.

Faltermayer, Edmund K. *Redoing America: A Nationwide Report On How To Make Our Cities And Suburbs Livable*. New York: Collier (PB), and Harper and Row (HB), 1968.

(3)

Feldman, L. D. and associates. *A Survey Of Alternative Urban Policies*. (Urban Canada: Problems and Prospects, Research Monograph 6.) Ottawa: Central Mortgage and Housing Corporation, 1971.
   This comparative study of policies in the U.S. and Great Britain in comparison with Canada forms a useful, although dry, reference.

PB (2)

Planning I: Urbanization As Planning

Fortune, ed. *The Exploding Metropolis*. New York: Doubleday, 1958.
    With chapters on renewal, urban sprawl, and the automobile, this work is easy reading and structured to be useful for single hour readings. It is, however, dated.
    (4)

Frankenberg, Ronald. *Communities In Britain: Social Life In Town And Country*. Harmondsworth: Penguin, 1966.
    (3)

Friedberg, M. Paul with Ellen Perry Berkeley. *Play And Interplay: A Manifesto For New Design In Urban Recreational Environment*. New York: Macmillan, 1970.
    This pictorial essay explores the condition of urban recreational space with considerable emphasis on the effect that existing playspaces have on children, the effect of non-space on juveniles, and the effect of inadequate open space on the elderly. Striking illustrations and provocative dialogue.
    HB (2)

Gans, Herbert J., ed. *People And Plans: Essays On Urban Problems And Solutions*. New York: Basic Books, 1968.
    (3)

Gerson, Wolfgang. *Patterns Of Urban Living*. Toronto: University of Toronto Press, 1970.
    (3)

Gertler, L. O., ed. *Planning The Canadian Environment*. Montreal: Harvest House, 1968.
    A reader of value as a supplemental item, the print in this edition is small, but chapters are short and, on the whole, easily readable by all. It is of value as a study of urbanization and planning in Canada. Studies include a general historical survey (superb) and essays on regional resource and recreational planning. It is of decided value.
    HB (1)

Gibberd, Frederick. *Town Design*. 5th ed. New York: Praeger, 1967.
    A comprehensive, well illustrated study of urban structures, this work begins with the whole town and then breaks it down into its component parts. The core, industrial, and housing areas are all fully covered in text and illustrations. Not only is it well written, but the illustrations are tied quite graphically to the text. It is an expensive reference with basic emphasis on urbanization in Great Britain.
    HB (2)

Gillie, F. B. *An Approach To Town Planning*. The Hague: Mouton, 1971.
    This is a textbook on planning.
    (3)

Ginger, R., ed. *Modern American Cities*. Chicago: Quadrangle Books, 1969.
    Not urban studies.
    (4)

The City In Print

Glazer, N., ed. *Cities In Trouble*. Chicago: Quadrangle Books, 1970.
    Not urban studies.

                                                                                                             (4)

Goodman, Charles. *Life For Dead Spaces*. New York: Harcourt, Brace and World, n.d..
    This reference is of value for developing student awareness and ideas on parks.

                                                                                                    OP (4)

Goodman, Paul. *Communitas*. 2nd ed., revised. New York: Vintage, 1960.
    This basic primer covers (1) historical and contemporary world-wide planning efforts, both practical and theoretical, and (2) the structure and nature of cities. Included in the latter are various suggested solutions to urban dilemmas in a wide range of areas, including work, leisure, and transportation. This is a generally valuable item.

                                                                                                    PB (2)

Goodman, Robert. *After The Planners*. New York: Simon and Schuster, 1971, and Ewing, David W. *The Human Side Of Planning: Tool Or Tyrant*. New York: Macmillan, 1969.
    Both of these works present personal and penetrating insights into the processes which hinder change. Both criticize existing methods of dealing with urban problems. Seeing these methods doomed to failure, both authors attack the 'sacred cows' that prevent the radical changes they feel are needed. The overemphasis of economic and structural, rather than people planning, is presented as one of the reasons for failure. They are compelling reading. The solutions offered are neither structural nor philosophical, but rather refreshingly provocative. Radical in the extreme, both works suggest solutions which are of interest to all students of the urban situation, providing insights which will aid in the investigation of one's own urban issues. Each book is complementary to the other and provides distinct views and commentary on our contemporary urban world.

                                                                                                    HB (2)

Gordon, Mitchell. *Sick Cities*. New York: Macmillan (HB), and Baltimore: Penguin (PB), 1963.
    Here is a broad journalistic study of the city, with discussions on traffic, pollution, public services and education, local government, and blight. This is a good study and interesting reading, but the style and structure make it awkward to use.

                                                                                                    HB (2)

Gutkind, E. A. *Twilight Of Cities*. New York: The Free Press, 1962.
    The nature of the exploding metropolis is dealt with following a good brief historical overview of the city. There is a study of living space vs. 'containerism' in this historical and contemporary examination of the human city and urban society.

                                                                                                    HB (2)

Planning I: Urbanization As Planning

Halprin, Lawrence. *Cities*. New York: Reinhold, 1965.
    Too expensive to be more than a library reference, this item contains a visual guide to the human side of the city.
OP (4)

Hansen, Niles M. *Twelve Cities*. New York: Harper and Row, 1969.
    Not urban studies.
(4)

Hauser, Philip. *The Study Of Urbanization*. New York: Wiley, 1965.
    Dated.
(4)

Haworth, Lawrence. *The Good City*. Bloomington: Indiana University Press, 1963.
(3)

Healy, Sean. *Town Life*. London: Batsford, 1968.
    An elementary historical and current survey of urbanization in England. Well illustrated, it is a useful item for general use.
HB (2)

Hedman, Richard and Fred Bair Jr. *And On The Eighth Day: Series Of Essays And Tableaux On Planner And Planning*. 2nd ed. Chicago: American Society of Planning Officials, 1967.
    A satire in prose and pictures, this work is a 'put-on,' a commentary on planning written by two planners. An inexpensive paperback, this work is a gem.
PB (1)

Higbee, Edward. *The Squeeze: Cities Without Space*. New York: William Morrow and Toronto: George McLeod, 1960.
    A study of space in the metropolitan area in terms of population, tax structures, suburbia vs. central city, rural-urban fringe, transportation and recreation. Highly readable.
PB (2)

Hirsch, S. Carl. *Cities Are People*. Toronto: Macmillan, 1968.
    This is a popularized, biographical, journalistic approach to the city that has minute studies of various world-wide locales. It is useful more as a school text and can help motivate students to an interest in urban affairs. Discussions include pollution, the automobile, and suburbia.
HB (2)

Hirsch, Werner Z., ed. *Urban Life And Form*. New York: Holt, Rinehart and Winston, 1965.
(3)

Hoyt, Homer. *The Structure And Growth Of Residential Neighborhoods In American Cities*. Washington: Federal Housing Administration, 1939 (available from Homer Hoyt Associates).

The City In Print

        This well illustrated collection of studies on the neighborhood is of historical value in both its text and maps. It is, however, dated.

        (4)

Hoyt, Homer. *According To Hoyt, 1916 To 1966.* Washington: Homer Hoyt Associates, n.d..
    In this collection of articles on the city, most are highly technical and of little value for the general reader. However, several are of definite use for the researcher.

        HB (4)

Hubbard, T. K. *Our Cities Today And Tomorrow.* Cambridge: Harvard University Press, 1929.
    Dated.

        (4)

Hurd, Richard M. *Principles Of City Land Values.* New York: The Record and Guide, 1924 (available from Homer Hoyt Associates).
    This is a valuable book when the misleading title is overlooked. The illustrations, maps, and diagrams of the cities and villages are superb. The study of the evolution of Paris is excellent. Other historical studies are likewise quite good. Topics discussed include site location, direction of growth, and utility distribution. Easy reading, this item is excellent.

        HB (2)

Jacobs, Jane. *The Death And Life Of Great American Cities.* New York: Vintage, 1961.
    An excellent source on the city, this book is highly critical and interesting. Following a decidedly humanistic approach to the city, it is a very good supplementary reader.

        HB/PB (2)

Keeble, Lewis. *Principles And Practice Of Town And Country Planning.* 4th ed. London: The Estates Gazette Ltd. (available in North America from the American Society of Planning Officials), 1969.

        (3)

Kent, T. J. *The Urban General Plan.* San Francisco: Chandler Publishing Co., 1964.
    This is an essential study of municipal planning. The general land use plan, its uses and structure are discussed in detail. It is of immense value for research and study.

        HB (2)

Krueger, Ralph R. and R. Charles Bryfogle, eds. *Urban Problems: A Canadian Reader.* Toronto: Holt, Rinehart and Winston, 1971.
    The selections in this large collection of articles related to the urban character of Canada were chosen for their suitability for secondary level use. Sections deal with the nature of cities, man in the city, urban sprawl and renewal, transportation, urban design, regional planning, urban government, and alternate futures.

        HB (2)

Planning I: Urbanization As Planning

Lauri, Peter. *Beneath The City Streets*. London: Allen Lane (The Penguin Press), 1970.
    Not urban studies.
(4)

Le Corbusier (Jeanneret-Gris, C. E.). *Concerning Town Planning*. New Haven: Yale University Press, 1948.
(3)

Levin, Melvin R., ed. *Exploring Urban Problems*. Boston: The Urban Press, 1971.
    Superior works exist.
(4)

Lewis, David, ed. *The Pedestrian In The City*. Princeton: Van Nostrand Reinhold, 1965.
    Available in the U.S. only, this is an excellent collection of studies on the topic.
(3)

Liston, Robert A. *Downtown: Our Challenging Urban Problems*. New York: Dell, 1968.
    This short paperback, written by a journalist, examines the major ills of American cities.
PB (2)

Lithwick, N. H. *Urban Canada: Problems And Prospects*. Ottawa: Central Mortgage and Housing Corporation, 1970.
    This document surveys urbanization in Canada and its future prospects. A must for both Canadians and Americans, it is the first official North American attempt to outline the problems and possible political alternatives for national policy. A heavy document, it is full of information and statistics, making it an excellent reference.
PB (2)

Little, Charles E. *Challenge Of The Land: Open Space Preservation At The Local Level*. New York: Pergamon, 1969.
    Written by the founder of the Open Space Institute, this work is essentially a manual for suburban municipal officials. It summarizes relevant knowledge on open space, with case studies, showing what can be done. A highly effective rendering of the topic, this title deals with specific techniques, both political and economic, which can be used to acquire and hold open space.
HB/PB (2)

Loewenstein, Louis K., ed. *Urban Studies: An Introductory Reader*. New York: The Free Press, 1971.
    Superior works exist.
(4)

Logie, Gordon. *The Urban Scene*. London: Faber and Faber, 1964.
OP (4)

The City In Print

Lucas, Rex A. *Minetown, Milltown, Railtown: Life In Canadian Communities Of Single Industry*. Toronto: University of Toronto Press, 1971.
    Not urban studies.

(4)

Lynch, Kevin. *Site Planning*. Cambridge: The M. I. T. Press, 1967.
    This work deals with urban planning from the viewpoint of site and location. The first half considers the interrelationships between the site and the natural and human environment. A very useful reference, this is the most complete work on the topic.

HB (2)

_____. *Site Planning*. 2nd ed. Cambridge: The M. I. T. Press, 1971.
    This edition adds over one hundred pages, updating and revising the previous information on the art of arranging the external physical environment. New data is added on ecology, the human use of space, and its psycho-social effects and design methods. A superb book.

HB (2)

MacGraw, Frank M., D. L. Phelps, <u>et al</u>. *The Rise Of The City: An Urban Approach To World Geography*. San Francisco: Field Educational Publications, 1971.
    This school text on urban geography focuses on three areas; the effect of man's use of land, the historical growth of cities, and urban development patterns and characteristics in the United States.

The first two sections are international, the third American in emphasis. Even though it is geographically oriented, there is a distinct urban studies emphasis. Well written, with hundreds of color photographs and dozens of maps and charts, this book is superb as a text. The authors have dealt both comprehensively and in depth with their subjects.

The teacher's edition includes an additional 96 pages of conceptual framework, 'enrichment activities' suggestions, a highly useful bibliography, and a glossary.

This title should be reviewed by all teachers of urban studies programs.

HB (1)

Meadows, Paul and Ephraim H. Mizruchi, eds. *Urbanism, Urbanization, And Change: Comparative Perspectives*. Reading (Mass.): Addison-Wesley, 1969.
    This college level collection of readings is distinctive because it draws from a wide range of disciplines. With world-wide coverage of urban patterns and problems, this volume focuses on urbanization as a social process. The 43 articles and the concise section leads provide highly useful reference material.

HB (2)

Meyerson, Martin, <u>et al</u>., eds. *Housing, People And Cities*. New York: McGraw-Hill, 1962.
    Dated.

(4)

Planning I: Urbanization As Planning

Meyerson, Martin. *Face Of The Metropolis*. New York: Random House, 1963.
    Dated.

(4)

Miles, Simon R. *Metropolitan Problems: International Perspectives. A Search For Comprehensive Solutions*. Toronto: Methuen, 1970.
    A volume of the Intermet Metropolitan Studies Series.

(3)

Moscow, Alvin. *City At Sea*. New York: G. P. Putnam, 1962.
    Not urban studies.

(4)

Moynihan, Daniel P., ed. *Toward A National Urban Policy*. New York: Basic Books, 1970.
    Here is a reader worthy of purchase. It deals with a wide spectrum of topics, providing current perspectives on population, housing, government, transportation, land use, pollution, poverty, and renewal in the city. New towns and urban designs are also included among the 25 topics covered. A successful compilation.

HB (2)

Mumford, Lewis. *The Urban Prospect*. New York: Harcourt, Brace and World, 1968.
    This is the latest comment by Mumford on the condition of the urban environment. Although the articles date from the early 1950's through the late 1960's, the earlier ones have supplementary remarks that bring them up to date. The broad range of topics include neighborhoods, urban landscapes, the automobile and highways, urban form, megalopolis (with Doxiadis' commentary on it), megalopolis vs. the regional city, and future prospects--both the ills and the remedies. This is a valuable work as it brings together remarks on the concepts of several individuals involved in analyzing the urban condition. A valuable book, it is much too esoteric for more than a reference.

HB/PB (2)

Nixon, G. Peter and Maurice A. Campbell. *Four Cities: Studies In Urban And Regional Planning*. Toronto: McClelland and Stewart, 1971.
    This is a well developed series of four case studies from Ontario.
They include:

    Windsor: A Study Of Urban Problems.
    Sarnia: A Study Of Annexation Problems.
    London: A Study Of Urban Renewal.
    The Waterloo-South Wellington Area: A Study In Regional Planning.

Each carefully outlines the historical background, specific conditions, political developments, plans, and problems of the city in question. Each is structured with questions for student use. It is a highly useful series.

PB (1)

Owen, Wilfred. *The Accessible City*. Washington: The Brookings Institute, 1972.
    This work updates Mr. Owen's exhaustive research and evaluation of urban transportation in North America, and goes beyond into the city as a whole. Public and private transport are dealt with in relation to urban design, community goals, housing, and metropolitan growth. It is highly readable, presenting a considerable amount of information in a digestible form.

HB (2)

Palmer, Michael. *Cities*. London: Batsford, 1971.
    A cursory overview, this book deals with the full spectrum of urbanization in less than 100 pages. A very useful item for an introduction to the subject for a slow reader.

HB (1)

Papageorgiou, Alexander. *Continuity And Change: Preservation In City Planning*. New York: Praeger, 1970.
    Superior works exist.

(4)

Problems Of American Society Series. Gerald Leinwand, general editor. New York: Washington Square Press, 1969ff.
    From this series, the following titles are available and applicable to urban studies:

The City As A Community
City Government
The People Of The City
The Slums
The Traffic Jam

Covering a number of topics, with an American emphasis, each volume has a common format. They are presented at a level that is quite useful for secondary school students. Well illustrated, they include both general text and brief readings.

PB (1)

Reissman, Leonard. *The Urban Process: Cities In Industrial Societies*. New York: The Free Press, 1964.
    These studies are based upon the major ideas of men such as Howard, Wright, and Mumford. Although it is specialized, this is an excellent item for those interested in urban theory.

HB/PB (2)

Richardson, Ronald E., George H. McNevin and Walter G. Rooke. *Building For People: Freeway And Downtown: New Framework For Modern Needs*. Toronto: The Ryerson Press, 1970.
    Superior works exist.

(4)

Planning I: Urbanization As Planning

Sert, Jose Luis. *Can Our Cities Survive: An ABC Of Urban Studies, Their Analysis, Their Solutions*. Cambridge: Harvard University Press, 1942.
    Dated.
    (4)

Seymour, Whitney North, Jr., ed. *Small Urban Spaces: The Philosophy, Design, Sociology And Politics Of Vestpocket Parks And Other Small Urban Spaces*. New York: New York University Press, 1969.
    The subtitle well describes the content of this sophisticated work. There is a great deal of valuable material in this reference.
    HB (2)

Shomon, Joseph James. *Open Land For Urban America: Acquisition, Safe Keeping, And Use*. Baltimore: The Johns Hopkins Press, 1971.
    Studying human needs for land, this work looks at parks, wildlife areas, and the land needs in both the present and the future. With an emphasis on a 'quality of life' criteria, the author surveys urban priorities, many of which now preclude the acquisition or holding of land for recreational use. A number of case studies on policies in specific cities are included. This is a useful and highly readable reference with an American emphasis.
    HB (2)

Simmons, James and Robert. *Urban Canada*. Toronto: Copp-Clark, 1974 Rev. Ed.
    A school text which presents a comprehensive view of the Canadian city, its images, origins, sectors, shapes, residents, and prospects for change. A highly informative and readable work, of use both in and outside the classroom.
    PB (1)

Spreiregen, Paul D. *Urban Design: The Architecture Of Towns And Cities*. (See 4.1)

Starr, Roger. *Urban Choices: The City And Its Critics*. Harmondsworth: Pelican, 1967 (PB), also titled *The Living End: The City And Its Critics*. New York: Coward-McCann, 1966 (HB).
    Superior works exist.
    (4)

Storm, Michael. *Urban Growth In Britain*. Toronto: Oxford University Press, 1967.
    A brief, well illustrated item on urbanization in England, this is primarily of value for its comparison with development in the U.S. and Canada.
    HB/PB (2)

Swatridge, L. A. *The Bosnywash Megalopolis: A Region Of Great Cities*. Toronto: McGraw-Hill, 1971.
    This school text is of general use, presenting as it does a concise and informative image of the Atlantic seaboard megalopolis. This work looks at the region as a whole, its past and present, and its five major urban centers. Profusely illustrated, this book is of immense use not only for study, but also for general reading.
    PB (1)

Swatridge, L. A. *Problems In The Bosnywash Megalopolis: Pollution, Transportation, Social Problems*. Toronto: McGraw-Hill, 1972.
    A supplement to *The Bosnywash Megalopolis*, an earlier book prepared by the same author, this title is equally important and valuable. As the topics listed in the subtitle would indicate, this work is very useful as either a reference or text.

    PB (1)

Tetlow, John and Anthony Goss. *Homes, Towns And Traffic*. 2nd ed. London: Faber and Faber, 1970.
    Superior items exist.

    (4)

Tietze, Frederick J. and James E. McKeown, eds. *The Changing Metropolis*. Houghton-Mifflin Research series, No. 10. Boston: Houghton-Mifflin, 1964.
    Dated.

    (4)

Tretten, Rudie W., ed. *Cities In Crisis: Decay Or Renewal*. Englewood Cliffs: Prentice Hall, 1970.
    Useful because of its readability, this book deals with a large number of urban conditions. Short and inexpensive, this reader is American oriented.

    HB/PB (2)

Tunnard, C. *The City Of Man*. New York: Charles Scribners and Sons, 1953.
    Dated.

    (4)

_____, and Boris Pushkarev. *Man-Made America: Chaos Or Control*. (See 5.1)

Tyrwhitt, J., ed. *The Heart Of The City: Towards The Humanization Of Urban Life*. London: Lund Humphries, 1952.
    Basically two books, Part 1 is a collection of brief sections by various planners and architects. It was written for the specialist and not for students.

    Part 2 deals with the core of various cities around the world. Each section is short, from one to only a few pages. Illustrated, it is of value in providing drawings, maps and photos of projects in more than 21 towns and cities. Although the layout is not well done, and it is dated by 20 years, this item is still quite valuable as a library reference. Sections on Chandigarh, Boston, Lausanne, Basel, and Hiroshima are quite useful. It is a good reference as a single library copy--if a copy can be found.

    OP (2)

Urban Affairs Annual Review. These annual collections deal with a variety of topics Of the volumes published or planned through 1972, the two volumes presented are of direct value for research in urbanization.

Planning I: Urbanization As Planning

    Schmandt, Henry J. and Warner Bloomberg, Jr., eds. *The Quality Of Urban Life*. Beverly Hills: Sage Publications, 1969.
        This volume includes studies by Gottmann, Greer, and Blumenfeld. The 20 chapters deal with urban life from a wide range of views. The probabilities and possibilities in the improvement of the quality of life are both dealt with. All essays deal with 'what we can get' and by what devices. A highly useful general research item.
        HB (2)

    Schnore, Leo F. and Henry Fagin, eds. *Urban Research And Urban Planning*. Beverly Hills: Sage Publications, 1967.
        Part 1 of this book concentrates on disciplinary analysis of urban problems. Part 2 deals with planning from cross-disciplinary perspectives. These essays are of value for research and analysis. Useful as a general reference.
        HB (2)

Van Cleef, Eugene. *Cities In Action*. New York: Pergamon, 1970.
    This is a general work with topics covering most aspects of urbanization. Each chapter is brief and quite readable. It is definitely a useful item.
    HB/PB (1)

Venetoulis, Ted and Ward Eisenhouer, eds. *Up Against The Urban Wall*. Englewood Cliffs: Prentice Hall, 1971.
    Superior works exist.
    (4)

Vernon, Raymond. *The Myth And Reality Of Our Urban Problems*. Cambridge: Harvard University Press, 1962.
    Dated.
    (4)

Wade, Mason, ed. *The International Megalopolis*. Toronto: University of Toronto Press, 1969.
    This collection of essays is focused on the theme of problems related to the Great Lakes megalopolis (Detroit-Windsor to Montreal). The first essay, by C. A. Doxiadis, is an excellent overview. Others deal with pollution, land use, transportation, political structures and administration, and the economic matrix of this two-nation metropolitan region.
    HB (2)

Wallace, David A., et al. *Metropolitan Open Space And Natural Process*. Philadelphia: University of Pennsylvania Press, 1970.
    (3)

Ward, Sol A. *Urban Planning And Architecture*. New York: Philosophical Library, 1971.
    Designed for use in computer programming.
    (3)

Warren, Roland L., ed. *Perspectives On The American Community*. Chicago: Rand-
McNally, 1966.
    Readings that can be found in better collections.

(4)

Weaver, Robert C. *Dilemmas Of Urban America*. New York: Atheneum (PB), and
Cambridge: Harvard University Press (HB), 1969.
    Superior works exist.

(4)

Weiner, Myron, ed. *Modernization: The Dynamics Of Growth*. New York: Basic Books,
1966.

(3)

Whitaker, Ben and Kenneth Browne. *Parks For People*. New York: Winchester Press,
1971.
    Here is a look at the ideas and forms of parks and other urban recreational spaces that serve the same function. Well illustrated, this presentation makes a strong case for human recreational space. Europe and the U.S. are both covered. It is a book worthy of inclusion in any collection.

HB (2)

Whyte, Willam H. *The Last Landscape*. Garden City: Doubleday, 1968.
    This is a long and essentially ponderous work on land-use planning. It has some interesting perspectives and is quite worthwhile, but its length is a major detracting point. With a sophisticated presentation of the topic, it is a useful reference.

HB/PB (2)

Wilhelm, Sidney M. *Urban Zoning And Land Use Theory*. New York: The Free Press,
1963.

OP (3)

Wingo, Lowdon, ed. *Cities And Space*. Baltimore: The Johns Hopkins Press, 1963.
    The articles by Gottheim and Haar in this reader are exceptionally good. The remainder are too sophisticated for general use.

PB (2)

Winter, Eric. *Urban Landscapes*. Scarborough: Bellhaven House, 1969.
    A good, basic introduction to urbanization, this work has a definite Canadian emphasis. It well serves as a teaser to a broad range of topics related to urbanization. An excellent item which is both highly readable and useful.

HB (1)

_____. *Urban Areas*. Scarborough: Bellhaven House, 1971.
    A superb item on urban sectors (Central Business District, residential, economic, and service), this book contains interesting illustrations and a large number of charts to supplement the text. A well balanced study with

Planning I: Urbanization As Planning

a geographical bias, it is similar in format to the other Winter title, *Urban Landscapes*.

HB (1)

Wolforth, John and Roger Leigh. *Urban Prospects*. Toronto: McClelland and Stewart, 1971.
   A superb introduction to the study of urbanization, this school text presents a balanced picture of the structure of cities in Canada. Using geography as a base, the authors outline the city's various functions, the factors of urban growth, the characteristics of urban regions in Canada, and prospects for the immediate future. Basic problems in Canadian cities are also dealt with. Well illustrated, this is also of use outside the classroom.

PB (1)

3.2 REGIONAL PLANNING

Ash, Maurice. *Regions Of Tomorrow: Towards The Open City*. New York: Schocken Books, 1969.

(3)

Breckenfeld, Gurney. *Columbia And The New Cities*. New York: Ives Washburn, 1971.
   Where some of the works listed here are exhaustive studies of particular new towns or national settings, this item provides a comprehensive overview of the world experience in new towns, including an extensive study of new towns in the U.S.. An associate editor of TIME, the author uses a distinct journalistic style. A general lack of illustrative material is balanced by an interesting delivery in this worthy reference.

HB (2)

Bunker, Raymond. *Town And Country Or City And Region?* Melbourne: Melbourne University Press, 1971.

(3)

Chapin, F. Stuart and S. F. Weiss, eds. *Urban Growth Dynamics In A Regional Cluster Of Cities*. New York: Wiley, 1962.
   This collection of sophisticated essays dealing with urban growth potentials and factors is of value for anyone who is delving into this area of study.

HB (2)

Clapp, James A. *New Towns And Urban Policy: Planning Metropolitan Growth*. New York: Dunellen, 1971.
   This work is quite complete, well researched, and interesting. Its format is, unfortunately, cluttered with many footnotes and details, relegating this informative work to reference use only.

HB (2)

Clawson, Marion. *Suburban Land Conversion In The United States: An Economic And Government Process*. Baltimore: The Johns Hopkins Press, 1971.

(3)

Friedman, John and William Alonso, eds. *Regional Development And Planning: A Reader*. Cambridge: The M. I. T. Press, 1964.
    This reader is a comprehensive collection of multi-disciplinary selections which deal with all aspects of the city and the region. The sections on location and spatial organization, resources and rural-urban relationships, are of particular value for reference. The section on the role of the city is of special value.

HB (2)

Gillie, F. B. *Basic Thinking In Regional Planning*. The Hague: Mouton, 1967.
    In this guide, or 'how to' work on regional planning, the full range of necessary considerations for comprehensive planning is reviewed. Special emphasis is placed on how to use raw data. It is a readable and worthy book.

HB (2)

Glikson, Arthur. *Regional Planning And Development*. Leiden: Aiu Sitjhoff's Vitgevers-maatschappij/n.v., 1955.
    A book of basic lectures collected on the subject.

HB (4)

Isard, Walter. *Methods Of Regional Analysis: An Introduction To Regional Science*. Cambridge: The M. I. T. Press, 1960.

(3)

Karp, Herbert H. and K. Dennis Kelly. *Toward An Ecological Analysis Of Intermetropolitan Migration*. Chicago: Markham, 1971.

(3)

Krueger, R. R., <u>et al</u>. *Regional And Resource Planning In Canada*. Toronto: Holt, Rinehart and Winston, 1963.
    Dated.

(4)

_____, et al., eds. *Regional And Resource Planning In Canada*. Revised ed. Toronto: Holt, Rinehart and Winston, 1970.
    This edition updates the 1963 volume with a number of new articles and extensive revision of the remaining essays. Although it deals with resource planning as well as urban planning, the topics lend themselves to the study of urbanization. An essential reader.

PB (1)

McLoughlin, J. Brian. *Urban And Regional Planning: A Systems Approach*. London: Faber and Faber and New York: Praeger (U.S. only), 1969.

(3)

Planning I: Urbanization As Planning

Merlin, Pierre. *New Towns: Regional Planning And Development*. Translated by Margaret Sparks. London: Methuen, 1971.
    This work covers new towns in England, Scandinavia, the Netherlands, France, the U.S.A., and Eastern Europe.
(3)

Orr, Sarah C. and J. B. Cullingworth. *Regional And Urban Studies: A Social Science Approach*. Glasgow: University of Glasgow and Beverly Hills: Sage Publications, 1969.
(3)

Osborn, Frederic J. *Green Belt Cities*. New ed. New York: Schocken Books, 1969. First published in 1946.
(4)

_____ and Arnold Whittick. *The New Towns: The Answer To Megalopolis*. 2nd ed. London: Leonard Hill, 1969.
    Quite a different reference from others reviewed, this work presents considerable analysis of the English new towns, their evolution and purpose. These detailed studies provide a good supplement to Ashworth's *The Genesis Of British Town Planning* (See 2.6).
HB (2)

Purdom, C. B. *The Building Of Satellite Towns*. New ed. London: Dent and New York: The Humanities Press, 1949.
    Dated.
(4)

Spiegel, Erika. *New Towns In Israel*. New York: Praeger, 1967.
    A highly detailed study of new towns in Israel, this work views the structures, land use, and government policy. Eight communities are studied in detail. A reference only.
HB (2)

Stein, C. S. *Toward New Towns For America*. Cambridge: The M. I. T. Press, 1957.
    Dated.
(4)

Strong, Ann Louise. *Planning Urban Environments*. Baltimore: The Johns Hopkins Press, 1971.
(3)

Tinbergen, Jan. *Development Planning*. New York: McGraw-Hill, 1967.
(3)

Von Hertzen, Heikki and Paul D. Spreiregen. *Building A New Town: Finland's New Garden City--Tapiola*. Cambridge: The M. I. T. Press, 1971.
    An expensive reference, this work is of value only if new towns are being dealt with in depth. The text is heavy going, with illustrations that are informative, but lack lustre.
HB (2)

Williams, Michael. *New Towns*. London: Heinemann, 1969.
    Here is a small paperback which briefly describes and illustrates several Scottish new towns, including Cumbernauld. Profusely illustrated, this geographical study is a valuable and inexpensive reference.

PB (2)

3.21 URBANIZATION IN ASIA, AFRICA, AND LATIN AMERICA

Bernheim, Marc and E. *From Bush To City: A Look At The New Africa*. New York: Harcourt, Brace and World, 1966.
    Not urban studies.

(4)

Beyer, Glenn H., ed. *The Urban Explosion In Latin America: A Continent In Process Of Urbanization*. Ithaca: Cornell University Press, 1967.
    These essays culminated from a 1966 conference and form one of the best single volumes reviewed to date on the subject of non-western urbanization. From a wide range of disciplines, this work presents both perspective and detailed information on its subject. Although some selections are quite sophisticated, it is a good reference.

HB (2)

Breese, Gerald, ed. *The City In Newly Developing Countries: Readings On Urbanism And Urbanization*. Englewood Cliffs: Prentice Hall, 1969. Part of the *Modernization Of Traditional Societies* series.
    A useful item, both in scope and content, this book covers the non-western world in detail. Readings, statistical data and concise summaries are used to cover major trends in urbanization, the role of cities in underdeveloped countries, their inhabitants, and the conditions of urban expansion. As a reference, this is the most complete work available on the non-western world.

HB (2)

Caldwell, John C. *Population Growth And Family Change In Africa: The New Urban Elite In Ghana*. New York: Humanities Press, 1968.
    This is a socio-economic study relating to urban conditions and problems. The readings are often dry and weighty, thus limiting it to a reference.

HB (2)

Dwyer, D.J., ed. *Asian Urbanization: A Hong Kong Casebook*. Hong Kong: University of Hong Kong Press, 1971.
    On the surface, this dry, scholarly work is of little interest to the general reader. However, beneath the statistics and arid prose, there is information of immense value. Sections on housing, resettlement, and squatters are all excellent and provide provocative comparisons with the Western urban condition. With very good illustrations, this is an excellent reference.

HB (2)

Planning I: Urbanization As Planning

Hance, William A. *Population, Migration, And Urbanization In Africa.* New York: Columbia University Press, 1970.
    Demographics is the major emphasis of this work which analyzes densities, migrations, urban problems, and includes a chapter of thumbnail sketches on several urban communities. Liberally sprinkled with maps, good photos, and documentation, it is a well written presentation. An excellent reference.
    HB (1)

Hanna, William J. and Judith L. *Urban Dynamics In Black Africa: An Interdisciplinary Approach.* Chicago: Aldine-Atherton, 1971.
    Over 115 cities are referred to in this sophisticated reference. Patterns of urban growth, migration, and ethnic and non-ethnic characteristics, and patterns of change are among the topics. This is a highly detailed work, but of decided reference value.
    HB (2)

Herbert, John D. and Alfred P. Van Huyck, eds. *Urban Planning In The Developing Countires.* New York: Praeger, 1968.
    A collection of monographs, this book deals with problems of implementing planning policy in the developing countries. Detailed studies center on India and Japan. A useful reference.
    HB (2)

Hourani, A. H. and S. M. Stern, eds. *The Islamic City: A Colloquium* (Papers on Islamic History, I). Oxford: Bruno Cassirer (HB) and Philadelphia: University of Pennsylvania Press (PB), 1970.
    In English and French.
    (3)

Krapf-Askari, Eva. *Yoruba Towns And Cities: An Inquiry Into The Nature Of Urban Phenomena.* Oxford: Clarendon Press, 1969.
    (3)

Oakley, David. *The Phenomenon Of Architecture In Cultures In Change.* Oxford: Pergamon, 1970.
    Although this work views structures in general, it leans heavily on housing.
    (3)

Okin, Theophilus Adelodun. *The Urbanized Nigerian: An Examination On The African And His New Environment.* Jericho: Exposition Press, 1968.
    This little book presents a glimpse into the traditional life style and use of space as contrasted to the changes brought about by urbanization. It gives a balanced view of the effects and problems of African Urbanization.
    HB (2)

Oram, Nigel. *Towns In Africa.* London: Oxford University Press, 1965.
    Viewing town growth, land tenure, town planning, housing, urban government, and future prospects, this is an excellent study of sub-Saharan urbanization. A goldmine of information.
    PB (1)

Rodwin, Lloyd. *Nations And Cities: A Comparison Of Strategies For Urban Growth.* Boston: Houghton-Mifflin, 1970.

Studies of regional and national planning in Venezuela, Turkey, Great Britain, France and the U.S.. Chapters One and Two compare policies in the various countries and comment on their successes. This is done with valuable insight into the advantages and disadvantages in each nation. Useful.

HB/PB (2)

_____ and Associates. *Planning Urban Growth And Regional Development.* Cambridge: The M. I. T. Press, 1969.

This is a collection of detailed observations, by a number of individuals, of examples of urban growth patterns and problems in the city and the region. It is of technical value as a reference. Examples used are Venezuelan.

HB (2)

Shibir, Saba George. *Recent Arab City Growth.* Kuwait: Kuwait Government Printing Press, 1967.

This is a unique reference. To date, it is the only book that deals with modern urbanization in the Arab world. Expensive, paperbound, and slow to arrive (at least three months by sea mail), it nevertheless cannot be recommended too strongly. The 680 pages include articles by the author which have appeared in Arab newspapers and journals between the years 1959-1967. The following is an abridged table of contents with this reviewer's comments in parentheses.

   Part I.   The Arab World in Time and Space (color or black and white photos and line drawings).
   Part II.   Arab Cities in Process of Mutation.
      Chapter 1.   Traditional Setting and Anatomy of Arab Town(s).
      Chapter 4.   Understanding Some Causes of Urban Difficulties.
      Chapter 6.   Public Housing Policy Needed in the Arab World.
      Chapter 11. Ibn Khaldun on City Planning, Sociology, and Architecture (a major Arab philosopher 1332-1405 A.D.).
   Part III. Selected City and Country Studies and Case Studies (including Jordan, Kuwait, Lebanon, Libya, Palestine, Saudi Arabia, Tunisia).
   Part IV.   Exposition, Exploration, and Expansion of Planning Concepts.
   Part V.   Scanning the Arab Urban Scene (including observations on comprehensive planning, aesthetics, urban government, residential patterns, technology, Arab architecture).
   Part VI.   Urban Formation.
   Part VII. Whither Planning.

In summary, this work is a compilation of comments, observations, analyses, and illustrations of the Arab world. The process of urbanization, as perceived by an Arab, is presented in a manner which is quite interesting. Photos are reproduced poorly by North American standards, but they do provide, in their hundreds, a good feeling for the nature and character of urbanization in North Africa and the Middle East. Although it is difficult to secure, it is well worth the effort.

Planning I: Urbanization As Planning

>   Source: Mail--Ministry of Information
>   Kuwait, Arabia
>   Cable--Alirshad
>   Telex--MGIKT 2030
>   Price: KD 9.000 (approximately $25.00 US/CAN)

PB (2)

3.22 URBANIZATION IN THE COMMUNIST WORLD

Fisher, Jack C., ed. *City And Regional Planning In Poland*. Ithaca: Cornell University Press, 1966.
> A unique work in English, this is a study of Communist planning policies and accomplishments of Polish, not Western, academicians and practicing planners. Detailed analysis is made of city, regional and national planning. Over 100 photos and maps provide illumination into the structure and fabric of Polish and, as such, Communist cities. A highly sophisticated reference.

HB (2)

Gutnov, Alexei, et al. *The Ideal Communist City*. New York: Braziller, 1968.

(3)

Harris, Chauncy D. *Cities In The Soviet Union: Studies In Their Functions, Size, Density, And Growth*. Washington: Association of American Geographers, 1970.
> Fifth in the monograph series of the Association of American Geographers. Probably the definitive work on urbanization in this area, this item utilizes geography as a framework to deal with the Russian city through history, the early Soviet period, and current characteristics of growth. It covers a wide scope, with Russian studies, a functional classification of cities in the Soviet Union, density, long-range trends, and growth patterns by district. An excellent reference.

HB (2)

3.3 URBAN SPRAWL AND SUBURBIA

Carver, Humphrey. *Cities In The Suburbs*. Toronto: University of Toronto Press, 1962.
> A useful and readable book, this is of immense value for studying the suburb. Well illustrated.

HB/PB (1)

Chinitz, B. *City And Suburb*. New York: Prentice Hall, 1964.
> A good study of the economic structure of the suburb, its transportation and planning. This book is valuable for research.

PB (2)

Clark, S. D. *The Suburban Society*. Toronto: University of Toronto Press, 1968.
> Although this study of the suburbs deals with Canadian cities (Toronto Metropolitan area), it relates to some American studies made earlier. In

general, it presents a detailed analysis of life in the suburbs. A good source of data, this is an excellent reference. The reading level is somewhat advanced.

PB (2)

Donaldson, Scott. *The Suburban Myth*. New York: Columbia University Press, 1969.
    Heavily laden with references to other studies, this item is nonetheless quite readable. A useful reference.

PB (2)

Dobriner, William M. *Class In Suburbia*. Englewood Cliffs: Prentice Hall, 1963.
    An excellent, complete and scholarly study on the suburb, this title is different from others reviewed on the same topic. Well documented and sophisticated, it is a reference that provides a good overview of other studies and findings.

PB (2)

Look editors. *Suburbia: The Good Life In Our Exploding Utopia*. New York: Cowles, 1968.
    A pictorial essay of American suburbia, this work is essentially a collection of *Look* articles. It is useful as a viewpoint of a way of life, a subculture with its own rules and codes of behavior. A useful reference.

HB/PB (2)

Neutze, Max. *The Suburban Apartment Boom: Case Study Of A Land Use Problem*. Baltimore: The Johns Hopkins Press, 1968.
    This work deals with land use and, more specifically, American trends in apartment dwellings and construction. A highly detailed study, of value primarily as a reference, it includes surveys on factors of centrifugal movement to the suburb as well as the interaction of land speculation and regulation.

PB (2)

Sobin, Dennis P. *The Future Of The American Suburbs: Survival Or Extinction*. Port Washington (N.Y.): Kennikat, 1971.
    This is a study of the U.S. suburb from the 17th Century, including the suburban mystique, its place in the metropolitan region, and future propects. A good book, it is interesting reading, and has a useful format.

HB (2)

3.4 MAJOR METROPOLITAN AREAS

Abu-Lughod, Janet L. *Cairo: 1001 Years Of The City Victorious*. Princeton: Princeton University Press, 1971.
    A superb reference which provides detailed information on this significant Arab city. The text is divided into three parts, the first part deals with the historical city (640-1800), the second part handles conditions and problems from 1800 into the republic period, and the third part covers the contemporary metropolis. Profusely illustrated, this expensive text is

Planning I: Urbanization As Planning

        highly recommended as a readable and comprehensive reference.

        HB (2)

Arthur, Eric. *Toronto: No Mean City*. Toronto: University of Toronto Press, 1964.
    A pictorial study of Toronto from its beginnings to the turn of the century, this book has a good balance of readable text and fine photographs. It is ideally suited as a reference.

        HB (2)

Bain, Richard P. and A. Lynn McMurray. *Toronto: An Urban Study*. Toronto: Clarke-Irwin, 1970.
    This volume is the first of a series dealing with Canada's major metropolitan areas. Not a text in the traditional sense, it is a compilation of photographs, maps, charts, diagrams and statistics. Presenting a view of Toronto as it has been, and as it is today, materials can be selected to study a number of topics or themes. The information included is presented in sections covering major urban patterns. Quite useful for supplemental reading.

        PB (1)

Britain Today Series. Scarborough: Bellhaven House.
    Consisting of six pamphlets on British villages and towns, three titles of this series are applicable to urban studies.

Neil, Eric M. *Crawley: A New Town*. 1971.
_____. *Newcastle: An Industrial City*. 1971.
_____. *Teeside: An Industrial Port Area*. 1971.

Each is about 30 pages long, illustrated with statistics, photos, and maps. The brief text is followed by a number of exercises.

        PB (2)

Carter, E. J. and E. Goldfinger. *County Of London Plan*. Harmondsworth: Pelican, 1945.
    Dated.

        OP (4)

Carter, Edward. *The Future Of London*. Harmondsworth: Pelican, 1962.

        OP (4)

Cities Series. London: Thames and Hudson, n.d.
    Twelve titles are available on major world cities. Authored by Martin Hurlimann, they are:

        Athens   *Hong Kong*   *Moscow & London*
        Bangkok   *Kyoto*   *Paris*
        Delhi & Agra   *Istanbul*   *Rome*
        Florence   *London*   *Venice*

These works are not urban studies.

        (4)

The City In Print

Cities Of The World Series. London: Phoenix House, n.d.
    Cities covered are:

        Brussels   *Paris*   *Istanbul*
        Cairo   *Vienne*   *Tokyo*
        Jerusalem *Athens*
        Munich   *Bangkok*

    These works are not urban studies.

                                                                                                                   (4)

Couperie, Pierre. *Paris Through The Ages*. (See 2.1)

Dancer, W. S. and A. V. Hardy. *Greater London*. Cambridge: Cambridge University Press, 1969.
        This work is of special value for its maps. Included are studies of the city, other communities in Greater London, and the new town of Crawley. Interesting photos, substantial statistics, and a highly informative text.

                                                                                                                   PB (1)

DeCarlo, Giancarlo. *Urbino: The History Of A City And Plans For Its Development*. Cambridge: The M. I. T. Press, 1970.
        This reference is quite specialized, but it is highly recommended for use in communities with populations of 15-20,000. Urbino dates from the 12th Century A.D., has a population of 20,000, and is a distinctive and colorful town to study. The book is well illustrated with maps and photos that provide for easy comparison with North American towns.

                                                                                                                   HB (2)

Dore, R. P. *City Life In Japan: A Study Of A Tokyo Ward*. Berkeley: University of California Press, 1967.

                                                                                                                   (3)

Doxiadis, Constantinos A., Doxiadis Associates and The Detroit Edison Company. *Analysis. Vol. I: Emergence And Growth Of An Urban Region: The Developing Urban Detroit Area*. Detroit: The Detroit Edison Company, 1966.
        This work deals, in order, with the North American setting, the Great Lakes Megalopolis, the Great Lakes area, and the Urban Detroit area. The illustrative material in this volume is of particular value for studies of urbanization in Canada and the United States.

                                                                                                                 HB (2)

_____. *Future Alternatives. Vol. II: Emergence And Growth Of An Urban Region: The Developing Urban Detroit Area*. Detroit: The Detroit Edison Company, 1967.
        This volume presents sections on Doxiadis' own methodology, the present situation and trends, and a large number of alternatives.

                                                                                                                   HB (2)

_____. *A Concept For Future Development. Vol. III: Emergence And Growth Of*

Planning I: Urbanization As Planning

An Urban Region: The Developing Urban Detroit Area. Detroit: The Detroit Edison Company, 1970.
    A variety of Doxiadis' ideas are presented here along with an in-depth study of future potentials and conditions. Included is a study of historical growth and current land use problems. The majority of this volume looks at a conceptual plan, with elaborated forecasts for the entire region, each sub-area, and transportation, land use, employment, services, and residential patterns. Prospects to the year 2000 are put forth in great detail with profuse illustrations. This entire series is of value for any library.
    HB (2)

ELEK Series. London: Elek Books, 1960-1969.

    Blunt, Wilfrid. *Isfahan: Pearl Of Persia.* 1966.
    Brion, Marcel. *Pompeii & Herculaneum: The Glory And The Grief.* 1960.
    _____. *Venice: The Masque Of Italy.* 1962.
    Landau, Rom. *Morocco: Marrakesh, Fez, Rabat.* 1967.
    Nims, Charles F. *Thebes Of The Pharoahs: Pattern For Every City.* 1965.
    Procopiou, Angelo. *Athens: City Of The Gods From Prehistory To 338 B.C.* 1964.
    Rice, David Talbot. *Constantinople: Byzantium-Istanbul.* 1965.

    These books are part of a series which has a general layout of historical background, a cultural survey, and the art found in each of the cities presented. Their major value is found in the approximately 100 illustrations (half in color). Ideal references at a reasonable price.
    HB (2)

The following were reviewed and were found not to be urban studies:

Esin, Emel. *Mecca The Blessed, Madinah The Radiant.*
Gaunt, William. *Flemish Cities.*
Lin Yutang. *Imperial Peking.*
Sordo, Enrique. *Moorish Spain.*
Swaan, Wim. *Lost Cities Of Asia.*
    (4)

Evenson, Norma. *Chandigarh.* Berkeley: University of California Press, 1966.
    A detailed study of this Indian city. Unfortunately, it is quite sterile. Full of detail and illustrated with plans of the development of this model city, the overview becomes lost in details. The photographs at the end are passable, though not outstanding.
    HB (2)

Feldman, Herbert. *Karachi Through A Hundred Years: 1860-1960.* 2nd ed. Karachi: Oxford University Press, 1970.
    Not suitable for urban studies.
    (4)

Fogelson, Robert M. *The Fragmented Metropolis: Los Angeles 1850-1930.* Cambridge: Harvard University Press, 1967.
    Quite a worth-well item, the illustrations in this book are valuable

for the perspectives they present on urban sprawl in this city. A suitable reference.

HB (2)

Fuermann, George. *Houston: The Once And Future City*. Garden City: Doubleday, 1971.
    Not urban studies.

(4)

Goldston, Robert. *New York: Civic Exploration*. New York: Macmillan, 1970.
    A visual and textual portrait of New York City as a human space, this unique work delves behind the facades of the city. The author presents a vivid image of the best and the worst, of plans and hopes, as well as the forces that prevent their being realized. Interesting reading.

HB (2)

Greater London Papers. London: School of Economics and Political Science, 1965.
    Davies, E. *Transport In Greater London*. #6.
    Self, P. *Town Planning In Greater London*. #7.
    Robson, W. A. *The Heart Of Greater London*. #8.
    Well designed and easily read, these references provide readings on three political and structural problems found in dealing with the ancient heart and the sprawling conurbation of Greater London.

PB (2)

Gunther, John. *Twelve Cities*. New York: Harper and Row, 1969.
    Not urban studies.

(4)

Hall, Peter Geoffrey. *The World Cities*. New York: McGraw-Hill, 1966.
    This study of major world cities is full of statistical information on major city development. Well illustrated with maps, it is a good general introduction to a number of major centers of urban civilization today.

HB/PB (1)

Harvey, E. Roy. *Sydney, Nova Scotia: An Urban Study*. Toronto: Clarke-Irwin, 1970.
    A highly detailed geographical study of this Canadian city, this work contains superb maps and photos. The current situation is quite well discussed, with interesting historical material. Considerable emphasis is placed on statistical information. A good reference.

PB (2)

Hull, Oswald. *London*. London: Macmillan, 1970.
    Superior items do exist.

(4)

International Urban Research Institute Studies. *The World's Metropolitan Areas*. Los Angeles: University of California Press, 1959.
    This short book presents an overview and gazetteer of the world's cities and urban areas both by continent and country by country. Dated.

OP (4)

Planning I: Urbanization As Planning

Lubove, Roy. *Twentieth Century Pittsburgh*. (See 2.6)

Meyerson, Martin and Edward C. Banfield. *Boston: The Job Ahead*. Cambridge: Harvard University Press, 1966.
   Not urban studies.
(4)

Morgan, W. T. W. *Nairobi: City And Region*. (See 7.3)

Morris, James. *Cities*. London: Faber and Faber, 1963.
   This work, written by a newspaper correspondent, is a personal view of 74 cities from all over the world. The perspective is neither scholarly nor popular, but rather an interesting glimpse of the mood in a diverse range of cities. It is of decided value as a reference.
HB (2)

National Capital Development Commission. *The Future Canberra*. Sydney: Angus Robertson, 1965.
   This is quite useful as a reference on a city that is being built entirely by plan, without the usual problems of previous development, or the haphazard development that results from no planning. Excellent maps and photographs of models clearly describe what can be done in the development of an entire city using complete planning control from the start.
HB (2)

New York City Planning Commission. *Plan For New York City*. 6 Vols. Cambridge: The M. I. T. Press, 1969.
   Five of these six volumes are detailed studies of each borough--the Bronx, Brooklyn, Manhattan, Queens, and Staten Island. Division is made by planning districts, each having maps, photographs, and other graphic materials. Good for general use and reference, these are relatively expensive and oversized books.
PB (2)

_____. *Critical Issues*. Vol. I of *Plan For New York City*. Cambridge: The M. I. T. Press, 1969.
   This is a superb work. The charts, diagrams, photos, foldout maps, and airphotos included are excellent. The text deals with the immediate needs and a plan for action, not future possibilities. These photographs give the best feel for New York City yet seen in any work and the comparisons with other cities are quite graphic and useful. An essential reference.
PB (2)

Patrick, James H. *Montreal: Port City*. Toronto: Ginn, 1969.
   A short pamphlet, this school text deals with the largest Canadian city. Illustrated, the reading level is quite elemental and, therefore, good for the poor reader. It is a good, simplified geographic study of the city.
PB (2)

Rand, Christopher. *Los Angeles: The Ultimate City*. New York: Oxford University Press, 1967.
    A journalistic view of this city and its urban region, this title is highly personal and narrative. Of little value for research information, it is quite valuable for reading to grasp the essence of this vast conglomerate from the viewpoint of one who sees the city as the model for the future.
        HB (2)

Regional Plan Association. *Urban Design Manhattan*. New York: Viking, 1969.
    An essential pictorial reference. Photographs of the city are very good, but they are surpassed by the excellent drawings and maps of networks, systems, future prospects, etc. Although expensive, it is an excellent reference.
        HB (2)

Rice, Mary J. *Chicago: Port To The World*. New York: Follett, 1969.
    Not urban studies.
        (4)

Robson, William A. *Great Cities Of The World*. New York: Macmillan, 1955.
    A comprehensive study of the city as an institution, this title has been replaced by a new edition. (See 1.1) Dated.
        (4)

Schwartz, Alvin. *Old Cities And New Towns: The Changing Face Of The Nation*. New York: Dutton, 1968.
    This school text is somewhat superficial, but well suited for the poorer student. Using Philadelphia as a focus, and well illustrated with plans and drawings, it represents the positive and negative aspects of North American cities. Bacon's proposals for Philadelphia are presented quite well in a number of drawings.
        HB (2)

Self, Peter. *Metropolitan Planning: The Planning Service Of Greater London*. London: Weidenfeld and Nicolson, and New York: Humanities Press (U.S. only), 1971.
        (3)

Senior, Derek, ed. *The Regional City: An Anglo-American Discussion Of Metropolitan Planning*. Chicago: Aldine, 1966.
    These papers from a seminar on metro planning held in 1964 cover regions in the U.S.A. and England. The work is useful as it includes a great deal of detailed information on New York, London, Washington, and the English New Towns.
        OP (4)

Spreiregen, Paul D., ed. *On The Art Of Designing Cities: Selected Essays Of Elbert Peets*. Cambridge: The M. I. T. Press, 1968.
    An essential reference, although relatively expensive, this work includes

Planning I: Urbanization As Planning

>eleven essays on Washington and several others on London, Paris, Rome, and Williamsburg. All are highly readable.
>
>>HB (2)

This Beautiful World Series. Tokyo and Palo Alto (Calif.): Kodansha International Ltd..
>This series of illustrated books and city guides is unique in that several of the titles deal with cities and present quite a good image and feel for each one. Among the titles reviewed, the following are recommended:

>Ando, Hikotaro. *Peking*. 1968.
>Johnson, Paul. *San Francisco*. 1970.
>Kim, Chewon. *Seoul*. 1969.
>Ryo and Banri Namikawa. *Istanbul*. 1972.
>n.a. *Moscow*. 1968.
>
>>PB (2)
>
>Due to their more conventional tourist orientation, the following are not recommended:
>
>*Vienna*.
>*Hong Kong*.
>
>>PB (4)

Thomas, David. *London's Green Belt*. London: Faber and Faber, 1970.
>>(3)

Toynbee, Arnold, ed. *Cities Of Destiny*. New York: McGraw-Hill, 1967.
>This oversized, expensive item is a valuable library reference. It is a beautiful work, with chapters on the major urban centers of history. The text is both readable and interesting, with photographs and other illustrations that more than warrant its purchase as a reference.
>
>>HB (2)

University of Amsterdam. Sociographical Department. *Urban Core And Inner City: Proceedings Of The International Study Week, Amsterdam, 11-17 September, 1966*. Leiden: E. J. Brill, 1967.
>Expensive, this reference has articles in both French and English. Although some are highly detailed, a sufficient number of the articles are unique enough to warrant the purchase of this title for reference. It is the most complete work of any reviewed that provides information on the delineation of core theory and study techniques.
>
>>HB (2)

Vass, Benjamin. *Toronto: A Photo Study Of Urban Development*. Toronto: McGraw-Hill-Ryerson, 1971.
>This is an excellent collection of photos, many of which show and compare the same site in the early 1950's and 1970. Lettering of the significant points in each photo allows for easy comparison. There is also good coverage of the CBD, general land use, residential areas, transportation, and the future. Well worth buying.
>
>>PB (1)

Wechsberg, Joseph. *Prague: The Mystic City*. New York: Macmillan, 1971.
    Not urban studies.
(4)

Williams, Oliver P., <u>et al</u>. *Suburban Differences And Metropolitan Policies: A Philadelphia Story*. Philadelphia: University of Pennsylvania Press, 1965.
(3)

3.5 URBAN FEATURES

Anderson, Stanford, ed. *Planning For Diversity And Choice: Possible Futures And Their Relations To The Man-Controlled Environment*. **Cambridge: The M. I. T. Press, 1968.**
    Containing a number of articles on future prospects, this reference is primarily of use for in-depth research.
HB (2)

Baier, Kurt and Nicholas Rescher, eds. *Values And The Future: The Impact Of Technological Change On American Values*. New York: The Free Press, 1969.
    Superior works exist.
(4)

Beckwith, Burnham Putnam. *The Next 500 Years: Scientific Predictions Of Major Social Trends*. New York: Exposition Press, 1967.
    This is a study of trends (not science fiction), of prospective history, of what will come (and not how). The projections on such topics as government, population, work and production, finance, agriculture, industry, commerce, cities, communication, education, family life, and crime, make interesting reading.
HB (1)

Bell, Daniel, ed. *Toward The Year 2000: Work In Progress*. Boston: Beacon Press (PB) and Boston: Houghton Mifflin (HB), 1969.
    A collection from the 1967 summer issue of *Daedalus*, this is an exceedingly useful reference. An **extremely** wide range of topics is dealt with in detail, including studies of society, technology, cities, political structures, scientific alternatives, privacy and communication prospects by 2000 A.D..
HB/PB (2)

Bell, Wendell and James A. Mau, eds. *The Sociology Of The Future: Theories, Cases, And Annotated Bibliography*. New York: Russell Sage Foundation, 1971.
    An interesting book, but **far** too detailed for general use.
(3)

Bertin, Leonard. *Target 2067: Canada's Second Century*. Toronto: Macmillan, 1968.
    This forecast of the future, in narrative form, is quite good, with short, readable chapters. Although **given** several poor reviews, this work

Planning I: Urbanization As Planning

> stands up well under careful scrutiny; it is excellent, well researched, convincing and exciting reading.
>
> HB (1)

Brown, Harrison, et al. *The Next Hundred Years: A Discussion Prepared For Leaders Of American Industry*. New York: Viking, 1963.
> Although a decade old, this work is of use in its analysis of man's existing and potential natural and technological resources. As such, it takes a different direction than most books on the future. An interesting comparative study to the Meadows book (listed below).
>
> PB (2)

Burhoe, Ralph W., ed. *Science And Human Values In The 21st Century*. Philadelphia: The Westminster Press, 1971.
> Religious rather than urban studies.
>
> (4)

Burke, John G., ed. *The New Technology And Human Values*. 2nd ed. Belmont: Wadsworth, 1972.
> Superior works exist.
>
> (4)

Calder, Nigel. *Living Tomorrow: Planning For The Future*. Harmondsworth: Penguin, 1970.
> A potpourri of glimpses, through use of photo, text, and jest, of what may stand before us. As much a workbook of ideas as it is a text, this item looks at what is and what could be, intermingled with vignettes on the foibles of man. An interesting work to be exposed to.
>
> PB (1)

Cook, Peter. *Architecture: Action And Plan*. (See 4.1)

_____. *Experimental Architecture*. (See 4.1)

De Jouvenal, Bertrand. *The Art Of Conjecture*. See Helmer, Olaf. *Social Technology*. (Listed below.)

DeWofle, Ivor, ed. *Civilia--The End Of Sub Urban Man: A Challange To Semidetsia*. (See 4.1)

Diebold, John. *Man And The Computer: Technology As An Agent Of Social Change*. New York: Praeger (HB) and Avon (PB), 1969.
> Written by one of the developers of the computer, this book employs interesting perspectives, but is of limited use for all but those deeply interested in the origin of the computer and its implications for society.
>
> HB (2)

Ernst, Morris L. *Utopia 1976*. New York: Greenwood Press, 1955.
> This is an intriguing study which was written at a time when 1976 seemed far distant. The projections deal with many aspects of urban life, many

The City In Print

        that came true, and just as many long dead as possibilities. Interesting reading as a comparison with today's projections.

      HB (2)

Fabun, Don. *The Dynamics Of Change*. Englewood Cliffs: Prentice Hall, 1967.
        This blending of surrealistic photographs and observations on the future, from both scientists and poets, opens the imagination to shattering changes in the human environment and spirit.

      HB/PB (1)

_____. *The Dimensions Of Change*. Beverly Hills: Glencoe Press, 1971.
        Supplementing *The Dynamics Of Change*, this work provides mind expanding images of a changing world, with investigations into the human environment, housing, energy, food, mobility, and communications. An unusual rendering of possible futures for urban man.

Note: A paperback edition of this work is available in 6 modules.

      HB/PB (1)

Foreign Policy Association. *Toward The Year 2018*. New York: Cowles, 1968.
        A collection of 13 essays on change, this work consists of future prospects on topics such as transportation, communication, computers, food, population, and economics. Interesting reading and well worth purchasing.

      HB (2)

Forrester, Jay W. *Urban Dynamics*. Cambridge: The M. I. T. Press, 1969.

      (3)

_____. *World Dynamics*. Cambridge: Wright-Allen Press, 1971.
        The technical nature of this work severely limits its general use, but its recommendation is required, if for no other reason, than because of its contents. Forrester is in the forefront of the "gloom and doom" futurists, gaining support from the Club Of Rome. It is a computer study, fleshed out with dialogue, of use to serious students of the future. A good reference.

      HB (2)

Futterman, Robert A. *The Future Of Our Cities*. New York: Doubleday, n.d..
        This humanistic approach to the city has chapters ideally suited for readings on the city of tomorrow. Besides the human evaluation, 10-page chapters deal with 17 U.S. cities, using a format which includes a basic map, statistics, highway arterial systems, and text. This work is of decided value and worth searching for.

      OP (2)

Gabor, Dennis. *Inventing The Future*. Harmondsworth: Pelican, 1963.
        Not urban studies.

      (4)

Goldstein, Kenneth K. *The World Of Tomorrow*. London: Collins and New York: McGraw-Hill (U.S. only), 1969.

Planning I: Urbanization As Planning

      In this study of the future, the text is rather elementary, but the visual content is excellent. Easy to comprehend, most aspects of a future urban environment are well covered.

                                                                                       HB (1)

Goracz, A., I. Lithwick, and L. O. Stone. *The Urban Future* from Urban Canada: Problems and Prospects, Research Monograph 5. Ottawa: Central Mortgage and Housing Corporation, 1971.
      A detailed, statistical, and arid work, it is nevertheless of immense use as a reference, having considerable information and data on forecasts for Canadian cities.

                                                                                       PB (2)

Gunn, James E. *Man And The Future*. Lawrence: University of Kansas Press, 1968.
      Not urban studies.

                                                                                           (4)

Hellman, Hal. *The City In The World Of The Future*. New York: M. Evans, 1970.
      A general survey of the future city, this work deals with future trends, new building techniques, housing alternatives for the future, enclosed city areas, city center reconstructions, new towns, alternate urban forms, and megastructures. Well illustrated, this is a useful reference.

                                                                                    HB (2)

_____. *Communications In The World Of The World Of The Future*. New York: M. Evans, 1969.
      Not urban studies.

                                                                                          (4)

_____. *Transportation In The World Of The Future*. New York: M. Evans, 1968.
      Written for high school level readers, this book is of immense value in providing text and illustrations of a large number of transportation systems in Canada and the U.S..

                                                                                    HB (2)

Helmer, Olaf. *Social Technology* (1966) and De Jouvenal, Bertrand. *The Art Of Conjecture* (1967). New York: Basic Books.
      Both of these items are rather weighty, but they are recommended for their impact on the art of forecasting. Helmer outlines the methods of the "Delphi" technique of forecasting. Developed from several Rand Corporation studies, this book is essential to anyone who wishes to pursue the study of futures with any degree of sophistication.

      De Jouvenal's book is also significant. Taken in conjunction with Helmer's study, forecasting is expanded to include methodology in economics, sociology, and political science.

      Both works are complex, but they are crucial in providing a basis of understanding for most of the future studies which have appeared since the mid 1960's.

                                                                                   Both HB (2)

The City In Print

Jackson, John N. *The Urban Future*. London: George Allen and Unwin, 1972.
(3)

Jenks, Charles. *Architecture 2000: Predictions And Methods*. London: Studio Vista and New York: Praeger (U.S. only), 1971.
    This work is not just a study of alternative architectural forms, although that is the primary focus. Trends in structures, life styles, transportation, and industrial design are covered with illustrations of proposals and explanatory text. A highly useful reference.
HB/PB (2)

Jungk, Robert and Johan Galtung, eds. *Mankind 2000*. Oslo: Universitetsforlaget, 1969.
    These studies on the future represent a number of perspectives, including international alternatives, technological promises, human goals and prospects for humankind, and the role of future research. This work is detailed and sophisticated compared to other works reviewed dealing with the future. Even so, it is of value as a reference.
PB (2)

Kettle, John. *Footnotes On The Future*. Toronto: Methuen, 1970.
    A look at Canada in the Year 2000. Particular attention is given to discussion of population, cities, resources, travel, transportation, communications, the home, government, work, and leisure.
PB (1)

Knelman, Fred H., ed. *1984 And All That: Modern Science, Social Change, And Human Values*. Belmont: Wadsworth, 1971.
    A reader on the sociology of science, dealing with technological order, technology and the environmental crisis, the scientific revolution, and the complexities of priorities between science and ecology.
(3)

Kostelanetz, Richard, ed. *Social Speculations*. New York: William Morrow, 1971.
    A superb reader, this book is loaded with provocative selections that include observations by Buckminster Fuller, Isaac Asimov, Herman Kahn, Anthony Wiener, and Athelstan Spilhaus, to name a few.

    Grouped around the four topics of "history" (to the future), technology, environment, and cities, this work is detracted from only by the total lack of any illustrative material.
HB/PB (2)

McHale, John. *The Future Of The Future*. New York: Braziller, 1969.
    An interesting work which presents a different viewpoint from previously reviewed books on technological change. As with Kahn (*The Year 2000*, see 10.1), McHale does not directly relate to urbanization, but deals with future world patterns. An excellent reference, well illustrated and interesting.
HB/PB (2)

Planning I: Urbanization As Planning

Meadows, D. H., et al. *The Limits To Growth*. (See 1.2)

Michael, Donald N. *The Unprepared Society: Planning For A Precarious Future*. The Tenth John Dewey Society Lecture. New York: Basic Books (HB) and Harper & Row (PB), 1968.
    This work, by a social psychologist, emphasizes the cultural ramifications of alternate futures. Irrationalities, already built into changing systems are viewed, along with institutionalized resistance to change, scarcity of time, cybernation, social engineering, and the challenges that face educators in dealing with curriculum needs for an unknown future. This is essential for the educator.
HB/PB (2)

Ofshe, Richard, ed. *The Sociology Of The Possible*. Englewood Cliffs: Prentice Hall, 1970.
    A reader on the future, this book has selections from Harry Harrison, P. J. Farmer, Edward Bellamy, B. F. Skinner, Aldous Huxley, Isaac Asimov, Walter Miller, Arthur C. Clarke, Frederick Pohl, and others. The topics cover social characteristics, urbanization, technological change, and political organization. This is an extremely interesting book.
HB/PB (1)

Parker, Stanley. *The Future Of Work And Leisure*. (See 6.2)

Perloff, Harvey S., ed. *The Future Of The U.S. Government: Toward The Year 2000*. New York: Braziller, 1971.
    A study of significance, but superseded by the other Commission on the Year 2000 book entitled *Toward The Year 2000* (above).
(4)

Reich, Charles A. *The Greening Of America*. New York: Random House and Bantam (PB only), 1970.
    A bestseller with a great deal to offer as a reference, this work is too significant to bypass. Whether or not you accept Reich's theses on different levels of consciousness and its effect on change, the details of his commentary bear exposure. Essential for reference.
HB/PB (2)

Reid, Clyde. *21st Century Man Emerging*. Philadelphia: Pilgrim Press, 1971.
    Not urban studies.
(4)

Rodwin, L., ed. *The Future Metropolis*. New York: Braziller, 1967.
    A collection of essays, this reader is of value in that it presents some of the earlier studies on The Future City. Drawing from a number of disciplines, this work presents a variety of perspectives which have had a marked effect in subsequent analyses of urban futures. As such, this is a useful reference.
HB (2)

The City In Print

Ruste, R. G. *American Heritage: Prognosis A.D. 2000*. New York: Exposition Press, 1967.
    A religious rather than urban orientation.

(4)

Schaller, Lyle E. *Impact Of The Future*. New York: Abingdon Press, 1969.
    A study of the future, this book weaves the future trends of society in general with the trends for the church. Twenty topics are dealt with, emphasizing social and economic prospects. Each section has a succinct summary followed by a short statement of implications for the church. This work is not sectarian, and as such, the emphasis, not found in books previously reviewed, has value for its religious focus.

PB (2)

Staff of the *Wall Street Journal*. *Here Comes Tomorrow: Living And Working In The Year 2000*. Princeton: Dow Jones Books, 1967.
    A series of articles collected from the *Wall Street Journal* that deal with population, computers, communications, energy, transportation, cities, the home, and medicine. The selections are both factual and interesting. A good reader.

PB (1)

Stevens, L. Clark. *"EST": The Steersman Handbook: Charts Of The Coming Decade Of Conflict*. New York: Bantam Books, 1970.
    Superior works exist.

(4)

Stulman, Julius. *Evolving Mankind's Future*. Philadelphia: J. B. Lippincott, 1967.

(3)

Toffler, Alvin. *Future Shock*. New York: Random House and Bantam (PB only), 1970.
    This book has been so well received that little more need be said. It brings together a tremendous amount of information and presents it in a readable form. Toffler's views of the future are explained by extensive study of present conditions and plausible trends.

HB/PB (1)

Wallia, C. S., ed. *Toward Century 21: Technology, Society, And Human Values*. New York: Basic Books, 1970.
    Twenty-four selections on speculations into changes in man and machine. A superb collection, too sophisticated for general use, but highly recommended as a reference.

HB (2)

3.6 URBAN THEORISTS

Doxiadis, Constantinos A. *Architecture In Transition*. London: Hutchinson, 1963.
    A study of the state of architecture from the perspective of the author's science of Ekistics, this work is well illustrated with photographs and line

Planning I: Urbanization As Planning

    drawings. Complete surveys of Doxiadis' projects worldwide and studies of the future are also included in this highly worthwhile book.

        HB (2)

Geddes, Sir Patrick. *Cities In Evolution: An Introduction To The Town Planning Movement*. London: Ernest Benn (HB) and New York: Harper and Row (PB, U.S. only), 1968.
    A reprint of the 1915 work by this most influential planner. More than the comment of a particular period, this is a basic source still in use today. Essential.

        HB/PB (2)

Hilberseimer, L. *The New Regional Pattern: Industries And Gardens, Workshops And Farms*. Chicago: Paul Theobald, 1949.
    A significant reference which presents an early view of linear city developments foreshadowing the more sophisticated concepts of Doxiadis, and including interesting projections towards the future--1970 and beyond. Illustrated.

        HB (2)

Howard, Ebenezer. *Garden Cities Of Tomorrow*. London: Faber & Faber, 1965.
    This current Faber edition of an 1898 classic includes additional chapters on the success of the author's ideas, forerunners in the theory of modern suburbia. Reference use.

        HB (2)

Mumford, Lewis. *Art And Techniques*. New York: Columbia University Press, 1952.

        (3)

Ostrowski, Walclaw. *Contemporary Town Planning From The Origins To The Athens Charter*. The Hague: International Federation For Housing and Planning, 1970.
    An interesting little book which looks at large scale urban concepts from the 1880's to 1934. Essentially a reexamination of the pre-World War II ideas of Soria, Howard, and Le Corbusier as well as other 'pioneer' planners and their proposals. A useful book for this topic.

        PB (2)

Reiner, Thomas A. *The Place Of The Ideal Community In Urban Planning*. Philadelphia: University of Pennsylvania Press, 1963.
    Idealistic and utopian concepts by major theorists and planners of the past 75 years and encapsuled in short, readable chapters containing the basic proposals with analysis and evaluation of each. Of value for everyone.

        HB (2)

Wright, Frank Lloyd. *The Living City*. New York: Horizon Press (HB) and New American Library (PB), 1958.
    A collection of several works of this most significant architect. This edition is of particular value in presenting a detailed study of Broadacre City, the major concrete urban proposal of Frank Lloyd Wright. Also included is *When Democracy Builds*. Primarily for reference use.

        HB/PB (2)

3.7 SPECIFIC TECHNIQUES OF FIELD STUDIES

Boon, Gordon S. *Townlook, Book 1: Observing And Recording By Maps In Urban Areas.* Oxford: Pergamon, 1969.
    Superior works exist.

(4)

Gibbs, Jack P., ed. *Urban Research Methods.* Princeton: Van Nostrand, 1961.
    A collection of readings dealing with methods of defining and limiting such topics as urban boundaries and characteristics. Analysis also deals with specific areas of the city, including urban-rural functional relationships. Excellent research data.

HB (2)

Jackson, J. N. *Surveys For Town And Country Planning.* London: Hutchinson University Library, 1963.
    A valuable, concise study in the use and development of land, this work presents useful methods for data collection and covers methods of survey, transportation, industry, and population.

HB/PB (2)

Lynch, K. *The Image Of The City.* The M. I. T. Press, 1960.
    This is one of the most influential works on urbanization and is of immense value for its presentation of field work techniques. Content is arranged in textual form for easy assimilation, and after initial orientation, questions and study approaches are introduced for in-depth field work. (See additional comment in 1.1.)

HB/PB (1)

Warren, Roland L. *Studying Your Community.* New York: The Free Press, 1969.
    An interesting and valuable work. For each aspect of the community, a short introduction discusses methods and forms of inquiry followed by a series of questions which have been successfully designed to be applicable to communities of any size. A goldmine of ideas and techniques, and a superb field research guide.

PB (1)

Williams, Edward A. (Director of Study). *Open Space: The Choice Before California.* The Urban Metropolitan Open Space Study. San Francisco: Diablo Press, 1969.
    This unique book is useful for presenting a method of classifying open space and proposals for massive land acquisition for public use. Of value for reference in the U.S. and Canada.

PB (2)

Planning I: Urbanization As Planning

3.71 URBAN MODELS

Hohauser, Sanford. *Architectural And Interior Models: Design And Construction.* New York: Van Nostrand Reinhold, 1970.
    An essential reference which goes into painstaking detail on how to construct models, materials valuable for use in model making, landscaping, and sources for "to-scale" supplementary pieces. A superb item for any library and well worth its price.
                                                                                 HB (2)

Janke, Rolf. *Architectural Models.* New York: Praeger, 1968.
    This well illustrated book deals with a full range of uses for models, presenting various types of models and how they can be used in specific circumstances. Model-making and photographing are also dealt with in detail.
                                                                                    HB (2)

Wilson, Forrest. *Architecture: A Book Of Projects For Young Adults.* New York: Van Nostrand Reinhold, 1968.
    With a unique approach, the author presents architecture as a study which can be dealt with on a "do it yourself" basis. Architectural form appreciation is developed through simple techniques of construction with simple materials. A very interesting and useful work for urban studies or art.
                                                                                    HB (2)

3.8 URBAN RENEWAL AND RENOVATION

Abrams, Charles. *The City Is The Frontier.* New York: Harper & Row, 1965.
    A study of urban renewal in the U.S..
                                                                                        (3)

Center for Policy Study (University of Chicago). *The Social Impact Of Urban Design.* Chicago: University of Chicago Press, 1971.
    A study of the impact on American slum dwellers of improved design in housing and recreation facilities. An ethnic rather than urban orientation.
                                                                                        (4)

Greer, Scott. *Urban Renewal And American Cities: The Dilemma Of Democratic Intervention.* A sophisticated study dealing with urban renewal in theory and practice. The most complete item available on this topic and an ideal reference.
                                                                                   PB (2)

International Federation For Housing and Planning. *Urban Renewal.* The Hague: IFHP, 1967.
    This book includes reports on 22 urban renewal projects in 14 countries throughout the world. Concise, well illustrated studies are reported in three languages. A highly useful reference.
                                                                                  PB (2)

Mandelker, Daniel R. *The Zoning Dilemma: A Legal Strategy For Urban Change*.
   Indianapolis: Bobbs-Merrill, 1971.

(3)

Medhurst, D. Franklin and J. Parry Lewis. *Urban Decay: An Analysis And A Policy*.
   London: Macmillan, 1969.
      Studies of English urban renewal.

(3)

Miner, Ralph W. *Conservation Of Historical And Cultural Resources*. Chicago:
   American Society of Planning Officials, 1969.
      A paperbound, mimeographed, and illustrated study of this topic. Well written, easy to read and comprehend, it is the only highly readable item in print on this topic.

PB (1)

Wilson, James Q., ed. *Urban Renewal: The Record And The Controversy*. Cambridge:
   The M. I. T. Press, 1966.
      A comprehensive reader with selections on economic aspects, relocation, community life, design, challenges and alternatives. An exhaustively complete collection (680 pages), with an exclusively American orientation, this work is suitable as a library reference for comparative purposes.

HB/PB (2)

Worskett, Roy. *The Character Of Towns: An Approach To Conservation*. London: Architectural Press, 1969.
      A pictorial study of cities as artifacts, with sites to be preserved and means by which this can be done. Selection, efficient use, priorities, both in individual buildings and areas, are dealt with. Complementary to Cullen's *Townscape* (see 1.1) and Gibberd's *Town Design* (see 3.1), this is a useful reference with good illustrations and a readable text.

HB (2)

4
Planning II: Cities as Architecture

The books included in this section examine in one way or another, the structure of the city, either in its whole, or in detailed study of its components. Man's impact on land in the city, structures and their use, and human needs of structures, are major thrusts of a good number of the works reviewed.

Historical perspectives are included, with reference to a number of superb items rich with illustrations.

Section 4.3 includes several of the less expensive works about major architects of the city. It should be noted that the list is far from complete, with many more expensive, lavish titles not included. These, and a number of other, less expensive works, are now being gathered for review and report in the next edition.

Section 4.4 deals with housing in its entirety. Works on urban renewal have already been examined in section 3.8. This section examines the full spectrum including political, social and economic, as well as structural aspects of housing.

Section 4.5 includes several titles which illustrate unplanned communities and structures.

Section 4.6 lists several items that deal with design aspects of the use of space. For theoretical and humanistic studies of space and its effects on man, refer to section 6.3.

A number of works published under the umbrella of architecture have been excluded, namely those which deal with highly specialized, professional aspects of architecture and engineering. Any of general interest or reference have been reviewed.

4.1 GENERAL WORKS

Auzelle, Robert. *Enclycopedia De L'Urbanisme*. Paris: Freal Vincent, 1950.
    This work is in French, out of print and unique in its conception. Consisting of two loose-leaf volumes with foldouts, it contains hundreds of studies with photographs in association with maps and diagrams, all of which can be removed and utilized in a continuously changing display of all con- concepts of the city. Coverage is world-wide and historical.
    OP (2)

Bacon, Edmund. *The Design Of Cities*. New York: Viking, 1967.
    This work is of unexcelled importance in its presentation of current and

historical city structure from the architectural point of view. Well illustrated with conceptual drawings, maps, and photographs, it is of unusual value in depicting the concept of 'form and function' in the city, from Greek times to the present.

HB (1)

Banz, George. *Elements Of Urban Form*. New York: McGraw-Hill, 1970.
A study with unique viewpoints on overall urban design, examining the multitude of functions which combine to influence the development of current urban environments. Balancing concepts of the world-wide city, traditional urban forms, and future prospects, chapters deal with the city as man's home and as a locus of conflicting needs and resources. A useful reference.

HB (2)

City Building Series. London: Studio Vista.

    Balfour, A., et al. *Portsmouth*. 1970.
    Burrough, T. H. B. *Bristol*. 1970.
    Cantacuzino, S., et al. *Canterbury*. 1970.
    Hickman, D. *Birmingham*. 1970.
    Hughes, Q. *Liverpool*. 1969.
    Nuttgens, P. *York*. 1970.
    Sharp, D., ed. *Manchester*. 1969.

Each book in the series includes a pictorial and textual catalogue of significant structures of the city surveyed.

(3)

Cook, Peter. *Architecture: Action And Plan*. London: Studio Vista and New York: Reinhold, 1967.
An interesting little book, lavishly illustrated with designs for future modules, residential complexes, and megastructures. A useful reference.

PB (2)

_____. *Experimental Architecture*. London: Studio Vista, 1970.
Of value for its illustrations alone, this book presents a broad spectrum of new ideas and concepts in architecture. Also containing commentary, it is of definite value as a reference.

HB (2)

Crosby, Theo. *Architecture: City Sense*. London: Studio Vista and New York: Praeger (U.S. only), 1965.
Superior Works exist.

(4)

DeWofle, Ivor, ed. *Civilia--The End Of Sub-Urban Man: A Challange To Semidetsia*. London: The Architectural Press, 1971.
An expensive, yet worthwhile reference, worthy of purchase for its illustrations alone. Dealing with potentials for a high density city of one million inhabitants, the author exposes and illustrates revolutionary con-

Planning II: Cities As Architecture

cepts in a striking study setting out ideas which run counter to many of the 'givens' permeating so many other works. A must for those looking at new urban design potentials.

HB (2)

DeWofle, Ivor. *The Italian Townscape*. London: The Architectural Press, 1963.
Photos and graphics present three faces of Italy: the tourist facade of monumental places and subjects; the not so pretty view of an industrial country with very real problems of blight; and the natural face of settlements not yet victimized by developers. A beautiful book which breathes life into the towns and cities of Italy.

HB (2)

Hilberseimer, L. *Contemporary Architecture: Its Roots And Trends*. Chicago: Paul Theobald, 1964.
Superior works exist.

(4)

Le Corbusier. *The Radiant City*. New York: Orion, 1967.
Of all the works by this influential planner-architect, this one is the most useful for the general reader, blending together text, charts, maps, diagrams, and photographs in such a way that much can be learned about the nature of the "radiant city." A must for reference. Expensive.

HB (2)

Malt, Harold Lewis. *Furnishing The City*. New York: McGraw-Hill, 1970.
Dealing entirely with fixtures, this book illustrates a multitude of various features from statues to phone booths and street lights. The effect of alternate types on man is dealt with in detail. A distinctive work, useful for reference.

HB (2)

Mumford, Lewis. *Sticks And Stones: A Study Of American Architecture And Civilization*. 2nd revised ed. New York: Dover, 1955.
A dated and yet significant work. As with Mumford's other major works, the impact of his ideas on urbanization is immeasurable. With his usual flair for words, the author discusses developments from 1870 through the late 1920's, examining the influence of earlier periods on North American architecture.

PB (2)

Neutra, Richard. *Survival Through Design*. New York: Oxford University Press, 1969.
A reprint of this 1954 work.

(3)

Rasmussen, Steen Eiler. *Experiencing Architecture*. Cambridge: The M. I. T. Press, 1968.

(3)

Rudofsky, Bernard. *Streets For People: A Primer For Americans*. Garden City: Doubleday, 1969.
    An odyssey through pedestrian spaces throughout the world. In his preface, the author notes that this work is the only one which deals with the street, although the street is such an important part of any city, town, or hamlet. Woven throughout, in text and illustrations, is the theme that the space called the street is habitable only if it is designed to meet man's needs, and scaled to his proportions. Examinations deal with the historical street, current examples, and alternate trends or propsects for the future. A good study.

                                                                                                       HB/PB (1)

Safdie, M. *Beyond Habitat*. Edited by John Kettle. Montreal: Tundra Books, 1970.

                                                                                                                  (3)

Scully, Vincent. *American Architecture And Urbanism*. New York: Praeger, 1969.
    Superior works exist.

                                                                                                                 (4)

Severino, Renato. *Equipotential Space: Freedom In Architecture*. New York: Praeger, 1970.

                                                                                                                 (3)

Smithson, Alison and Peter. *Urban Structuring*. London: Studio Vista, 1967.

                                                                                                                 (3)

Spreiregen, Paul. *Urban Design: The Architecture Of Towns And Cities*. New York: McGraw-Hill, 1965.
    This well structured study covers the entire spectrum of the city, the text being supplemented with hundreds of line drawings. Of decided value for reference.

                                                                                               HB/PB (2)

Spyer, Geoffrey. *Architect And Community: Environmental Design In An Urban Society*. London: Peter Owen, 1971.

                                                                                                                 (3)

Von Eckardt, W. *A Place To Live: The Crisis Of Our Cities*. New York: Delacorte, 1967.

                                                                                                                 (3)

Wall, D. and W. Borek. *Visionary Cities: The Arcology Of Paolo Soleri*. New York: Praeger, 1970.
    A visual experience of Soleri's megastructures, this graphics-design book is a work of art in itself.

                                                                                               HB/PB (2)

Whiffen, Marcus, ed. *The Architect And The City*. Cambridge: The M. I. T. Press, 1966.
    A collection of papers on such topics as the purpose of the city, tech-

Planning II: Cities As Architecture

nology, ecology, and urban renewal, this work is quite worthwhile in providing insights into many complicated areas of study. Suitable for reference.
HB (2)

4.2 HISTORICAL ARCHITECTURE

Braun, Hugh. *Historical Architecture*. London: Faber & Faber, 1953.
The purpose and function of each architectural period is given concise evaluation in this well illustrated work. A very good item.
HB (2)

Chadwick, George F. *The Park And The Town: Public Landscape In The 19th And 20th Centuries*. London: Architectural Press and New York: Praeger (U.S. only), 1966.
A study of park design and function.
(3)

Gloag, John. *A Guide To Western Architecture*. London: George Allen and Unwin, 1958.
A basic, superbly illustrated history from the earliest origins to the 20th Century.
HB (2)

Great Ages Of World Architecture. A series. New York: Braziller, 1963-1965.

    Alex, William. *Japanese Architecture*.
    Branner, Robert. *Gothic Architecture*.
    Brown, Frank E. *Roman Architecture*.
    Hoag, John D. *Western Islamic Architecture*.
    Lowry, Bates. *Renaissance Architecture*.
    MacDonald, William. *Early Christian And Byzantine Architecture*.
    Millon, Henry A. *Baroque And Rococo Architecture*.
    Robertson, Donald. *Pre-Columbian Architecture*.
    Saalman, Howard. *Medieval Architecture*.
    Scranton, Robert L. *Greek Architecture*.
    Scully, Vincent, Jr. *Modern Architecture*.
    Wu, Nelson I. *Chinese And Indian Architecture*.

The value of this beautiful series cannot be too highly emphasized. Available in both hardbound and paperbound editions, it is essential for any library and for anyone interested in architecture.
HB/PB (2)

Hobhouse, Hermione. *Lost London: A Century Of Demolition And Decay*. London: Macmillan, 1971.
A pictorial record of structures demolished in the face of vociferous pleas for their preservation, this book presents a visual discussion of possible criteria for preservation of distinctive structures.
HB (2)

The City In Print

James, E. C. *From Cave To Cathedral*. London: Pall Mall, 1965.
    A basic reference for a view of man's earliest and most extensive architectural activities, this is a detailed study of his place of sanctuary and worship from the paleolithic to modern times.

    HB (2)

Pevsner, Nikolaus. *An Outline Of European Architecture*. 7th ed. Harmondsworth: Penguin, 1963.
    A useful single volume study, superbly illustrated, on the history of architectural form from the fourth through the 20th Century.

    PB (2)

Rasmussen, Steen Eiler. *Towns And Buildings: Described In Drawings And Words*. Cambridge: The M. I. T. Press, 1969.
    A visual tour through the cities of the world, as seen from the pages of this translation of a 1949 Danish work. This translation synthesizes the work of others, bringing illustrations and ideas from a good number of works not otherwise available (out of print or in languages other than English). The city and its structures are looked at by random searching through Europe and Asia, from the 16th Century to the present. A superb book, the most graphic on architectural history and historical urban design yet reviewed.

    PB (2)

Rosenau, Helen. *Social Purpose In Architecture: Paris And London Compared, 1760-1800*. London: Studio Vista, 1970.

    (3)

_____. *The Ideal City In Its Architectural Evolution*. London: Routledge & Kegan Paul and New York: Harper & Row, 1959.
    An overview is given to each historical period. Well illustrated, this work gives good perspectives for each period, but is of value only for research.

    HB (2)

Sandstrom, Gosta E. *Man The Builder*. New York: McGraw-Hill, 1970.
    Profusely illustrated with photographs (colour and black and white) and easily understood diagrams, this work is further complemented with a highly readable text. An excellent reference. Expensive.

    HB (2)

Vitruvius. *The Ten Books On Architecture*. Translated by Morris Hicky Morgan. New York: Dover, 1960.
    Written in the First Century B.C., this is the oldest work on architecture in existence as well as the most influential reference on the Roman views of architecture. As a prime reference on symmetry, harmony, and proportion, it has also had a great impact on western architecture since the Renaissance.

    PB (2)

Planning II: Cities As Architecture

4.3 ARCHITECTS OF THE CITY

Evenson, Norma. *Le Corbusier: The Machine And The Grand Design*. (See 2.1)

Giedion J. *Walter Gropius*. New York: Reinhold, 1954. A basic biography of this leader of modern architecture. Valuable for research.
OP (2)

Le Corbusier. *The City Of Tomorrow*. Cambridge: The M. I. T. Press, 1971, and *Towards A New Architecture*. London: The Architectural Press, 1970.
These items are reprints of works introduced in the 1920's, presenting the early views of this most important 20th Century architect and planner. Both are well illustrated, with some very interesting ideas, formulated half a century ago, but still relevant, if not more so, in the far more complex urban world of today. Limited to use by those particularly interested in urban design and architecture.
HB/PB (2)

Lissitzky, El. *Russia: An Architecture For World Revolution*. Cambridge: The M. I. T. Press, 1970.
This English language translation of the 1930 German edition is of interest as being the primer of "Soviet realism" in architecture. The chief architect of this school, El Lissitzky's comments are of interest for their presentation of a unique architectural form so prevalent in the Soviet Union from 1917-1932. Supplementary material is added to the original manifesto, providing a well balanced view of this architect's ideas, so easily identifiable in Soviet urban design to this day. Illustrated. A useful reference.
HB (2)

4.4 HOUSING

Wiebenson, Dora. *Tony Garnier: The Cite Industrielle*. (See 2.1)

Beyer, Glenn H. *Housing And Society*. New York: Macmillan, 1965.
A comprehensive study of housing from both the human and practical points of view. Contains useful sections on the history of housing, construction, house design, ownership, sector location, and housing in the U.K., the U.S.A., Western Europe, and the developing world. Useful as a reference.
HB (2)

Fried, Joseph P. *Housing Crisis, U.S.A.* New York: Praeger, 1971.
A superb reference, the only one so far which looks at the causes of urban housing shortages, decay, and costs. Useful in the Canadian context because the conditions, and their root causes, are products of a mutual stage of development. Interesting reading, it is well documented with statements and judgements fully substantiated. A must.
HB (2)

Johnston, R. J. *Urban Residential Patterns: An Introductory Review*. London: G. Bell and New York: Praeger (U.S. only), 1971.

(3)

Matsushita, Ronald, ed. *Housing*. Toronto: McGraw-Hill, 1971.
  A Canadian oriented reader dealing with housing in general as well as more specific topics including the availability of housing, residential patterns and alternatives, housing tenancy and ownership, and privacy. A concise work, with short selections presented in a highly readable style. A good reference.

PB (2)

Mayer, Albert. *The Urgent Future: People, Housing, City, Region*. New York: McGraw-Hill, 1967.
  The text deals with the need for solving the increasing crisis in housing. The content is quite broadly world-wide, and amply illustrated throughout with diagrams and photographs. A good reference. Expensive.

HB (2)

Pawley, Martin. *Architecture Versus Housing*. London: Studio Vista and New York: Praeger (U.S. only), 1971.

(3)

Wheaton, William L. C., et al., eds. *Urban Housing*. New York: The Free Press, 1966.
  An extensive collection of readings on this subject with emphasis on the U.S., but also containing a good deal on urban housing in general. A valuable reference.

HB (2)

Wheeler, Michael, ed. *The Right To Housing*. Montreal: Harvest House, 1969.
  An exclusively Canadian source, this work consists of papers from the 1968 Canadian Conference on Housing, covering the full range of housing conditions and problems in Canada. An extremely useful and exhaustive reference.

PB (2)

4.5 VERNACULAR ARCHITECTURE

Allen, Edward. *Stone Shelters*. Cambridge: The M. I. T. Press, 1969.
  A visual and textual study of the making of buildings in a particular region of southern Italy. The heart of this work illustrates habitations built by the residents of several villages in the area. A beautiful book, with fascinating illustrations.

HB/PB (2)

Branch, Daniel P. *Folk Architecture Of The Eastern Mediterranean*. New York: Columbia University Press, 1966.
  A superbly illustrated book on vernacular architecture, with a particularly good section on Mykonos. Out of print, but a must to search for.

OP (2)

Planning II: Cities As Architecture

Goldfinger, Myron. *Villages In The Sun: Mediterranean Community Architecture.* New York: Praeger, 1969.

    Essentially an essay on 25 villages in Greece, Italy, Spain, Morocco, and Tunisia. The illustrations alone are excellent, but supplemented by an exceedingly worthwhile commentary. An essential reference.

HB (2)

Rudofsky, Bernard. *Architecture Without Architects.* New York: Doubleday, 1964.

    More comprehensive in area, but less detailed than the Branch item listed above, this is a superb complementary volume. It should be noted that both of these works are useful in the study of site, town form and function as well as study of the small town or settlement outside North America or northern Europe. These volumes fill a gap left by most architect oriented material.

PB (2)

4.6 URBAN DESIGN

DeChiara, Joseph and Lee Koppelman. *Planning Design Criteria.* New York: Van Nostrand Reinhold, 1969.

    This work is unique in itself from all others reviewed to date. An expensive, oversized book, this study collects together masses of visual data on master plans, land use, population, housing, transportation, city sectors and activities, the "cityscape," utilities, and zoning. Illustrations range from designs of power poles and types of zoning lots to city-wide development concepts.

HB (2)

Dober, Richard P. *Environmental Design.* New York: Van Nostrand Reinhold, 1969.

    This superbly illustrated study of the use of space is an expensive yet worthwhile reference. It deals with three major concepts: human habitation, design structure, and a sense of place.

HB (2)

Norberg-Schulz, Christian. *Existence, Space And Architecture.* London: Studio Vista and New York: Praeger (U.S. only), 1971.

(3)

5
Urban Transportation

Titles in this section are restricted to works dealing exclusively with this specialized topic. It should be noted that transportation is also covered to a lesser degree in a number of works reviewed in section 3.1.

5.1 GENERAL WORKS

Halprin, Lawrence. *Freeways*. New York: Reinhold, 1966.
    Essentially a visual study, dealing with the automobile, transportation, land use, and transportation alternatives. Profusely illustrated.
HB (2)

Hennessey, R. A. S. *Transport*. London: Batsford, 1966.
    A simplified study of transportation in England from the 18th Century to the present. This work is short, but covers the development of the railway, the automobile, and, finally, sea and air transport.
HB (2)

Hull, Oswald. *Transport*. London: Macmillan, 1971.
    Superior works exist.
(4)

Leibbrand, Kurt. *Transportation And Town Planning*. London: Leonard Hill, 1970.
(3)

Meyer, J. R., et al. *The Urban Transportation Problem*. Cambridge: Harvard University Press, 1965.
    A detailed study on transportation in the context of current urban change, presenting a concise examination of comparative cost factors and varying possibilities for solutions to the problem. With its great amount of detail and statistical information, this work is more suitable for reference than general use.
HB (2)

Mumford, Lewis. *The Highway And The City*. New York: Harcourt Brace and World and New York: Mentor, 1963.
    This work carries on from *The City In History*, at least regarding movement within the city. Dated.
PB (4)

Urban Transportation

Murin, William J. *Mass Transit Policy Planning: An Incremental Approach.* Lexington: Heath Lexington Books, 1971.

(3)

Owen, Wilfred. *Cities In The Motor Age.* New York: Viking, 1959.
    A study of transportation, the problems it creates, and suggested solutions.

OP (4)

_____. *Metropolitan Transportation Problem.* Revised ed. Washington: The Brookings Institute, 1966.
    This basic text discusses the historical antecedents, impacts, and the current and future problems of transportation. These aspects are covered in overview as well as with documentation on specifics.

HB (1)

Pell, Senator Claiborne. *Megalopolis Unbound: The Supercity And The Transportation Of Tomorrow.* New York: Praeger, 1966.
    This work used the narrative to present a humanistic look at the city and megalopolis of today and tomorrow with documentation on transportation in the United States.

HB (2)

Reynolds, D. J. *The Urban Transportation Problem* from Urban Canada: Problems and Prospects, Research Monograph 3. Ottawa: Central Mortgage and Housing, 1971.
    A study of population forecasts and prospects in Canada done for analysis of transportation needs and facilities to the year 2000, with emphasis on Canada's nine major cities. Much of value for research in this document.

PB (2)

Richards, Brian. *New Movement In Cities.* 2nd ed. London: Studio Vista and New York: Reinhold, 1969.
    This excellent, short work, of value for studies in transportation systems and proposals, is profusely illustrated with photographs and diagrams. A good complementary text to Owen's *Metropolitan Transportation Problem*, this item is a must.

PB (1)

Ritter, Paul. *Planning For Man And Motor.* London: Pergamon, 1964.
    Profusely illustrated, this work presents considerable detail on the nature of transit and its relationships to human need. This work, considered by some to be complimentary to the extensive Buchanan Report, is the English counterpart to the Tunnard work *Man Made America* which is commentated upon below. This oversized and expensive work is well suited for use as a reference.

HB (2)

Schneider, Kenneth R. *Autokind Vs. Mankind.* New York: W. W. Norton, 1971.
    A similar work in style to Gruen's *The Heart Of Our Cities* (1.1). There is no doubt that the author condemns the automobile, presenting a tract

The City In Print

       which is emotional, but not pedantic; one sided, but of value as a resource. This book is interesting to read, presenting legions of intriguing vignettes about the automobile and interesting cartoon illustrations. A highly readable reference.

                                                                               HB (2)

Smerk, George O., ed. *Readings In Urban Transportation.* Bloomington: Indiana University Press, 1968.
       Excellent, and on the whole, brief selections on transportation, including: public transport, the automobile, costs, mass vs. private transport, and government action. A good reference, useful and readable.

                                                                           HB/PB (2)

Stone, Tabor R. *Beyond The Automobile: Reshaping The Transportation Environment.* Englewood Cliffs: Prentice Hall, 1971.
       An interesting and useful selection which looks at the transportation crisis, alternate systems, environmental problems, and land use implications.

                                                                          HB/PB (1)

Tunnard, Christopher. *Man-Made America.* Montreal: McGill University Press (Canada) and New Haven: Yale University Press (U.S.), 1963.
       This work is unique in its perspective of the varied problems of urban landscape, industry, and open spaces, the book is well laid out and easy to use. A worthwhile reference.

                                                                         HB/PB (2)

United States Government Printing Office. *The Freeway In The City: Principles Of Planning And Design.* A report to the Secretary, Department of Transportation Washington: United States Government Printing Office, 1968.
       Profusely illustrated, this work deals with the topic as outlined in the subtitle, and is of immense value in that it clearly and in simple terms, discusses options and illustrates a full range of possibilities in a way that all can comprehend. This report emphasizes the aesthetic and the gestalt effect of freeways on a location and recommends various possibilities which can place the freeway in a city as part of a transportation network. Included in this study is detailed illustration of how transit can be integrated with freeways and how freeway-transit corridors can be best put to use for a human city. Much vitality to this work. A must.

                                                                           HB (2)

Williams, Ernest W. Jr., ed. *The Future Of American Transportation.* An American Assembly Book. Englewood Cliffs: Prentice Hall, 1971.
       An item for general studies in transportation. Insufficient urban content.

                                                                               (4)

Wolfe, Roy. *Transportation And Politics.* Toronto: Van Nostrand, 1963.
       A study in political geography and not at all related to urban studies.

                                                                               (4)

Urban Transportation

5.2 SPECIFIC OR TECHNICAL WORKS

Appleyard, Donald, Kevin Lynch and John R. Meyer. *The View From The Road*. Cambridge: The M. I. T. Press, 1964.
    An outsized book combining photographic and conceptual drawings in a presentation designed to deal with the "esthetics of highways." Boston is used in detail as an example. The high cost of this book limits its use to situations where considerable detail is required.
HB (2)

Blunden, W. R. *The Land Use Transport System: Analysis And Synthesis*. Oxford: Pergamon, 1971.
(3)

Buchanan Report (abridged). *Traffic In Towns*. Harmondsworth: Penguin, 1963.
    Well illustrated with photographs, maps, and schematic drawings, from the study of traffic patterns in Britain. This survey, with English plans and projects to cope with the multitude of traffic problems there, is easily compared to urban transportation conditions in North America. A vast amount of information is represented under one cover, but the research is now about 10 years out of date.
PB (2)

Davies, E. *Transport In Greater London*. See *Greater London Papers* in section 3.4.

Fruin, John J. *Pedestrian Planning And Design*. New York: Metropolitan Association of Urban Designers and Environmental Planners, 1971 (order from MAUDEP Press, P.O. Box 480, Massapequa, N.Y. 11758).
    This work investigates the planning and design of building and street spaces for comfortable and convenient human use. Dealt with in considerable detail are the problems current in North American cities; human physiological and psychological factors affecting planning and design; and traffic and space requirements of pedestrians. A heavy book, suitable for reference rather than general use, providing in-depth information not available in any other work reviewed to date.
PB (2)

Jellicoe, Geoffrey. *Motopia*. New York: Studio Books, 1961.
    This out-of-print title, of value as a library reference, has a good section on the history of transportation and the city, and is a must for its presentation of a future in which the automobile has entirely won over all other considerations in planning. Quite readable and well illustrated.
OP (4)

Martin, Brian V. et al. *Principles And Techniques Of Predicting Future Demand For Urban Area Transportation*. M. I. T. Report No. 3. Cambridge: The M. I. T. Press, 1961. Dated.
(4)

Roth, Gabriel *Paying For Roads*. Harmondsworth: Pelican, 1967.
    A dry text on the economic problems of transportation and their effects upon towns, planning, and mobility.

OP (4)

Thomas, David St. John. *The Rural Transportation Problem*. London: Routledge and Kegan Paul and New York: Humanities Press (U.S. only), 1963.

(3)

6
The City as a Human Process

Works in this section cover a wide range of human activities which occur in the urban setting.

Sections 6.1 and 6.2 include books with a sociological bias, dealing with group processes and interaction. The books contained in sections 6.1 and 6.2 should be compared to the works in section 3.1.

Sections 6.21 and 6.22 deal with group processes in urban settings in the non-Western or Communist world. General works on the city in these areas can be found in 3.21 and 3.22.

Section 6.3 introduces several titles in a relatively new field of social inquiry. The Sommer title, in particular, must be pointed out as being quite influential.

Sections 6.4, 6.5, and 6.6 include works which analyze the urban setting using the three disciplines of anthropology, political science, and economics.

Several titles have also been set aside in 6.11. Although there is a wide range of basic works on sociology in print, the three listed are recommended as being of particular use for anyone seeking a working knowledge in sociology at either the secondary or university level. Other worthwhile titles most certainly exist.

6.1 GENERAL WORKS

Bergel, E. E. *Urban Sociology*. New York: McGraw-Hill, 1955.
    A general text intended for university level use. Dated.
                                                    HB (4)

Beshers, Jane M. *Urban Social Structure*. New York: The Free Press, 1962.
    A worthwhile, yet difficult book, which is of value for comparative field work in social consequence in neighborhood clans, social structure, and occupational status. Reference use only.
                                                    HB (2)

Bicanic, Rudolf. *Problems Of Planning: East And West*. The Hague: Mouton, 1967.
    National economic planning, with insufficient urban studies content.
                                                          (4)

The City In Print

Bock, Philip K., ed. *Culture Shock: A Reader In Modern Cultural Anthropology*. New York: Knopf, 1970.
    Insufficient urban studies content.

(4)

Clark, S. D., ed. *Urbanism And The Changing Canadian Society*. Toronto: University of Toronto Press, 1964.
    A collection of readings dealing with the social values and institutions of the community.

OP (4)

Coser, Rose L., ed. *The Family: Its Structure And Functions*. New York: St. Martin's Press, 1964.
    Superior works exist.

(4)

Cox, Fred M., <u>et al</u>., eds. *Strategies Of Community Organization: A Book Of Readings*. Itasca: F. E. Peacock, 1970.
    Insufficient urban studies content.

(4)

Davidson, Bruce. *East 100th St*. Cambridge: Harvard University Press, 1970.
    Insufficient urban studies content.

(4)

Elias, C. E. Jr., ed. *Metropolis: Values In Conflict*. Belmont: Wadsworth, 1968.
    A very worthwhile collection of readings by urban specialists, dealing with social and cultural problems and conditions in the city. Authors include Kingsley Davis, Lewis Mumford, Robert Moses, William Whyte, David Reisman, Kevin Lynch, and Jane Jacobs. A must.

PB (1)

Etzioni, Amitai and Eva, eds. *Social Change: Source Patterns And Consequences*. New York: Basic Books, 1964.
    Insufficient urban studies content.

(4)

Fiser, Webb S. *Mastery Of The Metropolis*. Englewood Cliffs: Prentice Hall, 1962.
    Duplicated in later works. Dated.

(4)

French, Robert Mills, ed. *The Community: A Comparative Perspective*. Itasca: F. E. Peacock, 1969.

(3)

Frieden, Bernard J. and Robert Morris, eds. *Urban Planning And Social Policy*. New York: Basic Books, 1968.
    Superior works exist.

(4)

The City As A Human Process

Gallagher, James E. and Ronald D. Lambert, eds. *Social Process And Institution: The Canadian Case*. Toronto: Holt, Rinehard and Winston, 1971.
    A college reader.

(3)

Gist, Noel P. and Sylvia Fleis Fava. *Urban Society*. 5th ed. New York: Thomas Crowell, 1964.
    Dated.

(4)

Glazer, Nathan and Daniel P. Moynihan. *Beyond The Melting Pot: The Negroes, Puerto Ricans, Jews, Italians, And Irish Of New York City*. 2nd ed. Cambridge: The M. I. T. Press, 1970.
    A highly detailed item which does look at the race issue, but is of more particular use for its in-depth analysis of the sub-cultures and their condition over the past thirty years in New York City. This work is of limited use as a general reference, but invaluable as a sociological study.

HB/PB (2)

Greer, Scott. *The Urban View*. New York: Oxford University Press, 1972.
    In this wide ranging examination of the social and political processes of the city, the author has brought together a number of articles which examine the city as it is and as it is perceived. The American city since 1950 is analyzed in depth in this highly sophisticated work.

HB (2)

Gutman, Robert and David Popenoe, eds. *Neighborhood, City, And Metropolis*. New York: Random House, 1970.
    An updating of materials found in Hatt and Reiss, listed below. Some selections included here have been seen before in other readers, but that does not detract from the usefulness of this work for reference or research. There are some interesting readings, including units on the approach of urban sociology, urbanization, urban differentiation, the urban ecology, urban groups, social behavior in the urban environment, and urban policy.

HB (2)

Hatt, Paul K. and Albert J. Reiss, Jr., eds. *Cities And Society: The Revised Reader In Urban Sociology*. 2nd ed. New York: The Free Press, 1957.
    A collection of articles dealing with the entire spectrum of the city from the sociological point of view. Dated.

(4)

Haskins, C. P. *Of Societies And Men*. New York: Viking, 1960.

(3)

Hastie, Tom. *Home Life*. London: Batsford, 1967.
    An elementary and well illustrated study of home life from pre-Roman times to the early 20th Century in England. This school text is an adequate introduction to the study of society.

HB (2)

The City In Print

Hetzler, Stanley A. *Technological Growth And Social Change: Achieving Moderation*. London: Routledge and Kegan Paul and New York: Humanities Press (U.S. only), 1969.

(3)

Hughes, Helen MacGill, ed. *Cities And City Life*. Boston: Allyn and Bacon, 1970.
    Dealing primarily with American cities, this title in the *Sociological Resources For The Social Studies Series* contains some older and well known articles on the city (1/3), and more recent, articles completed in the late sixties (2/3). A heavy American bias, but of use as a reference.

PB (2)

Keller, Suzanne. *The Urban Neighborhood: A Sociological Perspective*. New York: Random House, 1968.
    An extremely comprehensive and readable study on the nature of neighborhoods in the modern city. This work is highly useful, but the terminology limits it to reference use.

PB (2)

Mann, Peter H. *An Approach To Urban Sociology*. London: Routledge and Kegan Paul and New York: Humanities Press (U.S. only), 1965.
    Far better introductions to urban sociology have been reviewed.

(4)

Mann, W. E., ed. *Canada: A Sociological Profile*. Toronto: Copp-Clark, 1968.
    This work is a significant collection of readings dealing with population, the family, social stratification, ethnic groups, urban phenomenon, political and economic institutions, media, and social change in Canada. Extremely readable, this is useful as a general reference.

PB (1)

_____. *Canada: A Sociological Profile*. 2nd ed. Toronto: Copp-Clark, 1971.
    Thirty-five articles update this significant Canadian source, replacing over 75% of the articles found in the earlier edition. A necessary reference which has increased its focus on urban conditions in Canada.

PB (1)

Marsh, Leonard. *Communities In Canada: Selected Sources*. Toronto: McClelland and Stewart, 1970.
    Superior works exist.

(4)

Mayer, H. M. and C. F. Korn, eds. *Readings In Urban Geography*. Chicago: University of Chicago Press, 1959.
    This basic reader, containing much technical and statistical information, leans toward studies which are primarily sociological and economic. Of definite value as a reference. Dated.

(4)

McDonagh, Edward C. and Jon E. Simpson, eds. *Social Problems: Persistent Problems*. Toronto: Holt, Rinehart and Winston, 1966.
    This reader includes an excellent summary at the beginning of each unit,

and contains valuable selections on mass culture, alienation, familial problems, and population, with several good readings on possible solutions.

PB (2)

_____. *Social Problems: Persistent Problems*. 2nd ed. Toronto: Holt, Rinehart and Winston, 1969.
This edition presents an entirely different thrust with a considerable number of new articles replacing dated material. Both editions have much to offer, with distinct perspectives mirroring the issues at time of publication.

PB (1)

McQuade, Walter, ed. *Cities Fit To Live In*. New York: The Macmillan Co., 1971.
Superior works exist.

(4)

Michelson, William. *Man And His Urban Environment: A Sociological Approach*. Reading: Addison Wesley, 1970.

(3)

Mills, C. Wright. *The Power Elite*. New York: Oxford University Press, 1959.
Dated, but still a good reference. This work is a classic study of the elites who regulate and control society.

PB (2)

Moore, Wilbert E. *Social Change*. Englewood Cliffs: Prentice Hall, 1963.

(3)

Morris, R. N. and John Mogey. *The Sociology Of Housing: Studies At Berinsfield*. London: Routledge and Kegan Paul and New York: Humanities Press (U.S. only), 1965.
Part of the *International Library Of Sociology And Social Reconstruction*.

(3)

Morris, R. N. *Urban Sociology*. London: George Allen and Unwin and New York: Praeger (U.S. only), 1968.
This well developed scholarly work is a detailed study and compilation of Louis Wirth's urban theories. A complex reference, primarily of use to the researcher.

HB/PB (2)

Pahl, R. E. *Patterns Of Urban Life*. London: Longmans, 1970 (available from Humanities Press, New York).
A study of social structure in England.

(3)

_____, ed. *Readings In Urban Sociology*. Oxford: Pergamon, 1968.
Including a review of applied theory over the last 10 years, this work looks at various approaches used in the discipline to analyze the urban fabric. Chapters also deal with urban social structure in Britain, Japan, Africa, Czechoslovakia, the U.S., suburbia, and the rural-urban continuum.

HB/PB (2)

The City In Print

Pahl, R. E. *Whose City?* London: Longmans, 1970 (available from Humanities Press, New York).

(3)

Palen, J. John and Karl H. Flaming, ed. *Urban America: Conflict And Change.* New York: Holt, Rinehart and Winston, 1972.
    A sociological analysis of urban life in the United States, including an historical analysis, a study of current patterns of urbanization, and evaluation of the organization of urban life styles, a look at a variety of urban problems, and suggestions on how change can be brought about. Thirty-five selections, concise, highly readable, and immensely useful as distillations of the current thought of a significant number of urban specialists. An essential reference, sophisticated in presentation and style, and yet of immense value as a single volume reference in the U.S. and Canada.

PB (1)

Rosenbloom, Richard S. and Robin Marks, eds. *Social Innovation In The City: New Enterprises For Community Development.* Cambridge: Harvard University Press, 1969.

(3)

Schlivek, Louis B. *Man In Metropolis.* Garden City: Doubleday, 1965.

(3)

Schnore, Leo F. *The Urban Scene: Human Ecology And Demography.* New York: The Free Press, 1965.

(3)

Seabrook, Jeremy. *City Close-Up.* London: Allen Lane (The Penguin Press), 1971.
    Not urban studies.

(4)

Sherif, Muzafer and Carl Hovland. *Social Judgement: Assimilation And Contrast Effects In Communication And Attitude Change.* New Haven: Yale University Press, 1961.

(3)

Shipman, George A. *Designing Program Action--Against Urban Poverty.* University (Ala.): University of Alabama Press, 1971.

(3)

Sirjamaki, John. *The Sociology Of Cities.* New York: Random House, 1964.
    A general introduction to the sociology of cities, with a study of both historical and modern urban characteristics. Economic and sociological characteristics are analyzed in this valuable reference.

HB (2)

Swanson, Bert E. *The Concern For Community In Urban America.* New York: Odyssey, 1970.

(3)

The City As A Human Process

Swanson, Guy E. *Social Change*. Glenview: Scott, Foresman, 1971.
    Superior works exist.

    (4)

Sweetser, Frank L. *Studies In American Urban Society*. New York: Thomas Crowell, 1970.
    A collection of essays found in other items reviewed. Superior works exist.

    (4)

Wager, W. W. *The City Of Man*. Baltimore: Pelican, 1963.
    Not urban studies.

    (4)

Warner, S. B., ed. *Planning For A Nation Of Cities*. Cambridge: The M. I. T. Press, 1966.
    A reader, sociological in orientation, on urban culture and subcultures, services, physical planning, and government responsibilities in American urban problems. A valuable reference.

    HB/PB (2)

Weaver, Robert C. *The Urban Complex*. Garden City: Doubleday, 1966.
    This work is quite dry, but does include good analyses and gives an exhaustive introduction to the topic of urbanization from the sociological point of view. Reference only.

    HB/PB (2)

Whyte, William H. *The Organization Man*. Garden City: Doubleday, 1956.
    This classic on urban institutions has some very useful sections devoted to the effect of modern societal trends upon suburban man. A must.

    PB (2)

Yin, Robert K., ed. *The City In The Seventies*. Itasca: F. E. Peacock, 1972.
    A reader, sophisticated in style, with a number of interesting studies, including ethnic sub-cultures, neighborhood change, government, environment, and urban dynamics. A distinctly American flavour permeates this work.

    PB (2)

6.11 GENERAL TEXTS IN SOCIOLOGY

Chinoy, Ely. *Society: An Introduction To Sociology*. 2nd ed. New York: Random House, 1967.
    One of many good introductions to sociological thought and techniques, with good units on the community and city, technology, authority, demographics and social control. A univeristy level text.

    HB (2)

Horton, Paul B. and Chester L. Hunt. *Sociology*. 2nd ed. New York: McGraw-Hill, 1968.
    Geared for secondary level use, this general sociology text is readable

and comprehensive, with interesting illustrations. A well balanced collection of readings blends into a text which deals with the full range of social characteristics, and contains much of value in the study of urban social processes.

    HB (1)

Supplements available for Horton's *Sociology*:

    Cohen, B. J. and H. Bailie. *A Study Guide And Source Book*. New York: McGraw-Hill, 1968.
        This item is a goldmine of statistics, raw data, and text questions geared to the text above. It has an excellent synopsis of each chapter and is a must for the teacher.

    PB (1)

    H. Bailie. *An Instructors' Manual*. This is also available, at about half of the cost of the above, but is of little value.

    (4)

Koller, Marvin R. and Harold C. Couse. *Modern Sociology*. New York: Holt, Rinehart and Winston, 1969.
    A standard, high-school level text on sociology, of value to the poorer student because it does not overburden the reader with excessive verbiage. Although this is a good, basic sociology, it does not breathe life into the subject.

    HB (1)

6.2 SPECIFIC STUDIES ON URBAN MAN

Bunge, William. *Fitzgerald: Geography Of A Revolution*. Cambridge: Schenkman, 1971.
    A biography of an in-town residential neighborhood of Detroit, this work weaves a delicate and moving story of social change from the community's early beginnings in the 19th Century through the riots of 1967 and beyond. Of all the works this reviewer has yet read on the Black situation, Mr. Bunge's visual, textual, and living essay provides the most personal glimpse into the lives of the people involved, while avoiding the sensational or clinical approach used in most of the other studies. An essential reference for the student of man.

    HB (2)

Cahn, Edgar S. and Barry A. Passett, eds. *Citizen Participation: Effecting Community Change*. New York: Praeger, 1971.
    A casebook for trainees on the experience of citizen participation in the U.S., containing thirteen studies on community dialogue, general concerns regarding citizen participation, and specific issues. A sophisticated, unique reference.

    HB (2)

Firth, Raymond, Jane and Anthony Forge. *Families And Their Relatives: Kinship In A Middle-Class Sector Of London: An Anthropological Study*. New York: Humanities Press, 1970. From *The International Library Of Sociology And Social Reconstruction*.

    (3)

Gans, Herbert J. *The Levittowners: Way Of Life And Politics In A New Suburban Community*. New York: Random House, 1967.

(3)

_____. *The Urban Villagers: Group And Class In The Life Of Italian Americans*. New York: The Free Press, 1962.
   This case study of a distinctive ethnic neighborhood in Boston presents an interesting and informative view of a way of life. An essential work.

PB (2)

Gottmann, Jean. *Megalopolis: The Urbanized NE Seaboard Of The United States*. Cambridge: The M. I. T. Press, 1961.
   A superb and exhaustive study of this area, comparable to the New York Metropolitan Region Study, and one of the significant works on U.S. urbanization, as well as one of the most influential. Valuable as a library reference.

HB/PB (2)

Henry, Edward L., ed. *Micropolis In Transition: A Study Of A Small City*. Collegeville (Minn.): Center for the Study of Local Government, St John's University, 1971.
   A detailed look at the small city in North America using St. Cloud, Minnesota as a focus. An up-to-date version of Warner's *Yankee City* (listed below), which includes chapters on problems, power structure, residents, taxing, utilities, and annexation. A decidedly useful reference.

HB/PB (2)

Heritage Of Sociology Series. Chicago: University of Chicago Press, 1964-1967.
   Of this series, the following titles are of value:

   Park, Robert E. and E. W. Burgess. *The City*. 1967.
   Pfautz, H. W., ed. *Charles Booth On The City: Physical Pattern And Social Structure*. 1967.
   Reiss, A. J. *Louis Wirth On Cities And Social Life*. 1964.
   Turner, Ralph, ed. *Robert E. Park On Social Control And Collective Behavior*. 1967.

The City is a major work in urban sociology, if not the most important in American urban sociology. The discipline was essentially established at the University of Chicago, and although these works date back to the early part of the century, they are essential as references for information on the beginnings of urban sociology, or the bases of so many of the present theories in the discipline. *The City*, by Park, is constantly referred to in most modern works, while the other three works present the foundation theories in man and his role and stresses in the urban setting, social organization, social planning, human ecology, collective behavior, and functional analysis. Useful reference works.

HB/PB (2)

Hollingshead, A. B. *Elmtown's Youth*. New York: Wiley, 1949.
    A classic study of youth and society in suburbia, similar in style to Warner's *Yankee City*. A useful reference.
                                                                    PB (2)

Hughes, Helen MacGill, ed. *Population Growth And The Complex Society*. Boston: Allyn & Bacon, 1972.
    This collection of 20 readings presents perspectives and information on a wide range of topics, including population characteristics in the U.S., Africa, Europe, and Japan. The effect of technology on population is also dealt with. A readable selection.
                                                                    PB (2)

Mann, W. E., ed. *The Underside Of Toronto*. Toronto: McClelland and Stewart, 1970.
    A reader with a broad content, dealing with skidrow, ethnic and other minorities or groups, institutions, and deviant behavior. A college level reader, with topics not seen elsewhere.
                                                                    PB (2)

New York Metropolitan Region Study Series. Garden City: Doubleday-Anchor, 1959.

> Chinitz, B. *Freight And The Metropolis*.
> Handlin, O. *The New Comers*.
> Helfgott, R. B. *Made In New York*.
> Hoover, E. M. *Anatomy Of A Metropolis*.
> Lichtenberg, R. M. *One-Tenth Of A Nation*.
> Robbins, S. M. *Money Metropolis*.
> Segal, M. *Wages In The Metropolis*.
> Wood, R. C. *1400 Governments*.

These eight volumes are exhaustive studies, but they are now dated.
                                                                    (4)

Berman, B. R. *Projection Of A Metropolis*. This is the final volume, resulting from the collective studies above.
                                                                    PB (2)

Vernon, R. *Metropolis 1985*. Although the material covered in this synthesis of the first eight volumes is detailed and dry, it contains a good deal of information for study and research.
                                                                    PB (2)

Niebanck, Paul L. *Relocation In Urban Planning: From Obstacle To Opportunity*. Philadelphia: University of Pennsylvania Press, 1968.
    Not urban studies, but rather relocation problems related to the elderly.
                                                                    (4)

Parker, Stanley. *The Future Of Work And Leisure*. London: MacGibbon and Kee, 1971.
    The first study on this subject to be reviewed. This work is a highly sophisticated and immensely useful reference.
                                                                    HB (2)

The City As A Human Process

Porter, John. *Canadian Social Structure: A Statistical Profile*. Toronto: McClelland and Stewart, 1967.
    Of immense value, this work contains brief explanatory introductions with statistical tables related to such topics as the demographic structure, family, economy, government, and leisure.
    PB (1)

Rose, Stephen M. *The Betrayal Of The Poor: The Transformation Of Community Action*. Cambridge: Schenkman, 1972.
    Superior works exist.
    (4)

Schaffer, Albert and Ruth C. *Woodruff: A Study Of Community Decision Making*. Chapel Hill: University of North Carolina Press, 1970.
    (3)

Seeley, John R., et al. *Crestwood Heights: A Study Of The Culture Of Suburban Life*. Toronto: University of Toronto Press, 1956.
    Similar to Warner's *Yankee City* (below), this sociological study deals with Canadian suburban life. Given a fictitious name, the community studied is seemingly a suburb of Toronto. A highly worthwhile piece of research and a superb reference.
    PB (2)

Stein, Maurice. *The Eclipse Of Community*. New York: Harper and Row and Cambridge: Princeton University Press, 1964.
    A very good item and a valuable reference, but heavy going for general use. Major American sociological studies of the city since the 1920's are included. The Lynds, Park, Warner, and other founders of American urban sociology are well covered.
    PB (2)

Vidich, Arthur J. *Small Town In Mass Society*. Cambridge: Princeton University Press, 1960.
    Dry, but containing a good deal of worthwhile information. This study of class structure and power in rural communities covers the village in America from 1850-1950.
    HB/PB (2)

Von Eckardt, Wolf. *The Challenge Of Megalopolis*. New York: Macmillan, 1964.
    This work is a well illustrated, easy to read, and simplified version of the original study by Gottmann (see 6.1). Of value for use as a basic study of this region, it is ideally suited for use in general reading.
    HB (2)

Warner, W. Lloyd. *Yankee City*. New Haven: Yale University Press, 1963.
    Completed in the mid 1940's, this narrative study of an imaginary community in New England is still relevant for studies on such topics as class structure, family status, and urban fringe change. This one volume abridgement is a useful reference.
    HB/PB (2)

6.21 URBAN SOCIETIES IN ASIA, AFRICA, AND LATIN AMERICA

Belshaw, Cyril S. *The Great Village: The Economic And Social Welfare Of Hanuabada, An Urban Community In Papua*. London: Routledge and Kegan Paul and Boston: Routledge and Kegan Paul (U.S. only), 1957.
    Dated.

(4)

Epstein, A. L. *Politics In An Urban African Community*. Manchester: The Manchester University Press, 1958.
    Dated.

(4)

Gamer, Robert E. *The Politics Of Urban Development In Singapore*. Ithaca: Cornell University Press, 1972.

(3)

Gore, M. S. *Urbanization And Family Change In India*. New York: Humanities Press, 1968.

(3)

Halpern, Joel M. *The Changing Village Community*. Englewood Cliffs: Prentice Hall, 1967.
    A study of rural-urban differences, current conditions, and factors affecting change in the village. This work includes case studies of Tepuztlan in Mexico (of Oscar Lewis fame) and a Serbian village. Useful.

HB/PB (2)

Harris, Marvin. *Town And Country In Brazil*. New York: W. W. Norton, 1956.
    This work is a "socio-anthropological study of a small Brazilian town," a county seat in central Bahia. Although researched two decades ago, this work is still topical as a study of how a community lives, governs itself and defines itself. A well rounded investigation into the culture, society, and institutions of this town in an isolated locale. A useful reference, sophisticated in approach, but interesting to read.

PB (2)

Lewis, Oscar. *Five Families*. New York: Mentor, 1959.
    Of his several earlier works, including *Life In A Mexican Village*, this book is of particular value in that it studies five villagers who move to Mexico City. A study of lower class urban peasants, it is particularly poignant. A highly useful reference. Other Oscar Lewis titles should be looked at.

PB (2)

_____. *Village Life In Northern India: Studies In A Delhi Village*. New York: Vintage, 1958.

(3)

Mangin, William, ed. *Peasants In Cities: Readings In The Anthropology Of Urbanization*. Boston: Houghton-Mifflin, 1970.
    Short readings dealing with urbanization in the newly developing world. Worldwide coverage, a bit detailed, but still of value as a reference.

HB/PB (2)

Mitchell, J. Clyde, ed. *Social Networks In Urban Situations: Analyses Of Personal Relationships In Central African Towns*. Manchester: The Manchester University Press, 1969.
    Far too dry and statistical to allow even the extraction of data. Much information, but presented in an indigestible form.

(4)

Miner, Horace, ed. *The City In Modern Africa*. London: Pall Mall, 1967.
    Approaching the topic from sociological criteria, this work fills a void on urbanization in sub-Saharan Africa. The essays, well written and informative, are suited to reference use.

HB (2)

Ross, Aileen D. *The Hindu Family In Its Urban Setting*. Toronto: University of Toronto Press, 1961.
    A superb study of traditional values compared to the changing values forced upon individuals and groups as they move from country to city in India. A good reference.

PB (2)

Stycos, J. Malone. *Children Of The Barriada: A Photographic Essay On The Latin American Population Problem*. New York: Grossman, 1970.
    A superb photographic study.

PB (2)

Sweet, Louise E., ed. *Peoples And Cultures Of The Middle East. Volume 2: Life In The Cities, Towns, And Countryside*. Garden City: Natural History Press, 1970.
    This reader includes selections that are equally divided between studies of the traditional village and the city in North Africa or the Near East. These anthropological studies present information not available in other sources. The six papers on the Arab city and its inhabitants are highly informative.

PB (2)

6.22 URBAN SOCIETIES IN THE COMMUNIST WORLD

No works reviewed to date.

6.3 SOCIAL PSYCHOLOGY AND ENVIRONMENTAL DESIGN

Bergel, E. E. *Social Stratification*. New York: McGraw-Hill, 1962.

OP (4)

Brown, Roger. *Social Psychology*. New York: Free Press, 1965.
    A general introductory text.

                                                                                                 HB (2)

Henry, Jules. *Culture Against Man*. New York: Random House, 1963.
    A popularization with a broad area of application, this book lends itself to general use and is a good introduction for the reader who is untrained in social psychology.

                                                                                 HB/PB (2)

Hughes, Helen MacGill, ed. *Crowd And Mass Behavior*. Boston: Allyn & Bacon, 1972.
    Not urban studies.

                                                                                             (4)

Mannheim, Karl. *Essays On Sociology And Social Psychology*. New York: Oxford University Press, 1953.
    One of the best collections of essays by this significant sociologist. Section 4 is of particular value in its introductory comments on social dynamics.

                                                                                 HB (2)

Mills, Theodore M. *The Sociology Of Small Groups*. Englewood Cliffs: Prentice Hall, 1967.
    Not applicable to urban studies.

                                                                                             (4)

Parsons, Talcott. *Social Structure And Personality*. New York: The Free Press, 1965.
    This work, by one of the most eminent social scientists of the 20th Century, is also one of the most difficult written in English. As in all his works, the author uses an exceedingly ponderous terminology to put forth ideas of considerable significance. Parsons has attempted to tie the social sciences together in one unified theory. For those who wish to study the subject in detail, other works by Parsons are also recommended, particularly *Towards A General Theory Of Action* (New York: Harper, 1951).

                                                                              HB/PB (2)

Perin, Constance. *With Man In Mind: An Interdisciplinary Prospectus For Environmental Design*. Cambridge: The M. I. T. Press, 1970.

                                                                                             (3)

Riesman, David. *The Lonely Crowd*. New Haven: Yale University Press, 1961.
    This work is of definite value in the study of mass social processes and the effects of modern urban life upon Western man.

                                                                               HB/PB (2)

Sommer, Robert. *Personal Space: The Behavioral Basis Of Design*. Englewood Cliffs: Prentice Hall, 1969.
    The most important book written in this field. This work is a study of designed space and its effect on human response. Topics dealt with include spatial behavior, the effect of distance (privacy), small group ecology

(lifespace), and specific designed space conditions and problems (including hospitals, schools, and other institutional spaces). This book is well written, interesting reading, and a highly useful reference.

HB/PB (2)

6.4 URBAN POLITICAL SYSTEMS

Adrian, Charles R. and Charles Press. *Governing Urban America*. 4th ed. New York: McGraw-Hill, 1972.
    This college level text on metropolitan political processes is of value as a reference.

HB (2)

Almond, Gabriel A. and Sidney Verba. *The Civic Culture: Political Attitudes And Democracy In Five Nations*. Boston: Little, Brown, & Co., 1963.
    An abridgement of the 1963 Princeton University Press publication, covering attitudes and participatory democracy in five countries, and including detailed analyses of feelings of competence and realization of involvement and participation. Of value as a general reference.

HB/PB (2)

Altshuler, Alan. *The City Planning Process: A Political Analysis*. Ithaca: Cornell University Press, 1965.
    A rather detailed study of Minneapolis-St. Paul.

(3)

Baldinger, Stanley. *Planning And Governing The Metropolis: The Twin Cities Experience*. New York: Praeger, 1971.

(3)

Banfield, Edward C. and J. Q. Wilson. *City Politics*. Cambridge: Harvard University Press (HB) and New York: Vintage (PB), 1963.
    An exclusively American study. Dated.

(4)

Banfield, Edward C., ed. *Urban Government: A Reader In Administration And Politics*. 4th ed. New York: The Free Press, 1969.
    This work deals with universal problems as well as situations and studies of particular American cities. A good many chapters are also applicable to Canadian urban political problems, and the general nature of the study makes it of value to readers in both countries.

HB (2)

Bellush, Jewel and Stephen M. David, eds. *Race And Politics In New York: Five Studies In Policy Making*. New York: Praeger, 1971.
    Useful in the American context, this work presents a re-examination of several "fundamental" conclusions concerning power and participation in city politics. The five areas dealt with are welfare, police, housing, education, and health. An essential comparative reference.

HB/PB (2)

The City In Print

Beyle, Thad L. and G. T. Lathrop, eds. *Planning And Politics: Uneasy Partnership*. New York: Odyssey Press, 1970.

(3)

Bollens, John C. *Communities And Government In A Changing World*. Chicago: Rand McNally, 1966.
    Far superior materials have been reviewed for use at any level.

(4)

Bonjean, Charles M., et al., eds. *Community Politics: A Behavioral Approach*. New York: The Free Press, 1971.

(3)

Crawford, K. G. *Canadian Municipal Government*. Toronto: University of Toronto Press, 1954.
    Dated. Superior works exist.

(4)

Danielson, Michael N., ed. *Metropolitan Politics: A Reader*. 2nd ed. Boston: Little, Brown, & Co., 1971.
    Updating the content of the earlier edition to reflect changes in the American political scene, this work covers a wide range of topics including urban and suburban conditions and problems, federal relationships, and prospects for the immediate future. Three-quarters of the material is new. A useful reference.

PB (2)

Downes, Bryan T., ed. *Cities And Suburbs: Selected Readings In Local Politics And Public Policy*. Belmont: Wadsworth, 1971.

(3)

Feldman, Lionel D. and Michael D. Goldrick, eds. *Politics And Government Of Urban Canada*. Toronto: Methuen, 1969.
    A reader on Canadian political, economic, and social institutions, including articles on political structure from the metropolitan scale to small towns, with a good balance between both large and small town political structure and institutions.

HB/PB (2)

Greer, Scott. *Governing The Metropolis*. New York: Wiley, 1962.
    Dated.

(4)

Hadden, Jeffrey K., Louis H. Masotti, and Calvin J. Larson, eds. *Metropolis In Crisis: Social And Political Perspectives*. 2nd ed. Itasca: F. E. Peacock, 1971.
    An up to date collection of readings providing broad perspectives on the current urban crisis in the U.S., the present state of the U.S. urban "civilization," specifics of the crisis (racism, crime, poverty, housing, education, environment, and finance), urban power, and the possible roles of

different sectors of society in solving current problems. The selections have been contributed by prominent politicians, urban theorists, and leaders in various segments of urban life. This is a highly worthwhile reference, heavy going with no illustrations, but packed with valuable information relevant to all of North America.

HB/PB (2)

Hawkins, Brett W. *Politics And Urban Policies*. Indianapolis: Bobbs-Merrill, 1971.
    Superior works exist.

(4)

Hawley, A. H. and B. G. Zimmer. *The Metropolitan Community: Its People And Government*. Beverly Hills: Sage Publications, 1970.
    A study of the problems on metropolitan consolidation and the strengths of local municipalities in a metro region. Although a study of U.S. cities, the problems, analysis, and conclusions are valid for Canadian application and study. Well stocked with useful statistics.

HB/PB (2)

Hunter, Floyd. *Community Power Structure: A Study Of Decision Makers*. Chapel Hill: University of North Carolina Press, 1953.
    Primarily a study of power structure of a hypothetical regional city, utilizing the *Yankee City* format in a study of political systems rather than social structure. This biography of a city is a study of power concentration and utilization. A worthwhile reference for depth study in power politics.

HB/PB (2)

Kaplan, Harold. *Urban Political Systems: A Functional Analysis Of Metro Toronto*. New York: Columbia University Press, 1967.
    A study of the first metropolitan federation system in North America (1953-1965), this is an analysis of the experience, including the metro policy-making system, the formal structure, and the inter-action of bureaucrats at the municipal, metro, and provincial level. Highly detailed, complicated at points, but still a highly useful reference. Number 7 in the *Metropolitan Politics Series*.

HB (2)

Kotler, Milton. *Neighborhood Government: The Local Foundations Of Political Life*. New York: Bobbs-Merrill, 1969.

(3)

Long, Norton E. *The Unwalled City: Reconstituting The Urban Community*. New York: Basic Books, 1972.

(3)

Loveridge, Ronald O. *City Managers In Legislative Politics*. Indianapolis: Bobbs-Merrill, 1971.

(3)

Madgewick, P. J. *American City Politics*. London: Routledge and Kegan Paul and Boston: Routledge and Kegan Paul (U.S. only), 1970.
    A title in the *Library Of Political Studies*, this is another general survey of the ingredients and participants in urban political structure in the U.S.. A useful comparative reference.

    HB (2)

Mahood, H. R. and Edward L. Angus, eds. *Urban Politics And Problems: A Reader*. New York: Charles Scribner's Sons, 1969.
    This highly useful reference includes several significant essays on urbanization in the U.S., trends in urban government and administration power in the community, suburban dilemmas, urban transportation, urban services, housing, regional and intergovernmental problems, and urban political potentials for the future.

    PB (2)

Milner, J. B., ed. *Community Planning: A Casebook On Law And Administration*. Toronto: University of Toronto Press, 1963.
    This work is a good companion to Haar's *Land Use Planning*, with a distinctly Canadian emphasis. Topics deal with the full range of planning problems and issues, emphasizing procedures rather than ironclad law. An absolutely essential reference.

    HB (2)

Nisbet, Robert A. *Quest For Community*. New York: Oxford University Press, 1953. Also published by Oxford University Press as *Community And Power* (1962). Dated.

    (4)

Phillips, Jewell C. *Municipal Government And Administration In America*. New York: Macmillan, 1960.
    Although dated, this is a superb reference for comparative studies of Canada and the U.S.. A detailed yet well laid out college text, dissecting local government by function (government and administration), and presenting a mass of information in easy terms and a scholarly, dry, but not unpalatable style.

    HB (2)

Plunkett, Thomas J. *Urban Canada And Its Government: A Study Of Municipal Organization*. Toronto: Macmillan, 1968.
    A survey of governmental organization in Canada covering systems used in major Canadian cities, and including some discussion of regional government.

    HB/PB (1)

Praeger Special Studies In International Politics And Public Affairs. New York: Praeger, 1970.
    A series of detailed studies of political processes in a number of world cities. Titles include:

Austin, Allan G., et al. *Urban Government For Metropolitan Lima.* 1970.
Calmfors, Hans, et al. *Urban Government For Greater Stockholm.* 1968.
Cattell, David T. *A Case Study Of Soviet Urban Government.* 1968.
Johnson, Katherine M. *Urban Government For The Prefecture Of Casablanca.* 1970.
Pusic, Eugen, et al. *Urban Government For Zagreb, Yugoslavia.* 1968.
Walsh, Annmarie H. *Urban Government For The Paris Region.* 1967.
Williams, Babatunde, et al. *Urban Government For Metropolitan Lagos.* 1967.

    Each volume deals with governmental organization, functioning, and services. Each text has much detailed information. Although the statistics are a bit dated, they are the most recent available in English on the cities dealt with, and therefore are of considerable interest.

HB (2)

Rabinovitz, Francine F. *City Politics And Planning.* New York: Atherton Press, 1970.

(3)

Robson, William A. *Local Government In Crisis.* 2nd revised ed. London: George Allen & Unwin, 1968.
    This work analyzes the current condition of local government in England. Erosion of local authority, centralization of functions, inadequate reform, and general neglect of local involvement in national policy decisions and programs is discussed and documented. A penetrating study of local government.

HB/PB (2)

Rogers, David. *The Management Of Big Cities: Interest Groups And Social Change Strategies.* Beverly Hills: Sage Publications, 1971.
    An expansion on a theme presented in an earlier work, *110 Livingston Street,* this interesting and valuable study covers conditions, problems, and attempted solutions in New York, Philadelphia, and Cleveland, with detailed analysis of obstacles to change. A superb and easy to use reference.

HB (2)

Rowat, Donald C. *The Canadian Municipal System: Essays On The Improvement Of Local Government.* Toronto: McClelland and Stewart, 1969.
    This reference, oriented to Eastern Canadian examples, is quite dry. Some parts of the work relate to the general Canadian example, and these sections make it quite useful as a reference.

PB (2)

Ruchelman, Leonard I., ed. *Big City Mayors: The Crisis In Urban Politics.* Bloomington: Indiana University Press, 1969.
    A distinctive work among those reviewed in that it deals with the particular character, politics, duties and responsibilities of big city mayors in the U.S.. Thirty two readings are presented on a dozen American cities. A superb reference.

PB (2)

Seashore, Stanley E. and Robert J. McNeil, eds. *Management Of The Urban Crisis: Government And The Behavioral Sciences.* New York: The Free Press, 1971.

(3)

Smallwood, Frank. *Greater London: The Politics Of Metropolitan Reform.* Indianapolis: Bobbs-Merrill, 1965.

A detailed study of the mechanics of politics in Greater London, this book is a bit esoteric, but exceedingly complete. Its extensive detail limits it to reference use.

PB (2)

Walsh, Annmarie H. *The Urban Challenge To Government: An International Comparison Of Thirteen Cities.* New York: Praeger, 1969.

Interesting and easily read, this is essentially a compendia and summation of studies completed in the International Urban Studies Project (see Praeger series above), with hypotheses projected on such topics as governmental organization, intergovernmental relations, urban public finance, and land tenure. Useful as a reference.

HB (2)

Willbern, York. *The Withering Away Of The City.* Bloomington: Indiana University Press, 1966.

A highly readable reference on the urban condition as seen from the viewpoint of public administration. Quite useful.

PB (1)

Williams, Oliver P. and Charles Press, eds. *Democracy In Urban America: Readings On Government And Politics.* 2nd ed. Chicago: Rand McNally, 1969.

The worthwhile selections included are found complete in books reviewed earlier.

(4)

_____, and Charles R. Adrian. *Four Cities: A Study In Comparative Policy Making.* Philadelphia: University Of Pennsylvania Press, 1963.

(3)

_____. *Metropolitan Political Analysis: A Social Access Approach.* New York: The Free Press, 1971.

An interesting little book, dealing with urbanism as a social process and, more significantly, the interaction of social and political processes. As such, this work is unique. Scholarly, and yet quite readable, it is a highly suitable reference.

HB (2)

Wilson, James Q., ed. *City Politics And Public Policy.* New York: Wiley, 1968.

(3)

6.41 URBAN LAW

Hagman, Donald G. *Urban Planning And Land Development Control Law*. St. Paul: West Publishing Co., 1971.

    A casebook on current, practical applied law in relation to urban planning. Although this work would be ordinarily too specialized for general reading, its use in comparison to provincial or state municipal acts will prove of great interest for those interested in the legal strictures of land use planning. With this limitation, this work can prove to be an interesting reference.

    Of added interest is the compilation in this work, with updating, of 19 other casebooks, including Haar's *Land Use Planning* (1959), Berger's *Land Ownership And Use* (1968), and F. Michelman's *Government And Urban Areas* (1970). As a final note, PPBS (Planning, Programming, and Budgeting Systems) is explained in detail.

                                                                                  HB (2)

Roberts, E. F. *Land Use Planning*. New York: Matthew Bender, 1971.

    Another thick tome on urban law containing a selection of cases and statutes (U.S.) on such topics as the neighborhood, noise, municipal powers, zoning, urban renewal, and controlling decision making. A useful, yet expensive, reference for those interested in law. Useful in Canada for comparison.

                                                                                  HB (2)

6.5 URBAN ANTHROPOLOGY

Adams, Bert N. *Kinship In An Urban Setting*. Chicago: Markham, 1968.

                                                                                     (3)

Audrey, Robert. *The Territorial-Imperative: A Personal Inquiry Into The Animal Origins Of Property And Nations*. New York: Delta, 1966.

    A worthwhile reference on this topic, it is a useful perspective on the basics of territoriality.

                                                                                 PB (2)

Eddy, Elizabeth M., ed. *Urban Anthropology: Research Perspectives And Strategies*. Athens (Ga.): University of Georgia Press, 1968.

    A guide to philosophical and specific cultural studies of urbanization in Latin America, Africa, and Costa Rica. A highly useful reference.

                                                                                 PB (2)

Hall, Edward T. *The Hidden Dimension*. Garden City: Doubleday, 1966.

    This work deals with space, its use and its effect upon man. Crowding and social behavior, space from the point of view of all the senses, and various cultural and intercultural responses to space are investigated. An excellent book, actually better than *The Human Zoo*, listed below, although not given the same publicity. Quite readable and definitely suited for general use.

HB/PB (1)

Harris, C. C. *Readings In Kinship In Urban Society*. Oxford: Pergamon, 1970.
A book with worldwide coverage of kinship characteristics.

(3)

Laumann, Edward O. *Prestige And Association In An Urban Community: An Analysis Of An Urban Stratification System*. Indianapolis: Bobbs-Merrill, 1966.

(3)

Mayer, Philip. *Townsmen Or Tribesmen: Conservatism And The Process Of Urbanization In A South African City*. 2nd ed. Capetown: Oxford University Press, 1971.
A highly detailed reference. Too scholarly and dry for general reading, but included because of its peculiar topic. A useful reference, well documented, on urban processes among the Blacks of South Africa.

HB/PB (2)

Morris, Desmond. *The Human Zoo*. Toronto: Clarke Irwin (HB) and New York: Bantum (PB), 1960.
An interesting study comparing animal behavior with that of human beings especially man in the urban setting. The urban animal is analyzed from its beginings to the present. As an anthropological study, this work rambles, but as a reading, it is quite interesting and throws a different slant on urban history, society, class, and groups.

HB/PB (2)

Pauw, B. A. *The Second Generation*. Capetown: Oxford University Press, 1963.
A sequel to the Mayer book listed above, this is a study of the family among urbanized Bantu in East London (South Africa). Too detailed for the general reader, this work is of use for in-depth research in urban anthropology.

HB (2)

Potter, Jack M., May N. Diaz and George M. Foster, eds. *Peasant Society: A Reader* (A title in the Little, Brown Series in Anthropology). Boston: Little, Brown & Co., 1967.
A college level reader covering a widely diverse selection of cultures and containing interesting selections on peasant society, economics, social organization, personality, and problems. A useful reference in the study of rural-urban characteristics.

HB/PB (2)

6.6 URBAN ECONOMICS

Andrews, Richard B. *Urban Land Economics And Public Policy*. New York: The Free Press, 1971.

(3)

The City As A Human Process

Alonso, William. *Location And Land Use: Toward A General Theory Of Land Rent.*
   Cambridge: Harvard University Press, 1964.
      Far too detailed for general use, but worthy of consideration as the
   germinal work in urban economics. A reference only.
                                                                    HB (2)

Bish, Robert L. *The Public Economy Of Metropolitan Areas.* Chicago: Markham, 1971.
                                                                       (3)

Brewis, T. N. *Regional Economic Policies In Canada.* Toronto: Macmillan, 1969.
                                                                       (3)

David, Philip. *Urban Land Development.* Homewood (Ill.): Richard D. Irwin, 1970.
                                                                       (3)

Gillespie, W. Irwin. *The Urban Public Economy* (Urban Canada: Problems and Prospects,
   Research Monograph 4). Ottawa: Central Mortgage and Housing Corporation,
   1971.
      Although detailed and dry, this document is of value for its 160 pages
   of statistics and information on Canadian urban economics.
                                                                    PB (2)

Goodall, Brian. *The Economics Of Urban Areas.* Oxford: Pergamon, 1970.
                                                                       (3)

Green, James L. *Economic Ecology: Baselines For Urban Development.* Athens (Ga.):
   University of Georgia Press, 1969.
                                                                       (3)

Leahy, William H., et al., eds. *Urban Economics: Theory, Development And Planning.*
   New York: The Free Press, 1970.
      This work is a commendable reader on urban economics, including classic
   and up to date selections on location theory, economic activity and urban
   economic hierarchies and economic planning. Articles are also included
   from other disciplines, providing a balanced overview of urban problems as
   they affect and are affected by economic forces. Several of the selections
   included are complex and statistical, but as a whole, the collection is
   unique, including good items not otherwise available in book form. A highly
   useful reference for the serious student of urban economics.
                                                                    PB (2)

Lithwick, N. H. *Urban Poverty* (Urban Canada: Problems and Prospects, Research
   Monograph 1). Ottawa: Central Mortgage and Housing Corporation, 1971.
      A document containing much valuable information on the sources and
   structure of poverty in Canada and its relation to public policy.
                                                                    PB (2)

Lowe, Jeanne R. *Cities In A Race With Time: Progress And Poverty In America's
   Cities.* New York: Random House, 1968.
      Not urban studies.
                                                                       (4)

Margolis, Julius, ed. *The Public Economy Of Urban Communities*. Baltimore: The Johns Hopkins Press, 1965.

(3)

Perloff, Harvey S. *Issues In Urban Economics*. Baltimore: The Johns Hopkins Press, 1968.

(3)

Reid, Timothy E. *Contemporary Canada: Readings In Economics*. Toronto: Holt, Rinehart and Winston, 1969.
    This reader, which includes a general study of economics, but will prove of value in that it includes articles related to urban conditions. Useful as a reference.

PB (2)

Richardson, Harry W. *Urban Economics*. Harmondsworth: Penguin, 1971.
    A highly useful basic text on urban economics, and the most useful item on the subject encountered to date. Topics covered include urban land values, growth, transportation, renewal, and municipal government financing.

PB (2)

Schmid, A. Allen. *Converting Land From Rural To Urban Uses*. Baltimore: The Johns Hopkins Press, 1968.

(3)

Simon, Arthur. *Faces Of Poverty*. New York: Macmillan, 1966.
    Not urban studies.

(4)

Stanbeck, Thomas M. Jr. and Richard V. Knight. *The Metropolitan Economy: The Process Of Employment Expansion*. New York: Columbia University Press, 1970.
    A good study of employment characteristics in metropolitan areas.

(3)

Thompson, Wilber R. *A Preface To Urban Economics*. Baltimore: The Johns Hopkins Press, 1965.
    An extremely detailed work, far too sophisticated and complex for general use, but still worthy of consideration in light of its impact on the field of urban economics. A basic reference work.

HB (2)

7
Urban Geography: The Morphology of the City

Books included in this section use the discipline of geography as a framework for analysis and evaluation. Several of the most significant works in this field of urban analysis have been included in section 1.2.

A number of works reviewed earlier as useful have now been rated as being dated and insufficient in light of newer material available in general works. Where other disciplines have updated their literature on urbanization, few adequate works have appeared in recent years which address themselves to the city using the discipline of geography.

General works in geography have not been included on the assumption that the user of this bibliography will have ready access to current geographies of an international, national, regional, or thematic nature.

7.1 GENERAL WORKS

Abler, Ronald, J. S. Adams, and P. Gould. *Spatial Organization: The Geographer's View Of The World*. Englewood Cliffs: Prentice Hall, 1971.
(3)

Beaujeu-Garnier, J. and C. Chabot. *Urban Geography*. London: Longmans, 1967.
An evaluation of the general urban condition today, and also of specific situations in various cities around the world, this work can be characterized as a regional study in urban geography. Specific urban function is dealt with in detail, using world-wide examples. Quite useful and different from previous works reviewed.
HB (2)

Bourne, Larry S. *Internal Structure Of The City: Readings On Space And Environment*. New York: Oxford University Press, 1971.
This sophisticated collection of readings deals with a wide range of topics, including:
   Nature of the City
   Urban Structure and Growth
   Urban Processes
   Urban Networks
   Urban Communities, Activities, Problems, and Prospects
The readings are up to date, not found in other collections reviewed to date. Using a number of urban oriented disciplines, this work provides a broad spectrum of information.
PB (2)

The City In Print

Briggs, K. *Field Work In Urban Geography*. London: Oliver and Boyd, 1970.
    Superior works exist.

(4)

Carter, H. and W. K. D. Davies. *Urban Studies: Studies In The Geography Of Wales*. London: Longmans, 1970 (available from The Humanities Press, New York).

(3)

Detwyler, Thomas R., ed. *Urbanization And Environment: The Physical Geography Of The City*. Belmont: Wadsworth, 1972.
    A collection of articles covering such topics as topography, climate, resources, soil, ecology, noise, and vegetation in the city. Essentially a college level reader in urban geography, this reference work contains much valuable information.

PB (2)

Dickinson, Robert E. *City And Region: A Geographical Interpretation*. New York: Humanities Press (U.S. only) and London: Routledge and Kegan Paul, 1964.
    As with *The Western European City* by the same author, this work is too detailed for general use, but is of great value as a reference. This book looks at urban regions world-wide and also at the region as a social unit, an urban center, focal point of urban-rural interaction, and as a locus of change. A worthwhile complement to *The Western European City*.

HB (2)

_____. *The City Region In Western Europe*. New York: Humanities Press (U.S. only) and London: Routledge and Kegan Paul, 1967.
    An abridged version of *City And Region* with content limited to Western Europe. See the other two Dickinson titles listed.

(4)

_____. *The Western European City*. New York: Humanities Press (U.S. only) and London: Routledge and Kegan Paul, 1961.
    A general, but highly detailed, study of the historical location and development of towns. The first part of the book covers Europe in general, while the second part is a detailed study of urban function, morphology, the historic city throughout Europe, and modern urbanism. This work is a good reference, having become one of the more influential urban geographies.

HB (2)

Duncan, Beverly and Stanley Lieberson. *Metropolis And Region In Transition*. Beverly Hills: Sage Publications, 1970.
    Superior works exist.

(4)

Everson, J. A. and B. P. Fitzgerald. *Settlement Patterns*. London: Longmans, 1969.

(3)

Urban Geography

Freeman, T. W. *Geography And Planning*. London: Hutchinson University Library, 1967.
> A short and concise work, covering such topics as physical limitations, rural land use, urban geography, and problems of urban location and relocation. A suitable reference.
>
> HB/PB (2)

Gentilcore, R. Louis, ed. *Canada's Changing Geography*. Scarborough: Prentice Hall, 1967.
> About one quarter of this book is devoted to urban geography, with five readings dealing with industrial distribution, the growth of Toronto, and urbanization on the prairies. The remainder of the book is devoted to other aspects of geography. Of use as a reference.
>
> PB (2)

Gottmann, Jean and Robert A. Harper, eds. *Metropolis On The Move: Geographers Look At Urban Sprawl*. New York: Wiley, 1967.
> (3)

Gunn, Angus M. *Patterns In World Geography*. Toronto: Gage, 1968.
> A school text with units covering population, urban centers from the geographical point of view, the historical city, and regional studies of Holland, France, and Japan. This book is devoted in large part to general aspects of geography, limiting coverage of the city to less than 25% of the text. Each chapter is available in paper-bound form.
>
> HB (2)

Highsmith, Richard M., ed. *Case Studies In World Geography*. Englewood Cliffs: Prentice Hall, 1961.
> Insufficient urban studies content.
>
> (4)

Hull, Oswald. *Frontiers Of Geography*. London: Macmillan, 1964.
> Insufficient urban studies content.
>
> (4)

Johnson, James H. *Urban Geography: An Introductory Analysis*. Oxford: Pergamon, 1967.
> A basic urban geography dealing with historic form, demographics, occupational characteristics, sectors of urban activity, current form, and urban geographical theory. An excellent reference, but too dry for general application.
>
> PB (2)

Jones, Emrys. *Human Geography*. London: Chatto and Windus and New York: Praeger (U.S. only), 1965.
> Dated.
>
> (4)

_____. *Towns And Cities*. London: Oxford University Press, 1966.
> Superior works exist.
>
> (4)

Lithwick, N. H. and Gilles Paquet, eds. *Urban Studies: A Canadian Perspective.*
    Toronto: Methuen, 1968.
        The title here is misleading. Essentially a collection of sophisticated geographical studies, this item is of immense value for its detailed analysis and for the author's attempt to develop a cross-disciplinary approach between economics and geography. A good reference for the urban geographer.

                                                                          PB (2)

Marshall, John Urquhart. *The Location Of Service Towns: An Approach To The Analysis Of Central Place Systems.* Toronto: University of Toronto Press, 1969.

                                                                             (3)

Mayer, Harold M., et al. *A Modern City: Its Geography.* Chicago: National Council for Geographical Education, 1969.
        Reprints of nine articles in the 1969 volume of the *Journal Of Geography* are included in this work. Among them are articles on urban structure, urban economic patterns, land use, transportation, and the prospects for megalopolis. This book, recommended as a reference, is good, solid urban geography.

                                                                          PB (2)

Morrill, Richard L. *The Spatial Organization Of Society.* Belmont: Duxbury Press (Wadsworth), 1970.

                                                                             (3)

National Council for Geographical Education. *Urban Geography.* Topics in Geography 1. Normal: Illinois State University, 1966.
        An essential reader containing a general survey of urban geography as well as specific theory, and including a good study of Christaller's 'Central Place Theory.'

                                                                          PB (1)

Pritchard, J. M. *Towns And Cities.* London: Dent, 1967.
        Superior works exist.

                                                                             (4)

Putnam, Robert G, Frank J. Taylor and Philip G. Kettle, eds. *A Geography Of Urban Places: Selected Readings.* Toronto: Methuen, 1970.
        A highly useful source book dealing with 1) definitions of urban geography, 2) the economic functions of cities, and 3) the effects of urbanization and the urban environment. Most of the readings included are reprints of recent articles in geographical journals.

                                                                       HB/PB (2)

Rose, A. J. *Patterns Of Cities.* Melbourne: Thomas Nelson, 1967.
        A good study of world urban patterns and detailed studies of Sydney (Australia) and Calcutta. The use of Australian examples for the study of basic urban geography is interesting, but limits its use in North America.

Urban Geography

>The last two chapters, though, dealing with the two urban centers noted above, make this work of value as a reference.
>
>>PB (2)

Smailes, Arthur E. *The Geography Of Towns*. 5th ed. Hutchinson University Library, 1966.
>A good general study which deals with the origin, setting, and morphology of towns. This work has become an indispensible source on urban geography.
>
>>HB/PB (1)

Stamp, L. Dudley. *Applied Geography*. Harmondsworth: Pelican, 1967.
>Superior works exists. Dated.
>
>>(4)

Taylor, G. *Urban Geography*. London: Methuen, 1964.
>Dated.
>
>>OP (4)

Turner, P. M. *Towns*. London: Macmillan, 1970.
>This interesting work on field exercises uses pictures, maps, statistics, and diagrams, with English examples, for dissection and in-depth analysis of the urban structure in England. A title in the *Topics In Geography Series*.
>
>>PB (1)

7.2 HISTORICAL GEOGRAPHY

Mitchell, J. G. *Historical Geography*. London: English University Press, 1963.
>This work is dry and a bit hard going, but has some worthwhile information on village site and development, town location and development, and a short historical study of transportation through the 19th Century. For reference use only.
>
>>HB (2)

Ward, David. *Cities And Immigrants: A Geography Of Change In Nineteenth Century America*. New York: Oxford University Press, 1971.
>A highly detailed and sophisticated study, dealing with urban growth in the U.S. from 1790-1910. A superb reference.
>
>>HB/PB (2)

7.3 INDUSTRIAL GEOGRAPHY

Alexandersson, Gunnar. *Geography Of Manufacturing*. Englewood Cliffs: Prentice Hall, 1967.
>This work is basically an economic geography, but also deals with distribution patterns of manufacturing in the urban area, and includes sections on manufacturing and its effects upon urban areas.
>
>>PB (2)

Estall, R. C. and R. O. Buchanan. *Industrial Activity And Economic Geography*. London: Hutchinson University Library, 1966.
    This work is much too technical for general reading, but has reference value for location and productivity of manufacturing complexes.
    HB/PB (2)

Gentilcore, R. Louis, ed. *Geographical Approaches To Canadian Problems*. Scarborough: Prentice Hall, 1971.
    Sophisticated selections on a broad range of Canadian geographical studies including industrial location, urban characteristics, and political structures. Highly specialized, but good reference material.
    PB (2)

Morgan, W. T. W. *Nairobi: City And Region*. Oxford University Press, 1967.
    A geographical study of the region, through evaluation of physical features, tribal structures, land use, and the city itself. A useful reference.
    PB (2)

Mulvihill, Donald F. and Ruth Cope Mulvihill. *Geography, Marketing, And Urban Growth*. New York: Van Nostrand Reinhold, 1970.
    A *Searchlight Book*. A detailed and sophisticated study in macro-economics, looking at the market function in large urban units. Although specialized, this work is a valuable reference.
    PB (2)

8
Urban Environment and Urban Ecology

A considerable number of books, of varying quality, have been written on the nature of the current ecological condition (or crisis, as many would substitute).

Excluded were books which could only be labelled as poor attempts to provide "information" on pollution and its effects. Partisan tracts, or books carelessly thrown together in the wake of public concern, do little to provide information on the condition, problems, or prospects, of the global environment.

Many worthwhile works were also excluded if they took a strictly biological, non-societal approach, or dealt with the situation without reference to the urban element.

Those that have been included can provide a wide range of perspectives on the condition and problems as seen by activists and scientists. It should be noted that Carson's *The Silent Spring* (8.1) and McHarg's *Design With Nature* (8.2) are the most comprehensive studies of ecosystems, while Adamson's *Pollution* (8.1) is a highly readable school text.

Other sources should be consulted for a far wider range of titles.

8.1 GENERAL WORKS

Adamson, Robert G. *Pollution: An Ecological Approach.* Scarborough: Bellhaven House, 1971.
    A useful and readable item on pollution in Canada, presenting studies which are succinct, Canadian in focus, and illustrated with easily comprehended graphics. A superb book on the environment.
                                                                                                    HB (1)

Barnett, John, ed. *Our Mistreated World: Case Histories Of Man's Pillaging Of Nature.* Princeton (New Jersey): Dow Jones Books, 1970.
    Twenty-nine articles collected from *The Wall Street Journal*, dealing with specific pollution problems as well as general ecological conditions. A good reader, factual and interesting.
                                                                                                    PB (2)

Carson, Rachel. *The Silent Spring.* Greenwich: Fawcett-Crest, 1964.
    As the precursor of all other books on the environment, this is a most significant work. The author highlighted the problems of pollution at a time when they were far less serious than they are today.
                                                                                                    PB (2)

The City In Print

Dansereau, Pierre, ed. *Challenge For Survival: Land, Air, And Water For Man In Megalopolis.* New York: Columbia University Press, 1970.

(3)

Dickinson, Robert E. *Regional Ecology: The Study Of Man's Environment.* New York: Wiley, 1970.

(3)

Eckbo, Garrett. *The Landscape We See.* New York: McGraw-Hill, 1969.
    Superior works exist.

(4)

Fairbrother, Nan. *New Lives, New Landscapes: Planning For The 21st Century.* New York: Knopf, 1970.
    This text is a valuable reference on urban ecology with a distinctive approach--an examination of a multitude of ways in which land is blighted or preserved. Illustrated with good photographs.

HB (2)

Editors of Fortune. *The Environment: A National Mission For The Seventies.* New York: Harper & Row, 1970.
    A good general reader.

PB (2)

Fuller, R. Buckminster, <u>et al</u>. *Approaching The Benign Environment.* Edited by Taylor Littleton. University (Alabama): University of Alabama Press, 1970.
    Not urban studies.

(4)

Goodman, Marshall. *Controlling Pollution.* Englewood Cliffs: Prentice Hall, 1967.
    A highly readable collection of articles on problems, current action, and solutions.

PB (1)

Gregory, Peter. *Polluted Homes.* Occasional Papers on Social Administration, Number 15. London: G. Bell, 1965.
    The text is limited to the urban environment in England, and as such is of use for comparative reference. However, the information on the structuring of public surveys is of great value to anyone who is interested in making up a questionnaire related to the urban environment.

PB (2)

Harmer, Ruth Mulvey. *Unfit For Human Consumption.* Englewood Cliffs: Prentice Hall, 1971.
    An interesting journalistic study of pesticides.

HB (2)

Herber, Lewis. *Crisis In Our Cities.* Englewood Cliffs: Prentice Hall, 1965.
    Superior works exist.

(4)

The Urban Environment And Urban Ecology

Maunder, W. J., ed. *Pollution: What It Is, What It Does, What Can Be Done About It*. Victoria: University of Victoria, 1969.
    This excellent item is a collection of articles by observers of pollution in the Northwest (U.S. and Canada) and covers all forms of pollution, means of combatting them, and future prospects (to 2000 A.D.). Its local character adds to its value.

PB (1)

MacNeill, J. W. *Environmental Management*. Ottawa: Information Canada, 1971.
    This study, prepared for the Privy Council Office, is of interest as being an "unofficial" position paper on the current state of the environment in Canada. Looking at population, urbanization, technology, and government, this survey investigates the problems and prospects of urban and rural environments as well as the state of air and water resources in general. The last chapter, on summary considerations, is of particular importance. This is the first North American attempt to develop a coordinated national policy on the environment and, as such, it is of utmost importance to Canadians. As an example of environmental policy, it is therefore also important to Americans.

PB (2)

McHale, John. *The Ecological Context*. New York: Braziller, 1970.
    A more detailed study of some of the topics covered in McHale's *The Future Of The Future* (see section 3.5), this work includes discussions of the biosphere, population, food, energy, and materials. Charts and schematics abound. A good reference.

HB/PB (2)

Mitchell, John G., ed. *Ecotactics: The Sierra Club Handbook For Environmental Activists*. New York: Pocket Books and New York: Simon & Schuster, 1970.
    The title explains the purpose of this interesting work which includes a number of readings presenting ideas on methods of action, rather than describing conditions and problems. A useful reference.

PB (2)

Morgan, Frank. *Pollution: Canada's Critical Challenge*. Toronto: The Ryerson Press, 1970.
    A school text including a considerable amount of recent information on pollution in Canada. A useful classroom reference. A title in the *Shaping Canada's Environment Series*.

PB (2)

Perloff, Harvey S., ed. *The Quality Of The Urban Environment. Essays On "New Resources" In An Urban Age*. Baltimore: The Johns Hopkins Press, 1969.

(3)

Read, Brian. *Healthy Cities: A Study Of Urban Hygiene*. London: Blackie, 1970.
    Not urban studies.

(4)

Vallentine, H. R. *Water In The Service Of Man*. Harmondsworth: Pelican, 1967.
   Not urban studies.

(4)

8.2 SPECIFIC STUDIES

DeVos, Anthony, et al., eds. *The Pollution Reader*. Montreal: Harvest House, 1968.
   A series of readings (each from 5-20 pages) on the pollution of soil, water, and air. Some readings are excellent, and all are useful.

PB (2)

McHarg, Ian L. *Design With Nature*. Garden City: Natural History Press, 1969.
   This work deals with a basic problem of our urban environment: the imbalance between social and economic values in relation to the ecology. Beginning with analysis of the existing natural processes, a scale of values is drawn up, based on degree of tolerance for interference by man. Each value-system is then mapped individually in shades from light to dark. When superimposed one on the other, the areas of least social cost and least danger to natural resources are defined in lighter tones. Both social and economic values are included, presenting a complete value-description of an area. Profusely illustrated with photographs, maps, charts, and schematic drawings which are quite good. Essential.

HB/PB (2)

SMIC (Study of Man's Impact on Climate). *Inadvertent Climate Modification* (1971), and SCEP (Study of Critical Environmental Problems). *Man's Impact On The Global Environment* (1970). Cambridge: The M. I. T. Press.
   These two works are not urban studies *per se*, but their content is too significant to bypass. Both provide considerable detail on man made influence on the global environment. Highly useful references.

PB (2)

9
Urban Demographics: Population

This section includes titles which relate to population conditions and problems in cities. A wider range of works available on the more general topic of world demographics have been excluded, including many worthwhile books which approach the study of population without reference to urban influences of consequences. A larger mass of poorer works, published to capture an unsuspecting, yet increasingly concerned public, have been excluded for obvious reasons. The works included will provide valuable insights into the world wide condition and its related problems, taken from the perspective of the urban setting. Other sources should be consulted for a more complete list of classic and worthwhile recent works in this field.

9.1 GENERAL WORKS

Borgstrom, Georg. *The Hungry Planet*. Revised ed. New York: Collier, 1967.
    A worldwide overview of the problems of population, food production, and natural resource depletion, this book is readable, well illustrated, and balanced with easy-to-comprehend statistical information.
                                                                                    PB (1)

Brown, Harrison and Edward Hutchings, Jr., eds. *Are Our Descendents Doomed: Technological Change And Population Growth*. New York: Viking, 1972.
    A general reader which deals with the consequences of rapid population growth, population planning, and population controls.
                                                                        HB/PB (2)

Clark, Colin. *Population Growth And Land Use*. London: Macmillan, 1967.
    A heavy work, dealing with population characteristics on a worldwide scale. Historical demographics, food supply, and the economics and politics of population growth, are all covered in this work, heavily laden with statistics. The last two chapters deal with urban population characteristics, focusing on industrial location and land use. A useful reference.
                                                                            HB (2)

Clark, John I. *Population Geography And The Developing Countries*. Oxford: Pergamon, 1971.
    A highly detailed study which presents a considerable body of data on urban demographics. Well illustrated, this work deals with the factors of population growth, population distribution, urban and rural diversity, and

employment. Separate sections deal with Latin America, Africa, South-West Africa, South Asia, East Asia, and Southeast Asia. Quite a good reference.

PB (2)

Cipolla, Carlo. *The Economic History Of World Population*. 4th ed. Harmondsworth: Pelican, 1967.
    This book, well documented and interesting to read, provides an historical perspective to population growth over the last 9000 years. A superb study.

PB (1)

Freedman, Ronald, ed. *Population: The Vital Revolution*. Garden City: Doubleday, 1964.
    Essential in conjunction with Cipolla (above), this book provides an interesting and comprehensive look at the problem of population. The full spectrum of population study, with demography-oriented, discipline-oriented and region-oriented readings is included.

PB (1)

Griffin, Paul F. *Geography Of Population: A Teacher's Guide*. The 1970 Yearbook of The National Council for Geographic Education. Palo Alto: Fearon, 1969.
    This work deals with world population and includes good representation of most of the world's areas. Although listed as a teachers' text, it can also be utilized as a worthwhile general reference.

HB (2)

Heer, David M. *Society And Population*. Englewood Cliffs: Prentice Hall, 1968.
    A study of general population characteristics (historical, present, and future), population processes, and socio-economic influences. Includes some superb sections and others of limited use. A title in the *Foundations Of Modern Sociology Series*.

HB/PB (2)

_____, ed. *Readings On Population*. Englewood Cliffs: Prentice Hall, 1968.
    A collection designed to supplement the book above. A title in the *Readings In Modern Sociology Series*.

PB (2)

9.2 HISTORICAL DEMOGRAPHICS

Glass, D. V., ed. *Population In History*. London: Arnold, 1965.
    Basically a reference for certain aspects of population study, this work covers European and North American demographic history from the 17th to the 20th Century. It is an essential reference for this area of population studies.

HB (2)

Urban Demographics

9.3 TECHNICAL DEMOGRAPHICS

Abrams, Charles. *Man's Struggle For Shelter In An Urbanizing World*. Cambridge: The M. I. T. Press, 1964.
    A technical study of population inflation and its urban pressures, much of this work relates to the problems of the under-developed world. A worthwhile supplement for reference.
HB/PB (2)

Stone, Leroy O. *Urban Development In Canada: An Introduction To The Demographic Aspects*. Ottawa: Information Canada, 1967.
    This book is technical and statistical, but so structured that most people should have little trouble in using it. Well illustrated with graphs and charts, it is an exhaustive and very useful reference.
PB (1)

10
Cybernetics and Urban Society

The works in this section are inclusive of two basic types-- books on automation and technology (and their impact), and books that speculate on the future of urban civilizations largely in terms of technology. In this latter field, many of the future oriented works should be compared to the more humanistic studies found in section 3.5.

10.1 GENERAL WORKS

Brightbill, Charles K. *The Challenge Of Leisure*. Englewood Cliffs: Prentice Hall, 1960.
    Insufficient urban studies content.

(4)

Bronwell, Arthur B., ed. *Science And Technology In The World Of The Future*. New York: Wiley, 1970.
    Insufficient urban studies content.

(4)

Buckingham, Walter. *Automation: Its Impact On Business And People*. New York: Mentor (PB) and New York: Harper and Row (HB), 1961.
    Insufficient urban studies content. Dated.

(4)

Delgado, Jose M. R. *Physical Control Of The Mind: Toward A Psycho-civilized Society*. New York: Harper, 1969.
    An essential reference written by one of the chief proponents of societal control through the use of bio-chemical techniques. This work presents the author's view of mental evolution and capacities, supported with extensive studies of past and ongoing experiments in behavioral control. An exceedingly complete bibliography is included.

HB/PB (2)

Demcyzynski, S. *Automation And The Future Of Man*. London: George Allen and Unwin, 1964.

(3)

Dunlop, John T., ed. *Automation And Technological Change*. Englewood Cliffs: Prentice Hall, 1962.
    Dated.

(4)

Ellul, Jacques. *The Technological Society*. New York: Vintage, 1964.
   A translation of an exceedingly significant philosophical study of man and technology.

(3)

Gabor, Dennis. *Innovations: Scientific, Technological, And Social*. Oxford at the University Press, 1970.
   An interesting little book which includes a critical review of 137 technological (power, transportation, communications, cybernetics, education), biological (agriculture and bio-engineering), and social innovations (human ecology, economic reforms, cultural stabilization). A very useful general reference.

PB (1)

Hall, Peter. *London 2000*. London: Faber and Faber and New York: Praeger (U.S. only), 1963.

(3)

Hamill, Peter H. *Plenty And Trouble: The Impact Of Technology On People*. New York: Abingdon Press, 1971.
   This work has a religious rather than a social sciences orientation.

(4)

Hellwig, Jessica. *Introduction To Computers And Programming*. New York: Columbia University Press, 1969.
   A relatively simple and easy-to-comprehend introduction to this topic. A good general reference.

HB (2)

Kahn, Herman and Anthony J. Wiener. *The Year 2000: A Framework For Speculation On The Next Thirty-three Years*. New York: Macmillan, 1967.
   This work deals with possible futures, presenting scenarios focused on technological developments and their effects. The approach here is extremely practical in that it takes present developments, projects them along the lines of developments in process, and examines what would be the most probable results. Scenarios of alternative futures are listed in order from the most to the least likely to take place within the next thirty years. The research done here has been accepted by the U.S. and Canadian governments, and also by the military and industrial elites of both countries. The very nature of this book--projection of a series of events being most likely to happen--places it in the role of possibly creating futures, rather than simply predicting them.

HB (1)

Kahn, Herman and B. Bruce Briggs. *Things To Come: Thinking About The 70's And 80's*. New York: Macmillan, 1972.
   An updating of the fine aspects of the projections made in *The Year 2000*. A number of these have come about in the five years since the first book was written, and the authors have integrated this information in a detailed study of the future through the 1980's. This book is a supplement

to the earlier work, which still stands on its own as being one of the most important of all books available on technological projections to the year 2000.

    HB (1)

Landers, Richards R. *Man's Place In The Dybosphere*. Englewood Cliffs: Prentice Hall, 1967.
    Superior works exist.

    (4)

London, Perry. *Behavior Control*. New York: Harper and Row, 1969.

    (3)

Martin, James and Adrian R. D. Norman. *The Computered Society: An Appraisal Of The Next Fifteen Years*. Englewood Cliffs: Prentice Hall, 1970.
    A significant title which analyses the impact of computers on every aspect of urban life. Exceedingly complete in the presentation of examples this book examines information on what computers are, what they can and cannot do, and their impact, both as promise and threat to man. Also examined are alternate control and use recommendations in urban planning, data collection, privacy, education, and societal control and protection. One of the best works on cybernetics reviewed to date and, as such, a superb reference.

    PB (2)

McLuhan, Marshall. *Understanding Media: The Extensions Of Man*. 2nd ed. New York: Signet, 1964.
    A personal statement, this rambling and valuable work deals with the past, present, and future in light of communications, offering commentary on a myriad of aspects of modern civilization.

    PB (2)

_____ and Quentin Fiore. *The Medium Is The Massage: An Inventory Of Effects*. New York: Bantam, 1967.
    Essentially a visual experience which assists the reader in perceiving the potentials of new technologies and social thought, this work probes the effects of change on the group and on the individual psyche.

    PB (2)

Mesthene, Emmanuel G. *Technological Change: Its Impact On Man And Society*. New York: Mentor (PB) and Cambridge: Harvard University Press (HB), 1970.
    Superior works exist.

    (4)

_____, ed. *Technology And Social Change*. Indianapolis: Bobbs-Merrill (PB) and Cambridge: Harvard University Press (HB), 1967.
    Superior works exist.

    (4)

Midura, Edmund M., ed. *Why Aren't We Getting Through: The Urban Communication Crisis.* Washington: Acropolis Books, 1971.
   Superior works exist.
   (4)

Philipson, Morris. *Automation: Its Implications For The Future.* New York: Vintage, 1962.
   OP (4)

Walker, Charles R., ed. *Technology, Industry, And Man: The Age Of Acceleration.* New York: McGraw-Hill, 1968.
   (3)

Wiener, Norbert. *Cybernetics: Or Control And Communication In The Animal And The Machine.* 2nd ed. Cambridge: The M. I. T. Press, 1961.
   (3)

10.2 SPECIFIC STUDIES ON TECHNOLOGY IN URBAN SYSTEMS

Aranguren, J. L. *Human Communication.* New York: McGraw-Hill, 1967.
   Written on a more sophisticated level than the Bryars item listed below, this book looks at communication "as transmission of information to elicit a response." Communication, in its various forms, the sociology of communication (techniques and content), and future prospects are dealt with in an interesting way. Quite good.
   HB/PB (2)

Ayres, Robert U. *Technological Forecasting And Long-Range Planning.* New York: McGraw-Hill, 1969.
   (3)

Bagdikian, Ben H. *The Information Machines: Their Impact On Men And The Media.* New York: Harper & Row, 1971.
   A Rand Corporation study, this detailed reference looks at the impact of technology on information flow, with emphasis on the interrelationships of the various forms of media. Present and possible future developments and characteristics are evaluated.
   HB/PB (2)

Braithwaite, Max. *Servant Or Master: A Casebook Of Mass Media.* Agincourt: Book Society of Canada, 1968.
   A brief, yet worthwhile study of news, editorializing, advertising, propaganda, education, and entertainment. Excellent.
   PB (1)

Bryars, Gerald D. and George R. Hall. *This Book Is About Communication: Book I.* Toronto: Ryerson Press, 1971.
   A useful high school level text on means of communication (talking, newspapers, magazines, records, radio, film, T.V.). Worthy of examination.
   HB (2)

Halloran, J. D. *The Effects Of Mass Communication With Special Reference To Television*. Working Paper No. 1, Television Research Committee. Leicester: The Leicester University Press, 1965.
    Dated.

(4)

Hancock, Alan. *Mass Communication*. London: Longmans, 1970.
    Similar to the Bryars' book listed on previous page, but more sophisticated and restricted to the study of English mass communications. A useful comparative reference.

PB (2)

Irving, John A., ed. *Mass Media In Canada*. Toronto: Ryerson, 1962.
    A review of communications and its various forms in Canada. Dated.

PB (4)

McLuhan, Marshall. *The Gutenberg Galaxy*. Toronto: University of Toronto Press, 1962.
    A collection of poetic statements and meditations on the nature of modern man, this intriguing work is an experience in itself.

HB/PB (2)

Meadow, Charles T. *Man-Made Communication*. New York: Wiley, 1970.

(3)

Meier, Richard L. *A Communications Theory Of Urban Growth*. Cambridge: The M. I. T. Press, 1962.
    Although dated, this work is of value in its presentation of characteristics of urban organization and communications. Much ground is covered in this easily read and useful reference.

HB (2)

Miller, Arthur R. *The Assault On Privacy: Computers, Data Banks, And Dossiers*. Ann Arbor: University of Michigan Press, 1971.
    A study of the technology and social problems of personal information, this complete and detailed work surveys the full range of data systems and the various ways in which information is collected. Quite a good treatment of a topic not dealt with elsewhere.

HB (2)

Prehoda, Robert W. *Designing The Future: The Role Of Technological Forecasting*. Philadelphia: Chilton, 1967.

(3)

Rose, John. *Automation: Its Anatomy And Physiology*. London: Oliver and Boyd, 1967.
    An introduction to the technology of computers and automation, this work is a good study of the science of cybernetics. No social or human effects are discussed.

PB (2)

Steinitz, Carl and Peter Rogers. *A Systems Analysis Model Of Urbanization And Change: An Experiment In Interdisciplinary Education*. Cambridge: Harvard University Press, 1968.

(3)

Thomas, Shirley. *Computers: Their History, Present Applications, And Future*. New York: Holt, Rinehart, 1965.
    Insufficient urban studies content.

(4)

11
Miscellaneous

This section includes several works providing exclusively visual or statistical information.

11.1 ILLUSTRATIVE MATERIALS

Asbell, Bernard. *Careers In Urban Affairs*. New York: Wyden, 1970.
    This is actually a "career" introduction book for professions practiced in an inner city area.

    (4)

Augustine, Herbert A., <u>et al</u>. *Canadian Stereograms*. n.p.: J. M. Dent (Canada), 1971.
    A useful collection of 56 stereograms, with illustrations of Canadian towns and cities making up more than 50% of the total. Well laid out for classroom use (information and questions on back of previous photo, with photo trio below). A superb visual item, with clear, concise photographs in black and white.

    PB (1)

Blair, C. L. *The Canadian Landscape*. Toronto: Copp-Clark, 1967.
    Dated.

    (4)

Branch, Melville C. *City Planning And Aerial Information*. Cambridge: Harvard University Press, 1971.
    Harvard City Planning Studies, 17.

    (3)

GEE! Group For Environmental Education. *Our Man-Made Environment, Book Seven*. 1214 Arch Street, Philadelphia, Pennsylvania, 19107.
    An excellent study of urbanization for intermediate grades, approaching the urban environment through visual presentations, and of use for students at all levels of achievement.

    PB (1)

Minshull, Roger. *Settlements From The Air*. London: Macmillan, 1971.
    A highly useful little paperback which illustrates 19 different settlement patterns and urban structures, with each section including a concise description of the location, followed by a comprehensive geographical exercise.

    PB (1)

Miscellaneous

Wilson, W. Harmon and Roman F. Warmke. *Life On Paradise Island*. Glenview: Scott, Foresman and Company, 1970.
    Although listed as a grade 5-8 text, this book has definite general use; a complex study of man as a group animal is hidden in the elementary text.
    PB (1)

11.2 COMPENDIA, STATISTICAL MATERIALS

Goodman, William I. and Eric C. Freund, eds. *Principles And Practice Of Urban Planning*. 4th ed. Washington: International City Manager's Association, 1968.
    An exceedingly comprehensive guide for local municipal officials covering a wide range of planning topics. Essential for reference.
    HB (2)

The Municipal Yearbook (1972): The Authoritative Resume Of Activities And Statistical Data Of American Cities. Washington: The International City Management Association, 1971.
    An annual publication, this source is a compendia of data for U.S. cities of 10,000 population or more, dealing with individual city activities as well as regional or national programs. Topics include socio-economic classifications, services, land use, and finance. A directory of municipal officials is also included. An excellent reference.
    HB (2)

National Council for Geographic Education. *Statistics For Geography Teachers*. Topics in Geography 2. Normal: Illinois State University, 1967.
    A reference containing much valuable information on such topics as urban population and usability of land.
    PB (2)

12
Periodicals and Journals

Hundreds of periodicals are available on the full range of urbanization. Most are technical and detailed, specialist sources and as such outside the scope of this bibliography. G. C. Bestor's *City Planning Bibliography* (Section 1.3) is an exhaustive reference, providing complete source and ordering information for 205 periodicals. The U.S. section covers a wide range of disciplines. The international section restricts itself more to the traditional urban disciplines, leaving out a number of periodicals which complement American counterparts in areas such as architecture, urban government, sociology, history, and geography. The Bestor bibliography does not include Canadian journals or periodicals, but this information is available in public, college and university libraries throughout Canada.

Several periodicals bear mention as being critical sources:

Ekistics
Athens Center of Ekistics
Box 471
Athens, Greece

    12 issues per year; $24.00 per year.

Planning, The ASPO Magazine
American Society of Planning Officials
1313 E. 60th St.
Chicago, Illinois, U.S.A.

    11 issues per year; $25.00 per year U.S.; $20.00 Canada & Mexico; $17.00 elsewhere.

Journal Of The American Institute Of Planners (Also *AIP Journal*)
American Institute of Planners
1776 Massachusetts Ave., N.W.
Washington, D.C. 20036, U.S.A.

    6 issues per year; $12.00 per year U.S.: $14.00 all other countries.

Periodicals

Sage Urban Studies Abstracts
Sage Publications, Inc.
P.O. Box 776
Beverly Hills, California 90210, U.S.A.

    4 issues per year; $30.00 per year individual; $50.00 institutional.

The Futurist
World Future Society
P.O. Box 30369
Bethesda Branch
Washington, D.C. 20014, U.S.A.

    6 issues per year; membership and/or subscription, $10.00.

Habitat
Central Mortgage and Housing Corporation
Ottawa, Canada

    3-6 issues per year; no charge.

13
Related Literature and Resources

Material in this section is included to provide a broader scope on the city. The city and its people as a subject of study cannot avoid the effect of the surrounding physical environment. Ecology, as related to the city, is becoming recognized as a very real need in dealing with the city and its problems. For this reason, material from the natural sciences has been included.

Science fiction has been included to give the reader material to help develop an open and inquiring mind regarding not only the future, but also the consequences of certain present trends in our society. The presentations are conjectural, but are all well handled as assessments of possible future worlds. In dealing with the city and its future, all is conjecture anyway. Science fiction is a highly digestible form with which to deal with the subject. The science fiction titles included are only those with a particular emphasis on future urban alternatives.

Several utopian and anti-utopian works are included, providing an introduction to the philosophy of urban existence as seen by men from the time of classical Greece to the present. As will be noted, several of the titles listed also appear in the section on urban oriented science fiction.

Finally, several titles have been included which contain a distinct artistic or humanistic approach to viewing the city. As such, they are complementary to the other approaches to studying the city.

13.1 IN THE NATURAL SCIENCES

Darling, F. Fraser and John P. Milton, eds. *Future Environments Of North America*. Garden City: Natural History Press, 1966.
    A collection of papers presented at a 1965 conservation conference. Decidedly a reference only, but quite valuable as such, this book includes comment on a wide range of topics related to man and his natural environment, ecology, and the interaction of man with nature. The section "Regional Planning and Development" is of great value, but other sections have specifically worthwhile and useful studies.

HB/PB (2)

Kormondy, Edward J., ed. *Readings In Ecology*. Englewood Cliffs: Prentice Hall, 1965.
    A study of ecology in scientific terms without reference to social conditions and problems. Not urban studies.

(4)

Related Literature And Resources

Odum, Eugene P. *Ecology*. New York: Holt, Rinehart & Winston, 1963.
    Predominently scientific in orientation and, as such, of little value for use in studying the urban environment.
    (4)

Richardson, Ronald E., <u>et al</u>., eds. *Developing Water Resources: The St. Lawrence Seaway And The Columbia/Peace Power Projects*. Toronto: Ryerson Press, 1969.
    Although not directly involved with the urban condition, the development of natural resources and the resulting industrial/transportation complexes is still of significance to the study of urbanization. The two areas studied are dealt with through historical as well as current developments.
    PB (2)

Sollers, Allan. *Ours Is The Earth: Appraising Natural Resources And Conservation*. New York: Holt, Rinehart & Winston, 1963.
    An ecological study dealing with the basic elements such as water, soil, forest, and minerals. A short work, of value for reference.
    HB (2)

13.2 IN SCIENCE FICTION

All the books listed below have value and, therefore, no coding is given. These items are of particular value in developing imaginative thinking regarding possible futures for society. The nature of science fiction titles is such that they go in and out of print quite rapidly, and therefore may well be available at the moment under a different publisher's imprint. All the titles listed here are paperbound except where indicated, and the publisher listed is the one who put out the most recent paperbound edition reviewed. For the most recent editions available, check *Books In Print* and *Paperback Books In Print*.

Included in the list below are five titles considered by the editor to be the best for portrayals of urban futures:

    Asimov, Isaac. *The Caves Of Steel*.
    Bamber, George. *The Sea Is Boiling Hot*.
    Harrison, Harry. *Make Room/Make Room*.
    Silverberg, Robert. *The World Inside*.
    Spinrad, Norman. *Bug Jack Barron*.

Asimov, Isaac. *The Caves Of Steel*. New York: Fawcett-World.
    A superb study of a civilization in which the masses are confined to an urban complex in which any view of the sky is reserved for the elites, and open air and space are held in horror. The resulting look at changes in attitudes to human values as we know of them is handled beautifully.

_____. *The Naked Sun*. New York: Fawcett-World.
    A sequel to the previous novel, the main characters of the above-mentioned society are confronted with a society which is its direct opposite.

The City In Print

Asimov, Isaac. *The Rest Of The Robots*. New York: Pyramid and Garden City: Doubleday (HB).
    An excellent study of the robot in a future world not far off. The paperback edition includes eight short stories.

Bamber, George. *The Sea Is Boiling Hot*. New York: Ace.
    A superb story of a not so distant future which is both plausible and horrific. Uncontrolled pollution has altered the existence of man in ways which can be seen developing today in microcosm. Here it is carried to extremes in a society which is understandably familar and frightenly bizarre. The story is well developed both in characterization and plot.

Sexual mores are described in considerable detail.

Brunner, John. *The Wrong End Of Time*. Garden City: Doubleday (HB only).
    Ostensibly a tale of B.E.M.'s (Bug Eyed Monsters), this entire novel is an investigation of life in the U.S. in the 1990's, fully plausible in light of some of the current trends in American life. Urban life, or better, urban decay, is portrayed with vivid reality. A graphic tale of a decadent society in collapse.

Charbonneau, Louis. *No Place On Earth*. New York: Fawcett-Crest.
    In the same line as *1984*, this gripping novel portrays a world enslaved by a dictatorship which controls not only all public actions of the individual, but also such private matters as marriage and child-bearing.
                                                                         OP

_____. *Psychedelic-40*. New York: Bantam.
    A good study of a possible future world in which a nation is controlled by an elite that holds absolute power through the use of drugs on the general populace.
                                                                          OP

Christopher, John. *The Death Of Grass*, or *No Blade Of Grass*. Harmondsworth: Penguin and New York: Avon.
    Man's dependence on nature is graphically illustrated in this novel of a future in which all forms of grass, including all the grains, die off. The effect on civilization is immediate and devastating.

_____. *The Long Winter*. New York: Fawcett-World.
    A study of a future in which natural forces, in this case a new and sudden ice age, force man to abandon cities in Europe. This results in the collapse of Western Civilization.

Galouye, Daniel F. *Simulacron-3*. New York: Bantam.
    Simulation of an entire society and mass control through polls is the theme of this novel. Polling is carried to an extreme and lives are played with as though human beings had literally become no more than statistics. Included is a presentation of the possibilities of artificial society creation and manipulation.
                                                                         OP

Related Literature And Resources

Harrison, Harry. *Make Room/Make Room*. New York: Berkley.
    A study of New York with a population of 35,000,000 in the year 1999. This book, dealing with overpopulation and the ensuing disintegration of living standards and society as we know it is both fascinating and horrifying. A modified form of this story has been used as the plot for the film "Soylent Green."

Heinlein, Robert. *The Green Hills Of Earth, The Man Who Sold The Moon, Methusalah's Children,* and *Revolt In 2100.* New York: Signet/New American Library.
    The author's novels and short stories come together to form a series on the future from 1975 to 2600 A.D.. All of this series is not yet published. The approach is interesting and many of the short stories are particularly good in portraying man in a plausible future.

Herbert, Frank. *The Dragon In The Sea,* or *21st Century Sub.* New York: Avon.
    A world of the future in which the major nations have exhausted their land resources and must now fight for those below the sea. A story of another plausible future.

Huxley, Aldous. *Brave New World*. New York: Bantam and New York: Harper & Row.
    A classic study of man in the future, decidedly of value for its study of a streamlined Eden.

Kornbluth, C. M. *The Syndic.* New York: Berkley and New York: Harper & Row (HB).
    A novel in which society has been gripped first by anarchy and then mob control. Interesting as a study of a non-social society.

Orwell, George. *Animal Farm.* Harmondsworth: Penguin and New York: Signet/New American Library, and New York: Harcourt, Brace, & Jovanovich (HB).
    Another basic study of human "potentials."

_____. *1984.* Harmondsworth: Penguin and New York: Signet/New American Library, and New York: Harcourt, Brace, & Jovanovich (HB).
    A core work in the study of urban futures.

Pohl, Frederick, ed. *Nightmare Age.* New York: Ballantine.
    A collection of essays and stories by Paul Ehrlich, Frederick Pohl, Robert Heinlein, Fritz Leiber and others. Topics include ecological disaster, overpopulation, over consumption, and the fragmentation of society. A highly intriguing reader.

_____, and C. M. Kornbluth. *Gladiator-At-Law.* New York: Ballantine.
    This study of a future urban civilization projects a society in which the great corporations have secured total power. Included are possible implications of social conditioning, with control of the masses through psychiatry and surgery.

_____, and C. M. Kornbluth. *The Space Merchants.* New York: Ballantine.
    A novel in which those in control of big business and advertising have secured power over North America.

Raphael, Rick. *Code Three*. New York: Berkley and New York: Simon & Schuster (HB).
   A future world of gigantic expressways in which the automobile has won total dominance as the means of transportation both within and between the cities. A superb study.

Roshwald, Mordecai. *Level 7*. New York: Signet/New American Library.
   A good study of a future in which nuclear war has forced man below the surface into a chaotic and horrifying society with a mole-like existence.

Sheckley, Robert. *The Status Civilization*. New York: Signet.
   The author describes a world in which non-conformists are memory-washed, and the earth altered and stratified by fear of the radical and non-conventional. Includes an excellent study of man in a radically altered future.

Silverberg, Robert. *The World Inside*. Garden City: Doubleday (HB only).
   A view of the North American continent in 2381 A.D., providing perspectives useful in dealing with the potentials of megastructures. While the world view presented is incomplete, the story does weave a complete picture of a society based upon a totally open sexual code.

   The story is set around life in a megastructure which contains 880,000 people in 1000 stories, individuals who never leave the structure, and exist in space impossible small by current standards (45.90 square feet per family). A plausible tale in light of some current proposals for future structures and control techniques for the masses.

Spinrad, Norman. *Bug Jack Barron*. New York: Avon and New York: Walker & Co. (HB).
   As a novel, this work is remarkable, and as a study of future social conditions, it is quite useful. A liberal use of descriptive phraseology is matched to the life style of Jack Barron, once a bohemian and now, twenty years later, a member of the establishment. Superb characterization and a gripping plot.

Wells, H. G. *The Shape Of Things To Come*. London: Corgi.
   A study of man and society from 1929-2106. First published in the early 1930's, this work looks at the period of 1929-1970, with interesting "projections" for the period 1970-2100.
                                                                                    OP

Young, Michael. *The Rise Of The Meritocracy, 1870-2033*. Harmondsworth: Penguin.
   A satirical novel of a world in 2034. The title gives a key to its approach, namely that of a "history" of a society based on merit.

13.3 IN PHILOSOPHICAL AND UTOPIAN LITERATURE

   This listing is to serve as an introduction to the philosophy of urban existence as seen through the writings of classical figures or modern commentators on our world. It is beyond the scope of the present work to list all the utopias that have been written, or comment on their content. However, the information given here

Related Literature And Resources

will be expanded at a later date. Also, with the complex and diverse availability of some, current sources are not listed. *Books In Print* should be consulted for any title sought. The date listed is the date of original publication or presentation.

A. Utopian and Anti-Utopian Works

    Andreae. *Reipublicae Christianopolitanae Descriptio.* (1619)
    Aristotle. *Politics.* (Books 1 and 7, ch. 4-12) (4th Century B.C.)
    Bacon, Francis. *New Atlantis.* (1629)
    Bellamy, Edward. *Looking Backward.* (1888)
    Campanella, Thomas. *The City Of The Sun.* (1623)
    Carpenter, Edward. *Forecasts Of The Coming Century.* (1897)
    Forster, E. M. *The Machine Stops.* (1928)
    Fourier, Charles. *Le Nouveau Monde Industriel Et Societaire.* (1829)
    Garnier, Tony. *Une Cite Industrielle.* (1917)
    Harrington, James. *Oceana.* (1656)
    Herzl, Theodor. *Oldnewland.* (1902)
    Hobbes, Thomas. *Leviathan.* (1651)
    Holmes, Edmond. *What Is And What Might Be.* (1911)
    Holmes, Edmond. *Tomorrow: A Peaceful Plan To Real Reform.* (1898)
    Huxley, Aldous. *Brave New World.* (1932)
    Machiavelli, Niccolo. *Discourses.* (16th Century A.D.)
    Machiavelli, Niccolo. *The Prince.* (16th Century A.D.)
    Mercier, Louis Sebastien. *Memoirs Of The Year 2500.* (1802)
    Mill, John Stewart. *On Liberty.* (1859)
    More, Thomas. *Utopia.* (1515)
    Morris, William. *A Dream Of John Ball.* (1888)
    Morris, William. *News From Nowhere.* (1891)
    Orwell, George. *1984.* (1948)
    Owen, Robert. *A New View Of Society.* (1813)
    Plato. *Republic.* (Books 2-7) (4th Century B.C.)
    Rousseau, Jean Jacques. *The Social Contract.* (1762)
    Thoreau, Henry David. *Walden.*
    Wells, H. G. *A Modern Utopia.* (1905)
    Zamiatin, Evgenii. *We.* (1924)

B. Titles Related To Utopias

    Bernari, Marie L. *Journey Through Utopia.* (1950)
    Bestor, Arthur E., Jr. *Backwoods Utopias 1633-1829.* (1950)
    Bloomfield, Paul. *Imaginary Worlds: Or, The Evolution Of Utopias.* (1932)
    Cohn, Norman. *The Pursuit Of The Millenium.* (Revised ed. 1957)
    Cole, Margaret. *Robert Owen Of New Lenark.* (1953)
    Gerber, Richard. *Utopian Fantasy.* (1955)
    Gide, Charles. *Communist And Cooperative Colonies.* (1930)
    Holloway, Mark. *Heavens On Earth.* (1951, 1966)
    Negley, Patrick. *The Quest For Utopia.* (1952)
    Walsh, Chad. *From Utopia To Nightmare.* (1962)
    Webber, Everett. *Escape To Utopia.* (1959)

C. General Works

Strauss, Leo. *The City And Man*. Chicago: Rand McNally, 1964.
Under initial scrutiny, this work would be passed by as too detailed and sophisticated for general use. But, on second look, these studies are of immense use for those seeking a close examination of urban history and/or the philosophical foundations of urbanization. A good reference.

HB (2)

White, Morton and Lucia. *The Intellectual Versus The City*. New York: Mentor (PB) and Cambridge: Harvard University Press (HB), 1962.
An interesting and useful text which traces the views of American intellectuals and artists on the American city. From Jefferson to Frank Lloyd Wright, views are presented through the reactions of more than twenty men toward urbanism in the U.S.. A well developed presentation of anti-urban thought, expressing the prejudice, fear, and distrust of cities so prevalent in American life. A detailed work, limited to use as a reference.

HB/PB (2)

13.4 IN THE ARTS AND HUMANITIES

Ashcom, Benjamin M., Morton A. Maimon, and Williams W. Reynolds. *Stories Of The Inner City*. New York: Globe, 1970.
Good for browsing, this is a small paperback collection of short stories looking at people and life in the city.

PB (2)

Blackburn, Paul. *The Cities*. New York: Grove Press, 1967.
A collection of poems on cities and city life.

PB (2)

Cahill, Susan and Michele F. Cooper, eds. *The Urban Reader*. Englewood Cliffs: Prentice Hall, 1971.
This is a provocative collection of humanistic city images. Major units are entitled: 1) Life Styles and City Psyches, 2) The Physical Environment, 3) Housing, 4) Minorities, 5) Economics, 6) Politics and Power Struggles, 7) Education, 8) Artists, 9) The Future, and 10) City People. This work has a U.S. orientation.

HB/PB (1)

Schoenfeld, Oscar and Helene MacLean, eds. *City Life*. New York: Grossman, 1969.
This book presents the city as seen through excerpts from works by Henry Adams, Malcolm X, S. N. Behrman, Robert Coates, Edith Wharton, O. Henry, Truman Capote, H. L. Mencken, James Thurber, Booth Tarkington, Ralph Ellison, John Dos Passos, and several dozen more. An interesting and useful collection.

HB (2)

Related Literature And Resources

Trachtenberg, Alan, Peter Neill, Peter C. Bushnell, eds. *The City: American Experience*. New York: Oxford University Press, 1971.
    A reader on urban culture which integrates essays, poetry, and excerpts from novels and diaries, this book presents images of the urban experience rather than glimpses of concrete urban conditions. As such, considerable insight is gained in understanding the mood of the immigrant, migrant, intellectual, worker, revolutionary, and planner in American life. Includes readings from authors covering the period 1849-1970 and photographs from the 19th Century to the present day. An excellent reference.
    PB (2)

Watson, Ernest W. *Course In Pencil Sketching: Book 1. Buildings And Streets. Book 2. Trees And Landscapes*. New York: Reingold, 1956.
    Covering the topics listed in the subtitles, these two books are of use for those interested in dealing with the city through artistic observation and presentation. Easy to use and read, both books are essential references.
    HB (2)

_____. *Perspective For Sketches*. New York: Reinhold, 1966.
    Also a useful reference in supplement to the two books above.
    HB (2)

14
Modular Materials

Several series are outlined below which present urban studies data and resources in unit segments rather than whole texts. The flexibility of this approach widens the scope of use, while providing the same, if not greater, quantity of information available for application.

14.1   MAJOR MODULAR SERIES

The City Of Man: A Modular Series.   Agincourt: General Learning Corporation, 1974-76.

>In 1974, a new series will be coming out which addresses itself specifically to urban studies. Included in each volume is a considerable number of illustrations. Each module is written by a practicing classroom teacher, with world-renowned academicians lending their expertise, and under the general editorship of R. Charles Bryfogle. Based on the assumption that no single text can be written to fulfill all the needs for information on the urban scene, this series is being structured to offer a variety of packages tailored to individual needs. Each major topic is clustered with titles that will include a 96 page general survey and 3 or more 64 page specialized titles to provide greater depth in the particular area. The end result will be a series which is comprehensive and yet sufficiently flexible to allow for the maximum options for selection of emphasis. The initial portion of this series, as planned for summer 1974, is as follows:

Primary Modules

>*The Canadian City*. A concise visual and textual examination of the major cities of Canada. Included in this compilation will be an essay on the unique character of Canadian urbanization.

>*The City In Print: An Annotated Bibliography*. A listing, with annotations, of over 1200 books on urbanization from all disciplines and perspectives, with comment on their suitability for general and reference use. The second part includes an extensive, annotated review of non-book, commercially available resources. This was compiled by the series general editor.

Modular Materials

Series Modules (topics listed without title) For 1974.

The City As Space. 5 modules.

A General Urban Geography. 96 pp.

The Function Of Cities: types of cities; economic, cultural and institutional functions; centripetal forces in urban development. 64 pp.

Urban Sectors: the core, commercial districts, grey zone, industrial sections, suburbs, urban-rural fringe; and urban hierarchies (city through ecumenopolis). 64 pp.

The City As Set Space: the shape of cities; the land; services; urban and regional land use; networks (communication, transportation, and utilities). 64 pp.

Urban Transportation. 64 pp.

The City As The Home Of Man.

Urban Sociology. 96 pp.

Urban Dynamics And Growth: location, movement, migration, typology, population, and the anatomy of urbanization. 64 pp.

Social Dynamics: the group; stratification; mass culture vs. specific subcultures; urban social characteristics and institutions. 64 pp.

Human Dynamics: the individual in the city; privacy; family, deviant behavior; identity; individual associations; innovation and conformity. 64 pp.

Government In The City. 64 pp.

Urban Economics. 64 pp.

Series For 1974-1976 Might Include:

The City As Perceived Space. 3 or 4 modules.

The Historical City. 3 or 4 modules.

The Future Metropolis. 5 modules.

The Prime Movers And Innovators In World Urbanization. 3 to 6 modules.

Your City Is Alive: A teacher's resource book.

Individual Modules:
 housing and urban renewal
 urban economics
 poverty and wealth in the city
 the dynamics of urban demographics--population in cities

Sociological Resources For The Social Sciences. Boston: Allyn & Bacon, 1969--.

<u>Episodes</u> <u>In</u> <u>Social</u> <u>Inquiry</u> <u>Series</u>. Thirty-six episodes are conceived, of sets containing 10 student booklets and 1 instructor's guide. Prices vary and are indicated along with the date and pages of each episode. With few exceptions, these works show a distinct U.S. orientation.

Social Mobility In The United States. (1970/46 pp./$5.50 per 10) Distinctly an American item. The sections on occupational prestige, elites, and theories of social stratification are concise and informative. A useful item, limited only by a general lack of illustrations. The teacher's guide provides sheets suitable for duplication. This item is quite good and does provide much of value for the teacher.

Images Of People. (1969/27 pp./$5.50 per 10) A short module on human perception and its effect on how we see the world around us. With American orientation, this item is of use in the classroom. It is limited by minimal illustrations and reliance on text alone to carry the message.

Family Size And Society (Not yet published)
Cities (Not yet published)

Titles not reviewed in this series (not urban studies):

Social Change: The Case Of Rural China
Science And Society
Small Group Processes
Religion In The United States
Family Form And Social Setting
Simulating Social Conflict
Leadership In American Society: A Case Study Of Black Leadership
Values In Mass Communications: A Study Of The Western Roles Of Modern Women
Delinquency
Population Change: A Case Study Of Puerto Rico
Contemporary Soviet Society
Transitions
The Early Twenties And The Late Sixties
Class And Race In The United States
Incidence And Effects Of Poverty In The United States
Testing For Truth: A Study Of Hypothesis Evaluation
Migration Within The United States
Divorce In The United States

<u>Readings</u> <u>In</u> <u>Sociology</u> <u>Series</u>.

Hughes. *Cities And City Life.* (See 6.1)
_____. *Crowd And Mass Behavior.* (See 6.3)
_____. *Population Growth And The Complex Society.* (See 6.2)

Modular Materials

Titles not reviewed in this series (not urban studies):

Life In Families
Racial And Ethnic Relations
Deliquents And Criminals: Their Social World
Trends And Change In Canadian Society
Social Organizations

Texts not reviewed:

Understanding Yourself And Your Society
High School Sociology
Understanding Society

Minor Modular Series

People And The City. Glenview: Scott Foresman, n.d..
Five modular units are produced to this point, with more seemingly on the way. Each booklet averages 48 pages, is well illustrated, and at a reading level suitable for elementary reading abilities. A teacher's manual, with tests for each module, is also available.

Moving In
Crime And Safety
Buyers Beware
Housing Conflicts
Speaking Up

These items are urban in focus, but too elementary for secondary use. An American orientation is noted.

Modules Available from Methuen Educational Ltd.

Edynbry, D. *New Towns*. London: Methuen, 1971. A title in the series *Get To Know*. This pamphlet investigates the structure of towns. Although elementary in approach, this work is of use for the study of English cities.

Armstrong, Warwick. *New Towns*. Wellington: Hick Smith, 1968. A title in the series *Geography Of The British Isles*. This module provides concise data on the British New Town.

Bloomfield, G. T. *Cities And Towns*. Wellington: Hick Smith, 1969. A title in the series *Geography Of The British Isles*. This title deals with urban development in England. Modern urban problems of a physical nature are briefly touched upon.

Ryder, T. T. *Urban Development*. Wellington: Hick Smith, 1969. A title in the series *Geography Of South America*. The nature and extent of the current urban explosion in Latin America is dealt with, along with sections on Brasilia and Ciudad Guayana. This work is of definite usefulness.

Part Two
Introduction

In the past four years, a wide range of materials related to urbanization, produced in Europe and North America, have come on the market. Very little of the material reviewed is more than 10 years old, with the bulk being less than three years old. But, as will be noted in the annotations, this currency does not necessarily denote suitability for use. A wide range of extremely useful materials exists, as does the range of poor and useless materials.

Included in this portion of the bibliography is comment on more than

        50   Maps
     100   Articles & Reprints
      25   Filmloops
      25   Simulations & Kits of Materials
     300   Filmstrip/Slide Sets
      25   Tapes & Records
      20   Overhead Transparencies Sets & Singles
      10   Books on Simulations

All materials made available for review are included, with comment on suitability and availability. The value code classification used in the book section is not suitable for classifying non-book material, therefore an item's usefulness can only be determined from the annotation. Order numbers have been indicated (in parenthesis) as has any other information of use in determining a material's value. Although few of the audio-visual materials have been prepared specifically for urban studies, many of the items reviewed provide excellent coverage of urban topics.

This listing has attempted to provide the user with a comprehensive selection of non-book materials on the city, with annotations as to their usefulness at the secondary school or community level. Many of the items reviewed have been set aside, without prejudice, as being too elementary or too sophisticated for general or school use.

Unfortunately, the only comprehensive listing of audio-visual materials is so specialized and expensive that it is usually only acquired by media wholesalers. Publishers's catalogues are not only scattered, but are also inconsistent in their listing of materials by subject area.

Therefore, the compiler has attempted to review all materials which could be even remotely suitable. Materials were selected for review by title from items referred to by colleagues, from journals, or from catalogues made available by distributors of non-book materials.

Most of the film and simulation or kit materials (Sections 16 and 17) included in this section of the bibliography are available to schools or organizations for preview. The few items that are not, are so noted. Because the materials in Section 15 are too easily duplicated, they are, in most instances, not made available for preview.

Materials have been divided into three catagories. In Section 15, materials are reviewed encompassing printed articles, reprints, maps, and other documents that are available on a steady basis from commercial sources. In Section 16, audio-visual materials are reviewed including filmstrips, slides, records, tapes (video and audio), and overhead transparencies. The last category, Section 17, includes simulation games or books on simulations, and kits of materials. In each section, materials have been placed under the listing of the manufacturer. Complete information regarding the Canadian, British, and U.S. distributor is given where this information is available.

A source guide for Part II can be found following the book source guide. Prices have also been included since a reference indicating prices is not readily available. It should be noted that these prices were valid only for the date they were reviewed and are subject to change.*

Excluded from this selection are all items which are patently ethnic, and not urban, in their orientation (for rationale, see the introduction to Part I).

The compiler would like to acknowledge the producers and distributors of the materials reviewed, all of whom have provided invaluable assistance in the rendering of this comprehensive list.

---

*It should be kept in mind that distributors *and prices* do change frequently with little or no notice.

15
Unbound Print Materials and Maps

A large range of commercially available reprints and articles are available. The selection below was chosen, by title, from catalogues listing more than 3000 titles on all subjects. Other sources of commercially available reprints have been found, but their materials have not yet been reviewed. In all cases, the single most important criterion for this review was the suitability for general use, be it in a school or in the community.

No attempt has been made to do more than list several maps. Other sources should be consulted, both nationally and locally.

> NOTE: Regarding other sources of unbound, print materials: it is outside the scope of this bibliography to cover, in detail, non-commercial sources of material. See a further note on this subject in 15.3.

15.1 REPRINTS AND PAMPHLETS

AAAS REPRINTS

    Source: Can./U.S./G.B. American Association For The Advancement Of Science.

    Price: $1.00 each, or 60¢ each for up to nine. Larger quantities are available at less cost (on the basis of length).

    Note: Largely a collection of articles on the physical sciences, four articles were reviewed, titled in such a way as to suggest application to urban studies.

Ekistics, The Science Of Human Settlements, C. A. Doxiadis. (12 pp.)
    A must. Doxiadis has summarized the full range of his theory on the nature of cities in this short article. Well illustrated.

The Experience Of Living In Cities, Stanley Milgram. (12 pp.)
    A 1970 article which looks at the quality of life in cities, emphasizing research in human adaptions to urban conditions. Interesting, but too sophisticated for general use. Better items exist in readers on urban sociology.

Man's Movement And His City, C. A. Doxiadis. (12 pp.)
    Reprint of a 1968 article. A well illustrated study of the city as a

system. Human needs for movement, and its impact on urban structures, is reviewed. Patterns of movement, from pre-urban communities to the future, are dealt with succinctly and interestingly.

Science And The City: The Question Of Authority, James D. Carroll. (12 pp.)
A 1969 article on the research and development activities of HUD (U.S.). Of no direct relation to urban studies.

ASPO REPORTS

Source: Can./U.S./G.B.   American Society Of Planning Officials.

Price: $5.00 each (for those listed)

Note: This organization operates a book and research reprint service. The newsletter provided with ASPO membership is of value for its rather complete listings of new books and reports. The reprints and reports available cover the technical or physical aspects of planning. The reports listed below were taken from a list of over 200 reports. Most of these reprints or reports are too technical for general use. Two are worthy of mention.

Land Use Classification Manual. 1962. (53 pp.)
A manual of definite value in setting up land use maps. The system used is the one most commonly used in the U.S. and Canada.

Planning Maps For Small Cities. 1967. (24 pp.)
A short manual on how to make land use maps.

BOBBS-MERRILL REPRINTS

Source: Can./U.S. Bobbs-Merrill Co., Inc.
G.B. Eurospan, Ltd.

Note: This company puts out more than 2000 reprints in a number of fields, including:

European History   Geography
American History   Economics
Anthropology   Sociology
      Political Science

Included in this listing are 87 titles selected because of their possible application to urban studies. Selection was made on the basis of title, and as such, the collection may be incomplete. The date of publication is indicated.

Prices vary, and are indicated following each title. Orders must be for $2.00 or more. Orders must include series prefix letter and number. No preview available on these items.

Unbound Print Materials And Maps

Most of the recommended articles listed below are academic in orientation, thereby limiting their usefulness, in most cases, to reference.

Geography Reprints

No. G-2. H. W. Ahlmann. *The Geographical Study Of Settlements: Examples From Italy, Denmark, And Norway.* 1928. (30 pp.)
 A highly detailed survey. Illustrated. 60¢.

No. G-14. B. J. L. Berry, et al. *Urban Population Densities.* 1963. (16 pp.)
 A statistical-technical study, updating Colin Clark's earlier studies of urban population densities in the early 1950's. 40¢.

No. G-17. J. R. Borchert. *The Twin Cities Urbanized Area.* 1961. (23 pp.)
 A detailed study of Minneapolis-St. Paul. Included are two fold-out maps which illustrate growth and density from 1900-1980. Useful. 80¢.

No. G-35. S. D. Chang. *The Historical Trend Of Chinese Urbanization.* 1963. (34 pp.)
 A survey from the second millenium B.C. to 1940. This item provides information not available elsewhere. A well illustrated and essential reference. 60¢.

No. G-36. "Johann Heinrich von Thunen," from *Rural Settlement And Land Use*, by M. Chisholm (Hutchinson University Library), 1962. (14 pp.)
 A summary of this geographer's concepts. 40¢.

No. G-67. B. J. L. Berry. *The Functional Basis Of The Central Place Hierarchies.* 1958. (8 pp.)
 A highly detailed analysis. 40¢.

No. G-71. J. Gottmann. *Megalopolis.* 1957. (11 pp.)
 A summary which serves as a useful reference and definition. Worthwhile purchase. 40¢.

No. G-83. C. D. Harris. *Location Of Salt Lake City.* 1941. (8 pp.)
 A classical study. 40¢.

No. G-85. C. D. Harris. *The Nature Of Cities.* 1945. (10 pp.)
 An essential reference which looks at the functions of cities, including a discussion of three major theories of analyses (concentric zone, sector, and multiple nuclei). 40¢.

No. G-105. T. Jacobsen. *Salt And Silt In Ancient Mesopotamian Agriculture.* 1958. (7 pp.)
 A highly detailed and useful article. 40¢.

No. G-147. n.a. *On Some Indications Of Stability In The Growth Of Cities In The United States And Some Spatial Aspects Of Urban Growth In The United States*. 1956. (33 pp.)
   Exceedingly detailed, statistical information. Of limited use. Dated. 60¢.

No. G-159. R. L. Morrill. *The Development Of Spatial Distributions Of Towns In Sweden*. 1963. (14 pp.)
   An interesting article which analyzes urban function and migration. 40¢.

No. G-161. I. Morrissett. *The Economic Structure Of American Cities*. 1958.
   Far too detailed for general use.

No. G-165. R. Murphey. *The City As A Center Of Change*. 1954. (14 pp.)
   A comparison between western Europe and China. An article which can be of considerable value as a reference. 40¢.

No. G-206. O. H. K. Spate. *Factors In The Development Of Capital Cities*. 1942. (9 pp.)
   A classical reference, this is still useful. 40¢.

No G-207. O. H. K. Spate. *Five Cities Of The Gangetic Plain*. 1950. (18 pp.)
   A well illustrated study on Benares, Cawnpore, Lucknow, Agra, and Allahabad. 40¢.

No. G-215. D. Stanislawski. *The Origin And Spread Of The Grid-Pattern Town*. 1946. (15 pp.)
   A study which begins with Mohenjo-Daro, carries on through Hellenic and Roman patterns, into the Renaissance and modern period. An essential reference. 40¢.

No. G-236. E. Ullman. *A Theory Of Location For Cities*. 1941. (11 pp.)
   A significant article on urban analysis. 40¢.

No. G-238. E. Ullman. *The Minimum Requirements Approach To The Urban Economic Base*. 1960.
   Far too detailed for general use.

European History Reprints

No. E-1. R. M. Adams. *Developmental Stages In Ancient Mesopotamia*. 1955. (12 pp.)
   A useful survey on the growth of Neolithic cultures in Mesopotamia. 40¢

No. E-23. H. C. Boren. *The Urban Side Of The Gracchan Economic Crisis*. 1958.
   A detailed, in-depth study, of limited usefulness.

No. E-68. H. Frankfort. *The Origin Of Monumental Architecture In Egypt*. 1941. (19 pp.)
   A well illustrated article detailing Egyptian urban design and architecture.

Unbound Print Materials And Maps

No. E-93. L. Haimson. *The Problem Of Social Stability In Urban Russia.* 1964.
    Not urban studies.

American History Reprints

No. H-109. J. J. Huthmacher. *Urban Liberalism And The Age Of Reform.* 1962.
    Not urban studies.

No. H-121. E. E. Lampard. *American Historians And The Study Of Urbanization.* 1961.
    Too specialized for general use.

No. H-196. P. F. Sharp. *Three Frontiers.* 1955. (8 pp.)
    A study of the Turner thesis of settlement patterns, using Canada, the U.S., and Australia for comparative purposes. Useful. 40¢.

Anthropology Reprints

No. A-162. S. W. Mintz. *The Folk-Urban Continuum And The Rural-Proletarian Community.* 1953-4.
    A detailed classical study of continuing usefulness. 40¢.

No. A-254. R. M. Adams. *Agriculture And Urban Life In Early Southwestern Iran.* 1962. (14 pp.)
    An anthropological survey which illustrates the changes which have taken place over 7000 years. Useful. 40¢.

No. A-258. C. M. Arensberg. *The Community As Object And As Sample.* 1961.
    Too specialized for general use.

No. A-320. K. Little. *The Role Of Voluntary Associations In West African Urbanization.* 1957. (17 pp.)
    A detailed article, but interesting and useful. 40¢.

Economics Reprints

Econ-1. F. G. Adams, et al. *Undeveloped Land Prices During Urbanization.* 1968. (10 pp.)
    A detailed analysis of urban land values. 40¢.

Econ-7. W. Alonso. *A Theory Of The Urban Land Market.* 1960 (8 pp.)
    Detailed and heavy going. 40¢.

Econ-9. W. Alonso. *What Are New Towns For?* 1970. (18 pp.)
    A useful article on the economics of new towns. 40¢.

Econ-22. n.a. *Note On The Economics Of Residential Zoning And Urban Renewal.* 1959.
    Too sophisticated for general use.

Econ-143. J. D. Herbert. *A Model For The Distribution Of Residential Activity In Urban Areas.* 1960.
    Too detailed for general use.

Econ-208. J. R. Meyer. "Urban Transportation," from *The Metropolitan Enigma,* ed. by J. Q. Wilson. (Harvard University Press) 1967. (27 pp.)
    An analysis of urban transportation alternatives. Useful. 60¢.

Econ-223. L. Moses. *The Location Of Economic Activity In Cities.* 1967. (11 pp.)
    A brief economic analysis of urban function. Detailed, but highly useful. 40¢.

Econ-224. L. Moses. *Value Of Time, Choice Of Mode, And The Subsidy Issue In Urban Transportation.* 1963.
    Too dated and detailed for general use.

Econ-229. R. F. Muth. *Economic Change And Rural-Urban Land Conversions.* 1961.
    Too detailed for use.

Political Science Reprints

PS-16. J. E. Bebout. *Management For Large Cities.* 1955.
    Dated.

PS-32. J. S. Bruner. *The Boss And The Vote.* 1946.
    A dated study of city politics.

PS-55. R. T. Daland. *Political Science And The Study Of Urbanism.* 1957.
    Dated.

PS-121. R. C. Hanson. *Predicting A Community Decision.* 1959.
    Dated.

PS-127. L. J. R. Herson. *The Lost World Of Municipal Government.* 1957. (22 pp
    An interesting piece which analyzes the then present problems of U.S. municipal financing. A useful comparison to today's metropolitan problems. 40¢.

PS-205. D. C. Miller. *Decision Making Cliques In Community Power Structures.* 1958. Dated.

PS-206. P. A. Miller. *The Process Of Decision-Making Within The Context Of Community Organization.* 1952.
    Dated.

PS-300. R. E. Wolfinger. *Reputation And Reality In The Study Of Community Power*. 1960. (8 pp.)
   An interesting article. 40¢

PS-302. R. C. Wood. *Metropolitan Government, 1975*. 1958. (14 pp.)
   Of interest as a summary of thought in the late 1950's as to what this decade had in store. A useful reference for forecasters. 40¢.

PS-346. n.a. *Political Life In The Urban Centers Of Senegal*. 1960. (17 pp.)
   Although dated, this work is a worthwhile reference. 40¢.

Sociology Reprints

S-7. E. C. Banfield. *The Political Implications Of Metropolitan Growth*. 1960. (17 pp.)
   A study of British and American Metropolitan growth, its impact on local governments, and the effect of change. Still topical and useful although more than a decade old. 40¢.

S-14. W. Bell. *Urban Neighborhoods And Informal Social Relations*. 1957.
   Dated.

S-53. W. F. Cottrell. *Death By Dieselization*. 1951.
   Dated.

S-66. K. Davis. *The Origin And Growth Of Urbanization In The World*. 1955. (8 pp.)
   Covering a period of 6000 years, this article outlines the growth of urban societies. 40¢.

S-86. W. H. Form. *Urbanization, Anonymity, And Status Symbolism*. 1957.
   Too specialized for general use.

S-104. S. Greer. *The Social Structure And Political Process Of Suburbia*. 1960. (12 pp.)
   A significant article which analyzes suburban population characteristics, housing types, degree and nature of social participation, and local political behavior. 40¢.

S-105. S. Greer. *Urbanism Reconsidered*. 1956.
   Too detailed and dated.

S-125. B. F. Hoselitz. "The Role Of Cities In The Economic Growth Of Underdeveloped Countries," from *Sociological Aspects Of Economic Growth*, by B. F. Hoselitz. 1960. (25 pp.)
   An article which provides considerable information, though unfortunately in a relatively complicated style. 60¢.

S-202. H. Miner. *The Folk-Urban Continuum.* 1952.
    Too specialized for general use.

S-212-213. W. F. Ogburn. *Social Trends,* 1957 and *Technology As Environment,* 1956.
    Too specialized for general use.

S-232. A. J. Reiss, Jr. *Rural-Urban And Status Differences In Interpersonal Contacts.* 1959.
    Too specialized for general use.

S-271. G. Sjoberg. *The Pre-Industrial City.* 1955. (7 pp.)
    A worthwhile discussion 40¢.

S-280. G. P. Stone. *City Shoppers And Urban Identification.* 1954.
    Dated.

S-320. L. Wirth. *Urbanism As A Way Of Life.* 1938. (24 pp.)
    One of the classics. An article which is essential for any study of urbanization. 40¢.

S-338. n.a. *City Hierarchies And The Distribution Of City Size.* 1958.
    Statistical. Too specialized for general use.

S-340. B. J. L. Berry. *City Size Distributions And Economic Development.* 1961. (15 pp.)
    An illustrated study of rank-size categorization and prime cities. Highly statistical, but still useful. 40¢.

S-341. B. J. L. Berry. *Alternate Explanations Of Urban Rank-Size Relationships.* 1958.
    A detailed study of city size and the rank-style rule. Too detailed for general use.

S-348. D. J. Bogue. *Urbanism In The United States, 1950.* 1955. (15 pp.)
    An interesting comparative piece. 40¢.

S-365. M. R. Davie. "The Pattern Of Urban Growth," from *Studies In The Science Of Society,* by G. P. Murdock. 1937.
    Dated.

S-374. n.a. *The World's Great Cities.* 1960. (22 pp.)
    A demographic study of the growth of cities. 40¢.

S-377. B. Duncan. *Patterns Of City Growth.* 1962. (11 pp.)
    A study of the patterns of urban growth from the 1920's. Statistical, but still useful. 40¢.

S-415. R. M. Haig. *Toward An Understanding Of The Metropolis.* 1926.
    Dated.

Unbound Print Materials And Maps

S-420. A. H. Hawley. *Metropolitan Population And Municipal Government Expenditures In Central Cities*. 1951.
   Too specialized for general use.

S-427. W. Isard. *Metropolitan Site Selection*. 1949.
   Dated.

S-435. L. Kish. *Differentiation In Metropolitan Areas*. 1954.
   Dated.

S-440. n.a. *The History Of Cities In The Economically Advanced Areas*. 1955.
   Too detailed and obtuse for general use.

S-484. n.a. *The Cultural Role Of Cities*. 1954. (24 pp.)
   A highly sophisticated investigation into types of cities, this article is significant in its world-wide scope and infusion of sociological, philosophical, and anthropological data. 60¢.

S-488. W. C. Robinson. *Urbanization And Fertility*. 1963. (17 pp.)
   An article which analyzes the factors of rural and urban population growth. This detailed study presents a good amount of significant data. 40¢.

S-498. C. F. Schmid. *The Ecology Of The American City*. 1958.
   Too detailed for general use.

S-501. L. F. Schnore. *The Myth Of Human Ecology*. 1961.
   Too detailed for general use.

S-530. H. Tisdale. *The Process Of Urbanization*. 1942.
   Dated.

S-535. R. B. Vance. "Metropolitan Dominance And Integration," from *The Urban South*, by R. B. Vance. 1954.
   Too detailed for general use.

S-554. E. Bott. *Urban Families*. 1955. (39 pp.)
   An extensive study of maritial roles and family interaction. Worthwhile. 60¢.

S-556. E. W. Burgess. *The Growth Of A City*. 1929.
   Too dated. Other sources are in print which present a fuller perspective of Burgess' model.

S-566. K. Davis. "Sociological Aspects Of Genetic Control," from *Genetics And The Future Of Man* by J. D. Roslansky. 1966. (31 pp.)
   A significant reference which presents a sober and balanced study of an extremely emotional topic. 60¢.

S-631. R. Sommer. *Studies In Personal Space*, 1959, *Leadership And Group Geography*, 1961, *The Distance For Comfortable Conversation*, 1962, and *Further Studies Of Small Group Ecology*, n.d.
  40 pages of significant data on the use of space and small group ecology. An essential distillation of Sommer's unique investigations. 60¢.

  NOTE ON BOBBS-MERRILL REPRINTS: Most of these articles are reprints from scholarly journals, and as such, their style and levels of complexity are relatively high in most instances. Many represent information not available from other sources.

EASTMAN KODAK COMPANY

  Source: US/Can/GB Eastman Kodak Co. or larger photographic shops.

  Price: As indicated.

Photointerpretation For Planners, Wojciech Wronski and Kenneth J. Davies. (Kodak Publication M-81) 1972. $1.75.
  This superbly illustrated pamphlet provides a visual survey of Metropolitan Toronto while it presents techniques in the use of aerial photographs. Written by two planners, this work is structured in such a manner that it is of use to both the professional and layman. Different types of aerial photographs are illustrated and commented upon, including the oblique, vertical, varying scale vertical, and the colour vertical.

  This manual is the best item yet reviewed on photointerpretation. Its use cannot be too highly recommended.

Photointerpretation For Land Managers, T. Eugene Avery. (Kodak Publication M-76) 1970. $1.50.
  Although related to physical rather than man-made features, this complementary manual presents concise comment and illustration on the use of the sterescope and colour photo in resource management and land survey. A brief note is made on sources of aerial photographs. Useful.

Photointerpretation And Its Uses, n.a. (Kodak Manual) 1968. $1.00
  A brief introduction on the subject, useful as a supplement to the two titles above.

HISTORY OF THE TWENTIETH CENTURY

  Source: Can/US/GB Available from local newsagents or BPC Publishing Ltd., Dept. D., P.O. Box 4, Radstack, Bath BA3 3RA.

  Price: Can/US 60¢; GB 3/6.

  Note: Of hundreds of "chapters" published separately in over-sized, well illustrated pamphlets, only one title is of direct application to urban studies.

Unbound Print Materials And Maps

The City: Heaven Or Hell. (Vol. 8, Chapter 115)
   One of the best items reviewed to date. Exceedingly compact, and yet comprehensive and penetrating studies on urban history, the urban way of life, traffic and the urban landscape.

LESSON AIDS SERVICE

   Source: Can/US/GB   British Columbia Teachers' Federation

   Price: Prices noted are for British Columbia Teachers' Federation members. For non-members, a surcharge is added.

   Note: For ALL ORDERS, the following applies:

   1. Cash prepayment with request or order sent on a school board purchase order form.

   2. A minimum order of $1.00.

   3. No preview outside British Columbia.

Title	Pages	Price	Number
Birth Of A Port, C. M. Defeiux.	17 pp.	$ .40	(#2082)
Building Human Values Into The Community, Dr. A. Hoffer	11 pp.	.25	(#2069)
The City As A Work Of Art, P. D. Spreiregen	6 pp.	.15	(#2084)
City Of The Future, R. Buckminster Fuller (*Playboy* reprint)	11 pp.	.20	(#2087)
The Concerned Majority, A. Rose.	7 pp.	.15	(#2071)
Concerning Human Values, R. R. Jeffels.	4 pp.	.10	(#2070)
Environmental Issues	5 pp.	.12	(#2094)
False Creek Development Concepts, Vancouver City Planning Department.	22 pp.	.75	(#2091)
Field Work In An Urban Setting.	5 pp.	.12	(#2079)
The Function Of The Ancient And The Modern City, H. Hoyt.	10 pp.	.25	(#2075)
The Futurists, editorial in *Time*.	5 pp.	.12	(#2072)
Industrial Parks.	4 pp.	.10	(#2077)
Instant Slum Clearance, J. Meyer.	6 pp.	.18	(#2088)
Intersection Flow Diagram, Vancouver City Planning Department.	1 p.	.02	(#2067)
Local Areas Of Vancouver U.C.S., Vancouver.	34 pp.	1.60	(#2068)
Man And The Space Around Him, C. A. Doxiadis	13 pp.	.30	(#2074)
The Oceans: Man's Last Great Resource, Sen. C. Pell	8 pp.	.20	(#2083)
Origin Of Cities, R. M. Adams.	10 pp.	.25	(#2066)
Our Southwestern Shores, Lower Mainland Regional Planning Board, Vancouver.	56 pp.	1.00	(#2092)
Planning--The Port And The City, W. E. Graham (Planner, Vancouver).	13 pp.	.30	(#2086)
Population Trends In The Lower Mainland, 1971-1986.	41 pp.	1.00	(#2089)
Population Trends In The Lower Mainland, Summary, Lower Mainland Regional Planning Board, Vancouver	4 pp.	.10	(#2090)

The Port Of Vancouver, J. A. Wallace   14 pp. $ .32   (#2073)
Public Transportation In Canadian Cities.   26 pp.   1.25   (#2093)
Some Facts About Modern City Concentration.   4 pp.   .10   (#2095)
Two Short Articles On Urbanization And Human Welfare. 9 pp. .22 (#2081)
Types Of Land Use.   4 pp.   .08   (#2078)
Urban Living.   10 pp.   .25   (#2085)
Urban Renewal.   3 pp.   .07   (#2076)

LIFE EDUCATIONAL REPRINTS

    Source: Can.   School Book Fairs
                   U.S.   Life Educational Reprint Program
                   G.B.   TIME-LIFE International

    Price: 50¢ each, with discounts for more than 4 copies.

    Note: All four are useful for the topic covered.

Air Pollution. Reprint No. 69. 1969.
    An article which analyzes the problem and recommends solutions.

Cars And Cities: On A Collision Course. Reprint No. 92. 1970.
    This reprint from *Fortune* provides a brief, visual survey of the problem of automobiles in cities. A distinctive American emphasis exists in this investigation of problems and solutions.

Cities For Tomorrow. Reprint No. 20. 1965.
    A well illustrated and concise article on the future of cities. Although slightly dated, the material is still topical and current.

Environment: What Can Be Done. Reprint No. 91. 1970.
    This article from *Fortune* presents a concise summary of the problems related to the environment in North America.

NATIONAL LEAGUE OF CITIES PUBLICATIONS

    Source: Can/US/GB   National League of Cities

    Price: As indicated. Full payment or public agency purchase order must accompany order.

    Note: The N.L.C., in addition to its monthly magazine--*Nation's Cities*, publishes a wide range of reprint articles, monographs, and reports of use to municipal officials. Some are of value to the citizen or student. The publications listed are those items selected from a wider range of specialized reports and *Nation's Cities* reprints.

Unbound Print Materials And Maps

Conference Proceedings

The City: Its Resources, Structures And Systems. 1970. (#21A)

Cities In The '70s. 1969. (#19A)

City Goals And The Human Environment. 1967. (#14A)

      Each set of these conference proceedings is prices at $5. Each is also too specialized for general use.

Reports

Recreation In The Nation's Cities: Problems And Approaches. 1968. (56 pp.) (#11C)
      This report identifies municipal recreation needs and problems, looks at various solutions, and outlines several planning methods used in 15 U.S. cities. A detailed, informative document. Of use as a general reference. $2.00.

New Concepts In Municipal Government. 1966.
      Dated.

Reprints

      An urban affairs portfolio is available, including a collection of 6 reprints on a wide range of urban problems in the U.S.. 152 pages @ $2.00. Each article is also available as a reprint.

Air Pollution. 1967. (4 pp.) (#404)
      This article assesses the extent and severity of air pollution in 65 SMSA's in the U.S.. 30¢.

Area Wide Planning. 1966. (4 pp.) (#216)
      An overview of area wide planning in 143 U.S. cities. A cursory look. 25¢.

Better Assessments For Better Cities. 1970 (32 pp.) (#237)
      A panel of experts present a manifesto and recommendations outlining approaches which could be used to improve urban financing. This article is of use as a general reference. 50¢.

Better Environments Through Zoning. 1965. (4 pp.) (#300)
      A summary of alternatives for urban environments and their zoning requirements. Useful. 30¢.

Center City Transportation. 1970.
      Superior surveys exist in the readings to be found in the book section.

Citizen Participation. 1968. (12 pp.) (#225)
    Two articles on the need for citizen participation. Several recommendations are included in this penetrating analysis. Highly recommended. 50¢.

City-County Consolidation. 1969. (12 pp.) (#232)
    An article which analyzes the advantages and disadvantages of consolidation. Useful. 50¢.

Downtown. 1967.
    Dated in light of more current information available in the book section of this bibliography.

The Elected City Official. 1966. (4 pp.) (#217)
    An interesting assessment of the profile of an average mayor and council member in cities, towns and villages in the U.S.. Useful data and perspectives can be gleaned from this article. 30¢.

Financing Our Urban Needs. 1969. (31 pp.) (#227)
    A panel of experts assess the problems and prospects of securing adequate funding. For cities in the U.S. in particular, federal, state, and municipal responsibilities are discussed. 50¢

Here Come The Hate Groups. 1964. (4 pp.) (#601)
    A brief summary of the characteristics of militant extremist groups. A useful and current guide. 25¢.

Industrial Development. 1965. (2 pp.) (#308)
    An assessment of the city's role in industrial location. Useful. 20¢.

Look At Urban Transportation. 1966. (8 articles) (#100)
    Reprints of 8 articles covering the full range of transportation problems in the U.S.. Useful. 50¢.

Municipal Law Enforcement. 1966. (#213)
    Dated.

Mobile Homes. 1965. (#304)
    Dated.

Noise. 1969. (#416)
    Dated.

Reorganizing City Government. 1970. (4 pp.) (#236)
    An article on the do's and don'ts of changing city charters. 30¢.

Skip Annexation. 1967. (3 pp.) (#229)
    An interesting comment on this topic. 25¢.

Solid Waste. 1970. (20 pp.) (#415)
    A summary of a larger, more extensive report on the status of solid waste and its controls in the U.S.. $1.00.

Unbound Print Materials And Maps

Urban Man And The Communications Revolution. 1968. (#224)
    Dated.

Wealth Out Of Waste. 1969. (4 pp.) (#410)
    A study of municipal waste and its economic value. 25¢.

What Kind Of City Do We Want? 1967. (32 pp.) (#220)
    A reprint of a round-table conference of 33 urban experts which assesses what our cities are and what we can have, depending on what we want. 50¢.

What Makes A City Councilman Tick? 1970. (4 pp.) (#235)
    A study of the motivations, attitudes and values of small town council members. 30¢.

SCIENTIFIC AMERICAN OFFPRINTS

    Source: Can/US/GB   W. H. Freeman and Company

    Price: 25¢ each (singly or in quantity). Payment must accompany orders for less than 100 copies. Price listed here includes postage.

    Note: Of the 895 offprints available, 15 were selected as being possibly suitable for urban studies, in either broad or narrow interpretation of the term. The checklist or catalogue available from the firm is free of charge. Many offprints are also available (in the social sciences) on primitive anthropology, macro-economics, and psychology (predominantly individual-nuclear).

The Agricultural Revolution, Robert J. Braidwood. 1969. (10 pp.) (No. 605)
    A well illustrated article, dealing with the early agricultural communities in the Middle East. A good reference piece.

The Assessment Of Technology, Harvey Brooks and Raymond Bowers. 1970. (11 pp.) (No. 332)
    An extract which looks at the broad social consequences of advancing or retarding particular technological developments (by government action). A highly useful essay with a distinctive chart which looks toward twenty broad areas of possible developments in technology (1970-2030).

Communication By Laser, Stewart E. Miller. 1966. (11 pp.) (No. 302)
    An extract on the characteristics of laser. A useful supplement to explain this significant technological innovation.

The Culture Of Poverty, Oscar Lewis. 1966. (9 pp.) (No. 631)
    A study of Puerto Ricans in Puerto Rico and New York. Cultural differences resulting from poverty are presented in this article by an eminent anthropologist. A well illustrated and useful reference.

The City In Print

An Early City In Iran, C. C. and Martha Lamberg-Karlovsky. 1971. (11 pp.) (No. 660)
    An article on Tepe Yahya, a Mesopotamian outpost which acted as a center of trade 55 centuries ago. Illustrated and useful.

The Economics Of Technological Change, Anne P. Carter. 1966. (9 pp.) (No. 629)
    An article now out of date (misleading if applied today). Research included compares 1947-1958.

A Neolithic City In Turkey, J. Mellaart. 1964. (11 pp.) (No. 620)
    An article which details a study of Catal Huyuk in Turkey. A well illustrated reference.

The Origin Of Cities, Robert M. Adams. 1960. (10 pp.) (No. 606)
    A reprint which surveys the initial congregations of man into ever-larger communities in Mesopotamia. Well illustrated.

Population, Kingsley Davis. 1963. (11 pp.) (No. 645)
    A once useful article which is now badly dated by new census information.

Population Density And Social Pathology, John B. Calhoun. 1962. (10 pp.) (No. 506)
    A study of rat behavior. The effect of confined space is dealt with, including extensive description, illustrations, and statistics.

The Present Evolution Of Man, Theodosius Dobzhansky. 1960. (7 pp.) (No. 609)
    An article which is too obtuse for general use.

The Renewal Of Cities, Nathan Glazer. 1965. (11 pp.) (No. 646)
    An article with perspectives and conclusions now badly dated in light of the events of the past eight years.

The Shelter-Centered Society, Arthur I. Waskow. (No. 637)
    Not urban studies.

The Urbanization Of The Human Population, Kingsley Davis. 1965. (15 pp.) (No. 659)
    This article appears elsewhere in books of readings. It details the distribution of urban populations worldwide and is highly useful. Concise, with superb illustrations.

World Population, Julian Huxley. 1956. (13 pp.) (No. 616)
    A well illustrated survey of the population crisis. Although dated by its publication in 1956, the greatest proportion of this article relates to historical trends in population on a world scale. A useful reference.

SYNOPSIS: VIEWPOINTS OF SOCIAL ISSUES--PROBLEMS AND REMEDIES

    Source: Curriculum Innovations, Inc.

    Price: $7.50 for a set of 30 (with teacher's guide)

Unbound Print Materials And Maps

Note: This is a 12 page magazine style booklet on various topics, with twenty issues annually. Essentially reprints of newspaper and magazine articles, these inexpensive items try to cover too much and cannot, therefore, be recommended. A teacher would find far greater value in spending this sum on the reproduction of articles which would be of direct use to his program of study.

Of the present topics available, the following have urban content (school use only):

Ecology. (SB 3)
Integrated Housing. (SB 18)
The Right To Privacy. (SB 11)
Transportation And The Environment Crisis. (SB 7)

ZEPHYRUS

Source: Canada   Urban Educational Materials
       US/GB   Zephyrus

Price: Can/US $1.50

Deschool Primer No. 3: Your City Has Been Kidnapped, W. Ron Jones. n.d. (64 pp.)

This is a very unique work, with 64 unnumbered pages. To quote the author, "This book is about the mystery and magic that is city life." Depending on your interests, it can serve as a textbook, a sensory guide, a source book for locating city treasure, an investigation manual into city institutions, or perhaps, a simple game book for a rainy day. As an educational effort, this book is not directed at a specific age group, academic discipline, or accredited course. It does not have questions at the beginning or end of chapters as there are no chapters or sequential ordering to the ideas in this book. It is possible to begin on any page and continue in any direction. It is hoped this book will encourage the use of the city as a classroom. In doing so, it will serve many purposes, the most valuable being the experience of serving as the director of one's own learning.

This book is an experience and must be seen to be appreciated. It is quite profusely illustrated.

15.2 MAPS AND VISUAL AIDS

CITY VIEW PRINTS

Source: Can/US   American Heritage Publishing Co.
         GB   Information not available

Price: $2.50 each

The City In Print

> Note: Aerial, "bird's-eye," views of these four cities as seen by artists of the day. These color reproductions provide considerable detail of urban form. Each print, in color, measures 15" by 21". Superb display items, of use in any classroom. No preview available on these items.

Boston, 1850. (No. 512)
Charleston, 1851. (No. 513)
New Orleans, 1851. (No. 511)
New York, 1850's. (No. 510)

JACKDAWS

> Source: Can/US Clarke-Irwin and Company, Ltd.
> GB   Jackdaw Publications, Ltd.
>
> Price: $3.50 each

Men And Towns. 1970. (Jackdaw No. 80)
This folder of data sheets includes the following:

1. 10 data sheets on the structure of cities, patterns of housing, detailed land use analysis, new towns, redevelopment, towns around the world, and the city of tomorrow.
2. 3 broadsheets on origins, growth and structure of towns.

A highly recommended individual study package.

The Port Of London. 1970. (Jackdaw No. 81)
This folder includes historical and current data on the port of London. Prints, maps, documents, photos, and data flesh out the package, providing a comprehensive image of the economic activities of the port.

LESSON AIDS SERVICE

> Source: Can/US/GB British Columbia Teacher's Federation
>
> Price: 2¢* or 3¢** each, or
> 10 for 16¢ (2¢ items) and
> 10 for 25¢ (3¢ items).
>
> Note: See note in section 15.1 regarding ordering of materials. All 2¢ sheets* are 8½" x 11" and the 3¢ sheets are 17" x 11". All are at a scale of 1:50,000 unless indicated. These items have been selected from a longer listing as being suitable for urban studies. No preview outside British Columbia.

A. City	Map Index	Map Coverage	Order #
Kamloops, B.C.	(921/9 W.)	City and Suburbs	(*2103)

164

Unbound Print Materials And Maps

Lower Mainland, B.C.	(48/124)	1:500,000	(*2177)
Medicine Hat, Alta.	(72L/2b)	1:25,000	(*2151)
Mombasa		1:50,000 Port and city	(*2701)
Exercise for map			(*2701A)
Niagara Falls, Ont.	(30M/3a)	1:25,000	(*2153)
Ottawa, Ont.	(31G/5g)	1:25,000 City Center	(*2154)
St. Johns, Nfld.	(1N/10 b,a)	1:25,000	(*2150)
Vancouver, B.C.	(92g)	1:250,000 City and Lower Mainland	(**2117)
Exercise for map			(*2117A)
Vancouver North	(92G/6 E.)	City Center and North	(*2106)
Vancouver North	(92G/6 E.)	West End and North Shore	(*2118)
Vancouver South	(92G/3 E.W.)	City South of 25th and Richmond	(**2122)
Vancouver Metro	(92G/3 E.W.)	Delta	(**2123)
Ventura, Calif.		1:24,000	(*2251)
Victoria, B.C.	(92B/6 W.)	City and Suburb	(*2102)
Victoria-Vancouver	(92S.E.)	1:500,000	(*2176)

B. Towns

Altona	(62H/4W.)		(*2116)
Arnida, Que.	(22D/6E.)		(*2109)
Lunenburg, N.S.	(21A/8W.)		(*2112)
Santa Rita, N.Mex.		1:24,000	(*2250)
Squamish, B.C.	(92G/11E.)		(*2121)
Airphoto of Squamish		8½" x 11"	(**2121A)
Whiting, Ind.		1:24,000	(*2252)

The maps listed above are photolith copies (black and white) of geological survey maps.

URBAN CHARACTERISTIC SURVEY MAPS

    Source: Can/US/GB Map Distribution Office

    Price: $2.00 per sheet

    Note: Of the 35 available for each area, the following are suitable for use and are available for general distribution. No preview available on these items.

Existing Land Use. Map 1.
Land Slope And Elevation. Map 2.
Density Of Coverage Of Land By Buildings. Map 3.
Heights Of Buildings. Map 4.
Population Distribution 1961, Generalized. (One dot represents 1000 persons.) Map 11.
Population Distribution, Updated. (One dot represents 50 persons.) Map. 12.

Estimate Of Daytime Population Distribution. Map 13.
Distribution Of Dwelling Units. Map 15.
Land Transportation Facilities. Map 18.
Port Facilities. Map 19.

15.3 SOURCES OF OTHER UNBOUND PRINT MATERIAL, MAPS, PHOTOS, AND LOCAL RESOURCES

It is outside the scope of this bibliography to cover in detail sources of material other than those available from regular distributors of material.

Local libraries should be consulted regarding photo collections, files of newspaper clippings, uncatalogued materials, maps, and other urban oriented materials.

Government agencies: Federal (National), Provincial (State), Regional, and Municipal (City). Those departments which deal with urban affairs usually have reports and other material available for public use.

Major developers usually have materials on their own projects available for public perusal.

Local special interest groups that are interested in the city will invariably have a fount of information, or contacts for such.

Aerial photographs can be obtained by purchasing prints from existing collections held by the U.S. and Canadian government. For further information, contact:

>   Map Information Office
>   U.S. Department of the Interior
>   Geological Survey
>   Washington, D.C. 20242

(Request the free pamphlet, "Status of Aerial Photography in the U.S..")

>   National Air Photo Library
>   Surveys and Mapping Library
>   Room 180
>   615 Booth St.
>   Ottawa 4, Ont.
>   Canada

Aerial photos can also be obtained from local or regional aerial survey companies. These private firms often have extensive files of materials available for purchase. Local municipal officials should be able to provide addresses of their own sources.

Unbound Print Materials And Maps

Map lists can be secured from :

    U.S. Geological Survey Maps
    Map Information Services
    U.S. Geological Survey
    Department of the Interior
    Washington, D.C. 20240

    Map Distribution Office
    Department of Mining and Technical Surveys
    615 Booth St.
    Ottawa 4, Ontario
    Canada

    This list is only a cursory introduction, but even as such, it will provide the interested reader with several sources for material on the city which is current, local, and otherwise just not available from conventional distributors.

It should be kept in mind by the reader that most local resources do not last long in print. As such, any listing would soon become out-dated. This is not to suggest that there are few materials. In fact, most larger cities have vast resources. What is required is the ferreting out and selection of the material of use.

A more detailed study on non-commercial international, North American, national, or local materials will be made available in the extensive resource guide to be published as part of *The City Of Man* series in early 1974. Information on this title will be available from the publisher, General Learning Press (Agincourt, Ontario).

16
Audio-Visual Materials

Many of the materials included in this section were prepared for school use. The reader can therefore assume that the comments made in the annotations reflect this. Some materials are exceptional, being of a quality which sets them apart, and useful equally in school and in the community. These items have been noted accordingly.

16.1 AN INTRODUCTORY COMMENT

The community should be investigated as a source of visual materials. Schools, or organizations, can build up a large slide collection with little cost above time and effort. The only cost outlay should be for the copying of slides secured from private sources.

Other local visual resources, such as videotapes or film, will be relatively scarce, but they should be sought. A considerable amount of material can be found if time is spent to hunt for it.

16.2 A NOTE ABOUT FILMS ON URBANIZATION

No attempt is being made in this bibliography to provide a list of film resources on urbanization. Several sources are suggested as preliminary sources of information.

    American Institute of Planners--1776 Massachusetts Ave. N.W., Washington, D.C. 20036[1]
    American Society of Planning Officials--1313 E. 60th St., Chicago, Ill. 60637
    Community Planning Association of Canada--425 Gloucester St., Ottawa, Can.[2]
    Central Mortgage And Housing Corporation--Ottawa, Can.[3]
    Housing and Urban Development, Dept. of--Washington, D.C.[4]
    National Film Board--Ottawa, Can.[3]

---

    1. State chapters of the AIP should be contacted as a possible source for materials.
    2. Provincial divisions or local chapters should be contacted as well.
    3. Local offices of CMHC and NFB can provide lists of resources.
    4. HUD has regional and project offices throughout the U.S..

Audio-Visual Materials

16.3 SLIDES AND FILMSTRIPS

BEACON FILMSTRIPS/FABBRE FILMSTRIPS (ENGLAND)

    Source: Can. Medex Can.
                   U.S. Medex Can.
                   G.B. Beacon

    Price: B/W $4.00; Color $7.00.

Ancient Babylonia. B/W, 37 frames. (No. 299)
    A filmstrip with clear photos, maps and reconstructions. This item is of limited value in light of good color items that are available.

Ancient Egypt. B/W, 38 frames. (No. 273)
    Same limitations as the item above.

Ancient Iraq. Color, 50 frames. (No. 479)
    A highly useful item, with frame included on Ur, Babylon, Ashur, Nimrud, Ninevah, and Ctesiphon. Clear, concise visuals and a complete manual. Decidedly worthy of viewing.

Imperial Rome. Color, 38 frames. (No. 364)
    Entirely composed of reconstructions of streets, buildings and homes. Elementary in focus.

Incas Of Peru. Color, 38 frames. (No. 221)
    A similar format to the one above. It is also elementary in focus.

CARWAL LTD. FILMSTRIPS

    Source: Can. Medex Can.
                   U.S. Medex Can.
                   G.B. Visual Information Service

    Price: $4.00

The Discoveries At Ur. B/W, 37 frames.
    Prepared for English religious studies, this filmstrip was done by Sir Leonard Woolley and the British Museum. A collection of photos dealing with the uncovering of Ur, including several reconstructions and frescoes. Of limited value in view of the color materials available.

THE CENTER FOR HUMANITIES, SLIDE SETS

    Source: Can. Center For Humanities, Ltd.
                   U.S. Center For Humanities, Inc.
                 G.B. Center For Humanities, Ltd. (Can.) No preview.

    Price: $120 for 2 carousel sets; $180 for 3 carousel sets.

    Note: This series of slide programs relates primarily to the arts and humanities (philosophy, general social sciences,

English) programs. Each is self contained, inclusive of two or three carousels (Kodak 80 slide), each containing 80 slides, records (one per carousel), and cassettes of the commentary. An extensive teacher's guide completes the full package. Although prepared for school use, those items recommended are suitable for use in the community.

A particularly noticeable ingredient of each set is its use of a broad range of art to express ideas. Photos are used infrequently--most ideas illustrated with art. Selection and appropriateness vary by set, as commented upon in the annotations.

Review of non-urban studies sets is recommended. This unique visual series encompasses the study of many of man's activities and deals with man in a manner that is both striking and compelling.

Art With A Message: Protest And Propaganda. 2 carousels. (No. 207)
    Two distinct units exist. Carousel one includes a study of art as a medium of influence from the 16th Century to today. Revolutionary art is dealt with in depth, analyzing the effect of visual imagery, symbols and cultural characteristics. Both "positive" and "negative" propaganda are dealt with. Good illustrations. A superb item.

Human Values In An Age Of Technology. 2 carousels. (No. 222)
    Beginning with stills from 2001, this presentation carries the viewer through the development of technology, from primitive man to the present. The effect of technology, on earlier civilizations and today, is unfolded, weaving a story from the ancient world's use of technology for survival to the positive and negative payoffs of the post-industrial society of today. A superb presentation, of particular value in the study of this aspect of urbanization.

An Inquiry Into The Nature Of Man: His Inhumanity And His Humanity. 2 carousel (No. 211)
    A beautiful presentation, with feeling for both man's inhumanity toward man and man's attempts to counter this inhumanity with good. Detail is given to war and ethics, degredation and philosophy. Unfortunately, this set is not urban oriented, and cannot therefore be recommended. But its review for other programs is recommended.

Law And Justice--Man's Search For Social Order. 2 carousels. (No. 220)
    Poor for any use. No urban studies content. Good visuals, but too many unrelated to the topic of discussion. Just not up to the calibre of others reviewed.

Audio-Visual Materials

Man--The Measure Of All Things. 3 carousels. (No. 201)
    A study of man's nature through his art. The ways in which man imposes himself on nature, and man's view of his place in the universe, are dealt with, presenting threads from the ancient world into the Twentieth Century. This set is an art education item only, with a presentation of art (as it was used to display the mood of man) from Egypt to the Twentieth Century. A useful item to preview for a humanities oriented program.

Man And His Environment: In Harmony And In Conflict. 2 carousels. (No.206)
    Another superb pair, with direct usefulness in an urban studies program. This presentation delves into man's perceptions of himself, of nature, and that man-created environment, the city. The conflicts, between man as a dependent element in nature, and man, as lord over nature, are dealt with in depth with great feeling.

Historical attitudes toward nature and the city are blended into a broader study of man's progress through change, continually inquiring as to "where is mankind going?"

Is the city the ultimate environment for man, or is it a place to be escaped from? Can the city be divorced from nature? It may pull man to itself as a light draws a moth, but will this be the betterment of man, or a prelude to doom? The city can be a place of miracles, or of man's greatest degredation. The city, a space created by man, has not been created for man. Space exists, but for whom? Can humanity survive the city, or has man spawned some evil creation of self-destruction? And, with less space and more people, whither goes man in the city of tomorrow?

As a sum total, this work is the best item yet reviewed for investigation of the *nature* of cities. The visuals are striking, the background music and commentary superb. This item can also be recommended for general use.

Man And His Values: An Inquiry Into Good And Evil. 2 carousels. (No. 219)
    This series sets a good mood, with questioning throughout as to what is good and what is evil. The impossibility of answering either query absolutely becomes fully evident. The double-headed, or double standards, of social groups are dealt with in detail, with particular emphasis on religion.

The nature of societal value systems is dealt with, looking at the nature of life (or death), civilized (or barbaric), love (or hate), convention (or change), and truth (vs. falsehood).

To the question of whether or not there exists a timeless, placeless, universal set of values, this program fields superb resources in ideas. A detractive note connot be avoided. The illustrations are obtuse, abstract, and decidedly diminish impact on an audience. Limited usefulness.

Man's Search For Freedom. 2 carousels. (No. 216)
   This superb item has a decided impact on an urban studies program, with application to urban history.

The nature of man, with his drives for security in some epochs, and unshackling in others, is looked at through cycles of freedom, and what they meant to various epochs, from Sumer to Egypt.

Freedom in the west, from classical Greece to the end of the Roman Empire, is set against earlier restraints on man. The return to total submission in the Dark Ages finishes a cycle which begins again in the face of the open inquiry and sheer intellectual recklessness of the Renaissance and Baroque.

The western experience is discussed, merging the mutual impact of the philosophical assumption of a rational man and the open endedness of free inquiry.

The impact of technology and change leaves a question as to whether the cycle is again completing, or if it is now broken. "Is change freedom, or will increased change bring about a renewed passion for security?" "What is freedom for?"

Man's Search For Identity. 2 carousels. (No. 221)
   Rather lifeless, and not urban studies oriented.

No Man Is An Island. 2 carousels. (No. 213)
   Although this item is not urban studies oriented, *per se*, it deserves mention. This pair is provocative. Dealing with alienation and societal change in western civilization, this study focuses on the alienated revolutionaries which follow:

>   Socrates
>   Christ
>   St. Francis of Assisi
>   Luther
>   Rousseau
>   Thomas Paine
>   Marx
>   Thoreau
>   Van Gogh
>   The American "Lost Generation" of the 20's
>   Today's alienation

An American orientation, but not overbearing. This pair will draw some surprising reactions from students.

Audio-Visual Materials

Toward The Year 2000: Can We Survive The Future? 2 carousels. (No. 237)
   This program presents a thesis that "the future is now." It does not delve into the nature of the world in the next three decades, but rather uses the ideas of Toffler, Skinner, Ardrey, Huxley, and Reich to weave an optimistic view of the future. This program will evoke mixed reactions, from bored to excited, as to its value and impact. It is recommended that this item be previewed prior to purchase.

COMMON GROUND FILMSTRIPS

   Source: Can.   Carman Canada
             U.S.   Carman US
             G.B.   Common Ground

   Price: Color $7.50 (double frame--$9.00), and B/W $4.00

   Note: All Common Ground filmstrips have extensive booklets, commentary and additional background.

The Ancient World Series

   Life In Ancient Mesopotamia. (No. 1B 714)
      This color filmstrip, with manual, depicts the landscape, climate, location, people, excavations and reconstructions. Liberal use is made of diagrams and reproductions of art remnants. A bit too elementary for secondary use, but of value for lower grades.

   Life In Ancient America. (No. 1B 780)
   Life In Ancient Egypt. (No. 1B 680)
   Life In Ancient Greece. (No. 1B 681)

      These three are similar to the first filmstrip. Their usefulness is decidedly limited to elementary urban studies. About 30 frames. A fifth item, *Life In Ancient Palestine,* has no application at any grade level.

   The Growth Of Rome. (No. 1B 682)
   Life In The Roman Empire. (No. 1B 713)

      Similar to the series above, this series is limited to use at elementary grades.

Introduction To The Industrial Revolution. B/W. 12 filmstrips.
   From this series, three filmstrips were reviewed.

   The County Town And London. (No. CGB 42)
      An interesting collection of contemporary views of life in early 19th Century England. Limited by its lack of color.

   Villages, Market Towns, And Resorts. (No. CGB 41)
      Similar to the title above.

The City In Print

Transportation In The 18th Century. (No. CGB 43)
    Of limited usefulness.

People Of Other Times Series

    Life In Early Georgian Times. (No. CGB 778)
    Life In Early Stuart Times. (No. CGB 776)
    Life In Elizabethan Times. (No. CGB 775)
    Life In Restoration Times. (No. 777)
    Life In Tudor Times. (No. CGB 774)

    These filmstrips (color drawings) provide extensive coverage of daily life in each of these five periods in England. The details on dress, housing, transportation, recreation, and values of both commoner and nobleman are of particular interest. The focus of these materials is elementary, but their use with poorly motivated secondary level students is recommended. Striking illustrations are found in this series.

Miscellaneous Items:

Greater London. Color. (No. CGB 975)
    A study of the geography, historical growth and urban characteristics of this metropolitan region. Of definite value.

The Growth Of London. (No. IA 813)
    London's history from Roman times through the 19th Century, as seen through charts, maps, photos and prints.

New York. Color. 27 frames. (No. CGB 794)
    A color filmstrip that surveys the metropolitan region, its history and significant features. Views of social and economic characteristics are included. A geographical study of definite usefulness.

Ports Of West Africa. (No. CGB 971)
    Of limited usefulness. More a study of economic geography than any urban characteristics.

The Rise Of Man. B/W. (No. CGB 494)
    Too limited (or over generalized) for use at any level.

The Town (Medieval). Color. (No. CGB 667)
    Color drawings, using an approach similar to the *People Of Other Times Series* above. Comments apply as for that series.

Village Life In Northern Nigeria. (No. CGB 598)
    A useful study for comparative studies, dealing primarily with the economic structure of village and town. A useful item with good illustrations.

Audio-Visual Materials

CURRICULUM GROUP ON URBAN STUDIES

    Source: Can. B.C. Teacher's Federation
                   US/GB Urban Education Materials

    Price: As Indicated.

    Note: Orders to the B. C. Teacher's Federation or the Urban Education Materials must be prepaid or requested by agency or school purchase order. No preview available.

Vancouver Urban History

    Vancouver 1792-1940. B/W. 100 slides.
        100 slides from the Vancouver Historical Archives collection dealing with the growth of Vancouver from its beginnings as a logging station, through its growth as the western terminus of the CPR, to its development as Canada's third largest metropolis. $60.00.

    Vancouver Metro, 1960-2000. Color and B/W. 100 slides.
        100 slides representative of Vancouver from the mid 1960's and early 1970's as well as extensive coverage of projects, plans and dreams for Vancouver's future. $60.00.

Both sets have descriptive packages including notes.

DENOYER-GEPPERT AUDIO VISUALS

    Source: Can. McIntyre Educational Media, Ltd.
                 U.S. Denoyer-Geppert Audio-Visuals
                 G.B. McIntyre Educational Media, Ltd. (Can.)

    Price: $35.00 each
    Note: The items listed below are sound filmstrip sets, each containing 2 filmstrips and 2 records or tapes.

The Great San Francisco Oil Spill. (No. 69715)
    This pair must be used with caution. The visuals are superb, dealing with the events which precipitated the spill, the cleanup efforts, and environmental effects. But the commentary leaves much to be desired. The perspective presented is one of overkill, with too great an emphasis on extreme environmentalist views.

Lifestyle 2000: Inquiry Into The Future. (No. 69716)
    This study presents four personal viewpoints about where we are headed. The title is misleading in that it does not look at the year 2000, but rather uses the 1970's as a base for four glimpses into the future.

Commentary is made by Hugh Downs, a television personality; Paolo Soleri, the visionary architect; Herman Kahn, futurist and policy maker; and Ray Bradbury, science fiction writer and philosopher of the potentials of man.

The set does not provide actual images of the world of three decades hence, but what it does do is to present the present in the context of future possibilities.

Of use in the school or community as an initial starting point for discussion of what might be, this program presents a definite optimistic view of the future.

New York City: An Environmental Case Study. (No. 69706)
An uncompromising look at the image and reality of New York, not as a city, but as a human environment. Superbly balanced with excellent photos, commentary, and music, this pair presents a focus on New York City not often seen, with a universality which makes it useful for schools not only in the U.S., but also in Canada. The human element is represented here with a depth not reached in any other item reviewed, on any topic.

Quite moving, this presentation looks at reality and myth, compelling the viewer to identify with man, and not the system. Short shrift is given to greed and carelessness, while much emphasis is laid upon the threat to the spirit of man.

Many questions are opened by this fast paced pair, with a mood set at the end which should pull the least involved student out of himself and into an awareness of one direction in which we are heading.

This pair is of decided value for community use.

DIANA WYLLIE, LTD. FILMSTRIPS

Source: Can. Carman Canada
U.S. Carman U.S.
G.B. Diana Wyllie

Price: Unless indicated, these color filmstrips are $7.50 (double frame $9.00).

Note: The Diana Wyllie filmstrips are of use for the community as well as the schools. All have extensive booklets, commentary and additional background.

Architecture

Prepared by the Royal Institute of British Architects. This filmstrip set is a good supplement to *Man-Made World* (listed below), and is definitely worthy of purchase and use. The photos are superb, with wide coverage. An English orientation in the commentary and visuals.

Construction.
This filmstrip looks at the ways material is used to form structures. Classical and modern structures are dealt with.

Design.
This filmstrip examines the social, economic and aesthetic factors that influence the appearance of buildings. Proportion, surface texture, and the impact on the surrounding environment are studied through a wide variety of styles and periods.

Materials.
A study of the impact of materials on mood and atmosphere of a structure. World-wide coverage, dealing with stone, wood, brick, metal, concrete, and glass, including a large number of building styles and periods.

Environment. Air Pollution.

Of all the pollution items yet seen, this set is the most graphic. It is worth purchasing for information on more than just the pollution issue. $18.00 for the pair.

1. *Local, Continental And Natural Pollution.*
    Striking photos dealing with visual pollution all over the world. A useful world-wide survey of urbanization.

2. *Industrial Pollution.*
    Similar to the item above, this filmstrip is quite good.

Life In A Mediterranean Village Of NE Spain (The Costa Brava). (No. DW-F14)
An interesting presentation on the structure and way of life of one Mediterranean village. A useful filmstrip for comparison with cities in the region.

Man-Made World.
A series of four color filmstrips produced by the Royal Institute of British Architects, viewing "environment as the totality of our physical surroundings—not only from an aesthetic but also from a social, economic and functional point of view." The booklets are superb teaching aids. This study of nature and man's impact on it is excellent on such topics as the city as art, and perceived use of space. About 37 frames each, this series relies on British examples to illustrate the topics dealt with.

DOUBLEDAY-MULTIMEDIA FILMSTRIPS

    Source: Can. City Films
              U.S. Doubleday Multimedia
              G.B. Feffer & Simons

City Life Series

City Life In Iran. (No. 194225)
City Life In Turkey I. (No. 194092)
City Life In Turkey II. (No. 194100)
City Life In West Pakistan. (No. 194076)
City Life In Yugoslavia. (No. 194084)

Mexico City. (No. 194308)
A Trip To Mexico City I. (No. 194472)
A Trip To Mexico City II. (No. 194480)

These items are poor. The commentary is 'cute, patronizing, and devoid of meaningful content. The filmstrips are further limited as they include considerable extraneous information not related to the urban condition.

Cities Of Mexico. (No. 194068)
This item is quite good and, unlike the others of the series, it is of definite use in a secondary school program.

EDUCATIONAL AUDIO-VISUAL INC.

    Source: Can.   Medex Canada
                  U.S.   Educational Audio-Visual
                  G.B.   Educational Audio-Visual (U.K.)

    Price: As indicated

Dr. Johnson's London. 152 frames. (No. SE 28442, with record 27920; with tape 29324)
This sound filmstrip is a study of 18th Century London with rich content on the city and its way of life. Included are analyses of the society, culture, and the kinds of lives led by both rich and poor citizens. A superb blend of music, commentary, and illustrations, this item is similar in approach to *Pepys's London* (listed below). Contains 107 frames on Johnson's London and 45 on the art of Hogarth and Rowlandson. General use. Canada - $14.50; U.S.- $13.75.

Elizabethan Age. (No. 96RF734 2 f/s with record, 96TF734 2 f/s with tape)
Detailed study of life in Elizabethan England, with too little application to urban history. Canada- $20.00; U.S.- $18.75.

Pepys's London. 59 frames. (No. SE 28400, with record 27900; with tape 29309)
In 17th Century London: A study of the man, the era, and the city. The plague years are dealt with in detail, as well as the Great Fire of 1666 (during which 60% of London was destroyed). A sound filmstrip with commentary and additional excerpts from Defoe's *Journal Of The Plague Years* and two short excerpts from *Pepys's Diary*. Good. Canada-$14.50; U.S.-$13.75.

Roman Civilization. (No. SE 28410/11 with record 27905; with tape 29308)
These two sound filmstrips are more a study of the civilization rather than the urban structure. They contain comparisons of Greek and Roman civilizations, studies of religion, literature, the great works of architecture and art (sculpture and friezes). Life in Roman cities and Roman military camps is also dealt with. Canada-$20.00; U.S.-$18.50.

Audio-Visual Materials

The Roman House. (No. SE 8035)
   One color filmstrip with notes. Superb reconstructions, plans, and dioramas of a typical house. Canada-$6.75; U.S.-$6.50.

Roman Society. (No. SE 28107/08)
   Two color filmstrips with notes. The focus of this pair is more on general history than urban history. Of limited value for urban history. Canada-$13.00; U.S.-$12.50.

Shakespeare's London. (No. 94RF341 with record; 94TF341 with tape)
   One filmstrip and record with commentary. Dealing with life in England from 1585-1615, this item is of limited value for urban studies. It has much more value for studies of Shakespeare's time, but little application to urban history. Canada-$14.50; U.S.-$13.95.

Urban Civilization. (No. 28456-58, with records LE 27911-13)
   Three filmstrips and three records make up this comprehensive set which ranges over the entire city, past and present. A brief historical survey is followed with a study of 19th Century foundations of the modern city. Emphasis is placed on the 20th Century, with in-depth studies of New York, Los Angeles, Stevenge (an English new town), and Pittsburgh (urban renewal in the U.S.). Major urban characteristics are dealt with, the emphasis being on transportation, new patterns of urban growth, and major problems and solutions. The illustrations in this set are excellent, with good commentary. A superb introduction or review of urban prospects and alternatives. Limited to school use. $40.00.

The Victorian Era. (No. 96RF327 with record)
   Although this item is not specifically urban, and is more a study of the period 1836-1901, these two filmstrips deal with much of value in the study of Victorian England. Topics include social class, the industrial revolution, urbanization, political reform, and the empire. A useful supplement. Canada-$20.00; U.S.-$18.75.

EDUCATIONAL CONSULTANTS, LTD, SLIDES

   Source: Can/US/GB Educational Consultants, Ltd.

   Price: Personal orders must be prepaid. School orders require a purchase order.

   Note: From a 1971 trip to China, 3 color films, 11 slide sets, and 3 instructional maps (23" x 35") have been produced. Of this entire collection, one slide set is related to urbanization. It is reviewed below.

Cities Of China. 20 slides. (No. 11)
   Twenty slides (on plastic view sheets), a detailed set of teacher's notes (5 pages), and a list of references (5 pages). This broad coverage presents a general view of life in two of China's cities—Shanghai and Canton. Architecture and social characteristics are dealt with in detail

in 17 of the 20 slides. As is, this set is worth purchasing. Useful.
$8.50.

EDUCATIONAL PRODUCTIONS, LTD., FILMSTRIPS

>   Source: Can/US North American Distributors seem to vary by locality.
>   No exclusive nationwide distributors have been noted. Educa-
>   tional Productions filmstrips can be purchased, however, from
>   Medex Canada.
>
>   G.B   Educational Productions, Ltd.
>
>   Price: $7.00 color; $4.50 B/W.

About London With Dickens. 1966. 32 frames. (No. C6362, col.)
   As the manual points out, every building illustrated still stands.
Although short, this item has value in studies of 19th Century London.

The Changing Face Of The London Region

   Early Times To 1800. 1960. 45 frames. (No. 5028, B/W)
   A useful item including aerial views, the physical setting, and more
   than 25 frames on the historical setting. Includes reconstruction,
   paintings, and old lithograph prints of city views.

   1800 To The Present Day. 1965. 45 frames. (No. 5039 B/W)
   Following a short overview of developments from 1800-1939, 35 frames
   look at some actual developments. A large number of illustrations and
   maps outline the progression over 130 years. The filmstrip closes with
   4 frames looking at immediate postwar London. Although dated, this is
   a highly useful historical item. Good for comparison to Canadian urban
   growth.

Both filmstrips have manuals.

Everyday Life In London. 1970. 39 frames. (No. C6407, col.)
   This filmstrip looks at the various functions of this city, including
commercial, industrial, administrative and residential. Useful.

Family Life In Liverpool. n.d.   31 frames. (No. 6632, col.)
   A general study of the city, its economic life, and one of its families.
A conventional geographical study, of limited use in an urban studies
program.

The Geographical Background Of The Bible. Part I: The Old Testament.

   Section I:*Assyria And Babylon*. 1969. 27 frames. (No. C6270, col.)
   An unlikely source, this filmstrip is a brief study of these two great
   urban-oriented civilizations. Photos of the geographical setting, ruins

Audio-Visual Materials

and frescoes present a view of this area from Assyrian through Roman times. The lack of reconstructions, and its brevity, limit its usefulness.

Great Cities Of The World.

Paris. 1970. 32 frames. (No. 6572, col.)
With a highly detailed manual of 44 pages, this is a highly useful filmstrip. It is more a study of places than people.

History Of London And Its People. 44 frames. (No. 5271, B/W)
This filmstrip shows maps, dioramas, and reconstructions of Roman London, as well as lithographs of more current epochs. Worthwhile.

The Medieval Town. 1970. 27 frames. (No. 6072, col.)
Largely made up of reconstructions and photos of remaining sites (Carcasonne, Avignon) and cathedrals. A very good study of medieval city life.

The Romans In Britain. 1970. (No. 6562, col.)
Reconstructions of Britain before and after the Roman invasion. Very good, but at an elementary level.

H. M. ELKINS CO., FILMSTRIPS

Source: Can/US/GB H. M. Elkins Co.

Price: As indicated.

Note: All are captioned filmstrips.

An Athenian Family. An exclusively elementary item. (No. 551)
Greek City Life. General studies and not urban oriented. (No. 180)
Historical London. Not reviewed. (No. 398)
Middle East City. General studies and not urban oriented. (No. 187)
Modern Venice. Similar limitations as the item above. (No. 400)
The Town. An exclusively elementary item. (No. 463)
Transportation In Equatorial Africa. Badly dated (1957) and limited to historical use. (No. 611)
The Walled Town--Carcasonne. Good detail of the city. Old photos. (No. 468)

The above filmstrips are $4.95 each.

Paris: City, Old And New. Not reviewed. (No. 737)

The above filmstrip is $6.00.

Cities And Highways. Map reading and not urban studies. Elementary. (No. 708)
Great Cities. (South America) General studies and not urban oriented. (No. 840)
Urban And Rural Interdependence. Not urban studies material. (No. 778)

The above filmstrips are $7.00.

The City In Print

ENCYCLOPEDIA BRITANNICA, INC.

    Source: Can/US/GB Encyclopedia Britannica, Inc.

    Price: As indicated.

    Note: Encyclopedia Britannica material has a bias toward general geographical studies. The items listed are commented upon with that understanding. Some items, in the sets discussed, are excluded because they have too little urban-oriented content. All are limited to school use.

Ancient Times. (No. 6424)
A series produced in association with the National Geographic Society. Five sound filmstrips in the series. $57.50 for five; $15.00 for each sound filmstrip.

Egypt--Land Of The Pharaohs. (No. 11473)
This striking item captures the mood of the Egyptian civilization and deals with the origins of the Egyptians, their values, the structure of their civilization, and the timelessness of their culture. Dozens of superb reconstructions. Although not directly urban in orientation, this item is a must.

The March Of Empires. (No. 11471)
The beginnings of man and the march of empires; the creative and the demonic in man; and the emergence of man and his civilizations (from the Sumerian to the Roman). Not urban, but a remarkable overview which should not be by-passed.

Mesopotamia--Cradle Of Civilizations. (No. 11472)
The lower Tigris-Euphrates as the homeland of urban civilization is the focus of this filmstrip, looking at agriculture and water control, the urban disciplines (architecture, law, religion) and the way of life in the ancient world. Superb illustrations (many from *Everyday Life In Ancient Times)* and good commentary. This item is quite moving, combining music, commentary, and a fast paced filmstrip. Superb reconstructions.

Tying history to Biblical events, these three items are superb and cannot be too highly recommended.

Adventures Into The Buried Past. (No. 11475)
A study of archaeology, with detailed summaries of the finding of the Dead Sea Scrolls and King Tut's tomb, the translation of hieroglyphics and cuneiform, and other major finds. A good item, but the significant reconstructions are included in the first three filmstrips. Of no value in an urban studies program.

Audio-Visual Materials

Jerusalem--Heart Of The Holy Land. (No. 11474)
    A study of the foundations of three religions and cultures, this item is largely a depiction of Biblical events taking place in Jerusalem from the end of the Roman Empire, through the Crusades, to the present day. The focus is Christian, with little on Judaic or Muslim impacts on the city or times, and with no urban orientation. Of no value in an urban studies program.

Cities Of Europe. (No. 8831-37)
    These are seven filmstrips representing themselves as studies of cities. They are, unfortunately, not even good travel-tourist studies. Inadequate.

The City Community. (No. 7800)
    Six captioned filmstrips similar to *The Town Community* below. Quite good. $6.00 each.

Living Things In The City. (No. 11720)
    Nine captioned filmstrips, looking at ecology in the city. This series is elementary in focus, with no suitability for secondary use. But, as an elementary level item, it warrants preview. $6.00 each.

Middle East And India.
    Three of the filmstrips in this series were previewed (*Bombay: Gateway To India,* No. 8571; *Village Of India,* No. 8572; *Village And City In Turkey,* No. 8576). All three have some good stills, but are not suitable for the study of urbanization. Others in the series are exclusively general geography material. Dated.

The Rise Of Civilization. (No. 10570)
    Six captioned filmstrips. Not suitable for secondary level urban studies, although possibly of use at the elementary level. Illustrations are crisp, informative and interesting, but quite juvenile in focus. $6.00 each.

The Town Community. (No. 7783)
    Six captioned filmstrips. Looking at a small community, its structure, history, quality of life, and problems, this series presents an interesting perspective for *elementary* use. Well worth previewing at the pre-secondary level. $6.00 each.

Single Items (captioned filmstrips at $6.00 each):

From the series *Ancient Rome* (No. 10860):

    Architecture Of Rome. (No. 10865)
        A superb collection of "before and now" illustrations of architectural sites, including the Forum, the Circus Maximus, and the Coliseum. For architectural history, this filmstrip is a must. Reconstructions are reprints of the study prints put out by the Encyclopedia Britannica as reviewed in section 16.7.

The City In Print

Living In Ancient Rome. (No. 10863)
    Using movie stills, this filmstrip looks at the lives of patricians, the poor, and slaves. Quite useful, this is the best filmstrip on Roman social life yet previewed.

From the series *The British Isles* (No. 10770):

Village, Town And City In The United Kingdom. (No. 10772)
    An interesting survey of urban form. Good illustrations.

From the series *Canada: People At Work* (No. 8770):

Farm And City In Ontario. (No. 8773)
    Elementary level material with a geographical, not urban studies, orientation. Quite dated.

Vancouver. (No. 8775)
    Similar to the title above.

From the series *Impressions Of Holland* (No. 8800):

Amsterdam. (No. 8802)
    Not suitable for urban studies.

From the series *Lands Of The Far East* (No. 8880):

Hong Kong. (No. 8881)
    A general geographical study, of no use in urban studies.

From the series *Mediterranean Europe* (No. 8900):

Two Spanish Towns. (No. 8902)
    An old filmstrip which has limited usefulness as a study of changeless country towns, their inhabitants and functions.

Villages In Greece. (No. 8906)
    Similar to the item above.

From the series *Mexico And Central America* (No. 8600):

Town And City In Mexico. (No. 8603)
    A general study of urbanization, but too dated for use.

From the series *The U.S. Interior West* (No. 11370):

Growth Of A Mining Town. (No. 11374)
    A look at Leadville, Colorado, once a Western boomtown and now a single resource town. Useful.

Audio-Visual Materials

From the series *The U.S. Midwest* (No. 11360):

    Chicago-Transportation Center. (No. 11363)
        A look at the factors of location, history, and current economic functions of this city. Useful.

From the series *The U.S. Northeast* (No. 11150):

    The Decision Making Cities. (No. 11154)
        A look at the functions of the large American megalopolis between Boston and Washington. The economic necessities of location in the megalopolis are clearly pointed out. Definitely useful.

From the series *The U.S. Pacific West* (No. 11310):

    Exploding Los Angeles. (No. 11314)
        A general overview of this city. Useful.

Single items from regular or sound filmstrip sets. (Captioned filmstrip at $6.00, set No. 11320, or as sound filmstrips at $11.00 with records, set No. 6428, and $13.00 with cassettes, set No. 6428K).

From the series No. 11320:

    Southern South America.
    Buenos Aires. (No. 11322)
        General, rather than urban studies.

Single items from sound filmstrip sets for $15.00 each.

From series No. 6420:

    Washington, D.C.: The City Freedom Built. (No. 11431)
        Just plain bad. Flags wave wildly and corn runneth over.

From series No. 6421:

    Southeast Asia: Singapore. (No. 11447)
        An interesting look at this island city state. Although there are some urban conditions outlined, it is largely a general geographical study.

FILMSTRIP HOUSE, INC.

    Source: Can. Carman
                  U.S. Filmstrip House
                  G.B. Information not available

    Price: As indicated

The City In Print

American Decades Series
Six sound filmstrips are included in each decade package ($50.00 each). These items are of academic interest only because a few items are urban oriented, and the producers of this series will not allow them to be bought separately.

The 1950s: Metropolis And Suburbia. (No. 4)
The 1960s: Megalopolis. (No. (No. 4)
The 1970s: Ecology And Survival. (No. 1)
Cities: The Reality. (No. 2)
Cities: The Dream. (No. 3)

These items blend graphics with photos. On the whole, they would be of little value (even if they were available). Superior items exist.

People And Places: Harlem (N.Y. City).
Two color sound filmstrips, cute, pedantic and quite outdated. Of no use at any level.

FOM FILMSTRIPS

Source: Can. McIntyre Canada
         U.S. Popular Science Publishing Company
         G.B. Information not available

Price: Not available

Note: All of these items are elementary in focus.

Back In Ancient Babylonia. 1955. (No. 732)
The City: Changes In American Life. 1966. (No. 828)
Introducing Leading Cities Series.
  Boston. 1962. (No. 789)
  Chicago. 1957. (No. 748)
  Philadelphia. 1960. (No. 777)
  San Francisco. 1958. (No. 759)
  Washington, D.C. 1960. (No. 769)

GAGE FILMSTRIPS

Source: Can/US Gage Educational Publishing, Ltd.
         GB   Information not available

Price: $28.00

Discovery Of The City. (No. 432572)
A filmstrip with record, teacher's manual and study prints. Art studies and not urban studies.

Audio-Visual Materials

Towers And Palaces. (No. 432576)
> A similar package dealing with the architectural history of 19th Century America. Too detailed an approach, in light of the price, for use in school or community.

GATEWAY FILMS

> Source: Can. Carman
> U.S. No one source
> G.B. Gateway

> Price: B/W, $4.00; color, $$7.50; double frame, $9.00

> Note: All in color unless otherwise indicated.

The Acropolis. (No. F25)
> Exclusively a study of this group of buildings. Better items exist.

Africa: Drift To The Town. (No. F11)
> 26 frames. A study of developing town life in Zambia with an anthropological theme. Limited to, but definitely useful for, courses with this emphasis.

Africa: Town Life. (No. F12)
> 29 frames. An overview of Cairo, Lagos, Abidjan, Kampala, Nairobi, Lusaka, Salisbury, Durban and Capetown. Decidedly useful.

Ancient Athens. (No. F19)
> A view of the monuments of Ancient Athens. Of limited value in light of other materials available.

Ancient Rome. (No. F21)
> A collection of photos of ruins and monuments, including several reconstructions and maps. Useful, but better items have been listed.

Berlin. (No. F33)
> 28 frames. Shown are the significant features of this divided city. An interesting study.

Egypt. (No. F7)
> Similar to *Life In Ancient Egypt* (below), and centering on Memphis, Karnak, Thebes and Abu Simbel.

Egypt: Town Life. (No. F6)
> 39 frames. A study of seven cities including Alexandria, Cairo, and Aswan. Decidedly useful.

Egypt: Village Life. (No. F5)
> 30 frames. As a comparative supplement to the item above, this filmstrip is quite good. A superb study of village structure and life.

The City In Print

    Hong Kong. (No. F28)
        41 frames. A geographical study that surveys the social structure, housing, and general urban structure of Hong Kong. Although some of the frames are of value, the full filmstrip has too many frames on extraneous topics.

    India: Town Life. (No. F15)
        45 frames. A brief look at Delhi, Benares, Calcutta, Bombay and Trichinopoly. Highly useful. An excellent item.

    Life In Ancient Egypt. (No. F3)
        A view of Egyptian monuments and artifacts rather than social life. Far better materials exist for urban history, but this item is quite good for art history.

    Peking. (No. F53)
        A filmstrip with some significant features, but much too short for the price. Only 19 frames.

    Pompeii. (No. F26)
        Similar in content to *Ancient Rome* (above).

    Ravenna. (No. F22)
        Similar to *Ancient Rome* (above), but a useful item in view of the absence of any other material on this city and period. Definitely an art filmstrip.

    Russia: Background To History II. (No. F50)
        Although an unlikely title, this color filmstrip is superb in its presentation of historical, classical and pre-revolutionary architecture in Russia. 40 frames.

    Russia: Leningrad. (No. F47)
        Similar to the item below. 32 frames.

    Russia: Moscow. (No. F46)
        A study of the old and new city, social characteristics and significant features. Definitely useful. 41 frames.

    Stockholm. (No. F20)
        A filmstrip that surveys the city, presenting significant features, transportation routes and current developments. 29 frames.

IMPERIAL FILM COMPANY

        Source: Can. Educational Progress Company, Ltd.
                          U.S. Imperial Film Company
                          G.B. Information not available

        Price: As indicated

Audio-Visual Materials

Daily Life In The Ancient World: Daily Life In The Tigris-Euphrates Valley
(Set No. 902-1 & 2) and *Daily Life in Classical Rome* (Set No. 902-3 & 4)
Four sound, color filmstrips, by far too elementary to be of use at the secondary or community level. Although daily life in these two epochs is dealt with, there is insufficient urban content to warrant use. $52.00 with records; $57.00 with cassettes.

The Development Of Western Civilization: The Italian Cities. (Set No. 602)
Six captioned, color filmstrips.

Milan: Cathedral Duomo. (No. 602-4)
Milan: Cathedral S. Ambrogio. (No. 602-5)
Ravenna: Echoes Of Empire. (No. 602-6)
Venice: Along The Grand Canal. (No. 602-3)
Venice: Cathedral Of St. Marks. (No. 602-2)
Venice: The Doge's Palace. (No. 602-1)

Exclusively architectural studies, too detailed for general or secondary school use. Good photographic content and worthwhile commentary. $46.75 for the set, or $7.75 each.

Exploring Ancient Civilizations. Group I. (Set No. 601)
Six captioned, color filmstrips. Basically architectural studies of the following areas:

Ancient Athens. (No. 601-2)
Ancient Mexico: The Maya. (No. 601-6)
Ancient Mexico: Pre-Aztec. (No. 601-5)
Baalbek And Jerash. (No. 601-3)
Egypt. (No. 601-4)
Rome And Pompeii. (No. 601-1)

A worthwhile set, with good photos and intelligent commentary. Group II is not urban oriented. $46.25 for the set, or $7.75 each.

Single Items
Captioned, color filmstrips at $7.75 each.

Living In 18th Century Virginian Cities. (No. 615-4)
Charlottesville, the University of Virginia, Alexandria, and Fredericksburg are centered upon, with photographic examples of colonial buildings and interiors. For such studies, this filmstrip is quite good.

Manila, Hong Kong, And Singapore. (No. 702-3)
A general survey with very little urban studies content.

Mexico City And Acapulco. (No. 701-4)
A general survey with very little urban studies content.

The City In Print

MCGRAW-HILL

    Source: Can. McGraw-Hill Ryerson, Ltd.
                   U.S. McGraw-Hill Book Co.
                   G.B. McGraw-Hill Book Co. (U.K.), Ltd.

    Price: As indicated

Middle East Geography Series. (No. 633630)
    Three filmstrips are entitled *Iran: Cities And Industries; Israel: Urban And Industrial Developement;* and *Turkey: Its Cities And Industrial Future*. Good illustrations for general geographical studies, but not urban oriented. Little is included for the study of urban form, function, conditions or problems. Decidedly elementary captions. $8.50 each.

Types Of Cities Set. (No. 641310-1)
    Eight filmstrips on different city types. This series is apparently geared for the lower elementary grades. $57.50 for the set, or $7.75 each.

Miscellaneous Filmstrips

City Life In Japan. (No. 159914-2)
    Not urban studies.

Japan: A Nation Of Cities. (No. 633614)
    A captioned filmstrip with up-to-date visuals. This item is a general economic geography item not suited for urban studies. $8.50.

Life In A Large City. (No. 401819-1)
    Of little value for urban studies.

The Middle Atlantic Seaboard Region: Great Cities: Megalopolis. (No. 402177X)
    Relatively recent (1963), this captioned filmstrip presents a balanced view of the area, characteristics, and conditions of the megalopolis on the U.S. east coast. The captioning does limit its use, but it is still worth considering. Limited to school use. $6.00.

MODERN LEARNING AIDS

    Source: Can/US/GB Modern Learning Aids

    Price: As indicated

City Planning. 24 frames. (No. 5391)
    A captioned color filmstrip which is designed to analyze the process of planning through the study of Chicago's public transportation and Boston's housing problems in the 19th Century. The major forces influencing decisions are outlined in this brief filmstrip, raising questions as to what is the proper solution. The 2 subsections are followed by a comment on what was done. Too brief and too cursory a survey. $7.00.

Audio-Visual Materials

Ghettos. 24 frames. (No. 5387)
    A brief look at the 19th Century American ghetto. Useful information, but far too short and cursory. $7.00.

Of 100 filmstrips on U.S. history, only these two are urban oriented. Both items deal with topics of interest, but are over priced for their length and are far too brief to deal with the complex topics attempted.

The City. (No. 182x7020)
    Three filmstrips prepared for Grades 4-6. Too elementary for general secondary use, these items have very effective visuals, presenting mood and information. The captions are simple and conceptual. Worthy of preview for use with students who require motivation or those who have reading problems. $18.00.

The Science Of Life Series: Man's Impact On His Environment.
    Urban oriented items from this series include the following:

Autoculture. (No. 6431)
The Population Explosion. (No. 6430)
Urban Industrial Encroachment. (No. 6429)

    All were prepared for elementary level use, but the superb visuals and more than adequate commentary make them suitable for use at lower secondary levels. Useful. $6.00 each.

MULTI-MEDIA PRODUCTIONS

    Source: Can. Visual Education Centre
                 U.S. Multi-Media Productions
                 G.B. Visual Education Centre (Can.)

    Price: As indicated

    Note: Without the conventional educational tone, or patronizing commentary, the dialogue of these items is to the point, laying out conditions and problems. They essentially say 'where its at' with neither gloss nor diatribe. A concise manual and effective teaching suggestions are included with each item.

The Growth Of Cities, Municipal Corruption, And Boss Tweed.
    Two filmstrips in color and black and white that deal with the issues of change and the inability of political structures (municipal) to contend with it. The specific study included is post Civil War New York City, but the conditions are studied, not just the the specific example. As such, this study has general application, more than just a little to Canadian programs. A highly interesting commentary with superb illustrations. Can.-$25.00; U.S.-$20.00.

The City In Print

Hogarth's London.
    A B/W item composed entirely of drawings by Hogarth. A matter-of-fact presentation, with the flavor of a documentary. Of limited use in light of the Educational Audio Visual item, *Dr. Johnson's London.* Can.-$15.00; U.S.-$9.00.

Latin America Today: Village And Metropolis.
    A superb pair of filmstrips with records. The subjects dealt with are:

- Conditions and problems in the Latin American city;
- Traditional rural existence and the effect of rising expectations;
- Rural to urban migrations;
- Historical development of the Latin American city--with effects on today's cities;
- Factors in urban location;
- Current crises and future prospects.

Can.-$25.00; U.S.-$20.00.

Topics In Ecology.
    The four filmstrips listed below comment on the American condition, but this does not detract from their usefulness. General use. Can.-$15.00; U.S.-$9.95 each.

The Automobile: Beyond Air Pollution.
    This item is of definite value in that it looks at the auto as more than a menace. The impact of the car in North America, its problems and obvious advantages, is dealt with in detail. It is a useful study of this transportation system. Mass transit is not discussed. The record is the same on both sides--one with the 'blip' and one without.

Prosperity Equals Pollution.
    Unequaled economic expansion since 1945 is looked at in light of the waste from this massive production, growth, prosperity and obsolescence. The economic goal of ever increasing production is balanced by the present parallel growth of waste. A graphic presentation. The best single item on pollution yet reviewed.

What Is Air Pollution?
    A study of the value and abuse of air, the impact of the industrial revolution on the environment, and the chemical effects on man of the use of fossil fuels. Considerable emphasis is put on the economics of pollution problems. Some alternatives are suggested. An excellent item, worthy of purchase.

What Is Pollution?
    An introductory filmstrip looking at the universal opposition to pollution and the individual disagreement on what is undesirable. What is the point beyond which pollution will not be tolerated? Can there be a universal, acceptable standard?

Audio-Visual Materials

As pointed out in the commentary, man pollutes to enrich himself, or to fulfill personal goals. The desire for material goods is not new, but the volume of goods available has increased fantastically since 1945, and with it, the volume of industrial wastes. The consumer revolution, planned obsolesence, and the many new non bio-degradable products, all are a product of a lifestyle which demands abundance by any means. Pollution is looked upon as a problem of industry, something caused by someone else, and not a result of demands for products and convenience.

NATIONAL FILM BOARD OF CANADA

      Source: Can/US/GB National Filmboard of Canada

      Price: As indicated

Planning The City.
    A long filmstrip (113 frames), this item looks at the work of the industrial designer, centering around the design aspects of Montreal's Metro. A highly useful item on transportation as well as design, the city itself as art, and the city perceived. Priced at $6.50 with record, there is but one caution: the blips are very faint--run it through once to get a feel for the spacing.

City Series.
    Each filmstrip has a manual which includes detailed notes on each frame. Badly dated. $5.00 each.

    Industrial City. (Toronto)
    Ottawa: Canada's Capital.
    Port City. (Halifax)
    Railway City. (Winnipeg)
    River City. (Montreal)
    Timber City. (Vancouver)

Our Growing Cities.
    A Central Mortgage and Housing Corporation filmstrip looking at both historical and current development of cities. A useful overview, but now badly dated. $5.00 with manual.

Renewing Our Cities.
    A color filmstrip dealing with urban renewal in Canada. Dated. $5.00 with manual.

Slide Sets (10 slides each)

Canadian Cities.

    Part I.   Vancouver, Victoria, Edmonton, Saskatoon, Regina, Winnipeg, Toronto, Ottawa, and Hamilton.

The City In Print

        Part II.   London, Windsor, Sudbury, Montreal, Quebec City, Fredericton, Saint John, Halifax, Charlottetown.

Montreal.

        Part I.   A useful set of 10 slides on the city in general, housing, and the city center.
        Part II.   Major buildings and transportation networks are illustrated in this set.
        Part III. Industrial characteristics are shown in this set.

Old Montreal.

        Part I.   Ville Marie.
        Part II.   Ville Marie.

These slides are highly useful at any level. $4.00 each.

NEW YORK TIMES FILMSTRIPS

        Source: Can.   Visual Education Centre
                      U.S.   New York Times Filmstrips
                      G.B.   Information not available

        Price: As indicated

The Cities: People And Their Problems. 5 filmstrips. Color.
    This set includes 5 records, each of which has commentary on one side, and worthwhile discussions on the topic with a *New York Times* editor and New York high school students on the other side. The 5 manuals contain written duplication of the recorded commentary only.

The Citizen In The Cities.
        This is a view of citizen participation, political controls, hindrances to involvement (the impersonal city, lack of community spirit, echelons of political control and bureaucratic hindrances).

Leisure In The Cities.
        A look at the variety offered by large cities. Alternatives in urban recreation and leisure are dealt with, and the issue of leisure time is covered in depth.

Living In The Cities.
        This deals with urban conditions and pressures in the U.S.. Housing problems, urban renewal and transportation are covered. Superb illustrations.

Schools In The Cities.
        Covers the dichotomy between urban and suburban schools. Such issues as available tax dollars, local control and busing are looked at in detail.

Audio-Visual Materials

Working In The Cities.
   Largely deals with rural migration to the cities, unemployment, job training, economic plight of the poor, and crime in the city.

This is a valuable series with a strong American focus. Can.-$105; U.S.-$98.00.

Crisis Of The Environment. 5 filmstrips. Color.
   This set includes 5 records, each of which has commentary with an audible signal on one side, the other being a student discussion with an expert. The 5 manuals contain the recorded commentary.

Breaking The Biological Strand.
   A study of the effect of pesticides and other man-made effects on the biosphere.

Man: An Endangered Species!
   A study that looks at the question of whether or not man is destroying his environment. Historical examples in the ancient world and the dust bowl of the '30's are examined as a prelude to a survey of the environment and American efforts toward its protection.

Population Explosion.
   A study illustrating the Ehrlich thesis on population explosion and its likely outcome, the Roman Catholic viewpoint on controls, and other perspectives and problems. Quite good.

Preserve And Protect.
   The history of conservation, and its lack, in the U.S.; pressures against conservation, and other aspects of the entire issue.

Vanishing Species.
   A study of wildlife extermination and extinction, including factors that cannot be avoided and those that can. One of the only two filmstrips yet reviewed on this topic (see Society for Visual Education Filmstrips).

Each filmstrip has several breaks in the commentary at points that are significant for discussion. A superb series, of use in and out of the classroom. Can.-$105.00; U.S.-$98.00.

The Embattled Metropolis. 1970. 1 filmstrip. B/W.
   This is with 1 record, one side being the commentary and the other, of two student panel discussions on the city. One ditto master on the topic (a worksheet) and one discussion manual is included.

This filmstrip looks at the inner city, suburbia and the urban region. As a study of the U.S. condition, it deals with conflicts between these three sectors. The need for metropolitan government is strongly stressed. An exclusive American orientation. Can.-$9.50; U.S.-$9.00.

The City In Print

Problems Of Cities. 1 filmstrip. B/W.
   The single record that accompanies this item is continuous on one side, and on the other it is spaced at intervals. A ditto master of the major U.S. megalopolitan clusters is included.

This item focuses on the United States, its urban problems and solutions. Material dealt with includes current conditions and problems, the historical city (from ancient Mesopotamia to the 19th Century U.S. city) and current programs to remedy urban ills. Good illustrations and commentary. Heavy American orientation.

PANA-VUE SLIDES

Source: Can.   Canfilm Screen Service
          U.S.   Pana-Vue
          G.B.   Information not available

Price: $1.00 per set of 5 slides (North America, Caribbean, and world): and 75¢ per set of 3 slides (Europe). Free catalogue on request.

Note: This producer has more than 1000 sets available. All are oversized, square color photos in 2" x 2" frames. No preview.

          These slides are decidedly tourist oriented. One other limitation is the unwillingness of the producer to sell individual slides from sets. But some of these sets are still of value. The catalogue lists quite a few items which can be of definite use in building up a local slide collection. The prices are low enough to warrant purchase, even if one or two items in a set are inapplicable for an urban studies program.

          Very wide coverage of the U.S., Europe, and Canada; adequate coverage of the Caribbean; and a small amount on Latin America, the Middle East, Asia, the U.S.S.R., and the Pacific.

RANK AUDIO VISUAL LTD.

Source: Can.   Carman
          U.S.   Information not available
          G.B.   Rank

Price: Unless indicated, B/W filmstrips are $4.00; color $7.50; and double frames $9.00.

Note: Unless indicated, all have booklets.

Early Civilization. Color. Double frame filmstrip. (No. 09.0506)
   A filmstrip limited by its double frame structure. Content is exclusively of ruins of Roman Civilization. Available elsewhere in single frame and slides.

Audio-Visual Materials

Historical London. Color. (No. 09.0772)
    A potpourri in color, neither an overview of epochs nor any historical progression. Far better items exist.

Hong Kong. Color. 26 frames. (No. 09.0704)
    Presents a view of the city and way of life. Useful.

The Land Of The Incas. Color. (No. 09.0703)
    This item looks more at present local culture rather than the historical urban culture. Not suitable for urban studies.

Leptis Magna. Color. (No. 09.0457)
    A study of the remains of Roman cities. Several good reconstructions and maps, but superior material exists.

London/New York/Tokyo. Color. (No. 09.0708)
    This item tries to cover too much, and includes too little information on each city.

The Medieval City. B/W. (No. S.11/08.0011)
    Elementary in focus and inferior to a number of filmstrips on the same subject from other distributors.

People In Ancient Egypt. Color. (No. 09.0292)
    Unsuitable for a secondary level urban studies program.

People In Ancient Greece. Color. (No. 09/0290)
    A study of the Greeks, their civilization, way of life, and religion. Far too elementary for secondary use.

People In Roman Times. Color. (No. 09.0291)
    Superior items exist.

Pompeii. Color. (No. 09.0456)
    Similar to *Leptis Magna* (above).

Social Life In The Mid-19th Century. Part I: *The Town.* B/W. (No. 08.0035)
    More suitable for the study of the industrial revolution than urban history.

SOCIETY FOR VISUAL EDUCATION

    Source: Can. Educational Film Distributors
                  U.S. Society For Visual Education
                  G.B. Society For Visual Education

    Price: As indicated

    Note: These materials are suitable mainly for school use.

The City In Print

America's Urban Crisis. 6 sound filmstrips. (No. 202-SAR with records, or No. 202-SATC with cassettes)

This series, leaning toward an environmental approach, has good visuals, adequate to excellent commentary, and a good balance between information and perspective. The American emphasis is not overbearing, with the urban condition in North America adequately represented. As such, this series is a good set for use in Canadian schools. A superb general series. $57.50.

Air Pollution Menace. No. 202-2)

Starting with blankets of killing smog (Donora, Pa.-1948, New York City-1966, and Chicago-1969), the sources of air pollution (combustion) are dealt with in depth. Political, scientific and industrial solutions are also outlined. The cost aspect is adequately discussed, as are the difficulties of industrial control and intermunicipal pollution control.

The Housing Crisis. (No. 202-6)

A look at the dream of suburbia, its realities, the shortage of housing (either good city apartments or low cost housing), and the resulting condition and problem of poor housing. Economic factors are dealt with, as are the processes that result in decay. Urban renewal, both as solution and creator of problems of displacement, closes off this filmstrip.

The Roots Of Our Urban Problem. (No. 202-1)

This filmstrip deals with the pollution and decay of the larger metropolitan areas. This overview regards the structure of cities (including central Bosnywash), the extent of urbanization, urban population statistics, factors of urban growth in the U.S.A., consumptive patterns, surface wealth and well-being, some of the underlying problems (pollution, traffic congestion, slums, overpopulation) and conflicting arguments as to the root causes.

Solid Waste--A New Pollutant. (No. 202-4)

Litter, garbage, cast-off containers (cars to cans), as well as the massive volume of non-durable goods (compared to the longevity of goods 50 years ago). This aspect of planned obsolescence is looked at fully. The problem of containers (plastic, aluminum, tin), the volume of paper waste (office, newspapers) is also dealt with. Disposal problems and current alternatives (landfill, recycling) close off this filmstrip.

The Transportation Crisis. (No. 202-5)

A look at urban traffic congestion, problems of mass transit and the private automobile, and the alternatives. The advantages, disadvantages, and costs of either rapid transit or automobile transportation are dealt with in depth.

Water Pollution--A Complex Problem. (No. 202-3)

A look at the source of urban water pollution (home refuse, sewage, industrial waste). This item is a detailed study of natural, industrial, sewage, and thermal pollution as well as the sheer volume of pollution in relation to the total supply of water available.

Audio-Visual Materials

Ancient Greece: Cradle Of Western Culture. (No. 385)

The Golden Age: The Ascendancy Of Athens. 480-448 B.C. (No. 385-4)
The Golden Age: The Greek Wars And The Decline Of Athens. 448-362 B.C. (No. 385-5)

These two items present an evaluation of the structure and culture of ancient Athens. Art, architecture, cultural mood and city religion are dealt with, as well as the general historical background and culture. Excellent.

The Rise Of The City-States. 750-480 B.C. (No. 385-3)
A study of the city-state, its structure, form and purpose. Illustrations are elementary in focus, but the commentary is quite good. This is the best Greek item yet reviewed.

Not reviewed: Number 1, *Aegean Era*; Number 2, *Age Of Migration*; and Number 6, *Rise Of Macedonian Power*. Numbers 3 and 4 require record (385-2RR). Number 5 requires record (385-3RR at $4.00). Filmstrips are $7.00 each.

Architectural Slides

Ancient Architecture. 14 slides. U.S./Can.-$5.60. (No. 250A)
Classical Architecture. 7 slides. U.S./Can.-$3.15. (No. 251A)
Medieval Architecture. 14 slides. U.S./Can.-$5.60. (No. 253A)
Renaissance Architecture. 8 slides. U.S./Can.-$3.60. (No. 254A)
Roman Architecture. 10 slides. U.S./Can.-$4.50. (No. 252A)

These sets present a glimpse of architectural features for the periods listed. Superior materials exist in filmstrip or slide form and are reviewed elsewhere in this bibliography.

Early American Architecture. 9 slides. U.S./Can.-$4.05. (No. 255A)
One of the few items yet reviewed on 18th or 19th Century North America. A valuable set, dealing with architectural styles in the 13 American colonies.

Modern American Architecture. 6 slides. U.S./Can.-$2.70. (No. 256A)
An interesting short set. Slides illustrate suburbia, a tenement block, a skyscraper apartment block, the UN, Manhattan, and Chicago's Merchandise Mart. Good.

The Ecological Crisis. 6 sound filmstrips. (No. C797-SAR with records, $69.00; C797-SATC with cassettes, $72.00)
Each filmstrip can be purchased separately at $10.00 with manual; records (3) for $5.50; tapes for $6.50. This series has good photos, striking graphics and good drawing. The commentary is both informative and provocative. A worthwhile series for urban studies programs with an ecological unit. Included is a broadsheet on population with detailed manuals. See also *America's Urban Crisis* (above). Topics covered here emphasize pollution as well, and may be more suitable to individual urban studies programs.

Evolution And Extinction.
> A study of planetary evolution, environmental change and species adaptation and extinction. One-half of this study looks at paleontology. The second half views man's effect on animal extinction (hunting, pesticides, and the clearing of wilderness).

Pesticides.
> A study of the benefits and side effects of pesticides, hard and soft, as well as the effect of accumulation, and resistent strains.

Population Statistics.
> A visualization of the oft-quoted population statistics, with good photos, drawing and commentary. Tape commentary reviewed had varying sound levels. Basically an introduction to the study of population, not ecology.

Population Trends.
> Continuing the topic above, with the effects of population growth, growth spirals, overcrowding, natural and artificial controls, and man's prospects.

Pollution.
> Included are such topics as the biological effect of pollution, and the green-house effect potential.

Some Ecological Considerations.
> An introduction to ecology, looking at the ecosystem, the food chain, the backlash of predator control, effects of river damming, the use of pesticides, and other man-made disasters.

Living In Mexico Today. (No. 273)
> Both filmstrips reviewed below have manuals containing printouts of the commentary.

The Historical Triangle: Mexico City, Cuernavaca, And Puebla. (No. 273-2)
> Leaning toward an elementary focus, this is primarily a general geographic study. Little urban content. $7.00. Requires record (No. 273-1RR) for $4.00.

Taxco, A Spanish Colonial City. (No. 273-3)
> A sound filmstrip on this preserved historical city. Good photos and commentary start this study which deals in depth with Spanish, colonial, and Mexican urban structure. Extraneous topics are covered. $7.00. Requires record (No. 273-2RR) for $4.00.

> Not reviewed: *Northern Mexico And The Central Highlands.* (No. 273-1)
> *Southern Mexico, The Lowlands And The Yucatan Peninsula.* (No. 273-4)

Medieval Towns And Cities. (No. 381-12)
> This captioned filmstrip is an elementary item only. $6.00.

The Middle West: Cities And Commerce. Captioned filmstrip. (No. 270-16)
   Too elementary for use. Content is largely economic geography with very little urban content. $6.50.

The Roman Way Of Life. 4 filmstrips. (No. 383)
   Two titles, *The People Of Rome* (No. 383-1) and *The Religions Of Rome* (No. 383-2), were not previewed. The record needed for the two titles below is No. F772-2RR for $4.00. The filmstrips are $6.50 each.

   Roman Architecture And Art. (No. 383-4)
      An elaboration of the item listed below, but too much emphasis is put on architectural detail for use by secondary students.

   The Roman Communities And Homes. (No. 383-3)
      A study of historical architecture from the Etruscans through the empire's rise and fall. Quite a useful item, if commentary is needed. Otherwise, better items have been noted elsewhere (without records) at less cost.

This Is The Soviet Union. Filmstrip series. Filmstrips are $7.00; records (No. 294-SAR) are $4.00; cassettes (No. 294-SATC) are $6.00.

   Housing In The Soviet Union. (No. 294-3; record No. 294-2RR; cassette No. 294-2TC)
      This filmstrip looks at environmental adaptation of housing in the U.S.S.R., housing in Siberia (frontier villages and towns), Moscow and its congestion. A superb overview.

   Transportation And Communication. (No. 294-7; Record No. 294-4RR; cassette No. 294-4TC)
      An overview of transportation systems, costs, comparative use (private vs. public transit) as well as a quick look at rail, road, air, and ship transport. The section of communication, an overview, presents a complete image. Sufficient urban-oriented content to warrant purchase. Ideal for comparison to North America.

   Urban Centers And Historical Background. (No. 294-2; record No. 294-1RR; cassette No. 294-1TC)
      A brief study of the urban history of the U.S.S.R., but largely of modern urban life and characteristics. A good study of urban problems and background. Cities dealt with include Smolensk, Kiev, Moscow, Leningrad, Bukhara, Samarkand, Tashkent. Good commentary.

The following items were not previewed:

   Agriculture. (No. 294-4)
   Land And Climate. (No. 294-1)
   Marketing And Merchandising. (No. 294-8)
   Schools And Recreation. (No. 294-50
   Science And Industry. (No. 294-6)

The City In Print

Sets Too Elementary For Secondary Use

> *Communities Around The World Series.* 6 filmstrips. (No. 284)
> *Families Of Modern Black Africa.* 2 filmstrips. (No. F307)
> *Prehistoric Man Through The River Cultures.* 2 captioned filmstrips. (No.381)
> *San Francisco: Our City And County.* 9 captioned filmstrips. (No. A209S)
> *Working In The U.S. Communities.* 8 filmstrips. (No. 201-SR or STC)

Single Items. Captioned filmstrips, most with manuals containing script.

> *Australia: Cities And Industries.* (No. 290-21)
> A geographic study, not urban oriented. Captioned filmstrip. $6.50.

> *Five Great Cities.* (No. 270-6)
> The five major cities in the Northeastern Megalopolis (Boston, New York, Philadelphia, Baltimore, Washington). Good photos and maps. A highly satisfactory overview. Captioned filmstrip. $6.50.

> *Living In China Today: Cities And City Life.* (No. 288-2)
> One of four filmstrips in the series. Some superb frames, but too few to warrant purchase. Essentially part of a series on general geographical studies. Requires record No. 288-1RR for $4.00. Filmstrip is $7.00.

URBAN MEDIA MATERIALS

> Source: Can. International Telefilm Enterprises
> U.S.   Urban Media Materials
> G.B.   Patterson Associates

People Of The City.
Two sound filmstrips with commentary. A very poor item, for little use at any level. A look at the ethnic multiplicity of New York is the pair's purported purpose, but an extremely unreal image is presented. Canada-$32.00; U.S.-$28.00.

Problems Of Our Cities. 6 color sound filmstrips and manual.

Introduction.
Housing.
Pollution.
Social Problems.
Traffic.
Urban Renewal.

A view of the "good urban life." The commentary is over-dramatic and lacks credibility, but the filmstrips themselves are good. Without the record, the photos are quite useful, adaptable to many classroom conditions. Canada-$68.00; U.S.-$61.50.

Audio-Visual Materials

Story Of A Great City: New York. 2 sound filmstrips. Color.
    For use in schools, this pair is of limited value. The recorded commentary is adequate, dealing with the city from its discovery to the early 1900's (filmstrip 1), and studies of the city as an economic center, transportation hub, administrative center and entertainment center (filmstrip 2). The 2nd filmstrip, presenting an overview of the city, is limited for use by its rosy view of New York. No problems or issues would seem to exist. A very unreal image is presented. Canada-$32.00; U.S.-$28.00.

V-DIA VERLAG HEIDELBERG AND JUNGER VERLAG FRANKFURT AND COLORWALD

    Source: Can. Medex Canada
                  US/GB DCA Educational Products

    Price: 60¢ each in sets; 70¢ each as singles ($10.00 minimum, or add 10%)

    Note: These items can be ordered direct from the producer, but the delivery time is from 2 to 4 months.

              These slides can be purchased as the beginnings of a slide collection, either as sets or as singles. The map and diagram items are of particular value and certainly warrant purchase. Preview of other items listed is recommended.

Acropolis. 16 slides. (No.41007)
    Map and diagram: #1
    Archaeological Remains: #2-16
These differ from the items in set No. 53006. #1 is quite good. Other frames are available on filmstrip.

Ancient Mesopotamia. 38 slides. (No. 41)
    Map of Fertile Crescent   #1, 32
    Landscape and Geography   2, 3
    Archaeological Remains   4, 16, 19, 24, 25, 31, 36, 37
    Art, Sculpture, Friezes   5-15, 17, 20-23, 26-30, 34, 38
    Reconstructions   33
These superb color slides deal with ancient Sumeria, Assyria and Babylon. Descriptive sheet available in English.

Ancient Mexico. 16 slides. (No. 42006)
    Map   #1
    Art, Sculpture, Friezes   2, 6, 11, 12
    Archaeological Remains   3-5, 7-10, 13-16
Some useful materials. Good photos.

Ancient Persia. 34 slides. (No. 43)
    Map   #1
    Landscape   2, 23
    Art, Sculpture, Friezes   3-5, 7, 9, 14-20, 22, 24-26, 28, 31-34
    Archaeological Remains   6, 8, 10-13, 21, 27, 29, 30
Descriptive notes are available in English. Quite good.

Ancient Peru. 19 slides. (No. 42003)
    Archaeological Remains   #1-6
    Art Pieces   7-19
Of limited value, but they are beautiful items.

Baroque And Rococo Architecture. 25 slides. (No. 53003)
    Architectural Diagram   #25
    Architectural Detail
        (Interiors)   1-6, 8-11, 13, 15-17, 19, 20, 22, 23
    Architectural Features
        (Buildings)   7, 12, 14, 18, 21, 24
Most of these items are of limited use, but the photos are superb. The diagram is useful.

Egyptian Architecture. 21 slides. (No. 53004)
    Maps and Diagrams   #1, 2
    Archaeological Remains   3-10, 17-19, 21
    Art, Sculpture, Friezes   11-16, 20
Descriptive notes are included for slides with detail (No. 1, 2, 12). Slides are labeled in English and German. Items 1 and 2 are particularly useful.

Etruscan Architecture. 12 slides. (No. I-12A)
    Archaeological Remains   #1-12
Interesting items, not available in filmstrips.

Florence. 24 slides. (No. 51011)
    Cityscape   #1
    Architectural   2-12
    Art, Sculpture and Friezes   13-24
Slides include commentary in English and German. Cityscape and architectural items are superb.

Greek Architecture. 20 slides. (No. 53006)
    Archaeological Remains   #1-20
Including Tiryns, Mycenae, Delphi, Olympia, Sounion, Acropolis (Athens). Of less value than others. Available on filmstrip.

Greek Architecture In Sicily. 19 slides. (No. 53028)
    Archaeological Remains   #1-9, 11-14, 16
    Friezes, Sculpture   10, 15
Of little value.

Herculaneum. 20 slides. (No. K203)
    Archaeological Remains   #1-12, 18
    Art, Sculpture, Friezes   13-17, 19, 20
Descriptive notes available in English. Good detail, but of limited value.

Audio-Visual Materials

The Hittites. 26 slides. (No. K825)
  Landscape   #1-3, 11
  Archaeological Remains   4, 5, 7, 9, 10
  Art, Sculpture and Friezes 6, 8, 12-26
 Commentary sheet is included. Excellent photos, but of limited value.

Istanbul. 15 slides. (No. 52001)
  Architectural Sites   #5, 6, 8, 10
  Archaeological Remains   11-15
  Art, Sculpture and Friezes 7
  Landscape and Geography   1
  Cityscape   2-4
 Useful illustrations. Commentary is in English and German on the slides.

Medieval Daily Life. 24 slides. (No. 97108)
  Illuminations of the *Manesse Song Manuscript*. Superb photos of Medieval life as illustrated in this book. Quite good! English commentary on the slides.

The Medieval Town. 10 slides. (No. 42002)
  Although some of the slides are of interest, this series is inferior to material available on filmstrips.

Minoan - Mycenean Architecture. 20 slides. (No. 42008)
  Landscape   #1, 3
  Archaeological Remains   1, 6-13, 15, 16, 20
  Maps, Diagrams   2, 4, 14, 17, 19
  Art, Sculpture, and Friezes 5, 15
 Superb color photos. Maps are striking. No descriptive notes, but the slides are in English as well as German.

Ostia. 19 slides. (No. 42004)
  Reconstructions   #1, 11
  Architectural Features   2, 4-6, 8, 10, 12, 14-16, 18, 19
  Art, Sculpture, and Friezes 3, 7, 9, 13, 17
 Although illustrations are superb, the two reconstruction items are probably the only two useful in a general study of urban history. Other characteristic Roman features are dealt with elsewhere.

Paestum. 16 slides. (No. 53027)
  Archaeological Remains   #1-13
  Art, Friezes   14-16
 Of limited value.

Pompeii-Roman House. 16 slides. (No. 53014)
  House Plan   #1 (including sheet with detailed commentary)
  Archaeological Remains   2-4, 6, 8-10, 12-15
  Art, Sculpture, and Friezes 5, 7, 11, 16
 Slides, of definite value, on artistic remains and ruins. Useful. Commentary on slides in English and German.

The City In Print

Renaissance Architecture. 17 slides. (No. 53106)
    Architectural Diagram   #17
    Architectural Detail
      (Interiors)   3-4, 12
    Architectural Features
      (Buildings)   1, 2, 5-11, 13-16

Most of these items are of limited value, but the photos are superb. The diagram is useful.

Roman Architecture I. 8 slides. (No. 53010)
These are 8 architectural features dealt with in other series.

Roman Architecture II. 15 slides. (No. 53011)
Here there are 15 architectural features dealt with elsewhere.

Romans In North Africa. 12 slides. (No. L1047)
Similar to the item above.

Rome--Monuments Of History. 36 slides. (No. 97101)
    Archaeological Remains   #3, 5-8, 13-16, 20-26, 33, 34
    Reconstructions   9 (superb)
    Art, Sculpture, and Friezes   1, 2, 4, 10-12, 17-19, 27
    Architectural Features   28-31, 35, 36
    Miscellaneous   32

Commentary sheet is included. Archaeological and architectural items are superb. The reconstruction is a must.

VISUAL INFORMATION SERVICE, LTD.

    Source: Can.   Medex Canada
              U.S.   Medex Canada
              G.B.   Visual Information Service

    Price: $4.00 each

    Note: All are poor. Sterile photos, some taken <u>out of focus</u>!

Ancient Athens. B/W. (No. 263)
Bignor Roman Villa. Color. (No. 300)
Classical Athens. B/W. (No. 11)
Greek Architecture In Europe. B/W. (No. 238)
Hadrian's Wall. Color. (No. 80)
Pompeii And Herculaneum. Color. (No. 287)
Roman Tripolitania. B/W. (No. 265)
Stones Of Ancient Greece. B/W. (No. 208)
Tales Of Old Rome. B/W. (No. 513)

VISUAL PUBLICATIONS FILMSTRIPS

    Source: Can/US   McIntyre Educational Media
              GB   Visual Publications, Ltd.

Audio-Visual Materials

Appreciation Of Architecture Series.

Elements Of Architecture. (No. 1)
Greek Architecture. (No. 2)
Roman Architecture. (No. 3)
Early Christian/Byzantine Architecture. (No. 4)
Romanesque Architecture. (No. 5)
Gothic Architecture. (No. 6)
Renaissance And Baroque Architecture. (No. 7)
18th And 19th Century Architecture. (No. 8)
Light And Color. (No. 9)

Each filmstrip has from 40 to 50 frames. The first eight are black and white while the ninth is in color. This series has good visuals of reconstructions, models, architectural designs, and photos of major examples of architecture in Western civilization. A superb introduction to Western architecture. $5.00 each for the first 8; $7.00 for No. 9.

History Of Western Art Series.

85 filmstrips are included in this series, covering the art history of man from the Paleolithic to the mid 20th Century. The subsections listed include filmstrips of use for the study of urban history. The number of filmstrips in each subsection is indicated in parens following the title.

Mesopotamian Art. (4) Good examples of temples, palaces, wall painting, etc.. Interesting.
Egyptian Art. (4) Examples of Egyptian art from the prehistoric to Ptolemaic periods. Good.
Art In The Greek World. (6) Minoan, Archaic to Hellenistic Greece, and Etruscan. Good.
Roman Art. (5) Much is included on the cities and architecture of Rome and its empire. Good.
Romanesque (architecture). (3) Covers most of Europe. Good.
Gothic Architecture. (4) From the 12th through 16th Centuries. Of limited value.
Architecture In Italy: Renaissance To Baroque. (3) Of limited value.
Architecture Outside Italy: Renaissance To Baroque. (2) Of limited value.
Architecture In The 18th And 19th Centuries. (4) Better items exist. Of limited value.
Architecture In The 20th Century. (6) Of limited value.

Each of the above filmstrips is in color and is priced at $8.00.

Looking At Things Series.

Materials. (No. 1) An examination of color and texture.
Classical Vista. (No. 2) An examination of art and architecture from the Renaissance to the 19th Century.
Romantic Vision. (No. 3) The 19th Century in imagery.
Industry And Revolt. (No. 4) A study of the transition from the gentle to the severe in the 19th Century (humanism to efficiency).

Modern Movement. (No. 5) The 19th Century revisited.
Viewpoints. (No. 6) A supplement to parts 1-5. An intriguing blend.
Environment. (Nos. 7 & 8) Two filmstrips which examine man and nature as seen through visual aspects of the environment.

This set is useful for a program designed to develop perception of the city as a living entity and the city as a work of art. A superb series, artistically, and of definite value in an urban studies program. $56.00 for the set or $7.00 each.

Looking Into History Series. Color.
Of this historical series, two filmstrips are of value in presenting an image of, and a feeling for, the period. Both have sufficient urban orientation to warrant use. $8.00.

The Triumph Of Industry, 1835-1860. (No. XV)
The End Of The Victorian Era, 1885-1910. (No. XVI)

Master Buildings. Color.
Five filmstrips on Durham, Chartres, St. Peter's, Vaux Le Vicomte, and Vierzehnheiligen. Too detailed for general use. $40.00 for the set or $8.00 each.

Modern Architecture. B/W
Eight filmstrips covering the period 1775-1960. Included is the description of innovative design through the 19th Century into the 20th Century. The work of Gaudi, Frank Lloyd Wright, Gropius, Le. Corbusier, and Mendelsohn are included. Visual display is given to Ronchamp (Le Corbusier), Lever House, the Seagram Building, the Gugenheim, Brasilia, and several New Towns.

This series is limited to those programs which are devoting considerable time to architecture. Series is $40.00 or $5.00 each.

Twentieth Century Environment.
Six filmstrips which present images that are neither related to ecology nor urbanization. Of no application to a program of urban studies.

WARREN SCHLOAT FILMSTRIPS

Source: Can.   Prentice Hall of Canada
          U.S.   Warren Schloat Productions
          G.B.   Information not available

Price: Single sound filmstrips are $22.50 and two filmstrip sets are $45.00.

Note: All sets come with <u>either</u> cassette or record; all sets have manuals.

Audio-Visual Materials

Air Pollution. 1972. (No. 464)
    This two filmstrip package presents scientific data related to the atmosphere and pollution as well as the human problem. Good photographs and diagrams are included in this useful set. The only detracting aspect is a commentary which sounds at times like the "scientific" introduction to a Grade B science fiction movie.

The Beer Can By The Highway. 1972. (No. 461)
    This single sound filmstrip is of little use in any program. The commentary is misleading and propagandistic, making too many unproven statements and comparisons.

History Of The City. 1972. (No. 465)
    Two sound filmstrips comprise this package. Not truly dealing with urban history, this program deals with cities only as a small part of a far broader study of civilizations from Sumer through to the modern era. The illustrations, in too many instances, are not representative of the point being made in the commentary. The commentary is too sophisticated for elementary use and too juvenile for secondary use.

Man And The City. 1972. (No. 467)
    This pair is of little use. The commentary does not match the illustrations. It is also indecisive and sterile. The visuals are, on the whole, lifeless, lackluster, and too often unsuitable for the topic being dealt with.

The Visual City. 1972. (No. 468)
    These four sound filmstrips cannot be recommended too highly. Based upon material contained in *The Language Of Cities*, by Fran Hosken, and similar to a slide set available from the author, this set illustrates a number of significant elements about the city, including what the city is; space and scale in the city; color, texture, and visual patterns in the city; and form and movement in the city.

From experience with the slide version (identical to the filmstrip, but without the sound commentary), the set can be of use in observing worldwide urban conditions, a number of elements which determine the character of cities, and for in-depth study of the city in its visual form.

The commentary becomes pedantic in spots, but, on the whole, the dialogue is well done. With or without the sound portion, this set is of decided use in school or community.

Water Pollution. 1972. (No. 453)
    Science oriented and not applicable to the study of urban ecology. Two sound filmstrips.

What Is Ecology? 1972. (No. 457)
    One sound filmstrip similar to the title above.

16.4 FILMLOOPS

The filmloop is a useful visual device even though it has several limitations. These items are usually available in a choice of two cassettes (Kodak and Technicolor brands). Specific machines are required to show either. In addition, filmloops can be available in 8mm. and Super 8mm. film. Caution should therefore be taken that proper machines are available for viewing.

HESTER FILM LOOPS

    Source: Can. McIntyre Educational Media
                U.S./G.B. Visual Publications Ltd.

    Price: $22.75 each

Awareness Series

Cities At Play. (No. EF103-82)
Cities At Work. (No. EF103-81)
Close-ups. (No. EF103-86)
Faces In The City. (No. EF103-60)
Forms Of The City. (No. EF103-87)
Moving City. (No. EF103-83)
Signs Of The City. (No. EF103-85)
Times Of The City. (No. EF103-88)
Where I Live. (No. EF103-84)

Filmloops in this series lack that certain spark that could have prevented them from being the lifeless works they are.

INTERNATIONAL COMMUNICATIONS FILMS

    Source: Can. City Films
                U.S. Doubleday Multimedia
                G.B. Feffer & Simons

    Price: $24.00 each

    Note: All of the items listed below come with study guides. Some of the films are dark and will require a brilliant screen and dark room.

Ancient Indus River Civilizations. (No. 3021)
    Studies of Mohenjo-Daro, Taxila, and Mogul India. Predominently views of ruins and sculpture.

Bangkok: The Nautical City. (No. 30625)
    A study of life on the river, but suited to regional geography, not urban studies.

City Life In Colombia. (No. 3401)
>Quite a lot is available in this film. Housing, from rich to poor (slums), comparisons of city and village life, transportation, river housing (similar to Hong Kong and Singapore), and the city marketplace. A worthwhile item to consider.

City Life In Eastern Europe. (No. 3706)
>Not urban oriented.

City Life In Middle America. (No. 3305)
>Views of Mexico City, its traffic congestion, land use, housing (rich and poor), and classic architecture. Of value for the study of world urbanization.

City Life In West Africa. (No. 4104)
>Views of modern, Western architecture as well as the more traditional portions of the African city. A good study.

City Markets And Stores Of Eastern Europe. (No. 3709)
>Not urban oriented.

Markets In Pakistan. (No. 3019)
>A useful study of the non-Western town which presents a concise view of the market function and way of life.

Marrakesh. (No. 21135)
>A good study of social life in this Northern African city.

People Of Eastern Europe. (No. 3707)
>Not urban oriented.

Small Town Life In Eastern Europe. (No. 3705)
>An interesting and useful view of small towns, their form, functions, and atmosphere.

Teotihuacan, Mitla, And Monte Alban. (No. 3312)
>Similar to the item below. Good photography of the sites and ruins.

Tikal: The Maya's First Great City. (No. 3313)
>A useful study of the ruins of this early Pre-Columbian city.

Tokyo's Population. (No. 3101)
>Studies of old and new in Tokyo, the Ginza, transportation and congestion.

Town Life In West Africa. (No. 4105)
>A view of social life in the Western African village and town. The mixture of traditional conditions and Westernization is quite well presented. A highly significant and useful film loop.

Warsaw. (No. 3701)
      Emphasizing the modern city of Warsaw, this film presents an image of land use, architecture, transportation, and social life. Remnants of World War II devastation are also shown.

PARK FILM LOOPS

    Source: Can./U.S. McIntyre Educational Media
                  G.B.   Information not available

    Price: $20.00 each

    Note: Of a much larger selection on general subjects, these items have limited usefulness. They are lifeless and poorly photographed. Movement on film is jerky and unnatural.

Amsterdam. (No. H8-023)
Modern London. (No. H8-062)
Montreal/Quebec. (No. H8-102)
Rotterdam. (No. H8-024)
Tokyo. (No. H8-009)

16.5 VIDEOTAPES

      To date, there is no nationwide source of videotapes. Instead, local sources should be sought. Many larger school boards tape programs directly. Local television stations certainly do, as do many individuals with the proper equipment. A caution should be noted. Until the copyright law is clarified, or until test cases are settled in the courts, such copying is often in violation of copyright. Even if the item to be copied will only be used for educational, or even personal, viewing, it can still be an "illegal" copy. Therefore, care should be taken in either requesting or copying material directly off the media. Local media stations should be able to clarify whether a program is "free" to copy or not.

In any case, this should not deter from the use of tapes. The videotape, especially with its reusability, is bound to become a major audio-visual tool for learning. Its use in the recording and replaying of local events should not be passed by. Local sources of privately secured tapes should also be sought. The major media companies, and an increasing number of large corporations, have videotapes available for loan.

16.6 RECORDS AND AUDIO TAPES

      Few records are presently available for urban studies. Several sources do exist, however, for audio-tapes. In no instance is preview possible. (In light of the ease of copying, this condition is understandable.)

Audio-Visual Materials

AAAS TAPES

      Source: Can/US/GB American Association for the Advancement of Science

      Price: $39.00

Urbanization In Arid Lands. (No. 72/70 I II III)
    Six three hour tapes from a long symposium held as part of an annual convention of the AAAS, these tapes are far too detailed for use at the secondary or community level. The individual presentations range from highly interesting to downright boring. Too many tend toward the latter.

CBC (CANADIAN BROADCASTING CORPORATION) TAPES

      Source: Can/US/GB CBC Learning Systems

      Price: ½ hour tapes are $6.00 each and 1 hour tapes are $12.00 each

      Note: No preview available on these items. All are of use for the community or school

Tapes Worthy Of Consideration:

Can The Urb Be Planned Anew? ½ hour. (No. 365)
    An interview with Hans Blumenfeld, the Canadian planner. Basically a survey of cities and their planning in Canada, this presentation is of definite value as an overall statement on urbanization. Included are comments on people and places (Le Corbusier, Jane Jacobs, Los Angeles, and New York).

Dead Cities. ½ hour. (No. 379)
    A presentation by the medieval historian, Professor Diane Hughes, this contrasts the fates of cities in the ancient world to the cities of today. The program ranges from views of the ancient, fortified, culture-oriented cities (Jericho, Mesopotamia) through the classical city of Greece and Rome; through the Medieval and Renaissance western city (based more on economic than cultural functions); and finally to the modern city, inheritor of this economic orientation. The possibilities of a "post civilization" era, suggested to be close upon us by Kenneth Boulding, rounds out this survey.

Interesting theses are developed in this lecture. Definitely a worthwhile item for the study of urban history.

Decisions In The Big City. 1 hour. (No. 253)
    An immensely useful tape which covers a wide range of topics. The first half looks at costs in the city, both political and economic, the role of advisor and politician, and power.

The second half hour deals with the politician and citizen, the role of expert, advocacy planning, the death or life of community, the ineffectiveness of local government, and the effects of rapid change. Comment and criticism are included from a diverse collection of individuals. This is a superb tape, of use in any classroom.

Future Shock. 1 hour. (No. 585)
      Alvin Toffler presents a lecture which exhaustively covers the major points made in his book. A bit long as is, but if dealt with in segments, this tape is a very worthwhile presentation. Worthy of purchase to use as is or abridged.

Ideology And Utopia. ½ hour. (No. 374)
      Another interview with Hans Blumenfeld, discussing the impact of Marxism and the communist state on urban planning in Russia. Professor Blumenfeld expands and develops this theme by comparison of Canadian, American, and Soviet conditions. A highly interesting commentary.

Mid-Canada Development Corridor. 1 hour. (No. 195)
      A distillation of comments made at the Lakehead Conference on Mid-Canada in 1964. Comments range on developmental planning, with reference to urbanization as it applies. Although this item is not directly urban in its orientation, it is a discussion of a topic crucial to Canada's trends in urbanization, namely concentration along the 49th parallel or a second band of urban concentration in Mid-Canada. A must for the study of cities and their future in Canada.

As is, this item is also significant for Canada studies other than those on urbanization.

New Towns. ½ hour. (No. 391)
      A panel of urban specialists investigates the pros and cons of new towns in the Canadian context. The alternatives of new towns vs. the rebuilding and renewal of existing cities are discussed. The participants, including Jane Jacobs, carry on a dynamic exchange. A highly useful and informative dialogue.

Technology: The Liberator. ½ hour. (No. 637)
      A presentation by an ardent pro-technologist. The basic theme stated is that nature is a tyrannical influence, while technology is a liberating force on man.

With its vigorous defense of technology, this tape is worthy of consideration. A multitude of examples are presented to defend the speaker's thesis. A contentious piece.

Transportation Theory. ½ hour. (No. 263)
      A third interview with Hans Blumenfeld, this time discussing urban transportation conditions. In a wide ranging presentation, Professor Blumenfeld comments on many of the conditions and problems which make up the total complexity of the present North American transportation situation. A fast moving, useful commentary.

Urbanizing In The Developing Nations. ½ hour. (No. 372)
      This tape deals with the process of rural to urban migration in India, Latin America (Venezuela, Peru), and Africa. Three interviews of McGill University Professors are included, presenting a sociologist, a social anthropologist, and a political scientist. Useful.

Audio-Visual Materials

The Urban Spaceship. ½ hour. (No. 702)
   An interview with Dr. C. M. Pedler, a visionary, environmentalist, and founder of the British Doomwatch group. In looking at whether or not the city is dying, an optimistic theme is developed that the future can be structured so as to allow for both man and cities. Habitation units and entire cities can be built which not only satisfy the needs of man, but also make use of techniques which allow for total recycling. Comments are also included by Frank Lloyd Wright, Arthur C. Clarke, and James Blish.

A wide ranging presentation, of interest for the study of the city today and its prospects tomorrow.

Utopias: Pros And Cons. 4 ½ hour tapes. (No. 366-369)
   This series is of definite use for the study of urban centered utopias, past and future.

   (No. 366) Dealing with utopias from Ancient Greece to the 20th Century, ideal states are discussed, including those of Plato, Thomas More, Swift, Robert Owen, H. G. Wells, and the other early 19th Century utopian socialists.

   Among all of the utopias presented, there is a notable and total lack of a rural-urban dichotomy, being replaced by idealized systems which assume a totally integrated, uniform, communistic, frozen, unchanging and static perfection.

   A very interesting item.

   (No. 367) The Anti-Utopias. This presentation is of immense value, focusing on the three main anti-utopian novels of the 20th Century, namely Zamitin's *We*, Huxley's *Brave New World*, and Orwell's *1984*. Looking at man bound to machines, all three anti-utopian works take a gloomy view of a future in which humanity is beaten down into an atomized existence devoid of all but fear.

   This tape is quite compelling.

   (No. 368) This third tape deals with mid 20th Century attempts to establish utopias. This tape is of interest, but of marginal use in urban studies. Individual anarchism and para-utopias are the two focii of this presentation.

   (No. 369) A philosophical discussion on utopias. Of no value for use in urban studies.

Items Previewed and Found Unsuitable For General Use:

Ancient Jericho. (No. 285)
   A study of anthropology without its application to urban history.

The City In Print

Architects In The Year 2000. (No. 378)
    Too personally biased. Not suitable.

Bombay, A Portrait In Sound. (No. 373)
    ½ hour. A general survey of the culture with no urban studies content.

Cabbagetown And Don Mills. (No. 526)
    Not urban studies, but rather a study of juvenile attitudes and life styles.

Cities: Design Environments. (No. 154-159)
    Six ½ hour tapes far too esoteric for use. Boring.

The Cybernetic State. (No. 719)
    Too esoteric.

Dynamic Change. (No. 675)
    A tape related to economics and management, not urban studies.

Ecology Of Institutions. (No. 420)
    A one hour tape of value for pure ecological studies, but not urban studies.

Mental And Physical Pollution Of The Canadian City. (No. 261)
    ½ hour. A look at the city through the eyes of an urban architect and a psychiatrist. Too esoteric for general or school use.

The Sociology Of Work In English Canada. (No. 403)
    Interpretations of studies conducted in Canada, including Porter's *The Vertical Mosaic*. Unfortunately, the presentation is boring.

Technological Forecasting. (No. 639)
    Energy resources projections, not urban studies.

The Urb Is Orbing. (No. 252)
    1 hour. A look at the city and its future. Comment is fielded by a number of academics from throughout the world. Although a good number of provocative ideas are presented, this tape is too loosely structured in its layout and too academic in content to be of use.

What Is A City? (No. 262)
    A look at the nature of cities, their promise and threat to mankind. Unfortunately, this presentation is quite boring.

URBAN MEDIA MATERIALS RECORDS

    Source: Can.   International Telefilm Enterprises
                    U.S.   Urban Media Materials
                    G.B.   Patterson Associates

Audio-Visual Materials

Discover The Sounds Of The City. 1970.
    Two records, with elementary level commentary, are included in this set. Unfortunately, the pair is of little use at any level. Much could have been done with sounds of a city, but too little variety is presented. To further limit its use, the set includes a printed manual which is of little aid in in giving directions for the use of the records. $14.50.

16.7 OVERHEAD TRANSPARENCIES

Many overhead transparencies are available, of varying quality in visual clarity and content, or of value to the study of urbanization. The recommended items are therefore only those which are of exceptional visual clarity and sufficient content to warrant use.

CREATIVE VISUALS

    Source: Can. Medex
                   U.S. Creative Visuals
                   G.B. Information not available

    Price: $7.00 per overhead transparency

Ancient And Classical Civilizations. (Set 900 AE) 8 OH's with overlays
Man's Progress. (Set 900 AA) 8 OH's with overlays
Medieval Civilizations. (Set 900 AF) 8 OH's with overlays

    These items are not suitable for use at the secondary level. Prepared for junior-secondary or elementary use, these transparencies lack the visual quality necessary for recommendation. Far too little information or too few ideas are presented for the price asked.

DCA TRANSPARENCIES

    Source: Can./U.S. Medex
                   G.B.   Information not available

    Note: These transparencies are concise in their content and exceptionally clear and vivid in visual quality.

Ancient Eurasian Centers Of Civilization And Trade Routes. (No. WH-2)
    A single transparency depicting the location of early civilizations in relation to movements of people. $3.15.

Ancient Middle Eastern Centers Of Civilization. (No. WH-10)
    A single transparency illustrating the development of civilizations from 5000 B.C. to 1600 B.C. $3.15.

Great Middle Eastern Empires, 486 B.C.-120 A.D.. (No. WH-13)
    A supplement to WH-12. $5.95.

The City In Print

Growth And Spread Of Middle Eastern Empires 1500 B.C.-100 A.D.. (No. WH-12)
   A transparency with two overlays. A useful supplement to the item above in illustrating Middle Eastern empires in relation to Indian and Chinese parallel empires. Urban centers are indicated for all three areas of Asia. $5.95.

Some Ancient Mediterranean Empires Before Rome. (No. WH-19)
   Focused on the Mediterrean, this OH (with 2 overlays) illustrates the empires and urban centers of the Assyrians, Egyptians, Phoenicians, and Greeks. $5.75.

Some Middle Eastern Kingdoms 2300-500 B.C.. (No. WH-11)
   A transparency with two overlays that covers the period from Sumerian Akkad to the Persian Empire. The major urban centers are indicated. $6.75.

A total of 45 7-color OH's are produced by DCA. These were selected from a larger number reviewed for their usefulness in the study of urban history. The remainder of the series is worthy of preview for a school AV collection. The excellence of the visuals cannot be overemphasized (series runs from the ancient world to the present day including European history, imperialism, the Communist experience, etc..

ENCYCLOPEDIA BRITANNICA TRANSPARENCIES

   Source: Can/US/GB   Encyclopedia Britannica

The Growth Of Medieval Towns. 8 over-view transparencies. (Series 30060)
   A series of prepared transparencies on the medieval town. The accompanying explanatory materials are quite useful. Although this set does not cover the entire subject of medieval urban structures, it is still quite useful. (Fenton-Wallbank Series) $14.50.

Historical Reconstruction Series

   Historical Reconstructions Of Rome. (History Series No. 5670)
      7 panels. $18.00 Catalogue.
   Historical Reconstructions Of Pompeii. (History Series No. 5680)
      4 panels. $12.00 Catalogue.
   Historical Reconstructions Of Ancient Greece. (History Series No. 6000)
      11 panels. $30.00 Catalogue.

   Sets of study prints depicting significant sites, with the bottom panel showing present conditions of the location, while the overlay presents the original condition. Useful historical materials. Study guide cards are included with each set, providing considerable information.

HAMMOND TRANSPARENCIES

   Source: Can. Book Society of Canada
             U.S. Hammond, Inc.
             G.B. McGraw-Hill Book Co. (UK), Ltd.

Audio-Visual Materials

Modern Urban Problems. An OH with 4 overlays. (No. 8433)
   This item is of value if the titling of "a typical U.S. city" is overlooked. The characteristics outlined deal with North American urban characteristics and changes (1947, 1957, 1967) in urban form and problems. The fourth overlay, looking at "urban America 1967" is of less use in Canadian schools, but of interest. $8.15 Can.-$7.50 U.S..

U.S.-Growth Of Industry And Cities. An OH with 4 overlays. (No. 8422)
   Periods dealt with are 1860, 1900, 1920, and 1960. Each looks at urban population in the U.S. and manufacturing location for each period. $8.15 Can.-$7.50 U.S..

Urban Crisis. 12 individual transparencies. (No. 8438)
   A U.S. orientation is noted in 8 of the 12 OH's. As such, this set is of too little use for Canadian schools, unless a look at specific U.S. conditions is required. $22.00 Can.-$20.00 U.S..

Each set includes a broadsheet of information, a map suitable for reproduction, and a simplistic quiz.

HUBBARD TRANSPARENCIES

        Source: Can. Visual Education Center
                  U.S. Hubbard Scientific Company
                  G.B. Information not available

Urban Growth. A set of 8 OH's with overlays. $35.00. (No. UST 5535) A must.

   OH 1. Growth of Urbanization (in the U.S.) 1870, 1900, 1930, 1961.
   OH 2. Growth of a Coastal City (San Francisco) 1853, 1870, 1900, 1920, 1966.
   OH 3. River City Growth (Memphis) 1826, 1850, 1900, 1950, 1967.
   OH 4. Inland City Growth (Denver) 1865, 1900, 1935, 1969.
   OH 5. City Shapes.
   OH 6. City Land Use.
   OH 7. Standard Metropolitan Areas (U.S.) 1970 Census.
   OH 8. World Cities--Ancient and Modern.

MCINTYRE TRANSPARENCIES

        Source: Can/US/GB McIntyre Educational Media

Geography Of Canada. 6 OH's with overlays and an extensive study guide.
    (Urban Set GC-C) $40.00.

   Population Distribution: Great Lakes/St. Lawrence Lowlands
   Toronto Land Use and Transportation Networks.
   Montreal Land Use and Transportation Networks (good material).
   Edmonton/Calgary Land Use and Transportation Networks (very useful).
   Vancouver Land Use and Transportation Networks.
   Winnipeg Land Use and Transportation Networks.

   A superb set of immense value for the study of urbanization in Canada.

The City In Print

VMI TRANSPARENCIES

        Source: Can.   Canfilm Screen Service
                      US/GB Visual Material, Inc.

City Government. (No. CG35)
    An OH with five overlays showing the three major forms of government common to the U.S. and Canada. Of definite use. $7.25.

Megalopolis I. (No. HG39)
    An OH with four overlays showing the growth of the Bosnywash Megalopolis. from 1850-1970. A useful item. $6.85.

Megalopolis II. (No. HG40)
    An OH with four overlays which indicates the influences effected by the Bosnywash Megalopolis. Of lesser value. $6.85.

Poverty In Urban Society.
    This set, although expensive, is worthy of consideration for use in the U.S. or Canada. The 41 OH's are divided between items which have identifiable U.S. content (19) and the majority which are North American in focus (22). Each overhead has clear visuals and concise commentary. The set is quite effective in its presentation, comprehensive in its scope, and distinctive in that it neither preaches nor excuses the condition of urban poverty.

The image and reality of urban poverty, its social, cultural and economic conditions, poor housing, and government attempts at action, are all dealt with in depth.

Each overhead has 3-6 overlays. An extensive teacher's manual is provided. Of definite use in preparing lesson materials.

The kit, which comes in a sturdy storage box, also includes 12 ditto transparencies, providing worthwhile exercises in policy decision-making, the evaluation of poverty, and role playing problem solving in poverty conditions.

This set is of use directly in the U.S.. In Canada, a majority of the overheads are useful as is, with the rest of use for comparative purposes. Many of the 19 with the U.S. content are in fact applicable to the Canadian situation. $123.00 Can.

17
Simulations and Multi-Media Kits

Two types of items are included in this section. Simulation games, or any device designed to place the user in a role playing situation, are included. As will be noted, some are designed for general secondary school use while some are not.

The other type of item included is the kit or packaged set of materials. This may be in the form of a full curriculum program, or it might be merely a collection of data and resources of use in the study or examination of a particular topic. Most of these kits include both printed and visual materials (either in the form of filmstrips or slides).

17.1 BOOKS ON SIMULATIONS

Several books are listed that contain lists, some annotated and some not, of simulations, parlour games, and activity kits.

Abt, Clark C. *Serious Games*. New York: The Viking Press, 1970.
    A scholarly study of simulations, as informational and behavioral educational tools. An essential reference on the philosophy, dimensions, potentials, and value of educational games and simulation techniques. Highly useful.

HB/PB (2)

Nesbitt, William A. *Simulation Games For The Social Studies Classroom*. New York: Thomas Crowell Co., 1971.
    Published for The Foreign Policy Association. A comprehensive study of simulation games, their purposes, types, value for classroom use, limitations, and advantages. The text is of use in itself, but this work's primary advantage is the full comprehensive listing of simulation games. A highly recommended work. A Must for the teacher.

PB (3)

Klietsch, Ronald G. *An Introduction To Learning Games And Instructional Simulations*. St. Paul (Minn.): Instructional Simulations, Inc., 1969.
    This work is a highly detailed, esoteric study of simulations. No direct review will be made of this item because of its limited usefulness to most teachers, but, for those involved in educational research in the area, or for those who desire many pages of 'educationalese' on this subject, the work is worth previewing. $10.00 U.S..

PB/Mimeo

Klietsch, Ronald G., F. B. Wiegman, and J. R. Powell, Jr. *Directory Of Educational Simulations Learning Games And Didactic Units*. St. Paul (Minn.): Instructional Simulations, Inc., 1969.
    More than 100 sheets, each listing a unit by title, developer, operating time, subject matter, number of participants, operating traits, cost (if available), and source of supply. A manual for school district A/V purchase. Cost $10.00 U.S. CAUTION: Many items listed are not available.
                                                                                                                                Looseleaf

Wing, Richard L., et al. *The Production And Evaluation Of Three Computer Based Economics Games For The Sixth Grade*. Yorktown (N.Y.): Board of Cooperative Educational Services, 1967.
    Included in this extensive report are three games (The Sumerian Game, The Sierre Leone Game, The Free Enterprise Game). The evaluation of the rationale, technical procedures and results are rather complete. Worthwhile.
                                                                                                                                 PB (2)

Zieler, Richard. *Games For School Use*. Yorktown (N.Y.): Board of Cooperative Educational Services, 1969.
    An extensive listing of commercial and educational games. Worthy of purchase and preview.
                                                                                                                                 PB (2)

17.2 SIMULATIONS AND MULTI-MEDIA KITS

ABT ASSOCIATES SIMULATIONS

        Source: Can/US/GB   ABT Associates, Inc.

Neighborhood.
    (Listed in Klietsch) Correspondence with the Wellesley Public School System (holders of the game) has resulted in the following information: The game is not in a distributable form, and will remain unavailable unless picked up for commercial production at some future time.

Simpolis.
    (Listed in Klietsch) No review copy was made available. This firm is unwilling to allow preview.

Urbcoin.
    (Listed in Klietsch) An unpublished simulation unavailable in any form.

BOARD OF COOPERATIVE EDUCATIONAL SERVICES SIMULATIONS

        Source: Can/US/GB   Board of Cooperative Educational Services

The Sumerian Game.
    (Listed in Klietsch and Nesbitt) This item is exclusively a computer-based game.

Simulations And Multi-Media Kits

The game itself is of limited use, not being a manual (boxed) game. However, the report on its implementation is quite worthwhile and inexpensive ($3).

EDUCATIONAL VENTURES SIMULATIONS

    Source: Can/US/GB Educational Ventures, Inc.

    Price: As listed

Community Decision Games. $4.95 each.

    Use Of Open Space
    New Highway
    New School
    Budgets and Taxes

Each game has three rounds, dealing with problems of conflict of interest and value conflict. Playable by six to thirty-six students, the game sets the players into six interest groups of equal size (government, industry and commerce, and citizen groups) with each group making choices in response to circumstances outlined. The degree of concensus, or lack of it, is then determined. The pressures for dialogue and compromise are a major element of these games.

24 reusable or consumable decision cards, three posters, and a four page teaching guide are included with each game.

Designed for grades 5-8, these games can be utilized through the senior secondary level. A simple game, playable in a short time.

The Game Of Sacrifice. $4.95.
    A five round game dealing with environmental problems, similar in design to the four *Community Decision Games*. Quite useful. Same grade level and use comments apply as to the games above.

Included in the package is another item, entitled *Mike's World, Your World*. This deals with the environment and is an exclusively elementary item. Also included is the *Land Use Game*, an elementary level simulation dealing with environmental issues in land use. This is for use in conjunction with a short text.

ENCYCLOPEDIA BRITANNICA SIMULATION

    Source: Can./G.B. Encyclopedia Britannica
               U.S.   Western Publishing Co., Inc.

    Price: $26.00 Can-$24.00 U.S.

Ghetto.
    A boxed simulation which deals with the mechanics of poverty, including emotional, physical and social conditions. This simulation is useful in

that it presents a situation into which the player can experience, vicariously, the economic pressures that drive slum dwellers into crime, welfare, and reaction. Designed for 7-10 players. Playing time: 1-2 hours. Not an exclusively American item, this game is of definite use in Canada for a look at urban poverty.

ENVIRONMETRICS SIMULATION

      Source: Can/US/GB   Environmetrics

City I.

(Listed in Nesbitt) This kit is a bit expensive. Run on a computer, its programming alone costs $500.00. That and its reliance on a computer limits its use.

GINN COMPANY URBAN STUDIES KIT

      Source: Can.   Ginn & Co. (Can)
                  U.S.   Ginn & Co. (U.S.)
                  G.B.   Ginn Ltd. (London)

Urban Action: Planning For Change. A multi-media kit. $268.00.

Included are: Filmstrips and other visual material (9)
                 Records (6)
                 Detailed information cards for student use (31)
                 Student workbooks
                 A planning guide and manual

This collection deals with urban history, the nature of urbanization, functions of the city, the city as art and culture, the urban neighborhood, future alternatives, and programs for change.

Evaluation: A dangerously provocative kit. Several rather considerable flaws exist, permeating the 'action' sections of this kit. Of greatest importance is this kits emphasis--one of 'action.' Although it may be fine for motivating 'action for change,' its use is limited to ghetto type conditions and is certainly not suitable for school use. (The assumption is that the secondary educational role in urban studies is not one of motivating the student toward radical confrontation on specific conditions.) This program is structured to take apathetic students, provide information and instill motivation, and then isolate a problem which can be carried through to solution. Unfortunately, this would be a real problem, with local political participants and forces, using tactics which would be selected to reinforce the motivation with success, no matter how extreme that tactic might be.

Besides development of radical student activism, this program is limited in use in that it requires a minimum of 117 hours to complete (with a maximum of 183 hours).

Simulations And Multi-Media Kits

HOLT, RINEHART AND WINSTON MULTI-MEDIA KIT

    Source: Can. Holt, Rinehart and Winston of Canada.
                   U.S. Holt, Rinehart and Winston, Inc.
                   G.B. Holt-Blond

    Price: $110.00

Fenton, Edwin. *The Humanities In Three Cities: An Inquiry Approach*.
An audio-visual kit of 11 filmstrips, 2 records, and ditto masters to deal with the three cities covered in the text, namely Athens, Florence, and New York. An expensive kit, the set provides a well balanced view of life in three periods and locations. Limited to school use.

The Athens section includes filmstrips of significant architectural forms and art, dittos on the city layout and brief readings from such classic writters as Plato. Also included is a selection on record of Sophocles' *Antigone*.

The Florence material includes 4 filmstrips on art and architecture in general, and Leonardo da Vinci in particular. There are dittos dealing with locations, as well as a selection on the city from Muller's *Uses Of The Past*, and a recording from *Leonardo Through His Notebooks*.

New York material is more diverse, dealing with art and architecture, but also life in the city. The sound recording of *West Side Story* is included for use here, along with other selections.

INSTRUCTIONAL SIMULATIONS MATERIALS

    Source: Can/US/GB. Instructional Simulations, Inc.

Impact.
An expensive group simulation designed to deal with community problems. Individual roles are predetermined in detailed biography cards. Without futher comment on its design, its cost markedly limits its use. For 2 large looseleaf books on roles and procedures, $160.00 is much too great a cost. It is just not worth $160.00.

Tracts.
An urban land simulation priced at $39.00. This game situation utilizes four community sectors as the focus of planning 16 city blocks (private land developers, urban housing developers, planning commission, industrial sector).

This simulation uses the same format as *Impact* (a looseleaf binder includes information, rules, maps, score sheets and four participant manuals).

The game has value in presenting a format for simulating the planning and zoning processes. Complicated, but still useful as a model for direct use and adaptation. Recommended for purchase by districts.

The City In Print

KAISER ALUMINUM COMPANY

    Source: Can/US/GB Kaiser Aluminum Company

Futures, by Dr. Olaf Helmer.
    Klietsch refers to this item as not being commercially available. Correspondence verifies that all supplies of this item have long been exhausted. Not available.

NATIONAL FILM BOARD (OF CANADA) MULTI-MEDIA KIT

    Source: Can/US/GB National Film Board (of Canada)

    Price: $46.00

City In Transition: Metropolitan Toronto. A multi-media kit.
For use in the study of urban geography. Included in the kit are:

- 4 Overhead Transparencies (Southern Ontario, Land Use--1965, The Site of Metropolitan Toronto, and Growth of The City)
- 9 Maps
- 1 Filmstrip, *City In Transition: Metropolitan Toronto*.
- 1 Book, *The Changing Face Of Toronto*, by Donald Kerr and Jacob Spelt.
- 4 Sets of Aerial Photos (35 copies each), Showing the City Center, North Central Metro, a portion of the Don Valley, and Don Mills.
- 30 Slides (10 on land use, 10 on geological features, and 10 on the port).

This kit is quite complete for the study of urban geography, but does not include sufficient material on other aspects of the city. It is therefore limited in its usefulness.

NEW TOWN: THE ENVIRONMENTAL GAME

    Source: Can.   Urban Educational Materials
                    US/GB Harwell Associates

    Price: As listed

New Town Games, created by a professional planner, are designed to complement any urban studies program. Developed in 1965 and revised in 1971, these games are designed for use at various levels (11 years old to adult).

Two basic formats are available:

    The New Town Educator's Kit, for community or secondary school use, or
    The New Town Professional Planner's Kit, for professional planners or university level courses.

The *New Town Educator's Kit* is available in two sizes, either a small kit, for 4 to 10 students, or a large set for 4 to 20 students. This simulation is both simple and effective, being sufficiently adaptive to allow use during hourly periods, or in larger blocks of time. It can be completed within two hours or can be effectively continued for more than 8 hours. This kit includes a concise 21 page manual, various building blocks, a mapboard, monopoly-like money, and tally sheets. Players buy and develop land and grapple with the dichotemy of personal accumulation of wealth and proper planning.

This simulation is the single best urban studies kit available. It can be picked up and used, by student or adult, with little prior preparation. The rules and procedures are only a little more complicated than *Monopoly*. As such, this simulation is of value for parlour, school, or community use.

The large format of the *New Town Educator's Kit* can be used in classes of up to thirty. With some roles doubled up, the process can be quite stimulating. In larger classes, two sets are recommended.

The *New Town Professional Planner's Kit* is available either as a straight gaming situation or for computer simulation. This format is far too complicated for general or school use. Playing time is open ended.

Prices of the *New Town Games* are:

    Small Format *Educator's Kit* (4-10 players): $20.00 Can.; $16.00 U.S.
    Large Format *Educator's Kit* (4-20 players): $30.00 Can.; $28.00 U.S.
    The *New Town Professional Planner's Kit*: $100.00 Can.; $90.00 U.S.
    Computer Program for Above Item (Write-up plus deck): $60 Can.; $50 U.S.

PROJECTION ARTS MULTI-MEDIA KITS

    Source: Can/US/GB   Urban Educational Materials

A Multi-Media Kit On The Toronto Centered Regional Design Concept.

    Each kit contains: Teacher Resource Materials
                          25 Student Resource Material Booklets

    Teacher Resource Materials:
        Teacher Resource Text
        Design For Development In Ontario (120 page book)
        Status Report On The Toronto Centered Region (20 page book)
        Overhead Transparencies of Aerial Photos Illustrating the Design
            Concepts of
                Recreation Potential
                Urban Corridor
                Limited Growth Centers
                Growth Points
                Problem Areas
        4 Topographic Maps 1:25000 Showing Toronto Centered Region
        12 Overhead Transparencies or Maps Illustrating The Major Components
            of The Design Region.

35mm Slide Sets On
- Outdoor Recreation--Summer
- --Winter
- Existing Planning Problems--Sprawl
- --Congestion
- --Housing
- Unique Physiographic Features--Kettle Lakes
- --Moraine

Student Resource Material Booklets:
This booklet includes
- Printed copies of aerial photos
- Printed copies of maps illustrating the major components of the design region
- Basic summary of the regional design concept
- Statistical data on trends and problems inherent in the region

A highly useful collection of material. Although based on Metropolitan Toronto, this kit is of use for both comparative purposes and as a basis for the study of other metropolitan areas. $120.00.

Urban Planning Kits.
4 kits are now available, covering, in depth, the cities of
- Montreal
- Toronto
- Winnipeg
- Vancouver

Each kit includes the following:
- 2 large aerial mosaics (3' x 5') with imprinted vinyl overlays
- 20 enlarged photos on plasticized cards
- 100 work sheets of enlargement photos
- 20 overhead transparencies of enlargement photos
- 10 washable marking pens
- 6 topographic maps of the urban area
- 1 each: teaching guide, census data book, and land use map.

This kit cannot be recommended too highly. The material included is of direct use in the classroom. The teaching guide is superb, and the quality of the material included quite high. In all, these sets are of immense value for either direct study in the communities involved, or for comparative purposes. The massive amount of material available permits a complete in-depth comparison and analysis to take place in the classroom. $100.00.

PSYCHOLOGY TODAY GAMES

Source: Can/US/GB Psychology Today

The Cities Game.
An inexpensive (less than $10.00) game which deals with crises rather similar to American ghetto problems. This game, with its simple board and

Simulations And Multi-Media Kits

playing instructions, is suitable more for parlour use than for classroom use. Limited to 4 players.

SIMILE SIMULATIONS

    Source: US/GB Simile II
                   Can.   Harry Smith and Sons (Canadian prices slightly higher)

Metro Politics.
A sample is available for $3.00. An 18-35 student kit is $25.00. A simple, book form simulation (a book to each participant or pair). This simulation has much to offer, is easy to learn and instruct, and can be played in a short time. Good.

Object: To secure group acceptance of one of four alternative governmental forms.

Sitte.
A sample is available for $3.00. A 35 student kit is $50.00, a 25 student kit is $35.00. Similar in format to the item above. Good.

Object: Land use control and manipulation.

SIMSOC

    Source: Can. Collier Macmillan
                  U.S. Free Press
                  G.B. Collier Macmillan Publishers

Simsoc: Simulated Society, by William A. Gamson.
Reviewed was the participants' manual, a book of assigned simulations and readings to be used in conjunction with conventional classroom discussion and readings. Exceedingly complicated for secondary level use. At the cost quoted, a class set (essential for success in the simulation) is just too expensive. $4.50 for each student manual.

S.P.R.I. KIT

    Source: Can/US/GB McGraw-Hill

S.P.R.I. Kit On Air Pollution.
This kit, although expensive, is a highly useful collection of materials on air pollution in Pittsburgh, Toronto and Vancouver. Each box includes the following:
Instructor's Manual (1)
Student's guide (31)
Air Pollution (readings) (11)
Pittsburgh, Toronto, Vancouver (11 each)   Maps, Graphs, Statistics
Maps of The Three Cities
Manual on Air Pollution Experiments

The City In Print

>   2 Records, With One Side Each On Air Pollution in Each of The Three Cities (the 4th side is blank).
>   3 Filmstrips on Air Pollution in Each of The Three Cities

A vast amount of highly useful material. $139.00.

URBAN DYNE

>   Source: Can/US/GB   Urban Dyne

Urban Dynamics.
    A complex simulation game designed to involve its four players in a wide range of problems and prospects of urban life.

Far too complex for use at the secondary school or community levels. $95.00 U.S..

URBAN LAND USE EDUCATIONAL KIT

>   Source: Can/US/GB   School of Economic Science
>
>   Price: $38.00 Can.
>
>   Note: This kit includes:
>   1 set of 58 slides, commentary and teaching notes
>   1 article on property taxes (well written and laid out, of use to student citizen)
>   1 pamphlet
>   Student packets (30) of 6 parts
>   1 free showing of the film *One Way To Better Cities* (film manual included in kit)

This kit is an essential learning tool for a full understanding of urbanization in North America. The full package is easy to use, well laid out, well researched and presented.

The visual material, some of which is presented on sheets for student use, is of value for use in the English speaking world. The student material can be used with little prior preparation.

The topics dealt with are:
    Property tax
    The mechanics of site value tax
    Australian examples of site value taxation
    Basic economic terms
    What gives value to land?
    The law of rent
    The effect of progress and the misuses of land

A superb kit worthy of review for school or community use.

Addenda, Part I

1.1 BASIC INTERDISCIPLINARY WORKS

Bacon, Edmund N. *Design Of Cities*. Revised Ed., New York: Studio/Viking Press, 1974.

This revised edition is a gem. This book is still one of the most beautiful works available on urbanization as well as being one of the most significant and substantive in the area of urban design. The author presents a visual image of historical and current preceptions of space and its use. This revision reflects the author's development, and the general sophistication in our concepts of space, over seven years. Minor revisions are made in some sections, rendering them even more visible. Mr. Bacon has also added new sections that tie space and its use to larger, more complex urban/human systems. This revision renders this work as useful for the 1970s as the first edition was for the late 1960s. A work of definite use for reference.

HB (2)

Hammond, Mason, with the assistance of Lester J. Barton. *The City In The Ancient World*. Cambridge: Harvard University Press, 1972.

This work is of value for two portions of its content. The first 5/8 of the book contains a concise, readable, scholarly, and complete survey of the development and growth of cities from their emergence and expansion in the Near East through to the later Middle Ages. Devoid of bias or personal thrusts, the text is interesting reading. Exhaustively complete, this study is comparable in significance to Mumford's *The City In History*. Of equal, if not greater, importance is the extensive bibliography provided at the end of this book. It is annotated, structured for easy use, and incredibly complete. The bibliography is undoubtedly the most thorough one available in English dealing with urban history through the Middle Ages. Balance is given to all aspects of urban existence and activity, with coverage extending to the entire world. Most of the works reviewed are in English, with supplemental listings of significant works in other languages. For the bibliography alone, this book is worthy of purchase.

HB (2)

Hiller, Carl E. *Babylon To Brasilia: The Challenge Of City Planning*. Boston: Little, Brown and Co., 1972.

Written for a juvenile audience, this work is a brief urban history and a glimpse at the city today, including vignettes on the form of cities, major urban planners (L'Enfant, Haussmann, Howard, Wright, Le Corbusier,

Addenda

and Doxiadis), new towns, and approaches to rebuilding the city.

This book is a short work in which the author has presented an intriguing introduction to cities for the beginner. Eminently suitable for school use.

HB (1)

Lewis, David, ed. *The Growth Of Cities*. London: Elek, 1971.
    A worldwide perspective is given to urban growth in general and housing in particular. Profusely illustrated, this work includes studies of growth patterns, or lack of patterns, in Europe, the U.S., and the underdeveloped world. As a reference, this compendia is of significance both for its informative text and the precise visual essays. Well developed, complete and yet concise, the essays included present a diverse range of perspectives on the dynamic city and its inhabitants both in the developed and underdeveloped world.

HB (2)

Skinner, B.F. *Beyond Freedom And Dignity*. Toronto: Bantam Books (PB), 1972 and New York: Knopf (HB), 1971.
    This work, serialized in the *New York Post* and *Psychology Today* (August 1971) is undoubtedly one of the most significant comments on the nature of man and what must be done to correct man's faults (as seen by B. F. Skinner). If accepted and <u>implemented</u> <u>fully</u>, *1984* would seem to be a truly free society by comparison. Whether you accept or reject Skinner's thesis, his evaluation of mankind, with extreme recommendations for the remedy of man's shortcomings, is compelling reading. The mere fact that this work has been received <u>with</u> <u>favor</u> by individuals and organizations of some considerable political and economic influence makes this work an essential one to be read by anyone concerned about the future of man and society.

HB/PB (1)

1.2 BASIC DISCIPLINE-ORIENTED REFERENCES

Bailey, James, ed. *New Towns In America: The Design And Development Process*. New York: John Wiley, 1973. (Published under the auspices of the American Institute of Architects.)
    Based on material gathered in a 1971 conference on new towns, this work examines 32 new towns in the U.S.. The first section of this book is unique, with glimpses of these new towns (from Philadelphia, 1685 to Fort Lincoln, Washington, D.C., 1972) illustrated with a map and concise textual introduction covering one or two pages.

In addition to more elaborate detail on some of the new towns, the rest of the book examines the designing of new communities, the various processes involved in planning one, and alternatives to future urban growth in the U.S..

Addenda

> Good visuals, a precise and readable text, and an intriguing introductory layout combine to make this work exceedingly useful. An essential reference.
>
> HB (2)

Dosman, Edgar J. *Indians: The Urban Dilemma*. Toronto: McClelland and Stewart, 1973.

> Most North American studies of ethnic groups in the city have fallen outside the scope of this urban studies bibliography. This work does fit because it deals with the manner in which the Canadian Indian fits, or fails to fit, into the Canadian city. In fact, this book is a unique study of rural-to-urban migration in North America.
>
> Avoiding the usual pitfalls of sociological research, this study uses a number of approaches and techniques to arrive at a well rounded image of Indian life in cities. Included in this book is a study of the Indian Act and its effects, government policy toward the Indian in the past 100 years, and the three major groups of urban Indians--those who are affluent, those who are best labeled as "welfare" Indians, and those who have tried to maintain a balance between their culture and the demands of urban life.
>
> Mr. Dosman closes with a concise summary of the problem, with telling comments on solutions which only await acceptance by the dominant majority.
>
> PB (1)

Dyos, H. J. and Michael Wolff, eds. *The Victorian City*. see 2.6

Helmer, John and Neil A. Eddington, eds. *Urbanman: The Psychology Of Urban Survival*. New York: The Free Press, 1973.

> This collection of compelling essays provides the reader with a considerable amount of insight on a wide range of group behavior patterns in cities. Included are studies on the psychological pressures of urban life, "to work" movement stresses, the rules of queuing, mass apathy, social control, privacy, and interaction among urban dwellers.
>
> This collection is unusual in that the essays are current, eminently compatable, interesting to read to the point of pleasure, and devoid of superficial generalities or erudite pomposity. And yet, the proofs and justifications for conclusions made are readily apparent. This work is evidence of a very successful application of the tools of social psychology to the urban condition.
>
> HB (1)

Lofland, Lyn H. *A World Of Strangers: Order And Action In Urban Public Space*. New York: Basic Books, 1973.

> The first work to systematically develop <u>and</u> <u>explain</u> individual or group reactions to urban life conditions, this book provides an incredible range of insights on how we identify and cope with the urban environment.

Both the pre-industrial and modern city is analyzed. Anonymity, and how we use it, is explained along with detailed outlining of the devices used to either avoid or make us part of the city and its inhabitants. This journey provides the reader with the means to better understand how he does operate, or how he could cope, with the urban maze. An intriguing work.

HB (1)

Moss, Robert. *The War For The Cities*. New York: Coward, McCann and Geoghegan, 1972. Also published under the title *The Urban Guerillas*. London: Temple Smith, 1972.

Not directly oriented to the study of the city, this work is yet an essential reference. The author presents a highly readable portrayal of the successes and failures of violent urban based revolutions worldwide. Areas examined in depth include Ulster, Quebec (the FLQ), and for most of the book, the various Latin American cities which have been struck by paramilitary and terror organization.

What is of value to the urban specialist or generalist is the author's analysis of the ingredients and characteristics of urban guerilla technique. Considerable space is given over to the analysis of what conditions foster or deter this form of violent, non-productive response. For this, if for nothing else, this book is critical reading.

HB (1)

Newman, Oscar. *Defensible Space: Crime Prevention Through Urban Design*. New York: Macmillan, 1972.

Based upon a three year study of urban environments in the U.S., this work examines the effect that architectural design can have upon social interaction, group attitudes, an individual's personal lifespace and neighborhood.

The author proves his point. There is a relationship between design and the incidence of crime. Thus, the findings should be studied by those involved in building our cities and by those interested in maintaining the city as a place for man to live without fear.

Defensible Space has a universal application. The study may be American, but the problem is caused by design and not cultural conditions. As such, it has direct application to any other nation's cities.

Some solutions are suggested by the author. The significance of this book, though, is in its examination and illustration of the problem. The evidence is balanced and telling. It should convince even the greatest skeptic. Engrossing, well illustrated, and precise in its portrayal of decay and its alternatives, this is an excellent item.

HB (1)

Richardson, Boyce. *The Future Of Canadian Cities*. Toronto: New Press, 1972.
Although mistitled, this work is of considerable influence in that it

Addenda

is the only current work which assesses the present urban condition throughout Canada. A broad spectrum of topics are dealt with, including the role of the Federal government (and the CMHC), the growth of regional government, public transportation, the growing political power of the poor, and the impact of resource development on Canadian cities. Interesting reading.

HB (1)

Sutter, Ruth E. *The Next Place You Come To: A Historical Introduction To Communities In North America*. Englewood Cliffs: Prentice-Hall, 1973.

The author approaches the telling of this urban history in a unique manner. Based upon a wide range of studies (historical, anthropological, sociological, political, and economic), the reader is provided with an interesting and comprehensible treatise on how communities developed and matured from their pre-Columbian (pre-European) settings, through the colonial period, and into the 20th Century.

This provocative and stimulating book examines various pre-European cultural locations, early urban transplant patterns in the various European colonial ventures, the 19th Century solidification of some community contexts, and the emergence of new urban patterns which arose in the face of changed political and economic trends.

A short work, with an immense amount of data, *The Next Place You Come To* weaves these trends into the present. A unique contribution to the study of urban history, this work is essential reading for the urban historian, and interesting reading for the generalist or casual reader.

PB (1)

1.3 BIBLIOGRAPHIES, INDEXES, AND ABSTRACTS

Bell, Gwen, et. al.. *Urban Environments And Human Behavior: An Annotated Bibliography*. Stroudsburg (Pa.): Dowden, Hutchinson and Ross, 1973.
Too highly specialized for general use.

(3)

Chandler, Tertius and Gerald Fox. *3000 Years Of Urban Growth*. New York: Academic Press, 1974. A title in the series *Studies In Population*.

Providing statistical data on the city throughout history, this book is the result of thirty years of research and compilation of data. This effort to provide population information on cities over such a long period is successful. Of use at any level, *3000 Years Of Urban Growth* is a reference of immense value, of use at any level.

This is the only work in existence that details such data. The tables included provide exhaustive coverage of

> Cities of Europe 800-1850 (with maps)
> Cities of the Americas, Africa, and Asia 800-1850 (with maps)
> The Largest Cities of the World 1360 BC to 1850 AD.

Addenda

>   Cities, 1360 BC - 150 AD. (by country and area)
>   The World's Largest Cities (overview), 800-1825
>   The World's Largest Urban Areas
>   Cities of the World; 1300-1850 (an overview)
>   Top Cities on Each Continent, 800-1850
>   Bibliography (exhaustive)
>   List tabulating location of cities not located on the maps.

Time gaps between the various tables is from 300 to 500 years. More recent periodic tables have shorter spans. The introduction carefully lays out methods used to arrive at specific figures. Comment is also made regarding sources and reliability of data. The perusal of the introduction is <u>essential</u>.

Although expensive, this work is of critical necessity for both the urban specialist and generalist.

HB (1)

Hammond, Mason, with the assistance of Lester J. Bartson. *The City In The Ancient World*. (See 1.1)

Shillaber, Caroline. *A Library Classification For City And Regional Planning*. Cambridge: Harvard University Press, 1973. A revision of Pray and Kimball's *City Planning Classification* of 1913.
    This brief work provides a comprehensive listing classification for planning materials and documents. Of use in organizing large collections.

HB (2/3)

Showers, Victor. *The World Of Figures*. New York: John Wiley, 1973.
    This significant work is a compendia of data of particular use for those involved with cities. The data is current, comprehensive and highly legible. More than 50% of the work includes urban data, including:

>   largest cities
>   largest metropolitan areas
>   highest, oldest, warmest, coolest cities
>   precipitation and cities
>   highest buildings, universities, libraries
>   and a gazateer of countries and cities
>   (comprising more than 300 pages)

A reference of value for any use.

HB (1)

White, Brenda. *Source Book Of Planning Information*. Hamden (Conn.): Linnet Books (CA/US) and London: Clive Bingley (GB), 1971.
    This resource work includes data on sources for a wide range of bound and unbound print or other urban oriented material. Although this book is focused on English sources, the discussion of different types of sources for material is of value for use in North America. A necessary text for

Addenda

libraries.

HB (2)

Whittick, Arnold, ed. *Encyclopedia Of Urban Planning*. New York: McGraw-Hill, 1974.
     This work is essential for all libraries, urban information/communication services, and all professional or research facilities. This 1200 page work provides several types of encyclopedic reference including comment on the terminology, major figures in the field, and major planning concepts. The terminology and concepts included are discussed in depth and illustrated. Short, concise biographies, are included on the individuals dealt with, with emphasis on their impact on the study and development of the city.

But of the greatest significance are the studies of urban development by country. All countries are not represented, but most are at least commented upon. Anglo-America, Europe, (both east and west), and the Soviet Union are covered in depth, while nations of Latin America, Asia and Africa are dealt with in varying degrees of completeness. One unfortunate omission is Mainland China.

But even though all countries are not included, these sections prepared by a local urban specialist or a professional well acquainted with the country, are of measurable value. Content for these units includes:

    demographics and other characteristics
    planning legislation and administration
    urban management and development
    historical urban patterns and current developments
    future prospects and problems; patterns of growth

These segments are substantial, objective and informative. Of definite use for reference.

HB (2)

2.1 GENERAL WORKS IN URBAN HISTORY

Alagoa, Ebiegberi Joe. *The Small Brave City State: A History Of Nembe-Brass In The Niger Delta*. Nigeria: Ibadan University Press, and Madison: The University of Wisconsin Press, 1964.
    Not urban studies.

(4)

Carter, F. W. *Dubrovnik (Ragusa): A Classic City-State*. London: Seminar Press, 1972.
    A detailed study of the history and sphere of influence of this city-state from its founding in the 7th Century A.D.. Exhaustively complete, this work is the first in English to examine this city. Most of the book emphasizes the commercial and political history of the city rather than the city itself.

HB (3)

Addenda

Cassell London Series. (Cont.)
> Metcalf, Priscilla. *Victorian London.* London: Cassell, 1972.
>> Similar in format to the titles reviewed to date, this work is probably the most useful, with text that gives life to each decade portrayed. Profusely illustrated with photos and contemporary drawings, this work presents vivid images of this city at a time when it was THE metropolis. Intriguing.

HB (2)

Handlin, Oscar and John Burchard. *The Historian And The City.* Cambridge: The M. I. T. Press, 1963.

(3)

Hibbert, Christopher. *London: The Biography Of A City.* London: Longmans, 1969.
> Profusely illustrated, this work is a highly readable portrait of London from its Roman beginnings through the 19th Century. Basically a social history, the author provides the reader with intriguing glimpses of London life for close to 2000 years, with emphasis on the 15th-19th Centuries.

HB (2)

Hugo-Brunt, Michael. *The History Of City Planning: A Survey.* Montreal: Harvest House, 1972.
> Beginning with the ancient Near East, the author presents a highly readable and unfortunately virtually unillustrated, picture of the growth of cities through the 19th Century. A remarkably wide area is covered, including not only Europe and the Near East, but also Asia during the Middle Ages and Russia. The 19th Century is exhaustively dealt with, focusing on Europe, Russia, the U.S.A. and Canada.
>
> A useful reference which supplements existing works.

HB (2)

Join-Lambert, Michel. *Jerusalem.* London: Elek, 1958.
> This work covers the history of Jerusalem from its origins in the Second Millenium, B.C. through the periods of Jewish and Roman dominance, the Muslim period, and down to the end of the Latin kingdom of Jerusalem (12th Century A.D.). This book is illustrated, adding a visual perspective to a well developed textual history. Interesting reading.

HB (2)

Kenyon, Kathleen M. *Jerusalem: Excavating 3000 Years Of History.* London: Thames and Hudson, 1967.
> This beautiful book is not an urban history, but rather a detailed archaeological study.

(4)

Kimmich, Christoph M. *The Free City: Danzig And German Foreign Policy, 1919-1934.* New Haven: Yale University Press, 1968.
> A study on the international relations and not the urban characteristics

Addenda

       of this city. (4)

Levine, Herbert J. *Hitler's Free City: A History Of The Nazi Party In Danzig, 1925-1939*. Chicago: University of Chicago Press, 1973.
    No urban studies content.
(4)

Maclagan, Michael. *The City Of Constantinople*. London: Thames and Hudson, 1968, and New York: Praeger, 1968.
    A study of art and general history with little urban content.
(4)

McKelvey, Blake. *The City In American History*. London: George Allen and Unwin, and New York: Barnes and Noble, 1969.
    A collection of contemporary observations tied together with concise commentary. An intriguing collection of readings.
HB/PB (2)

Mohl, Raymond A. and James F. Richardson, eds. *The Urban Experience: Themes In American History*. Belmont: Wadsworth, 1973.
    A reader in American urban history.
(3)

PLANNING AND CITIES SERIES

Ward Perkins, J.B. *Cities Of Ancient Greece And Italy: Planning In Ancient Antiquity*. New York: Braziller, 1974.
    Following the format set by the series, the author outlines the general flow of cities and city planning in Greece, the Hellenistic world, and the Roman Empire. The text is succinct and useful.

The illustrations are the core of the work, and bear up to the usual high quality maintained by the series. The illustrations, including maps, photographs and diagrams, alone warrant use of this book.

The best illustrated work on the classical city available.
HB/PB (1)

in PLANNING AND CITIES SERIES

De La Croix, Horst. *Military Considerations In City Planning: Fortifications*. New York: Braziller, 1972.
(3)

Richardson, James F. *The American City: Historical Studies*. Waltham (Mass.): Xerox College Publishing, 1972.
    A collection of readings presented in an impalatable format. This work would be difficult to use. Subject matter is covered is dealt with elsewhere.
(4)

Addenda

2.2 ANCIENT CITIES

Champdor, Albert. *Babylon*. London: Elek and New York: G. P. Putnam's (U.S. only), 1958.
    An illustrated study of this ancient world capital, with considerable space given to translation of contemporary accounts of the city and its inhabitants from the 18th Century B.C. to 539 B.C..

    HB (2)

Hamblin, Dora Jean. *The First Cities*. New York: Time-Life Books, 1973.
    This work is a hodge-podge of vignettes in archaeology which sporadicall touch upon early towns and cities. There is, in fact, little urban content, and the thrust of the coverage, as suggested by the titles, is never delivered. An average archaeological study, this work is definitely not urban history by any stretch of the imagination.

    (4)

Mellaart, James. *Catal Huyuk: A Neolithic Town In Anatolia*. London: Thames and Hudson, 1967.
    An archeological study and not an urban history.

    (4)

2.3 CLASSICAL (GREEK AND ROMAN) CITIES

Jones, A. H. M. *The Greek City: From Alexander To Justinian*. Oxford at the Clarendon Press, 1971.
    A reprint of the original 1940 edition, this work presents detailed material on the Hellenistic city (in re-arranged detail than in the author's earlier work, *The Cities Of The Eastern Roman Provinces*, reviewed earlier in this section). Where the first work looks at cities by geographical location, *The Greek City* analyzes the city in terms of political and institutional development. A highly useful and concise concluding chapter examines the achievements and accomplishments of Greek cities. This section alone makes the book worthwhile. An essential reference.

    HB (2)

Ward-Perkins, J. B. *Cities Of Ancient Greece And Italy: Planning In Ancient Antiquity*.
    see 2.1 under PLANNING AND CITIES series.

2.4 MEDIEVAL CITIES

Lopez, Robert S. and Irving W. Raymond. *Medieval Trade In The Mediterranean World: Illustrative Documents Translated With Introductions And Notes*. New York: W. W. Norton, n.d..
    This collection of translated documents and commentary, woven together with concise prefatory notes, is of use to the reader seeking contemporary

Addenda

information on aspects of the economic functions of medieval cities. Although not urban in its orientation, the text does provide a wealth of data to complement the modern statements on medieval urban life.

PB (2)

Powicke, Michael R. *The Community Of The Realm. The Borzoi History Of England, Volume II 1154-1485.* New York: Knopf, 1973.
    A general history with a short chapter on the community in medieval England. Insufficient urban content in the total work.

(3)

2.45 BYZANTIUM AND THE MUSLIM WORLD (600-1600 A.D.)

Downey, Glanville. *Ancient Antioch.* Princeton: Princeton University Press, 1963.
    A condensed version of the work listed below. Covering a time period from the Hellenes to the end of the Eastern Roman Empire (Byzantium). A heavy work, useful as a reference.

HB (2)

Downey, Glanville. *A History Of Antioch In Syria From Seleucus To The Arab Conquest.* Princeton: Princeton University Press, 1961.

Lapidus, Ira M., ed. *Middle Eastern Cities: Ancient, Islamic And Contemporary Middle Eastern Urbanism, A Symposium.* Berkeley: University of California Press, 1969.

(3)

2.5 RENAISSANCE AND BAROQUE CITIES

Buck Brother's Panorama Of London 1749. (See 11.1)

Burckhardt, Jacobs. *The Civilization Of The Renaissance Of Italy.* New York: New American Library (Mentor), 1960, and New York: Harper & Row, 1958. Note: The NAL ed. (unillustrated) is available in 1 vol. The H & R ed. (illustrated), is available in a 2 vol. set.
    Based on two distinct versions of the original work (published in German in 1860), each has its own distinct flavour and stamp. The work is a marvel in presenting an immensely rich view of the world of Renaissance Man. Although not urban in its focus, the considerable detail presented on the way of life both public and private, provides the reader with clear images of the city and its inhabitants in Renaissance Italy. Highly readable.

Cochrane, Eric. *Florence In The Forgotten Centuries: A History Of Florence and The Florentines In The Age Of The Grand Dukes.* University of Chicago

Addenda

>Press, 1973.
>>Not urban history.

(4)

Lane, Frederic Chaplin. *Venice: A Maritime Republic*. Baltimore: Johns Hopkins, 1973.
>Not urban history.

(4)

Pred, Allan R. *Urban Growth and Circulation of Information: The United States System of Cities, 1790-1840*. Cambridge: Harvard University Press, 1973.
>Otherwise, far too sophisticated for any but academic use, this work does contain unique data on information circulation before the telegraph (or radio and tv). Detail is included on data flow in newspapers, by post, via commercial transactions, and interurban travel. The last two chapters of the book analyze general patterns of communication and information flow. Portions of this work are of definite use for general reference.

HB (2,3)

Visscher, C. J. *London Before The Fire*. (See 11.1)

2.6 NINETEENTH CENTURY AND INDUSTRIAL CITIES

Cherry, Gordon E. *Urban Change And Planning: A History Of Urban Development In Britain Since 1750*. Henley-on-Thames: G.T. Foulis, 1972.
>A well illustrated book which investigates the full spectrum of planning in the English city during the industrial period. This book examines changes in ideas, use of land, and technology, and the effect of each on the city. Coverage extends through the late 1960s. A useful reference.

HB (2)

Coleman, B. I., ed. *The Idea Of The City In Nineteenth Century Britain*. London: Routledge and Kegan Paul, 1973.
>Emphasis is placed in this book upon events and attitudes that are not particularly urban. Insufficient urban studies content.

(4)

Dyos, H.J. and Michael Wolff, eds. *The Victorian City*. London and Boston: Routledge and Kegan Paul, 1973. Two volumes.
>This monumental work is a reference without bounds. It is, without exception, the most useful reference work in or out of print on the 19th Century. Woven among the more than 900 pages is a vast accumulation of contemporary images, photographs and lithographs (434), assessments of the Victorian city, and a wide range of selections on monumental conditions and trivia.
>
>The format is academic, and each contributor has his own style and degree

Addenda

of sophisticated presentation, but on the whole this set is usable as a general reference or for reading curled up in front of a month-long fire. A pair of definitely valuable volumes for use as a library reference.

Note: The retail cost of this set exceeds $75.00.

HB (2)

Green, Constance McLaughlin. *Washington: Capital City, 1879-1950*. Princeton: Princeton University Press, 1963. Volume 2 of a set (Volume 1, now out of print, is *Washington: Village And Capital, 1800-1878*).
    A ponderous work, superceded by more usable studies.

(4)

Griffith, Ernest S. *A History Of American City Government*. Volume One *The Conspicuous Failure, 1870-1900* and Volume Two *The Progressive Years And Their Aftermath, 1900-1920*. (See 6.4)

Lubove, Roy. *The Urban Community: Housing And Planning In The Progressive Era*. Englewood Cliffs: Prentice-Hall, 1967.

(3)

McMahon, William. *South Jersey Towns*. New Brunswick: Rutgers University Press, 1973.
    Local studies, not urban studies.

(4)

Metcalf, P. *Victorian London*. (See 2.1)

Reps, John W. *The Making Of Urban America: A History Of City Planning In The United States*. Princeton: Princeton University Press, 1965.
    This beautiful book includes over 300 maps, models, lithographs, and plans illustrating the growth of cities in colonial and republican America. The text combines contemporary comments with a lively analysis of the factors which resulted in the founding and growth of a wide range of American Cities.

HB (2)

Smith, Charles Manly. *Curiosities Of London Life, Or Phases, Physiological And Social, Of The Great Metropolis*. London: Frank Cass, 1972. No. 15 in the *Cass Library Of Victorian Times*.
    First published in 1853, this work chronicles the life of London's street dwellers and workers. An on-the-spot, contemporary view of a different time. A superb piece.

HB (2)

Smith, Duane A. *Rocky Mountain Mining Camps: The Urban Frontier*. Bloomington: Indiana University Press, 1967.
    Insufficient urban studies content.

(4)

Addenda

Summerson, John. *The London Building World Of The Eighteen-Sixties*. London: Thames and Hudson, 1973.

(3)

Sutcliffe, Anthony. *The Autumn Of Central Paris: The Defeat Of Town Planning, 1850-1970*. Montreal: McGill-Queens University Press, 1971. Studies in Urban History, 1.

(3)

Thernstrom, Stephen and Richard Sennett, eds. *19th Century Cities: Essays In The New Urban History*. New Haven: Yale University Press, 1969.

(3)

Thomas, Brinley. *Migration And Urban Development: A Reappraisal Of British And American Long Cycles*. London: Methuen, 1972.
    Concentrating on the period 1870-1913, this work deals with the factors of mass intra-national migration in the U.S. and G.B.. An intriguing book which is unfortunately too complex for general use.

(3)

n.a. *The Grand Panorama Of London (1844)*. (See 11.1)

2.7 CITIES IN PRE-EUROPEAN ASIA AND AFRICA

Rosman, Gilbert. *Urban Networks In Ch'ing China And Tokugawa Japan*. Princeton: Princeton University Press, 1973.
    This sophisticated examination of the pre-modern, pre-industrial pre-western city in China and Japan includes studies of the patterns of urbanization in the highly efficient cities of East Asia. Also included is a discussion of social and economic structures and functions. An intriguing comparison of Peking, Edo (Toyko), and the prevalent hierarchy of cities finishes the work.

    Drawn from sources in Chinese and Japanese, this work is a unique reference the first reviewed dealing with the city in pre-European East Asia.

HB (2)

3.1 GENERAL WORKS ON PLANNING: URBANIZATION AS PLANNING

Bathke, W. L. and W. A. Haney, eds. *Land Management In The '70s: Concepts And Models*. San Francisco: San Francisco Press, 1972.

(3)

Bell, Gwen and Jaqueline Tyrwhitt, eds. *Human Identity In The Urban Environment*. Hammondsworth: Penguin, 1972.
    A collection of articles which have appeared in *Ekistics* in the past ten years. An interesting collection.

(3)

Addenda

Center for the Study of Instruction. *Man's Settlements*. New York: Harcourt, Brace and Jovanovich, 1972.
    An elementary level examination cluttered with extraneous information. Slick, but vacuous.
(4)

Chapin, F. Stuart, Jr. *Urban Land Use Planning*. 2nd ed. Urbana: University of Illinois Press, 1972.
(3)

Chen, Kan, ed. *Urban Dynamics: Extensions And Reflections*. San Francisco: San Francisco Press, 1972.
    A collection of essays assessing the urban dynamics model formulated by Jay Forrester.
(3)

Claire, William H., ed.. *Handbook On Urban Planning*. New York: Van Nostrand Reinhold, 1973.
    Superior works exist.
(4)

Cowan, Peter, ed. *Developing Patterns Of Urbanization*. Beverly Hills: Sage, 1970.
    Articles come mostly from Volume 6, No. 3 of the journal *Urban Studies*.
(3)

Cowan, Peter, et. al., eds. *The Future Of Planning*. Beverly Hills: Sage, 1973.
    A series of essays on the future of planning.
(3)

Elazar, Daniel J. *Cities Of The Prairie: The Metropolitan Frontier And American Politics*. (See 6.4)

Eisenstadt, S. N. and Stein Rokkan, eds. *Building States And Nations*. 2 Volumes. Beverly Hills: Sage, 1973 (Vol. 1) and 1974 (Vol. 2).
    Insufficient urban stuides content in this intriguing, sophisticated study of national development patterns.
(4)

Everson, J. A. and B. P. Fitzgerald. *Inside The City*. London: Longman, 1972.
    No. 3 in the series *Concepts In Geography*.
(3)

Ficker, Victor B. and Herbert S. Graves, eds. *Social Science And Urban Crisis: Introductory Readings*. New York: Macmillan, 1971.
    A repeat of articles found elsewhere, with too many dated selections. This junior college level text is superseded by other works reviewed.
(4)

Addenda

Frieden, Bernard J. and William W. Nash, Jr., eds. *Shaping An Urban Future: Essays In Memory Of Catherine Bauer Wurster*. Cambridge: The MIT Press, 1969.

(3)

Gibberd, Frederick. *Town Design*. 6th Edition, revised and enlarged (metricated). London: Architectural Press, 1970.
 The major revision only seems to be the metrication of the text. Although the illustrations are old, the text still is of definite value for reference use.

HB (2)

Goldwin, Robert A., ed. *A Nation Of Cities: Essays On America's Urban Problems*. Chicago: Rand McNally, 1968.
 Superior collections of readings have been reviewed.

(4)

Gutman, Robert, ed. *People And Buildings*. New York: Basic Books, 1972.
 A sophisticated collection of readings on the ecology of buildings; on the effects of man made structures on man.

(3)

Haar, Charles M., ed. *Law And Land: Anglo-American Planning Practice*. Cambridge: Harvard University Press, 1964.

(3)

Halprin, Lawrence. *Cities*. Revised ed. Cambridge: The M. I. T. Press, 1972.
 A reprint of the 1963 ed., long out of print, with the addition of a 14 page epilogue. This book, mostly of illustrations rather than text, provides a wide range of rich visual experiences on the city. Of use for casual reading and serious comparative research.

PB (1)

Harrington, Michael. *The Accidental Century*. Harmondsworth: Penguin, 1968.
 Not urban studies.

(4)

Harris, Fred R. and John V. Lindsay, co-chairmen. *The State Of The Cities: Report Of The Commission On The Cities In The '70s*. New York: Praeger, 1972.
 A highly political study which outlines the findings of the Commission. A significant document for views on how the political establishment interprets the urban condition in the U.S.

HB/PB (2)

Harvey, Edward B., ed. *Perspectives On Modernization: Essays In Memory Of Ian Weinberg*. Toronto: University of Toronto Press, 1972.
 Too little urban content to warrant use.

(4)

Addenda

Hoskin, Fran P. *The Functions Of Cities*. Cambridge: Schenkman Publishing Co., 1973.

(3)

House, Peter W. *The Urban Environmental System: Modeling For Research, Policy-Making And Education*. Beverly Hills: Sage, 1973.

(3)

Kulski, Julian Eugene. *Land Of Urban Promise*. Notre Dame: University of Notre Dame Press, 1967.
    A look into the state of urban design in the Northeastern part of the U.S., this work illustrates and comments on the foundations and fabric of urban space, including detailed analysis of the status of urban renewal, urban transportation, recreational planning, new towns, and urban design in the northeastern megalopolis. Idealistic in its approach and comments, this is a commendable reference on the state of the city in the late 1960s.

HB (2)

Jackson, John N. *The Canadian City: Space, Form, Quality*. Toronto: McGraw-Hill Ryerson, 1973.
    This title presents an up to date compilation of academic thinking about the city in Canada and the world. It investigates both the physical structure and human fabric of the city in Canada. The photos lack sparkle, but the charts are quite useful. Heavy going, this work is not light reading, but as a general reference, it cannot be recommended too highly.

PB (2)

Lewis, David, ed. *Urban Structure*. London: Elek, 1968.

(3)

Lynch, Kevin. *What Time Is This Place?* Cambridge: The M. I. T. Press, 1972.
    A study of the sense of time and the biological rhythms of man and how these senses affect our perception of the city.

(3)

Mann, Roy. *Rivers Of The City*. New York: Praeger, 1973.
    Of value for the specialist or for general reading, this book outlines the ecology of 15 rivers in Europe and North America. Included in this well illustrated reference is an assessment of historical use, current use(s), and prospects for more aesthetic or leisure use of the urban waterway.

Designed to inform rather than provide copious proofs, *Rivers Of The City*, presents a strong case for diminished economic or transportation uses. This theme recurs throughout the text, following the authors' predilection for human use of riverbanks.

The visuals, with the exception of several maps, are quite good. A useful reference text.

HB (2)

Addenda

Mass, Nathaniel J., ed. *Readings In Urban Dynamics*, Volume 1. Cambridge: Wright-Allen Press, 1974.

(3)

Mayerovitch, Harry. *Overstreet: An Urban Street Development System*. Montreal: Harvest House, 1973.
    This work illustrates and comments upon the feasibility of building over streets, to not only separate pedestrian from vehicular movement, but most important, to make use of that space now reserved solely for the use of motor vehicles. An interesting book, *Overstreet* presents a thesis with a concise text and comprehensible graphics.

HB (2)

McKeown, James E. and Frederick I. Tietze, eds. *The Changing Metropolis*, Second Edition. New York: Houghton-Mifflin, 1971.
    This collection of readings is divided between analysis of the explosive forces which divide the American city (schools, ghettos, police and poverty) and the less explosive, but equally important alternatives in urban design, the planning process, and metropolitan politics. A concise collection of short, readable essays.

PB (2)

McLoughlin, J. Brian. *Control And Urban Planning*. London: Faber and Faber, 1973.
    A study of the discipline of planning and not applicable to the study of the city.

(4)

Michel, John. *City Of Revelation: On The Proportions And Symbolic Numbers Of The Cosmic Temple*. London: Garnstone Press, 1972.
    As the subtitle indicates, this is a study of numerology and not urban studies.

(4)

PRAEGER SPECIAL STUDIES IN INTERNATIONAL POLITICS AND PUBLIC AFFAIRS.

Hodge, Patricia Leavey and Philip M. Hauser. *The Challenge Of America's Metropolitan Population Outlook, 1960-1985*. Prepared for the National Commission on Urban Problems. New York: Praeger, 1968. Dated.

(4)

Spatt, Beverly Moss. *A Proposal To Change The Structure Of City Planning: Case Study Of New York City*. New York: Praeger, 1971.
    Limited usefulness.

(4)

Taylor, John L. (ed.). *Planning For Urban Growth. British Perspectives On The Planning Process*. New York: Praeger, and London: Pall Mall, 1972.
    Selected proceedings of a seminar held in 1970 at the American University of Beirut for senior planners in the Middle East.

(3)

Addenda

PRAEGER SPECIAL STUDIES IN U.S. ECONOMIC AND SOCIAL DEVELOPMENT

Abrams, Charles, with the assistance of Robert Kolodny. *Home Ownership For The Poor: A Program For Philadelphia.* New York: Praeger, 1970.

(3)

Blecher, Earl M. *Advocacy Planning For Urban Development: With Analysis of Six Demonstration Programs.* New York: Praeger, 1971.
A useful and sophisticated study of citizen participation processes in the U.S.. Of use only for detailed research and comparison.

HB (2)

Lewis, Jordan D. and Lynn (eds.). *Industrial Approaches To Urban Problems. Discussions Of Housing, Transportation, Education, And Solid Waste Management Issues.* New York: Praeger, 1972.
Based on papers presented at a 1970 conference.

(3)

O'Connor, John R., et. al. *Exploring The Urban World.* New York: Globe Book Company, 1972.
An elementary level textbook on the growth of cities and their current status worldwide.

HB (2)

Rechy, John. *City Of Night.* New York: Grove, 1963.
Not urban studies.

(4)

Rudnick, Raphael. *In The Heart Of Our City.* New York: Random House, 1973.
A collection of poems with no urban studies content.

(4)

Schnore, Leo F. ed.. *Social Science And The City: A Survey Of Urban Research.* New York: Praeger, 1968.
The contents of this book are lifted from portions of Volume One of the *Urban Affairs Annual Reviews* published by Sage. Since the full rendering is available in paperback form, the complete work is recommended.

(4)

Siegan, Bernard H. *Land Use Without Zoning.* Lexington (Mass.): Lexington Books, 1972.

(3)

Spelt, Jacob. *Urban Development In South Central Ontario.* Toronto: McClelland and Stewart, 1972.

(3)

Stewart, Murray, ed. *The City: Problems Of Planning.* Harmondsworth: Penguin, 1972.

(3)

Addenda

Taylor, Nicholas. *The Village In The City: Towards A New Society*. London: Temple Smith, 1973.

(3)

URBAN AFFAIRS ANNUAL REVIEW (series continued)

Bloomberg, Warner, Jr., and Henry J. Schmand, eds. *Power, Poverty And Urban Policy*. Beverly Hills: Sage, 1968.
  Involved predominantly with ethnic and not urban issues.

(4)

Crecine, John P., (ed). *Financing The Metropolis: Public Policy In Urban Economics*. Beverly Hills: Sage, 1970.

(3)

Hawley, Willis D. and David Rogers, eds. *Improving The Quality Of Urban Management*. Beverly Hills: Sage, 1974.
  This volume provides a wide range of essays on civic bureaucracies and governmental structure. Included are selections on current urban governmental structure, non-innovational forms of change, decentralization innovational forms of change, and barriers to change. A useful selection for the serious researcher.

HB (2)

Orleans, Peter and William Russell Ellis Jr., eds. *Race, Change And Urban Society*. Beverly Hills: Sage, 1971.
  Predominantly involved with ethnic and not urban issues.

(4)

Hahn, Harlan, ed. *People And Politics In Urban Society*. Beverly Hills: Sage, 1972.

(3)

Masotti, Louis H. and Jeffrey K. Hadden, eds. *The Urbanization Of The Suburbs*. Beverly Hills: Sage, 1973.
  A superb collection of articles on the origins, social processes, government, economics, problems and prospects of suburbia. Scholarly selections, with fresh perspectives on the character of suburbs. Interesting reading.

HB (2)

Wager, W. Warren. *Building The City Of Man*. New York: Grossman, 1971.
  Not urban studies.

(4)

Webber, Melvin M. et. al. *Explorations Into Urban Structures*. Philadelphia: University of Pennsylvania Press, 1964.

(3)

Addenda

Wilson, James Q. ed. *The Metropolitan Enigma: Inquirier Into The Nature And Dimensions Of America's "Urban Crisis."* Rev. Ed. Cambridge: Harvard University Press, 1968.

(3)

Wright, W. D. C. and D. H. Stewart. *The Exploding City.* Edinburgh at the University Press, 1972.

(3)

3.2 REGIONAL PLANNING

Chisholm, Michael, et. al., eds. *Regional Forecasting.* Hamden (Conn.): Archon Books, 1970. Volume XXII of the Colston Papers of the Colston Research Society (GB).

(3)

Friedmann, John. *Urbanization, Planning And National Development.* Beverly Hills: Sage, 1973.
   Updating information and perspectives presented in an earlier work (*Regional Development And Planning.* Cambridge: M. I. T. Press, 1964), the author elaborates on the theory and practice of regional urban development in this sophisticated study of the urban regional structure worldwide. Specific emphasis is placed upon urban development in Chile and Venezuela, or upon theoretical aspects of the study. A useful reference for the serious researcher.

HB (2/3)

Gertler, L. O. *Regional Planning In Canada: A Planner's Testament.* Montreal: Harvest House, 1972.
   A current assessment of the state of urban and regional planning in Canada.

(3)

Hall, Peter, et. al. *The Containment Of Urban England.* Volume One. *Urban and Metropolitan Growth Processes, Or Megalopolis Denied.* London: George Allen and Unwin, and Beverly Hills: Sage, 1973.

Hall, Peter, et. al. *The Containment Of Urban England.* Volume Two. *The Planning System: Objectives, Operations, Impacts.* London: George Allen and Unwin, and Beverly Hills: Sage, 1973.
   This massive, two volume work encompasses the totality of urban growth in England. This set is the definitive study of urban growth and its planning in Great Britain.

Urban And Metropolitan Growth Processes includes studies of urban growth from 1801-1939, the beginnings of planning, and analysis of the philosophical base for the urban planning legislation that followed World War II.

Addenda

The major portion of this volume analyzes the development of metropolis and megalopolis, with chapters on the anatomy of metropolitan England, megalopolitan growth dynamics, and case studies on growth patterns in 5 urban areas. The last chapter assesses the problems and successes of planning during the last quarter century in comparison with previous eras of planning legislation and urban growth.

The Planning System delves into an entirely different series of conditions. This parallel volume examines the 1947 planning system, the role of planners, the impacts of residential mobility, the role of developers, land values and their impact on urban growth, housing trends, and new towns.

The last section of this volume arrives at a conclusion regarding the effectiveness of the total planning process. The last chapter outlines a number of policy alternatives to the various problems and processes that make up the totality of urban growth dynamics.

This work is the result of the work by a project team. The contributors are members of this team, and as such the various segments are the coalescence of a group process. The results are intriguing.

An essential reference, both for the data contained and for the process used and illustrated by the content.

HB (2)

Pass, David. *Vallingby And Farsta: From Idea To Reality*. Cambridge: The M. I. T. Press, 1973. First published in Sweden in 1969.

(3)

3.21 URBANIZATION IN ASIA, AFRICA, AND LATIN AMERICA

Fathy, Hassan. *The Arab House In The Urban Setting. Past, Present And The Future*. London: Longman for the University of Essex, 1970.

(3)

Field, Arthur J., ed. *City And Country In The Third World: Issues In The Modernization Of Latin America*. Cambridge: Schenkman, 1970.

(3)

Gulick, John. *Tripoli: A Modern Arab City*. Cambridge: Harvard University Press, 1967.

Although prepared over a decade ago, this work has a freshness which recommends its use. Dealing with a wide spectrum of urban functions, *Tripoli* provides the reader with an in-depth analysis that gives life to the city, providing a balance of facts and interpretations. A highly readable book.

HB (2)

Addenda

Jakobson, Leo and Ved Prakesh, eds. *Urbanization And National Development*. Beverly Hills: Sage, 1971. Volume One of *South And Southeast Asia Urban Affairs Annuals*.
    A highly sophisticated and useful reference containing current data.
(3)

Johnson, E. A. J. *The Organization Of Space In Developing Countries*. Cambridge: Harvard University Press, 1970.
(3)

Rabinovitz, Francine F. and Felicity M. Trueblood, eds. *Latin American Urban Research*. 2 volumes. Beverly Hills: Sage, 1971 (volume 1) and 1972 (volume 2).
    Considerable amounts of up-to-date material is to be found in these volumes. Although detailed and scholarly in orientation, this pair is one of the most useful references available on Latin American urbanization.
HB (2)

Scobie, James R. *Argentina: A City And A Nation*. 2nd ed. New York: Oxford University Press, 1971.
    A general history of Argentina. Not an urban history.
(4)

3.3 URBAN SPRAWL AND SUBURBIA

Goldston, Robert. *Suburbia: Civic Denial*. New York: Macmillan, 1970.
    An angry work, this book penetrates the vastness of suburbia and finds a wasteland. Assuming megalopolitan expansion to be doomed, the author sees the present suburban form as incompatible with human life. With this viewpoint, a piercing analysis of suburban life (predominantly in the Boston-Washington megalopolis) is unfolded. Illustrated, this work is presented in a style which compels reading from start to finish.
HB (2)

Masotti, Louis H. and Jeffrey K. Hadden, eds. *The Urbanization Of The Suburbs*. (See 3.1)

3.4 MAJOR METROPOLITAN AREAS

Abbott, Berenice. *New York In The Thirties*. New York: Dover, 1973. A reissue of a 1939 work which was then titled *Changing New York*. Text by Elizabeth McCausland.
    The core of this book is the collection of 97 photos which illustrate this city in another age. More than nostalgia, this work gives life to the urban condition of another epoch. An incredible range of rich images.
PB (2)

Addenda

Baine, Richard P. *Calgary: An Urban Study*. Toronto: Clarke, Irwin and Co., 1973.
    Similar to other titles in the Clarke Irwin Urban Studies Series (*Toronto* and *Sydney, Nova Scotia*, reviewed in 3.4), this work is a compilation of a wide range of data on the history, functions, land use, population, and current status of Calgary. Profusely illustrated with maps, charts, graphs, and photos, this work is of immeasurable value in providing the data needed to understand the structure and state of this city. A highly useful book.

PB (1)

Cooper, John Irwin. *Montreal: A Brief History*. Montreal: McGill-Queens University Press, 1969.
    A poor format, difficult to use.

Donnison, David, <u>et. al</u>., eds. *London: Urban Patterns, Problems, And Policies*. (See 6.2)

Evenson, Norma. *Two Brazilian Capitals: Architecture And Urbanism In Rio de Janeiro And Brazilia*. New Haven: Yale University Press, 1973.
    The text of this work delves heavily into the details of urban development in these two cities. The level of complexity reached limits the usefulness of this work for all but the most intensive research. What does make this work of immense value for general use are the 240 photos, maps and diagrams. These alone make this book an essential reference. The visuals provide clear images of these cities of stunning architectural innovation and abject squalor. An even split is made in presenting views of Rio de Janeiro and Brazilia.

HB (2)

Fried Robert C. *Planning The Eternal City: Roman Politics And Planning Since World War II*. New Haven: Yale University Press, 1973.

(3)

Frisch, Michael H. *Town Into City: Springfield, Massachusetts, And The Meaning Of Community, 1840-1880*. Cambridge: Harvard University Press, 1972.
    Too detailed and specialized a study for general use.

(3)

Glazebrook, G. P. de T. *The Story Of Toronto*. Toronto: University of Toronto Press, 1971.
    In his inimitable style, Professor Glazebrook renders the history of Toronto into a presentation which is both readable and exhaustively complete. A useful supplemental reference with distinctive perspectives.

HB (2)

Goldston, Robert. *London: The Civic Spirit*. New York: Macmillan, 1969.
    Similar in format to the other Goldston book in this section (*New York:*

Addenda

Civic Exploitation), this illustrated work leads the reader through the city, providing images and scenes that give the city life. A dismal picture is portrayed, of a city at a crossroads, and seemingly headed toward oblivion. An interesting and unique reading of this city.

HB (2)

Laredo, Victor, with captions by Thomas Reilly. *New York City: A Photographic Portrait*. New York: Dover, 1973. (This collection of photographs first appeared in 1964 under the title *New York People And Places*, New York: Reinhold.)

The author-photographer has captured much of the essence of a New York of the early 1960s. The strength of this work is in its examination of the changing cityscape and the people of New York. An intriguing study.

PB (2)

Powell, Allen, ed. *The City: Attacking Modern Myths*. Toronto: McClelland and Stewart, 1972.

Based upon seminars and discussions held in 1970-71, this work includes essays on a wide range of urban problems, their causes, and the major participants. Unfortunately, the content is limited to detailed study of the Toronto region.

PB (2)

Price, John A. *Tijuana: Urbanization In A Border Culture*. (See 6.21)

Price, Ray. *Yellowknife*. Toronto: Peter Martin, 1967.

An interesting little history of this northern settlement. Not urban oriented.

(4)

Spelt, Jacob. *Toronto*. Don Mills: Collier-Macmillan, 1973.

Of the several works reviewed to date that deal with the Toronto region, this work provides the greatest depth. Limited to use as a reference by its level of reading, this work encompasses the city and distills an image supported with substantial detail. The balanced coverage given to the historical city, the city's current economic and political structure, and to Toronto's habitability result in a well rounded work which provides the reader with a text which is informative and readable.

PB (2)

The Blue Guides. London: Ernest Benn, and Chicago: Rand McNally, various dates.

Athens And Environs   new edition in prep.
London   10th ed.   (1973)   HB/PB
Paris   3rd ed.   (1968)   HB
Rome And Environs   1st ed.   (1971)   HB/PB

These tourist guides are the most complete reviewed to date. Good maps are included.

HB/PB (2)

Addenda

Whalen, Richard J. *A City Destroying Itself: An Angry View Of New York*. New York: William Morrow, 1965.
    An interesting book in light of what has happened to New York since 1960.

PB (2)

Wurman, Richard Saul and John Andrew Gallery. *Man Made Philadelphia: A Guide To Its Physical And Cultural Environment*. Cambridge: The M. I. T. Press, 1972.
    This work is a guide to Philadelphia's urban environment; a guide as to how one sees and experiences the city. This intriguing balance of photos, maps, text and imagery provides the reader with a comprehensive perception of the city. Historical and current data is included. Of definite value for reference or general reading.

HB/PB (1)

3.41 URBAN CITY CENTRES (NEW HEADING)

From the main body of this edition, the following titles contribute to an understanding of the urban core. While titles found elsewhere in the bibliography may well include comment on the urban center, these works are predominantly centered on this area.

    Lynch, Kevin. *The Image Of The City*. p.5.
    Liston, Robert A. *Downtown*. p.37.
    Tyrwhitt, J., ed. *The Heart Of The City*. p.42.
    New York City Planning Commission. *Plan For New York City: Manhattan*. p.57.
    Regional Plan Association. *Urban Design Manhattan*. p.58.
    University of Amsterdam. Sociographical Department. *Urban Core And Inner City*. p.59.

Gruen, Victor. *Centers For The Urban Environment: Survival Of The Cities*. New York: Van Nostrand-Reinhold, 1973.
    This work is ostensibly a study of shopping centers, but it goes far beyond this to examine, in considerable depth, the multi-functional center. A good number of case studies are provided to lend example and illustration to the concepts discussed.

This far ranging reference examines the dynamics of attraction to regional or metropolitan centers, with definite preference given to the multi-functional center. Since most of these occur as part of a changing urban core, this work is of significance in the examination of what the downtown area can be. Well illustrated, the book provides a balanced view of alternative possibilities in what the author labels "the emerging new urban pattern."

HB (2)

Addenda

Murphy, Raymond E. *The Central Business District*. Chicago: Aldine-Atherton, 1972.
    Also published by Longman in Great Britain. Material in this book is predominantly a decade or two out of date. Most of the content is available in the other works listed in this section.

(4)

3.5 URBAN FUTURES

Calder, Ritchie. *How Long Have We Got?* Montreal: McGill-Queen's University Press, 1972.
    Not urban oriented.

(4)

Bell, Daniel. *The Coming Of Post-Industrial Society: A Venture In Social Forecasting*. New York: Basic Books, 1973.

(3)

Burns, Jim. *Arthropods: New Design Futures*. New York: Praeger, 1972.
    A collection of artistic expressions on today and tomorrow. Unfortunately, there is too little that is concrete and usable.

Dahinden, Justus. *Urban Structures For The Future*. Translated by Gerald Onn. New York: Praeger, 1972.
    This profusely illustrated work is the most comprehensive compilation of futuristic urban design in print. The author examines various aspects of the current urban scene with visual glimpses of the past and a diverse range of future options. Leaning toward various design alternatives, this book is a massive source of urban alternatives on personal through megalopolitan scales. An essential reference for the study of the future of cities.

HB (2)

Esfandiary, F. M. *Up-Wingers: A Futurist Manifesto*. New York: John Day, 1973.

This work is a highly personal exhortation on the prospects for the future. *Up-Wingers* is what it claims, a manifesto for confirmed futurists.

Esfandiary's earlier work, *Optimist One*, is mild in comparison to this critique of the present and proposal for the future.

Either of these works is essential reading for anyone wishing to have a balanced perspective on what the future could be.

PB/HB (2)

Gabor, Dennis. *The Mature Society*. London: Secker and Warburg and New York: Praeger, 1972.
    A personal essay.

(4)

Addenda

Harrison, Harry and Theodore J. Gordon, eds. *Ahead Of Time*. Garden City: Doubleday, 1972.

(3)

Jackson, John N. *The Urban Future: A Choice Between Alternatives*. London: George Allen and Unwin, 1972.

(3)

Maddox, John. *The Doomsday Syndrome*. New York: McGraw-Hill, 1972.
    This work was written as a complaint against superficial, alarmist projections of "future prophecies of calamity." The author uses superficial, alarmist evaluations to refute the arguments of those he opposes. Superior works exist on the future.

(4)

Mass, Nathaniel J., ed. *Readings In Urban Dynamics*. (See 3.1)

McHale, John. *World Facts And Trends*. 2nd ed. (See 11.2)

McReynolds, David. *We Have Been Invaded By The 21st Century*. New York: Praeger, 1970.
    A hodge-podge on today and not tomorrow. More suitable reference material has been noted.

(4)

Negroponte, Nicholas. *The Architectural Machine: Towards A More Human Environment*. Cambridge: The M. I. T. Press, 1970.
    A general discussion of machines assisting architectural design now in use or likely in the near future, this work includes comment and illustrations of not only techology but also potential impacts on man. The effect of man-machine interaction is dealt with exhaustively and interestingly. A useful reference.

HB/PB (2)

Peccei, Aurelio. *The Chasm Ahead*. New York: Macmillan, 1969.

(3)

Phillips, Bernard S. *World Of The Future: Exercises In The Sociological Imagination*. Columbus: Charles E. Merrill, 1972.

(3)

Richards, Fred and A. C. Richards. *Homonovus: The New Man*. Boulder (Colo.): Shields Publishing Co., 1973.
    Too esoteric for general use.

(4)

Theobald, Robert. *Futures Conditional*. Indianapolis: Bobbs-Merrill, 1972.
    A wide ranging book which presents more than 60 vignettes selected to

Addenda

help the reader perceive the future. Taking the stance that our future must be preconditioned and preset (planned for), the author has chosen from writers of science fiction, newspaper journalists, social scientists, futurists, and others to present humorous and glum glimpses of the future. An unusual book which is interesting and informative.

HB (2)

Toffler, Alvin, ed. *The Futurists*. New York: Random House, 1972.
    Essays by prominent futurists.

(3)

Urban, G. R., ed. *Can We Survive Our Future: A Symposium*. London: The Bodley Head, and New York: St. Martin's Press, 1972.

(3)

Vermilye, Dyckman, ed. *The Future In The Making: Current Issues In Higher Education*. San Francisco: Jossey-Bass, 1973.
    No urban content.

(4)

3.71 URBAN MODELS

Berry, Brian J. L., ed., with the assistance of Katherine B. Smith. *City Classification Handbook: Methods and Applications*. New York: Wiley-Interscience, 1972.
    Unnecessarily obtuse, even for research.

(4)

3.8 URBAN RENEWAL AND RENOVATION

Doxiadis, C. A. *Urban Renewal And The Future Of The American City*. Chicago: Public Administration Service, 1966. Available from the American Society of Planning Officials.
    This work surveys the experience of urban renewal in the U.S. from its beginnings in the mid 1960s. A good number of Mr. Doxiadis' unique graphics are included to illustrate the concepts discussed. The author blends the U.S. experience with suggestions based upon his science of Ekistics. The present and future prospects for the U.S. are dealt with in relationship to current trends and future alternatives worldwide. An essential reference of use both for its text and the graphics.

PB (2)

Fraser, Graham. *Fighting Back: Urban Renewal In Trefann Court*. Toronto: Hakkert, 1972.
    This reference work is a political history of urban renewal in Trefann Court (Toronto). Written by a journalist, it is essentially a case study which uses narrative and dialogue to give life to the problems which faced the residents of this area slated for demolition. This presentation of

Addenda

their struggle to retain their homes, and their ultimate victory, is both highly readable and exhaustively complete in its documentation. A worthwhile, interesting book.

HB/PB (2)

Jones, M. A. *Housing And Poverty In Australia*. Carleton (Victoria): Melbourne University Press, 1972.
This scholarly work is of value for anyone seeking comparative data. The Australian approach to housing, slum clearance, development, subsidies, and the myriad other aspects of state policy, is unique and of interest when compared to national policies in the U.S., Great Britain, and Canada. Heavy going, this work is well documented and is of value primarily to the serious researcher.

HB (2)

Kaplan, Harold. *Urban Renewal Politics: Slum Clearance In Newark*. New York: Columbia University Press, 1963.
Dated.

(4)

Kennet, Wayland. *Preservation*. London: Temple Smith, 1972.

(3)

Lipsky, Michael. *Protest In City Politics: Rent Strikes, Housing And The Power Of The Poor*. Chicago: Rand McNally, 1970.
A heavy work which delves into the rent strike movement in New York City. The process of protest is documented, with objective and documented analysis of the housing conditions which led to the problems, the direct causes and results. The resultant conclusions of both cause and effect are applicable to pressures found in large metropolitan areas of Canada and the United States. A useful reference.

HB/PB (2)

Turner, John F. C. and Robert Fichter, eds. *Freedom To Build: Dweller Control Of The Housing Process*. New York: Macmillan, 1972.
This work examines the state of housing worldwide. Taking a particular stance, the authors build a case for the idea that dweller control will mean cheaper and better homes than those built under government or corporate programs. The contributors are experienced in the housing field either in the U.S. or the rest of the world. Although long and detailed, this book provides the reader with considerable data, sufficient to allow for some far reaching conclusions. Good.

HB/PB (2)

4.1 GENERAL WORKS ON PLANNING II: CITIES AS ARCHITECTURE

Bacon, Edmund N. *Design Of Cities*. Revised Ed., see 1.1.

Addenda

Boudon, Philippe. *Lived In Architecture: Le Corbusier's Pessac Revisited.* Cambridge: The M. I. T. Press, and London: Lund Humphries, 1972.
    A translated edition of a work first published in 1969 by Dunod (Paris). Obtuse.
(4)

Conrad, Ulrich and Hans G. Sperlich. *The Architecture Of Fantasy: Utopian Building And Planning In Modern Times.* New York: Praeger, 1962.
    Translated, edited and expanded by C.C. Collins and G.R. Collins. Too esoteric for all but the most specialized research.
(3)

Cook, Peter, et. al., eds. *Archigram.* London: Studio Vista, 1972.
    This work is a collection of images of the future. Illustrating several dozen innovative technological architectural concepts, *Archigram* provides intriguing glimpses of moving cities, "plug-in" cities, modular homes, capsule housing units, living pods, portable and other adaptable living units. A useful reference.
HB (2)

Negroponte, Nicholas. *The Architectural Machine: Towards A More Human Environment.* (See 3.5)

Nuttgens, Patrick. *The Landscape Of Ideas.* London: Faber and Faber, 1972.
(3)

Prak, Niels Luning. *The Language Of Cities: A Contribution To Architectural Theory.* The Hague: Mouton, 1968.
(3)

4.2 HISTORICAL ARCHITECTURE

Geddes, Patrick. *City Development: A Study Of Parks, Gardens, And Cultural Institutes.* New Brunswick: Rutgers University Press, 1973.
    A facsimile of the original 1904 report to the Carnegie Dunfermline Trust.
(3)

Hitchcock, Henry Russell, et. al. *The Rise Of American Architecture.* New York: Praeger, 1970.

Palladio, Andrea. *The Four Books Of Architecture.* New York: Dover, 1965.
    First published in 1570, this edition is an unabridged and unaltered republication of an English edition published in 1738.
(3)

Addenda

Shvidkovsky, O. A., ed. *Building In The USSR, 1917-1932*. London: Studio Vista, 1971.

(3)

4.3 ARCHITECTS OF THE CITY

Brett, Lionel. *Architecture In A Crowded World: Vision And Reality In Planning*. New York: Schocken Books, 1971, and under the title *Parameters And Images*, London: Weidenfeld and Nicholson, 1970.

(3)

Halprin, Lawrence. *Notebooks: 1959-1971*. Cambridge: The M. I. T. Press, 1972.
Too personal and esoteric for all but the most specialized use.

(4)

n.a. *The Architecture Of Paul Rudolph*. New York: Praeger, 1970.
A collection of photos and drawings illustrating this architect's projects. Supplemented with an introduction by Sibyl Moholy-Nagy and comments by Paul Rudolph, this work is of interest for its superb visuals on new town concepts and megastructure design. Lavish illustrations add to the value of this reference.

HB (2)

4.4 HOUSING

Lang, Jon, et. al., eds. *Designing For Human Behavior: Architecture And The Behavioral Sciences*. (See 6.3)

4.5 VERNACULAR ARCHITECTURE

Rapoport, Amos. *House Form And Culture*. Englewood Cliffs: Prentice-Hall, 1969.
This work is a comprehensive review of vernacular architecture throughout the world. Data is presented on the elements which affect housing style and form (materials, construction, and technology). Considerable textual and visual detail is given in providing a well balanced analysis of social and cultural consideration which affect house design and settlement patterns. The author presents information on universal constants in house design as well as the detail for specific cultures. A unique reference for this subject.

PB (2)

4.6 URBAN DESIGN

Pundt, Hermann G. *Schinkel's Berlin: A Study Of Environmental Planning*.

Addenda

Cambridge: Harvard University Press, 1972.
An intriguing work, but far too esoteric for any use but that of detailed academic reference.

(3)

5.1 GENERAL WORKS (URBAN TRANSPORTATION)

Creighton, Roger L. *Urban Transportation Planning*. Urbana: University of Illinois Press, 1970.

(3)

Schreiner, John. *Transportation: The Evolution Of Canada's Networks*. Toronto: McGraw-Hill Ryerson, 1972.
Insufficient urban studies content.

(4)

5.2 SPECIFIC STUDIES IN URBAN TRANSPORTATION

Currie, A. W. *Canadian Transportation Economics*. Toronto: University of Toronto Press, 1967.
Insufficient urban studies content.

(4)

Hebert, Richard. *Highways To Nowhere: The Politics Of City Transportation*. Indianapolis: The Bobbs-Merris Co., 1972.
Diagnosing the condition of urban transportation in five U.S. cities, the author presents a highly personalized accounting of successes and failures. The text is close set, unbroken by visuals, but its style is both penetrating and interesting. Sufficiently massive to limit this work to reference use only.

HB (2)

Robinson, John. *Highways And Our Environment*. New York: McGraw-Hill, 1971.
Written by a conservationist, this book exudes a distinct anti-automobile bias. Even with this one-sided analysis, it is both unique and essential reading.

With the use of concise text and a well balanced selection of photos, the author examines the history of roads and transportation in the U.S., the interstate and urban freeway, the city street, and the myriad human environmental effects of our present automobile oriented culture. Interesting perspectives are presented on the effects of suburbia on life styles and the results of visual and other road network blight. Good and bad examples of freeway design are presented in this useful reference item.

HB (2)

Addenda

6.1 GENERAL WORKS (THE CITY AS A HUMAN PROCESS)

Lenz-Romeiss, Felizitas. *The City: New Town Or Home Town*. New York: Praeger, 1973.
    Unnecessarily obtuse.

(4)

Weinberg, S. Kirson. *Social Problems In Modern Urban Society*. Second Edition. Englewood Cliffs: Prentice-Hall, 1970.
    A study of race relations, poverty, youth, the elderly, and deviant behavior. Although set in an urban context, this work provides little perspective on the "urbane" aspects of these problems. Insufficient urban orientation.

(4)

6.2 SPECIFIC STUDIES ON URBAN MAN

Brody, Eugene B., ed. *Behavior In New Environments: Adaptation of Migrant Populations*. Beverly Hills: Sage, 1970.
    This highly esoteric work contains several essays of particular value in the study of rural-urban migration in North and South America. Included are case studies dealing with American Appalachia, Mexican Americans in Texas, New York City, Santiago (Chile), and several detailed studies on the process of adaptation.

Although highly sophisticated, this book does have several chapters that contain information worthy of being extracted. This reference is of value for the serious researcher into the processes of rural-urban migration.

HB (2/3)

Donnison, David, et. al., eds. *London: Urban Patterns, Problems And Politics*. Beverly Hills: Sage, 1973.
    This volume explores a number of social characteristics of London in the late 1960s and early 1970s. Included in this sophisticated selection are studies of social planning, employment trends, social polarization, slum conditions and problems, urban stresses on man, local politics, and the current feel of the city.

Although detailed and sophisticated, this work is of particular value for research.

HB (2)

Eden, Lynn. *Crisis In Watertown: The Polarization Of An American Community*. Ann Arbor: University of Michigan Press, 1972.
    This narrative study examines the tensions of conflict brought about by the current social state in the U.S. Urban content is extraneous.

(4)

Addenda

Gale, Fay. *Urban Aborigines*. Canberra: Australian National University Press, 1972.
    Although a scholarly work, this book bears mention as a useful general reference. Considerable detail is presented on the urban situation of aborigines in Australia, of a people coming from a stone age culture into the 20th Century in one step. A unique reference.
    HB (2)

Jones, F. Lancaster. *Dimensions Of Urban Social Structure: The Social Areas Of Melbourne, Australia*. Toronto: University of Toronto Press, 1973.
    (3)

Lynd, Robert S. and Helen Merrell Lynd. *Middletown: A Study In Modern American Culture*. New York: Harcourt, Brace and World, 1929, and by the same authors, *Middletown In Transition: A Study In Cultural Conflicts*. New York: Harcourt, Brace and World, 1937.
    Reprints of the earlier editions, these works stand as basic studies of the American community which include detailed study of work, leisure, family life, education, religion, and community activity in the 1920s and 1930s. *Middletown In Transition* is a sequel to the earlier work, examining the same community after eight years of depression and New Deal reforms. Both of these works are gems. Besides being basic studies in urban sociology and urban anthropology, they are intriguing examinations of a community frozen in time, in a way of life now long past. These two works stand as compelling comparisons to present communities, especially the myths that surround them.
    PB (2)

Radford, Elizabeth. *The New Villagers: Urban Pressure On Rural Areas In Worchestershire*. London: Frank Cass, 1970.
    Too specialized for general use.
    (4)

Shannon, Lyle and Magdaline. *Minority Migrants In The Urban Community: Mexican-American And Negro Adjustment To Industrial Society*. Beverly Hills: Sage Publications, 1973.
    Little urban content is to be found in this study of social conditions among several minorities in the United States.
    (4)

Suttles, Gerald D. *The Social Order Of The Slum: Ethnicity And Territory In The Inner City*. Chicago: University of Chicago Press, 1968.
    A very sophisticated rendering, this work presents detailed data on the human ecology of a community in the U.S., detail which is distilled into a readable form. Topics include institutional and communicative techniques, specific ethnic value systems, and various slum groups, including gangs. An intriguing study, with a general application throughout North America and Europe.
    HB/PB (2)

Addenda

_____. *The Social Construction Of Communities*. Chicago: The University of Chicago Press, 1972.
    This work is a scholarly reaction to the concepts of territory as presented by Ardrey and Morris. Rejecting the assumed aggressive, hostile "parochialism" suggested by the earlier territorialists, the author weaves an interesting accounting of community within a system of differentiation and competition.

HB (2)

6.21 URBAN SOCIETIES IN ASIA, AFRICA, AND LATIN AMERICA

Caldwell, John C. *African Rural-Urban Migration: The Movement To Ghana's Towns*. New York: Columbia University Press, 1969.

(3)

Price, John A. *Tijuana: Urbanization In A Border Culture*. Notre Dame: University of Notre Dame, 1973.
    An interesting study which analyzes this border city in terms of its relationships with the U.S. and the rest of Mexico. Considerable space is given to providing a description of the city and its way of life. Included is extensive analysis of that portion of Tijuana's culture which is vice-ridden and deviant.

HB/PB (2)

Richardson, Miles. *San Pedro, Columbia: Samll Town In A Developing Society*. New York: Holt, Rinehart and Winston, 1970. A title in the series of *Case Studies In Cultural Anthropology*.
    A short college level study of a small community of under 2000 people. Although sophisticated in its approach, this work is interesting as a general reading on the form, function, and life of a small Latin American town.

PB (2)

6.22 URBAN SOCIETY IN THE COMMUNIST WORLD

Simic, Andrei. *The Peasant Urbanites: A Study Of Rural-Urban Mobility In Serbia*. New York: Seminar Press, 1973.
    A study of peasant migration to Belgrade, this anthropological work examines the process of transculturation, adjustment to urban conditions, and the role of rural culture and tradition in the context of the city. A well documented, detailed study that is readable and intriguing.

HB (2)

6.3 SOCIAL PSYCHOLOGY AND ENVIRONMENTAL DESIGN

Gutman, Robert, ed. *People And Buildings* (See 3.1)

Addenda

Lofland, Lyn H. *A World Of Strangers: Order And Action In Urban Public Space*. (See 1.2)

Sommer, Robert. *Design Awareness*. San Francisco: Rinehart Press, 1972.
(3)

6.4 URBAN POLITICAL SYSTEMS

Alford, Robert R. *Bureaucracy And Participation: Political Cultures In Four Wisconsin Cities*. Chicago: Rand McNally, 1969.

Benson, George C. S. *The Politics Of Urbanism: The New Federalism*. Woodbury (N.Y.): Barron's Educational Series, 1972.
  Not suitable for urban studies.
(4)

Cox, Kevin R. *Conflict, Power And Politics In The City: A Geographical View*. New York: McGraw-Hill, 1973.
(3)

Daland, Robert T., ed. *Comparative Urban Research: The Administration And Politics Of Cities*. Beverly Hills: Sage Publications, 1969.
  Incredibly obtuse and unreadable.
(4)

D'Antonio, William V. and William H. Form. *Influentials In Two Border Cities: A Study In Community Decision Making*. n. p.: University of Notre Dame Press, 1965.
  Not influential.
(4)

Davis, Morris and Marvin G. *Metropolitan Decision Processes: An Analysis Of Case Studies*. Chicago: Rand McNally, 1969.
(3)

Elazar, Daniel J. *Cities Of The Prairie: The Metropolitan Frontier And American Politics*. New York: Basic Books, 1970.
  This extensive work investigates the impact of traditional American institutions (frontier migration, sectionalism, and federalism) on 17 midwestern cities. A reference of considerable value and complexity.

Feldman, Lional D. and Michael D. Goldrick. *Politics And Government Of Urban Canada: Selected Readings*. 2nd ed. Toronto: Methuen, 1972.
  Contrary to the usual understanding of a revision, this work either duplicates the 1969 edition or adds articles which predate that edition. Very little new information is actually provided, with some of the remaining sections becoming rapidly dated. This work is still a worthwhile reference, providing data on Canadian urban political processes not found elsewhere in book form.

Addenda

Gordon, Daniel N., ed. *Social Change And Urban Politics*. Englewood Cliffs: Prentice-Hall, 1973.

    A reader with a majority of readings first published before 1963. Most of the current articles deal with the black minority problem in the U.S. rather than urban issues. Superior, and more recent, works do exist.

(4)

Gordon, Diana R. *City Limits: Barriers To Change In Urban Government*. New York: Charterhouse, 1973.

(3)

Griffith, Ernest S. *A History Of American City Government*. Volume One, *The Conspicuous Failure, 1870-1900*, and Volume Two, *The Progressive Years And Their Aftermath, 1900-1920*. New York: Praeger, 1974.

    This two volume set explores the historical development of civic government during a critical fifty year period. This highly readable pair presents the reader with general perspectives on the growth and maturation of American urban political systems, but most important, this picture is balanced with a diverse range of contemporary details which give life and reality to the trends presented as a framework.

Beginning with the emergence of the railroad, and its considerable impact on the city, the first volume delves into the realities of the frontier city and then passes on to a comprehensive study of the growing pains of American cities, as evidenced in the widespread growth of corruption, and the problems of providing public services and facilities in the face of a non-urban climate of opinion. A considerable portion of this volume analyzes the growing patterns of financial and political power within the city and between cities and either the various state governments or the federal government.

The second volume examines the effect of the wave of urban reform which characterized the early 20th Century. This volume adroitly deals with the realities and problems of the city before, during, and just after the First World War. The last chapter outlines unsolved problems that were to rise and plague the city during the 1930s and 40s.

This work is of immeasurable value in that it provides a rare picture of how American cities got to where they are. This pair is recommended for general reading or for reference.

HB (2)

Soon to be published by the author is a work which will tie earlier urban development to the period outlined in this set. *The Foundation Of*

Addenda

Traditions, 1775-1870, will be published shortly.

Published earlier, and now available in reprint from De Capo Press, is *A History Of American City Government: The Colonial Period* (published 1938, reprint 1972).

Hebert, Richard. *Highways To Nowhere: The Politics Of City Transportation.* (See 5.2)

Hahn, Harlan. *Urban-Rural Conflict: The Politics Of Change.* Beverly Hills: Sage Publications, 1971.
    A study of urban and rural forces in Iowa politcs.
(3)

Hoiberg, Otto G. *Exploring The Small Community.* Lincoln: University of Nebraska Press, 1955.
    Limited exclusively to use in small rural communities. Little urban application.
(4)

Kammer, Gladys M., <u>et. al.</u> *The Urban Political Community: Profiles In Town Politics.* Boston: Houghton-Mifflin, 1963.
    Dated.
(4)

Lipsky, Michael. *Protest In City Politics: Rent Strikes, Housing, And The Power Of The Poor.* (See 3.8)

Lorimer, James. *A Citizen's Guide To City Politics.* Toronto: James Lewis and Samuel, 1972.
    Dated.
(4)

Masson, Jack K. and James D. Anderson, eds. *Emerging Party Politics In Urban Canada.* Toronto: McClelland and Stewart, 1972.
   This work examines the beginnings and growth of partisan politics in Canadian cities. Readings are included on historical perspectives, the specific political structure of several Canadian cities, and the prospects for local party politics. Unfortunately, this work has the limitation of so many studies on the politics of urban Canada, namely that the author seems to perceive urban Canada as being only Toronto. This work does extend to other cities, but the preponderance of emphasis and data deals exclusively with Toronto.
PB (2)

Parker, R.S. and P.N. Troy, eds. *The Politics Of Urban Growth.* Canberra: Australian National University Press, 1972.

Addenda

A study of Australian urbanization.

(3)

Power, John, ed. *Politics In A Suburban Community: The N. S. W. State Election In Manly, 1965*. Sydney: Sydney University Press, 1968.
    Too specialized for general use.

(3)

PRAEGER SPECIAL STUDIES IN INTERNATIONAL POLITICS AND GOVERNMENT (Cont.)

Cannon, Mark W., <u>et</u>. <u>al</u>. *Urban Government For Valencia, Venezuela*. 1973.

Richardson, Ivan L. *Urban Government For Rio De Janeiro*. 1973.

PRAEGER SPECIAL STUDIES IN U.S. ECONOMIC, SOCIAL AND POLITICAL ISSUES

Hirsch, Werner Z. and Sidney Sononblum, eds. *Governing Urban America In The 1970s*. New York: Praeger, 1973.

(3)

PRAEGER SPECIAL STUDIES IN U.S. ECONOMIC AND SOCIAL DEVELOPMENT

Hirsch, Werner Z., ed. *Los Angeles: Viability And Prospects For Metropolitan Leadership*. New York: Praeger, 1971.

(3)

Rogers, David. *110 Livingston Street: Politics And Bureaucracy In The New York City School System*. New York: Vintage, 1969.
    Insufficient urban studies content.

(4)

Sewell, John. *Up Against City Hall*. Toronto: James Lewis and Samuel, 1972.
    John Sewell was first elected as a Toronto alderman in 1969, following three years of work with Trefann Court residents (see *Fighting Back*, 3.8). His challenge of the pro-development majority then on council is related in this personal account of the "realities" of metropolitan politics. Stimulating reading.

HB/PB (1)

Stedman, Murray S., Jr. *Urban Politics*. Cambridge (Mass.): Winthrop Publishers, 1972.

(3)

Stein, David Lewis. *Toronto For Sale: The Destruction Of A City*. Toronto: New Press, 1972.
    Too detailed for general use and becoming dated.

(4)

Addenda

Warren, Roland L. *The Community In America*. 2nd ed. Chicago: Rand McNally, 1973.
    A college level textbook.
(3)

6.5 URBAN LAW

Babcock, Richard F. *The Zoning Game: Municipal Practices And Politics*. Madison: The University of Wisconsin Press, 1966.
    This concise work not only analyzes the practitioners of zoning but also delves into the purpose and principles of zoning. Well written, this book comments on the practice of zoning in terms of mystique and reality. *The Zoning Game* is a comprehensive and readable treatise. Highly recommended.
PB (2)

6.6 URBAN ECONOMICS

Bryant, R. W. G. *Land: Private Property/Public Control*. Montreal: Harvest House, 1972.
(3)

First National City Bank, Economics Department. *Profile Of A City*. New York: McGraw-Hill, 1972.
    Written by practicing economists, this hard headed, realistic, and refreshingly readable economic assessment of an American city is essential reading for the generalist or specialist. The realities of urban life are examined, not just for New York City, the focus of the study, but for any American city. The full range of economic oriented urban problems are delved into, using an approach which is precise, clean and understandable. Illustrated with several dozen well chosen photographs and easily understood graphs.
HB (2)

Ginzberg, Eli. *New York Is Very Much Alive: A Manpower View*. New York: McGraw-Hill, 1973.
    Insufficient urban studies content.
(4)

Haring, Joseph E., ed. *Urban And Regional Economics: Perspectives For Public Action*. New York: Houghton-Mifflin, 1972.
    This collection of readings deals with poverty, housing, transportation, public services, crime, urban financing and regional coordination. A refreshing array of essays which are highly readable, up-to-date, and informative.
PB (2)

Addenda

Hartwick, John M. and Ronald W. Crowley. *Urban Economic Growth: The Canadian Case*. Ottawa: Information Canada, 1972.

(3)

Hirsch, Werner Z. *Urban Economic Analysis*. New York: McGraw-Hill, 1973.
   This complex book is a useful reference for general use. Although it is highly sophisticated, it is one of the most readable urban economic texts yet reviewed. A wide range of topics are dealt with, including the economics of urbanization, the economics of services and urban finance, and urban micro-macro economics. Little statistical analysis is included. In its place is a concise survey of recent theoretical and empirical findings in this rapidly expanding field. Each chapter is complete and self contained. Of definite use for the generalist.

HB (2)

Schreiber, Arthur F., et. al., eds. *Economics Of Urban Problems: Selected Readings*. Boston: Houghton Mifflin, 1971.
   These supportive readings share a similar level of sophistication with the work above. They are also current and decidedly usable.

PB (2)

Schreiber, Arthur F., Paul K. Gatons and Richard B. Clemmer. *Economics Of Urban Problems: An Introduction*. Boston: Houghton-Mifflin, 1971.
   This text studies the conditions of urban growth in the United States in terms of its economic impacts and determinants. Detailed examination is made of urban poverty, housing, transportation, pollution, and crime. The work also includes a summary statement regarding the future trends and potential solutions to the various conditions and problems outlined.

The book is problem oriented, and as such it presents and identifies areas of agreement and controversy. In doing so, the authors also provide the reader with a comprehensive image of these problems in terms of their economic impacts and restraints.

This work is one of the few urban economic texts that are generally readable and current. Although presented in a sophisticated style and format, it is recommended for general reference use.

PB (2)

7.1 URBAN GEOGRAPHY (THE MORPHOLOGY OF THE CITY)

Bourne, L. S., et. al., eds. *The Form Of Cities In Central Canada: Selected Papers*. Research Publication No. 11, Department of Geography, University of Toronto. Toronto: University of Toronto Press, 1973.

(3)

Bourne, L. S. and R. D. MacKinnon, eds. *Urban Systems Development In Central Canada: Selected Readings*. Research Publication No. 9, Department of

Addenda

        Geography, University of Toronto. Toronto: University of Toronto Press, 1972.

Briggs, K. *Introducing Towns And Cities*. London: University of London Press Ltd., 1974.
    This school laboratory type text and workbook relies heavily upon central place theory application. Exercises are also included on town/city classification, patterns of city size, location, and inter-urban dynamics.

    Unfortunately, this exercise format relies too heavily on detailed geographical/statistical model analysis and application. No overall perception permeates through the heavy screen of dry, academic study. Suitability limited to university level, specialized geography classes... if then.

PB (2,4)

Carter, Harold. *The Study Of Urban Geography*. Toronto: Macmillan of Canada, 1973. Also published in London: Edward Arnold, 1972.
    An updated compilation of research and models used in urban analysis in this discipline.

(3)

Johnson, James H. *Urban Geography: An Introductory Analysis*. Second Edition. Oxford: Pergamon, 1972.
    Slightly revised, this edition elaborates on its bibliographical content and adds several short segments which update the work. Illustrations remain unchanged.

PB (2)

Swartz, Robert D., et. al., eds. *Metropolitan America: Geographical Perspectives And Teaching Strategies*. (See 11.2)

7.2 HISTORICAL GEOGRAPHY

Ali, Jamil. *The Determination Of The Coordinates Of Cities: Al Bīrūni's Tahdīd Al-Amākin*. Beirut: University of Beirut, 1967.
    An intriguing title, but unfortunately this work is exclusively a mathematical treatise.

(4)

Lagerberg, C. S. I. J. and G. J. Wilms. *Profile Of A Commerical Town In West-Cameroon*. Tilburg (The Netherlands): Tilburg University Press, 1974.

(3)

Addenda

8.1 GENERAL WORKS ON THE URBAN ENVIRONMENT AND URBAN ECOLOGY

Grava, Sigurd. *Urban Planning Aspects Of Water Pollution Control*. New York: Columbia University Press, 1969.

(3)

Mann, Roy. *Rivers In The City*. (See 3.1)

Rutledge, Albert J. *Anatomy Of A Park: The Essentials Of Recreation Area Planning And Design*. New York: McGraw-Hill, 1971.
    Similar to McHarg's *Design With Nature* in impact and usability, this work is essential reading for the generalist or specialist. Well illustrated, *Anatomy Of A Park* is just that, a well structured, fully illustrated anatomical examination of the components of parks, their detail and overall character. Included in this book is a history of parks in the U.S., people oriented needs (aesthetic and functional), various development plans, discussion of the site design process, and plan evaluation. Many types of parks are illustrated by maps and graphics. The process of clarifying park needs is outlined in simple and complete terms in this essential reference.

HB (1)

Weidner, Charles H. *Water For A City: A History Of New York City's Problem From The Beginning To The Deleware River System*. New Brunswick: Rutgers University Press, 1974.
    This study begins in the 18th Century and ends during World War II. A potentially technical and obtuse topic has been given life and vitality by the author. This work is a summation of historical events and human happenings, and trends of continual growth and expansion, woven together into a presentation which balances historical information with the human elements of an ongoing problem. Intriguing reading.

HB (2)

9.2 HISTORICAL DEMOGRAPHICS

Rosenwaike, Ira. *Population History Of New York City*. Syracuse: Syracuse University Press, 1972.
    A detailed and intriguing work which examines the characteristics of people of New York City from the city's founding through the mid-20th Century. Exhaustively complete and highly readable.

HB (2)

Westoff, Charles F., et. al. *Family Growth In Metropolitan America*. Princeton University Press, 1961.
    Dated.

(4)

Addenda

9.3 TECHNICAL DEMOGRAPHICS

Passonneau, Joseph R. and Richard Saul Wurman. *Urban Atlas: 20 American Cities, A Communication Study Notating Selected Urban Data At A Scale Of 1:48,000.* (See 11.1)

10.1 GENERAL WORKS ON CYBERNETICS AND URBAN SOCIETY

Cook, Peter, et. al., eds. *Archigram.* (See 4.1)

Elsner, Henry, Jr. *The Technocrats: Prophets Of Automation.* Syracuse: Syracuse University Press, 1967.
    This work examines the philosophy, origins, and history of the technocrat movement. The depth and range of technocrat thoughts are bizarre and alien to any of the current political or economic ideologies. This book provides a firm understanding of what these ideas are. A world order based on technocracy would be incredibly different. This work illustrates how different.
                                               HB (2)

Leach, Gerald. *The Biocrats: Implications Of Medical Progress.* Revised ed. Harmondsworth: Penguin, 1972.
                                                    (3)

Theobald, Robert. *Habit And Habitat.* Englewood Cliffs: Prentice-Hall, 1972.
                                                    (3)

11.1 MISCELLANEOUS ILLUSTRATIVE MATERIAL

Buck Brothers' *Panorama Of London, 1749.* London: Sidgewick and Jackson, 1972.
    This facsimile of a 1749 engraving unfolds to more than 10 feet, illustrating the north bank of the Thames from Westminster to Tower Bridge. A superb item. A concise and informative guide is provided.
                                                   HB (1)

Chandler, Tertius and Gerald Fox. *3000 Years Of Urban Growth.* (See 1.3)

Passonneau, Joseph R. and Richard Saul Wurman. *Urban Atlas: 20 American Cities, A Communication Study Notating Urban Data At A Scale Of 1:48,000.* Cambridge: The M. I. T. Press, 1969.
    This oversized, expensive reference includes maps which provide detailed data on the following cities:

       Atlanta   Boston   Chicago (In Two Parts)

Addenda

> Cincinnati   Cleveland   Denver   Detroit (In Tow Parts)
> Houston   Los Angeles (In Two Parts)   Miami
> Milwaukee   Minneapolis-St. Paul   New Orleans
> New York (In Two Parts)   Philadelphia   St. Louis
> San Francisco (In Two Parts)   Seattle   Washington, D.C.

Showers, Victor. *The World Of Figures*. (See 1.3)

Visscher, Hollar and de Witt's *London Before The Fire: A Grand Panorama*.
    London: Sidgewick and Jackson, 1973.
        Similar to the item above. Superb.
                                                                    HB (1)

n.a. *The Grand Panorama Of London From The Thames*. London: Sidgewick and
    Jackson, 1972.
        Similar to the items above, unfolding 12 feet. Highly useful.
                                                                    HB (1)

11.2 COMPENDIA, STATISTICAL MATERIALS

McHale, John. *World Facts And Trends*. 2nd ed. New York: Macmillan (HB) and
    New York: Collier (PB), 1972.
        This work presents short textual passages and a considerable number of charts, maps, and schematics to illustrate a wide range of changes in the biosphere, society, and urban institutions. A vast amount of material on the future has been distilled into highly visible graphic presentations. A reference of immeasurable significance.
                                                               HB/PB (1)

Swartz, Robert D., et. al., eds. *Metropolitan America: Geographical Perspectives And Teaching Strategies*. The 1972 Yearbook of the National Council for Geographical Education. Oak Park (Illinois): NCGE, 1972.
        A collection of readings followed by a section on teaching strategies. This work is superseded by other works available. The readings are lifeless and the teaching strategies overburdened with dry, academic geographica analysis.
                                                                        (4)

Wisniewski, Richard, ed. *Teaching About The City*. Washington: National Council for the Social Studies, 1972. 42nd Yearbook.
        The purpose of this work was to address itself to the immediate realities and problems facing humans in the city. Too much emphasis is given to ethnic problems, neglecting the city and its condition.

Addenda

13.2 RELATED LITERATURE IN SCIENCE FICTION

Brunner, John. *The Squares Of The City*. New York: Ballantine, 1965; *Stand On Zanzibar*. New York: Ballantine, 1968; *The Sheep Look Up*. New York: Harper and Row, 1972.

The Squares Of The City leads off this trio of sombre views of the immediate future with the telling of the collapse of a city. Although not central to the plot, the delicate fabric of urban existence is graphically illustrated through the viewing of the last days of a majestic showplace metropolis. With a setting of dissension, conflict and anarchy, the breakdown of urban services, of normal urban growth and dynamism run amok, so the inevitable occurs, a complete societal collapse. This is an engrossing book.

Stand On Zanzibar and *The Sheep Look Up* both deal with a future grim by any standards. Lack of concern and action in the 1970s have had their toll on the late 1980s and early 1990s. A continuing lack of concern and personal greed have not solved problems in this dismal future. In both works, a morass of decay has replaced the positive, creative impetus of today. Apathy and berserk behavior are the norm, a very frightening norm. The value of these works is in their capacity to present a vivid, day by day, human image of a world totally alien to our own current psychological state, but so close, so possible if our technology and will is not channeled to solve our problems. *Stand On Zanzibar* has won acclaim as being one of the most brilliant science fiction novels ever written. It is also one of the best and most realistic protrayals of a potential urban future, and with this, our civilization. *The Sheep Look Up* is of equal poignancy and value.

PB

Harrison, Harry, ed. *The Year 2000: An Anthology*. Garden City: Doubleday, 1970.

A collection of original stories about the quality of life at the turn of the century. Although not oriented to urban conditions, this collection is of interest in viewing 13 different immediate futures.

HB/PB

Mason, Douglas R. *The End Bringers*. New York: Ballantine, 1973.

This superb novel is a portrayal of a world in which man has relinquished all power to robots; robots which in turn have decided that man is redundant. A powerful study of a world remolded into the image of its makers, and how some few humans regain control of their own destinies.

PB

Wylie, Philip. *The End Of The Dream*.

Set in the year 2023, this hard hitting novel portrays a world in collapse between 1970-2010. Holding to an unswerving image of a world collapsing as a result of environmental abuse, a grim picture is painted of the future of man. Although the telling of the world-wide effects of the collapse is spotty for details, the specific vignettes are well done and recommend this work for general use.

13.3 UTOPIAN LITERATURE

Armytage, W. H. G. *Heavens Below: Utopian Experiments In England, 1560-1960.* (1961)

Hertzler, Joyce, Oramel. *The History Of Utopian Thought.* New York: Cooper Square, 1965.
> A reprint of the original 1923 edition. Exhaustively complete.

Manuel, Frank E. *Utopias And Utopian Thought.* (1965)

13.4 RELATED ARTS AND HUMANITIES

Boyle, Thomas and James Merritt, eds. *The Urban Adventurers.* New York: McGraw-Hill, 1972.
> Little urban content in this collection of literary vignettes.
>
> (4)

Jonas, George. *Cities.* Toronto: Anansi, 1974.
> Little urban content.
>
> (4)

Schwarz, Hans. *Painting In Towns And Cities.* London: Studio Vista, and New York: Watson Guptill Publications, 1969 (available in Canada from Collier Macmillan).
> An intriguing little book which illustrates and comments on approaches to painting or drawing city scenes. This work is superb in clearly illustrating how to draw townscapes. Of use, in particular, for the non-artist.
>
> HB (1)

14.1 MAJOR MODULAR SERIES

Justice In Urban America Series. Boston: Houghton-Mifflin, 1969-1970.
> Six modular units of about 80 pages each, with a well structured balance between text and illustrations.

Ranney, George Jr. and Edmon Parker. *Landlord And Tenant.*
> Through the use of short case studies, this brief school text leads

Addenda

the reader through the problems of renting and its controls and abuses. Of use in Canada and the U.S., this work presents a precise overview balanced with sufficient data to enable the user to search out answers to many of the problems of renting in North America. A highly useful introduction.

Zevin, Jack and Richard Groll. *Law And The City*.
Following the same format, this module explores the structure of U.S. city and its legal system. Useful for study of the social and institutional makeup of cities, *Law And The City* looks at new towns, old cities and the controls that regulate the American city.

Other titles in the series with little urban content:

Crime And Justice, Law And The Consumer, Poverty And Welfare and *Youth And The Law*.

SOCIOLOGICAL RESOURCES FOR THE SOCIAL STUDIES

Cities: Where People Live And Why. (1973/58 pp./$9.25 per 10).
This work deals with residential patterns in the U.S., the problems of suburbanization, racial segregation, and population movement in the New York Metropolitan Region.

Although the examples are exclusively American, this module has definite application for the study of residential characteristics in all of North America. The illustrative material is of definite value, as is the entire module.

SOCIOLOGICAL RESOURCES FOR THE SOCIAL STUDIES (ADDITIONAL TITLES REVIEWED)

Family Size And Society. (1972/55 pp./$9.25 per 10).
A study of family growth and its effect on world population growth, this module discusses such topics as the ideal in family size, the social determinants of family size and childbearing, the effect family size has on the quality of life, and the patterns of family size worldwide. A case study is provided on India and its population status. Of use in the study of family size and urbanization.

14.2 MINOR MODULAR SERIES

The Noble And Noble African Studies 14.1 Program. New York: Noble and Noble, 1971. Available in Canada from Clarke, Irwin and Company.

Addenda

Clifford, Mary Louise and Edward S. Ross. *Challenge Of The City: The Urban African*. ($1.45/64 pages)

    The student text is of value for classroom use. Coverage is extensive, with a view of both the Moslem cities of North Africa and the city of sub-Saharan Africa. Although a general overview, an amazing amount of material is crammed into this short work. Illustrated with colour photos, this module provides a comprehensive image of the city in Africa. Of definite value for use in class sets.

A teacher's guide ($1.25/95 pp.) is available. It was prepared for use with the entire series of 11 modules.

A student's manual or activity book is available, but is of little value.

Addenda, Part II

15.1 REPRINTS AND PAMPHLETS

ADVISTORY COMMISSION ON INTERGOVERNMENTAL RELATIONS PUBLICATIONS

      Source: Single copies, ACIR
  CA/US/GB: Multiple copies, Superintendent of Document

       Price: Single or multiple copy, $1.70 (pre-paid in U.S. funds)

        Note: This single document is part of larger series on SUBSTATE REGIONALISM AND THE FEDERAL SYSTEM.

A LOOK TO THE NORTH. (Stock Number 5204-00051)
(1974)

This report includes readable and <u>current</u> assessments of the process of metropolitan government and urban political processes *in Canada*. The chapters on Toronto, Winnipeg and Vancouver are balanced against chapters on provincial patterns of urban growth (Ontario, Quebec, New Brunswick, and British Columbia).

For Canadians, this is the most recent and usable publication available on urban political processes for Canadian cities.

ASSOCIATION OF AMERICAN GEOGRAPHERS PUBLICATIONS

      Source: Can./U.S./G.B. AAG, Commission on College Geography Publications.

       Price: Resource Papers; $1 each (1-9 cop.), lesser cost by volume.
                Technical Papers; $1 each.

Resource Papers

Addenda

Metropolitan Neighborhoods: Participation And Conflict Over Change, Julian Wolpert, et. al. 1972. (51 pp.)
   A detailed study of community organization and change. Although much of this work is too detailed for general use, portions are of value. The introductory section on neighborhood attributes and the specific neighborhood studies are of value for general reference.

The Political Organization Of Space, Edward W. Soja. 1971. (54 pp.)
   This study of territoriality and human ecologies is too sophisticated for general use.

Residential Mobility In The City, Eric Moore. 1972. (50 pp.)
   Too sophisticated for general use.

Social Processes In The City: Race And Urban Residential Choice, Harold M. Rose. 1969. (34 pp.)

Society, The City And The Space-Economy Of Urbanism, David Harvey. 1972. (55 pp.)
   Too sophisticated for general use.

The Spatial Expression Of Urban Growth, Harold M. Mayer. 1969. (57 pp.)
   A highly sophisticated study of use in its examination of the characteristics which define cities, world patterns of urban growth, and most important, the examination of changing patterns of urban growth and expansion. The data provided for emerging urban forms is unique to this paper.

Theories Of Urban Location, Brian J. L. Berry. 1968. (25 pp.)
   Too specialized for general use.

Simulation Of The Urban Environment, Barry M. Kibel. 1972. (126 pp.)
   Too obtuse for general use.

Visual Blight In America. Peirce F. Lewis, et. al. 1973. (48 pp.)
   Four dozen photographs for the three essays and two commentaries are included in this resource book. Using geographical perspectives as a base, the authors extend their view of visual blight to the entire human experience. A highly useful and recommended book.

CENTER FOR URBAN DEVELOPMENT RESEARCH REPRINTS

   Source: Can./U.S./G.B. Center for Urban Development Research, Cornell University.

   Price: As indicated. Article reprints are free to libraries and 50¢ to others.

Addenda

Article Reprints

Architectural Preservation: Europe-French And English Contributions; United States-The Government's Role, Stephen W. Jacobs. 1966. (43 pp.)
    A useful survey of historic and current policies and attitudes toward preservation of historically significant buildings and districts.

Control Of Urban Land Subdivision, John W. Reps and Jerry L. Smith. 1963. (21 pp.)
    Dated.

The Metropolitan Area Concept: An Evaluation Of The 1950 SMA's, Allen G. Feld. 1965. (20 pp.)
    Too specialized for general use. Dated.

Metropolitan Area Mobility: A Comparative Analysis Of Family Spatial Mobility In A Central City And Selected Suburbs, Warren E. Kalbach, et. al. 1964. (5 pp.)
    Dated.

Planning The City Of The Socialist Man, Jack C. Fisher. 1962. (15 pp.)
    Although dated, this reprint has some value in its concise evaluation and illustration of city planning in Eastern Europe.

Requiem For Zoning, John W. Reps. 1964. (12 pp.)

Socialist City Planning: A Reexamination, Zygmunt Pioro, Milos Savic, and Jack C. Fisher. 1965. (12 pp.)
    A useful examination of the city in the communist world.

The Soviet City, B. Michael Frolic. 1964. (25 pp.)
    Although a decade old, this essay is of value in that it provides concise text and illustration on the development of several new towns around Moscow. A useful document.

The Tidewater Colonies: Town Planning In The 17th Century, John W. Reps. 1963. (12 pp.)
    A concise presentation on this topic. Illustrated.

Urban Analysis: A Case Study Of Zagreb, Yugoslavia, Jack C. Fisher. 1963. (17 pp.)
    An interesting and concise history of the development of this intriguing Balkan city. Although the illustrations are not reproduced that precisely, they are still useful. An all around useful essay.

An Urbanization Pattern For The United States: Some Considerations For The Decentralization Of Excellence, Oliver C. Winston. 1967. (9 pp.)
    Too specialized for general use.

Addenda

Variations In Urban Population Structure, George C. Myers. 1964. (7 pp.)
Dated.

Miscellaneous Papers

Soviet Urban And Regional Planning And Administration, Michael Frolic. 1963. (34 pp.)
A bibliography of Western and Soviet sources available in English. Although dated, this item is still of use as an introductory source. $1.50.

Research Reports

Lysander New Town, O. M. Ungers and Tilman Heyde. 1970. (225 pp.)
Too detailed for general use.

Residential Sectors And Urban Expansion, Phillip D. Peters. 1964. (106 pp.)
Too detailed for general use.

A Visual Approach To Regional Planning, Robert L. Mann. 1969. (81 pp.)
This highly visual document graphically presents ways in which a region can be analyzed and understood. A tremendous amount of useful information and perspectives can be extracted from this work. $3.50.

INSTITUTE OF INTERNATIONAL STUDIES PUBLICATIONS

Source: Can./U.S./G.B. Institute of International Studies

Price: As indicated. Payment in advance for monographs. Reprints available as single copies at no cost.

International Population And Urban Research Monographs And Reprints

Monographs: A wide range of detailed monographs are available. Two are of particular note:

World Urbanization 1950-1970
Volume I: *Basic Data For Cities, Countries, And Regions*, Revised ed. Population Monograph Series, No. 4 (1969).
Volume II: *Analysis Of Trends, Relationships, And Development*, Population Monograph Series, No. 9 (1972).
This pair is a veritable goldmine. Although not as up to date as the *1971 UN Demographic Yearbook* (published 1973), the data provided here is exhaustively complete for cities of 100,000 or more.

Although detailed, the text is quite readable and the charts and statistic tables, which make up the majority of the work, are decidedly useful.

Addenda

The second volume provides some updating of data, but goes beyond to give a perspective on the nature of urban growth worldwide.

An essential reference for the generalist and specialist, or for use at any educational level (high school through university). Vol. I: 321 pp. $3.00. Vol. II: 319 pp. $3.00.

Reprints

None reviewed to date.

INSTITUTE OF URBAN AND REGIONAL DEVELOPMENT PUBLICATIONS

Source: Can./U.S./G.B. Institute of Urban and Regional Development.

Price: As indicated for all orders. In the U.S., prepayment or billing. For orders outside the U.S., either from individuals or institutions, for a total of less than $5.00, materials will be sent free of charge. For orders totaling more than $5.00, billing will be allowed.

Note: Of a wide range of working papers, reprints, mongraphs, and reports, the following were selected for review. The balance from information provided, were assumed to be sufficiently complex or technical to limit their use to academic research.

Analysis Of Bart Impacts On Bay Area Land Use, Douglass B. Lee, Jr. 1972. Reprint No. 78.
　　Too technical for general use.

The City As A Mechanism For Sustaining Human Contact, Christopher Alexander. Working Paper No. 50.
　　This paper examines the nature of human contact with cities, including psychological analysis of its effect on individuals and society. A wide ranging, sophisticated, useful document dealing with normal and abnormal contact patterns. (49 pp.) $1.00.

The City Is Dead--Long Live The City, Janet Abu-Lughod. Monograph No. 12.
　　Too sophisticated for general use.

The Development Features Of Great Cities Of Asia, Richard L. Meier.
　I: (1969) Working Paper No. 112.
　II: Japanese, Chinese, And Indian. (1970) Working Paper No. 124.
　III: Housing, Urban Expansion, And Growth Policies. (1970) Working Paper No. 113.
　IV: Physical Expansion, Institution Building, And Political Crisis In Karachi And Bangkok. (1971) Working Paper No. 157.
　　These four papers combined are an incredible resource on the modern Asian city. Part I provides precise details on the means used by Dr.

Addenda

Meier to analyze the cities examined. These simple techniques are of use to anyone. The body of this paper delves into the nature of two Asian cities Bangkok and Seoul.

Part II extends this survey to comment on Tokyo, Hong Kong, Taipei, and six Indian cities.

Part III studies urban housing policies in Seoul, living space in Tokyo, planning for Singapore, Ahmedabad and Tehran, and urbanizing of rural residents in Bangkok.

Part IV singles out two cities for examination, focusing on problems which hinder effective modernization and change.

These four papers are readable and comprehensive; they provide the reader with a distinctive feeling of what these Asian cities are like today. Although listed as being at just the working paper stage, this intriguing four part series is more complete than many texts reviewed. (287 pp.) $5.50.

The Economics Of Urban Size, William Alonso. (1971) Reprint No. 81.
Too technical for general use.

The Environmental Quality Of City Streets: The Resident's Viewpoint, Donald Appleyard and Mark Lintell. (1972) Reprint No. 77.
This short essay is an interesting and informative study of the impact of light and openness, traffic volume, opportunities for interaction, privacy, and territory on residents of a street. A sophisticated, illustrated work with general usefulness. (18 pp.) 25¢.

The House As Symbol Of Self, Clare Cooper. (1971) Working Paper No. 120.
Based upon Jungian concepts of the self, this work examines the psychological effect of the home on man. A useful comparative device which is sophisticated and intriguing. (50 pp.) $1.00.

The Metropolitan Experience, Claude S. Fischer. (1972) Working Paper No. 195.
Examining the social psychological aspects of urban life, this paper includes data on normal and deviant behavior, factors of individual residential choice and associations, the effect of the urban and suburban experience, and individual responses to the urban condition. A vast amount of data in interesting perspectives are contained within this sophisticated study. (72 pp.) $1.50.

Modeling Urban Change, Martin H. Krieger. (1971) Reprint No. 65.
A computer model explanation.

Newark: Community Or Chaos, Leonard J. Duhl and Nancy Jo Steetle. (1969) Reprint No. 52.
Not urban studies.

Addenda

The Performance Of Cities: An Assessment Of Hong Kong And Its Future,
Richard L. Meier. (1970) Working Paper No. 136.
A study of trade and economic competition. Too detailed for general use.

The Post City Age, Melvin M. Webber. (1968) Reprint No. 38.
Too detailed for general use.

The Post-Industrial Family, Martin H. Krieger. (1971) Reprint No. 76.
Not urban studies.

The Question Of City Size And National Policy, William Alonso. (1970) Working Paper No. 125.
Too detailed for general use.

Resident Dissatisfaction In Multi-Family Housing, Clare Cooper, et. al.
(1972) Working Paper No. 160.
This interesting paper investigates the living environment of multi-family housing. Included is comment on negative social status, the character of this type of environment, services and amenities, the usual lack of community, and incidence of crime. A well written, intriguing study. (54 pp.) $1.00.

Resource Conserving Urbanism In South Asia, Richard L. Meier.
IV: *The Development Of Greater Bombay.* (1972) Working Paper No. 154.
V: *Further Explorations Of Potentials For New Bombay.* (1972) Working Paper No. 186.
These papers present detailed information on the city in relationship to Asia and India, urban services and facilities, transportation, communications, housing, and the factors of change. Of definite value. (117 pp.) $2.50.

What Are New Towns For? William Alonso. (1970) Reprint No. 64.
A detailed, sophisticated study of new towns. (18 pp.) 25¢.

LESSON AIDS SERVICE

Canadian Cities: Their Health, Malaise And Promise, D. Cappon 6 pp. $ .15 (2073)

The Case For Optimism. FUTURIST book review. 7 pp. $ .17 (2090)

The History Of Canadian Settlement. N. Pearson 13 pp. $ .33 (2091)

An Overview Of World Trends. L. B. Brown. 14 pp. $ .35 (2099)

Physico-Chemical Control Of The Mind. FUTURIST book review. 10 pp. $ .25 (2087)

Addenda

The Significance Of The City. E. Edinborough. 4 pp. $ .10 (2086)

Urban Renewal. S. H. Pickett. 6 pp. $ .15 (2071)

SCIENTIFIC AMERICAN OFFPRINTS

An Earlier Agricultural Revolution, Wilhelm G. Solheim II, 1972. (9 pp.) (No. 675)

A short essay on a recent discovery of agricultural communities in Southeast Asia which predate the beginnings of communal life in the Middle East by some 5000 years. This well illustrated article is of definite value for the urban historian.

Communication, John R. Pierce. 1972. (13 pp.) (No. 677)

A highly useful and concise examination of the alternate means of mass communication now available.

Communication And The Community, Peter C. Goldmark. 1972. (8 pp.) (No. 678)

This article begins with the premise that cities exist because they enhance communication. The effect of mass communication systems are commented upon in terms of their potential impact on the modern city and the quality of urban life. A useful reading.

Communication And Social Environment, George Gerbner. 1972. (10 pp.) (No. 679)

A study of the effects of mass communication on human behavior and attitudes. A sophisticated study which still has application for general use.

UNIVERSITY PROGRAMS MODULAR SERIES

Source: Can./U.S. General Learning Press
G.B. Eurospan

Price: Approximately $1.00 each.

Note: The original monographs listed below are from a wider selection of papers on economics, sociology, history, political science and psychology. All are academic in level or approach, with the items listed below of value for specific content not readily available from other sources.

The Economics Of Pollution Control And Environmental Quality, A. Myrick Freeman III. 1971. (27 pp.)

Several useful diagrams and succint summaries of technological options for pollution control render this academic paper of use for general use.

Addenda

The Metropolitan Frontier: A Perspective On Change In American Society,
Daniel J. Elazer. 1973. (20 pp.)
This well developed article examines the impact of frontier expansion on the U.S., with a focus on the effects this expansion had on social change. A concise list of frontier conditions is listed using a modified version of Turner's thesis. Of equal importance is the segment relating to the impact of urbanization on frontier existence and the reverse westernization of the U.S. An intriguing paper which bears close attention.

Personal Space, Darwyn E. Linder. 1974. (23 pp.)
Too detailed for general use.

Policy Making In American Cities: Comparisons In A Quasi-Longitudinal, Quasi - Experimental Design. Heinz Eulau. 1971. (16 pp.)
Too detailed for general use.

The Urbanization Of The United States. Alan Olmstead and Eugene Smolensky. 1973. (23 pp.)
This summary paper on the process of urbanization in the U.S. examines the various processes that resulted in urban concentration, specialization, and industralization.

Utopian Myths And Movements In Modern Societies, Joseph R. Gusfield. 1973. (33 pp.)
This monograph is significant for two features. The first is in its discussion of social and political utopias and utopian thought from More's *Utopia* through Skinner's *Walden II*. The paper also delves into the commonly held belief that utopian ideals are currently on the decline. Rejecting this position, the author convincingly illustrates in what ways utopian belief and application is still prevalent in social and political processes, particularly in the area of technology, modernization, Marxist socialism and futurism.

15.2 MAPS AND VISUAL AIDS

ARCHITECTURAL PRESS. 9-13 Queen Anne's Gate, London SW1H 9BY.

Lifescape: Pack1/Introduction: The Way Things Are. by Pat Haikin.

Lifescape: Pack2/Home, Neighborhood, And Community. by Anthea Holme.
This collection deals with the way of life in cities during the last century through the end of this one.

The illustrations provide for a very rich mix of visual experiences (supplemented with text) that graphically bring home to the viewer the human element of the city.

Addenda

These sets are of immeasurable value...with considerable impact potential for the study of the human city. The examples are incidentally English, but in fact they reflect the universal character of urban man.

An inexpensive and highly versatile learning package.

Each set includes 24 loose-sheet (8½" x 11" or larger), 24 question cards, and an overall guide sheet. Each segment of the study is colour coded.

Source: CA Urban Educational Materials
         US/GB Architectural Press Ltd.

Price and Note: ₤1.50 each (₤1.20 for 10 or more). Teacher's guide @30p.

For shipments from England, allow for 6 weeks for deliver. Available by air at ₤1 each (airfare).

16.3 SLIDES AND FILMSTRIPS

CENTER FOR HUMANITIES

An Inquiry Into The Future Of Mankind: Designing Tomorrow Today. (No. 258, 1974). A two slide tray set.
   This is the best single item yet reviewed on the future. It comments and illustrates alternative views of where it is we are going and the various ways we might get there. The set provides a balanced view of alternatives, includes comment on alternative means of evaluating future prospects (scenarios, probability curves, Delphi techniques, genius forecasting, and inventing).

Considerable comment is made regarding the alternative of an unalterable future vs. a future created (invented) by man. How probable is it that we could design the future? This question is assessed in tandem with a tight evaluation of major world problems which will have significant impact on any future (food, population, and the general quality of life). In particular, detailed comment is made on the future of cities, with a wide ranging discussion of form alternatives.

The pair close with a wide ranging discussion of the technology vs. a controversy.

This beautifully illustrated set presents a very positive view of man.

An excellent introductory piece for any study of the future, and particularly for the study of urban alternatives.

Addenda

Conflict In American Values: Life Style Vs. Standard Of Living. (No. 242, 1973)
    A two slide tray set. Not urban studies.

The Mass Mind: Conformity And Individualism. (No. 244, 1974)
    A two slide tray set. Insufficient urban studies content.

URBAN MEDIA MATERIALS (Continued from page 206)

Ecology Of The Urban Environment. 6 captioned color "shortstrips." 36 frames each. (Set UMM 406) (1972)
    Housing Patterns
    Population
    Sanitation
    Water Supply
    Air Pollution
    Urban Wildlife
    Designed for use at the intermediate level, these filmstrips have supervisuals, of use at the secondary level as well. Some of the best illustrations on these topics yet seen. $37.50 for the set, or $7.00 each.

Man And The Environment. 2 color F/S with record (UMM 505 - $35.00) or cassette (UMM 505C - $37.00). (1973)
    This pair takes a distinctive stance on the place of man in the ecology of earth. Man's dependence and interaction with the biosphere is woven into a larger view of the nature and charater of the total biosphere. Good visuals, dramatic (possibly overly dramatic) dialogue in this useful study.

Note: This company has a number of superb elementary level sets with an urban focus.

17.1 BOOKS ON SIMULATIONS

Cohen, Robert, et. al. *Psych City: A Simulated Community.* New York: Pergamon, 1973.
    (3)

Gibbs, G. E., ed. *Handbook Of Games And Simulation Exercises.* Beverly Hills: Sage, 1974.
    This is the most comprehensive study of simulations available. Close to 2000 games/simulations are reviewed, but of equal importance, this compilation includes listings of other bibliographies and books in English, magazines and periodicals, and books about gaming. Organizations involved with serious gaming are also listed.

    The author includes copious information regarding sourcing for this material. Immensely useful for the simulation specialist.
    HB (2)

Addenda

17.2 SIMULATIONS AND MULTI-MEDIA KITS

CLASSROOM DYNAMICS SIMULATIONS

    Source: Can./U.S./G.B. Classroom Dynamics

    Price: For those listed, $21.50 each.

Confrontation In Urbia.
A simulation involved with community/youth confrontation. Not urban studies. Booklet form.

Urban America.
A book form procedure dealing with "some of the problems facing cities in the United States." This two week, 20-36 student role playing simulation deals with four or more problems identified for a small town environment. Students are required to fit themselves into specific roles, acting thereafter as decision makers. The format of the booklet lends itself to easy duplication. A simple exercise to utilize with 20 or more students in time segments of 45-50 minutes. A useful simulation.

INTERACT SIMULATIONS

    Source: Can./U.S./G.B. Interact

    Price: $10.00 each, including the right to duplicate material within the actual school purchasing the simulation.

    Note: These easy to use simulations are packaged single sheets bound by a plastic strip binder. This single booklet can be easily disassembled for duplication. Student information is provided on an easily comprehensible single sheet. For use over 2-3 weeks with up to 35 students.

Cope: A Simulation Of Adapting To Change And Anticipating The Future.
A simulation which places the role players into five future time situations. Participants experience the stresses and anxieties caused by rapid change. Technological changes create direct challenges. A highly useful situation to create awareness of future possibilities, and the future itself.

Balance: A Simulation Of Four Families Caught In Ecological Dilemmas.
This simulation creates an understanding of the process whereby choices are made between economic and social values on the one hand and ecological values on the other. All of the role players are urban dwellers. A useful role playing device. A three hour version for use outside of school is also provided.

Ecopolis: A Simulation Of A Community Struggling To Solve Ecological

Addenda

Problems.
   An elementary school adaptation of *Balance*.

Pressure: A Simulation Of Decision-making In Local Government.
   Similar to the simulations above in general usefulness in school, this role playing process breathes some very real life into the study of a local government. Some slight adaptation will be necessary for use in Canada.

Note: Interact simulations are prepared by secondary school teachers. From the quality of the examples seen to date, the user of this bibliography is recommended to investigate the other two dozen or so simulations available on other school topics.

Appendices

APPENDIX ONE: Book Source Guide

This source guide indicates whether publishers of books listed in this bibliography have subsidiaries, have copublishing arrangements or particular agents in the United States, Canada, Great Britain, and in some cases, Europe, for the books in *City in Print*. In Appendix One, this information is supplied in brief with the name of the original publisher followed by the names of the sources in the different countries listed above. The detailed national names and full addresses of these sources are listed in Appendix Two. To use these appendices, first locate the publisher's name in the left-hand column in Appendix One and read across the page. A straight horizontal line in the lists on the right-hand side indicates that no source exists in that country. If a source name *is* discovered, turn to Appendix Two and find that name in the alphabetical listing; the full address will be found there as well.

Companies having subsidiaries in other countries with exactly the same name are listed in Appendix One with the letters representing the alternate country behind the publisher's name, as in "Scott, Foresman & Co. (US)." An asterisk beside the name of the distributor in Appendix One indicates that the address will be found in the "Additional Listings" as the end of Appendix Two.

This source guide is provided for those who may find it necessary to go directly to the publisher for certain works, however, customers are urged to first apply to their local bookseller for assistance in acquiring any book listed. *Books in Print* should also be consulted to see whether additional national imprints exist.

City in Print lists the publisher of record for the titles reviewed. Where simultaneous or complimentary editions are known, they are listed with the bibliographic information in the text.

The distributors listed have been authenticated as of March 1974, but since distributors often change with little notice, please bear in mind that some of these may no longer be accurate.

PUBLISHER	CANADA	US	GREAT BRITAIN/EUROPE
Abingdon	G. R. Welch	Abingdon	
Academic Press Inc.	Renouf*	Academic Press (US)	Academic Press (GB)
Ace	Simon and Schuster (CA)	Ace	
Acropolis	Smithers-Bonellie	Acropolis	
Addison-Wesley	Addison-Wesley (CA)	Addison-Wesley (US)	Addison-Wesley (GB)
Aiu Sitjthofts Vitgevers Maatschappij/n.v.			Aiu Sitjthofts Vitgevers Maatschappi/n.v.
Akademiforlaget		Scandinavian University Books	Eurospan
Aldine		Aldine	European Bookservice
Allen Lane	Longman Canada		Allen Lane
Allyn and Bacon	Macmillan of Canada	Allyn and Bacon	Macmillan (London) Ltd.
American Society of Civil Engineers		American Society of Civil Engineers	
American Society of Planning Officials		American Society of Planning Officials	
American University of Beirut	Burns and MacEachern	Syracuse University Press	Transatlantic Book Service
Angus & Robertson	Thomas Nelson (CA)		Angus and Robertson (UK) Ltd.
Architectural Press	General Publishing		Architectural Press
Archon Books		Shoe String Press	
Arnold (E.J.)	Dent (CA)	Aldine	Arnold (E.J.)
Association of American Geographers		Association of American Geographers	
Atheneum	Hollinger House	Atheneum	Transatlantic Book Service
Australian National University Press		International Scholarly Book Service	
Avon	Barrdawn Sales	Avon (US)	Avon (GB)
Ballantine	Ballantine (CA)	Ballantine (US)	Pan
Bantam	Bantam (CA)	Bantam (US)	
Barron's Educational Series	Burns and MacEachern	Barron's	Silco Bks Ltd.*
Basic Books	General Publishing	Basic Books	P.A.G.E.S.
Batsford	Copp Clark		Batsford
Beacon Press	Saunders of Toronto	Beacon Press	Transatlantic Book Service
G. Bell	Clarke, Irwin		Bell
Bellhaven House	Book Society of Canada		Heineman
Berkley	Barrdawn Sales	Berkley	
Blackie	Copp Clark		Blackie
Bobbs-Merrill	Fitzhenry and Whiteside (pb, texts)	Bobbs-Merrill	Eurospan
	Thomas Allen and Son (trade)		
The Bodley Head	Copp Clark		The Bodley Head
Book Society of Canada	Book Society of Canada	Books Canada (US)*	
Braziller	Doubleday Canada	Braziller	Transatlantic Book Service
E. J. Brill		Humanities Press	E. J. Brill
The Brookings Institute	McGill-Queens University Press	The Brookings Institute	George Allen and Unwin
Bruno Cassirer	Oxford University Press (CA)	Oxford University Press (US)	Bruno Cassirer
Cambridge University Press	Macmillan of Canada	Cambridge University (US)	Cambridge Univ. Press (GB)
Frank Cass		International Scholarly Book Service	Frank Cass
Cassell	Collier-Macmillan		Cassell
Central Mortgage and Housing Corporation	Information Canada	Canada House*	Books Canada*

PUBLISHER	CANADA	US	GREAT BRITAIN/EUROPE
Chandler	Copp Clark	Chandler	International Textbook Co.
Chatto and Windus	Clarke-Irwin		Chatto and Windus
Chilton	Thomas Nelson (CA)	Chilton	
Clarke, Irwin	Clarke, Irwin	Books Canada (US)*	
Collier	Collier-Macmillan	Macmillan Inc., N.Y.	CCM Publishers
Collier-Macmillan	Collier-Macmillan	Macmillan Inc., N.Y.	CCM Publishers
William Collins	Collins (CA)		Collins (GB)
Columbia University Press		Columbia University Press	American University Publishe Group
Congressional Quarterly		Congressional Quarterly	
Copp Clark	Copp Clark		
Cornell University Press		Cornell University Press	I.B.E.G.
Coward McCann and Geoghegan	Longman Canada	Coward McCann and Geoghegan	Transatlantic Book Service
Cowles	General Publishing Co.	Cowles	
Creative Educational Society	J.M. Dent	Creative Educational Society	
Crowell	Fitzhenry and Whiteside	Thomas Y. Crowell	
John Day	Longman Canada	Day	
Delacorte	Fitzhenry and Whiteside	Dial	Transatlantic Book Service
Dell	Dell (CA)	Dell (US)	
Delta	Fitzhenry and Whiteside	Dell (US)	
J.M. Dent	J.M. Dent (CA)		J.M. Dent (GB)
Detroit Edison		Detroit Edison	
DEV-SCO Publications	Longman Canada		
Dodd Mead	Hollinger House	Dodd Mead	Transatlantic Book Service
Doubleday	Doubleday Canada	Doubleday (US)	Doubleday (GB)
Dowden Hutchinson and Rose		International Scholarly Book Service	Wiley (GB)
Dover	General Publishing	Dover	Tiptree Book Services
Dow Jones		Dow Jones	Constable and Co. Ltd.*
Duckworth	Copp Clark		Duckworth
Dunellen		Dunellen	Transatlantic Book Service
Dutton	Clarke Irwin	Dutton	Transatlantic Book Service
Duxbury	Wadsworth (CA)	Wadsworth (US)	Prentice Hall (GB)
Eckbo, Dean, Austin and Williams		Eckbo, Dean, Austin and Williams	
Edinburgh University Press		Aldine	Edinburgh University Press
Edward Arnold	Macmillan of Canada	St. Martin's Press	Edward Arnold
Elek	Griffin House		Elek
English Universities Press	Musson		English Universities Press
Ernest Benn	General Publishing		Ernest Benn
M. Evans	Hollinger House	Lippincott	Transatlantic Book Serivce
Exposition Press		Exposition Press	
Faber and Faber	Oxford University Press (CA)		Faber and Faber
Fawcett		Fawcett	
Fearon	Clarke, Irwin	Fearon	
Field Educational Publications	MacMillan	Field Educational Publications	Field Educational Corporatior
Follett	McGraw-Hill Ryerson	Follett	McGraw-Hill Book Co. (GB)
Freal Vincent			Freal Vincent*
The Free Press	Collier Macmillan	Macmillan, Inc.	CCM Publishers
Gage	Gage		
Garnstone Press	Copp Clark		Garnstone
General Learning Press	GLC Educational Materials and Services	General Learning Press	Eurospan
George Allen and Unwin	Methuen		George Allen and Unwin
Ginn	Ginn (CA)	Ginn (US)	Transatlantic Book Service

PUBLISHER	CANADA	US	GREAT BRITAIN/EUROPE
Glencoe Press	Collier Macmillan	Macmillan Inc.	CCM Publishers
Globe	Book Society of Canada	Globe	
Greenwood Press		Greeenwood Press	Westport Publications Ltd. (Eurospan)
Grossman	Fitzhenry and Whiteside (Random House) (CA) (National Publishing)*	Viking	Transatlantic Book Service
Grove Press		Grove Press	
Hakkert	Hakkert		Books Canada, Ltd. (GB)
Hamlyn	Hamlyn (CA)		Hamlyn (GB)
Harcourt Brace Jovanovich	Longman Canada	Harcourt Brace Jovanovich (US)	Harcourt Brace Jovanovich (GB)
Harper and Row	Fitzhenry and Whiteside	Harper and Row (US)	Harper and Row (GB)
Harvard University Press		Harvard University Press	Oxford University Press (GB)
Harvest House	Harvest House	Books Canada (US)*	
D.C. Heath	Heath (CA)	Heath (US)	Heath (GB)
Heinemann	Book Society of Canada		Heinemann
Hick Smith	Methuen	Harper and Row	
Holt Rinehart and Winston	Holt Rinehart and Winston (CA)	Holt Rinehard and Winston (US)	Holt-Blond
Hodder and Stoughton	Musson Book		Hodder and Stoughton
Homer Hoyt Associates	Urban Educational Materials	Homer Hoyt Associates	
Horizon	Smither and Bonellie (Thomas Allen) (Trade)	Horizon	Transatlantic Book Service
Houghton-Mifflin	Thomas Nelson (CA) (Educational) Thomas Allen (Trade)	Houghton Mifflin	Eurospan
Humanities Press		Humanities Press	
Hurst	Nelson, Foster and Scott		Hurst
Hutchinson	Nelson, Foster and Scott (trade) Dent (CA) Educational		Hutchinson Publishing Group
Hutchinson University Library	Dent (CA)	Humanities Press	Hutchinson Publishing Group
Indiana University Press	Fitzhenry and Whiteside	Indiana University Press	American University Publisher's Group
Information Canada	Information Canada	Books Canada (US)*	
International City Managers Association		International City Managers Association	
International Federation of Housing and Planning		American Society of Planning Officials	International Federation of Housing and Planning
Richard D. Irwin	Irwin Dorsey*	Irwin	European Book Service
James Lewis and Samuel	Belford Book Distributing Co.	Books Canada (U.S.)*	Books Canada (GB)*
Johns Hopkins	Copp Clark	Johns Hopkins	I.B.E.G.
Kennikat Press	Urban Educational Materials	Kennikat	
Knopf	Random House (CA)	Knopf	Pandemic Ltd.*
Kodansha International	Fitzhenry and Whiteside	Kodansha International	George Allen and Unwin
Kuwait Government Printing Press			Kuwait Government Printing Press
Lancer		Lancer (US)	Lancer (GB)
Leicester University Press		Humanities Press	Leicester University Press
Leonard Hill	Copp Clark	Intext	International Textbook Co. Ltd.
Lexington	Heath (CA)	Heath (US)	Heath (GB)
Linnet Books		Shoe String Press	
Lippincott	Hollinger House	Lippincott	Blackwell Scientific*
Little, Brown	Hollinger House	Little, Brown	Eurospan

PUBLISHER	CANADA	US	GREAT BRITAIN/EUROPE
London School of Economics and Political Science			London School of Economics and Political Science
Longman Canada	Longman Canada	Harcourt, Brace Jovanovitch	Longman Group
Lund Humphries	Clarke, Irwin		Lund Humphries
McClelland and Stewart	McClelland & Stewart*	Books Canada* (US)	
MacGibbon and Kee	General Publishing Co.		MacGibbon and Kee
McGill-Queen's University Press	McGill-Queen's University Press (CA)		McGill-Queen's University Press (GB)
McGraw Hill	McGraw Hill-Ryerson	McGraw Hill (US)	McGraw Hill (GB)
Macmillan (London) Ltd.	Macmillan of Canada	St. Martin's Press	Macmillan (London) Ltd.
Macmillan of Canada	Macmillan of Canada	St. Martin's Press	Macmillan (London) Ltd.
Macmillan, Inc., New York	Collier-Macmillan	Macmillan, Inc.	CCM Publishers
Manchester University Press		Humanities Press	Manchester University Press
Markham		Markham	Eurospan
Matthew Bender		Matthew Bender	
Maudep Press		Maudep	
The Medieval Academy of America		The Medieval Academy of America	
Melbourne University Press		International Scholarly Book Service	Angus and Robertson (UK) Ltd.
Mentor		New American Library	New English Library
Methuen (CA)	Methuen (CA)		Methuen (GB)
Methuen (GB)	Methuen (CA)		Methuen (GB)
The M.I.T. Press	General Publishing	The M.I.T. Press (US)	The M.I.T. Press Ltd. (GB)*
William Morrow	G. J. McLeod	Morrow	Transatlantic Book Service
Mouton		Humanities Press	Mouton
Ejnar Munksgaard			Munksgaard*
National Council for Geographic Education		NCGE	
Natural History Press	Doubleday Canada	Natural History Press	Transatlantic Book Service
New American Library Paperbacks	Har-Nal Distributors* General Publishing	New American Library	New English Library
New American Library Hardbacks	G. J. McLeod	World Publishing Co.	New English Library
New Press	New Press	Books Canada	
New York University Press		New York University Press	English Universities Press Ltd.*
W.W. Norton	G. J. McLeod	Norton	Transatlantic Book Service
Odyssey	Fitzhenry and Whiteside	Bobbs-Merrill	Eurospan
Oliver and Boyd	Longman		Oliver and Boyd
Orion	Macmillan of Canada	Viking	Transatlantic Book Service
Oxford University Press	Oxford University Press (CA)	Oxford University Press (US)	Oxford University Press (GB)
Pall Mall	Burns & MacEachern	Praeger	Pall Mall
Pan	Penguin Books Canada*	Pelican/Penguin	Pan
F.E. Peacock		F.E. Peacock	European Book Service
Pelican/Penguin		Pelican/Penguin	Penguin
Pergamon		Pergamon (US)	Pergamon (GB)
Peter Owen	Smithers and Bonellie	Humanities Press	Peter Owen
Philosophical Library	Book Centre	Philisophical Library	C. W. Daniel
Pilgrim Press	McGraw Hill-Ryerson	McGraw Hill (US)	McGraw Hill (GB)
Pitman	Copp Clark	Pitman (US)	Pitman (GB)
Pocket Books	Simon and Schuster (CA)	Simon and Schuster (US)	Transatlantic Book Service
Praeger	Burns and MacEachern	Praeger	Transatlantic Book Service
Prentice Hall	Prentice Hall (CA)	Prentice Hall (US)	Prentice Hall (GB)
Princeton Univ. Press		Princeton University Press	Oxford University Press (GB)
G.P. Putnam's	Longman Canada	Putnam's	Transatlantic Book Service
Pyramid	Barrdawn Sales	Pyramid	

PUBLISHER	CANADA	US	GREAT BRITAIN/EUROPE
Quadrangle	Fitzhenry and Whiteside	Quadrangle	Transatlantic Book Service
Rand McNally	Thomas Allen, (Trade) Gage (Educational)	Rand McNally (US)	Rand McNally (GB)
Random House	Random House (CA)	Random House (US)	European Book Service
Reinhart Press	Holt Reinhart and Winston (CA)	Holt Reinhart and Winston (US)	Holt Blond
Reinhold	Van Nostrand Reinhold (CA)	Van Nostrand Reinhold (US)	Van Nostrand Reinhold (GB)
Robert Speller		Robert Speller	
Routledge and Kegan Paul	General Publishing		Routledge and Kegan Paul
Russell Sage Foundation	General Publishing	Basic Books	P.A.G.E.S.
Rutgers University Press	Griffin House	Rutgers University Press	Transatlantic Book Service
Ryerson Press	McGraw Hill-Ryerson	McGraw Hill (US)	McGraw Hill (GB)
Sage Publications		Sage Publications (US)	Sage Publications Ltd.
San Francisco Press		San Francisco Press	
St. Johns University Press		St. Johns University Press	
St. Martin's Press	Macmillan of Canada	St. Martin's Press	Macmillan Ltd.
Schenkman	GLC Educational Materials and Services	General Learning Press	Eurospan
Schocken	Book Centre	Schocken	
Scott Foresman	Gage	Scott Foresman (US)	Scott Foresman (GB)
Charles Scribner's	John Wiley (CA)	Scribner's	Transatlantic Book Service
Seminar Press	Longman Canada	Seminar Press, Inc. (US)	Seminar Press Ltd. (GB)
Signet	Har-Nal Distributors*	New American Library	New English Library
Sidgewick and Jackson	Griffin House		Sidgewick and Jackson
Simon and Schuster Paperbacks	Simon and Schuster (CA)	Simon and Schuster (US)	Transatlantic Book Service
Simon and Schuster Hardbacks	General Publishing	Simon and Schuster (US)	Transatlantic Book Service
Studio Vista	Collier-Macmillan	Macmillan Inc.	Studio Vista
Sydney University Press		International Scholarly Book Service	Angus and Robertson (UK) Ltd.
Syracuse University Press	Burns and MacEachern	Syracuse University Press	Transatlantic Book Service
Temple Smith			Temple Smith
Thames and Hudson	Oxford University Press (CA)		Thames and Hudson
Paul Theobald		Theobald	
Thomas Nelson	Thomas Nelson (CA)	Thomas Nelson (US)	Thomas Nelson (GB)
Time Life Books	Time Life Books (Mail Order)	Time Life Books (Mail Order)	Time Life International
	GLC Educational Materials (Educational)	General Learning Corporation (Educational)	Eurospan
	Hollinger House (Trade)	Little Brown (Trade)	
Tundra	Tundra	Books Canada (US)	
United States Government Printing Office		United States Government Printing Office	
Universitets Forlaget		Universitets Forlaget	Dawson's of Pall Mall*
University of Alabama	Book Centre	University of Alabama	Transatlantic Book Service
University of California Press		University of California Press (US)	University of California Press (GB)
University of Chicago Press		University of Chicago Press (US)	University of Chicago Press (GB)
University of Georgia Press		University of Georgia Press	Transatlantic Book Service
University of Glasgow Press	Methuen	Sage Publications (US)	University of Glasgow Press
University of Hong Kong Press	Oxford University Press (CA)	Oxford University Press (US)	Oxford University Press (GB)
University of Illinois Press		University of Illinois Press	

PUBLISHER	CANADA	US	GREAT BRITAIN/EUROPE
University of Kansas Press		University of Kansas Press	
University of Michigan Press	Longman Canada	University of Michigan Press	Transatlantic Book Service
University of Missouri Press		University of Missouri Press	Transatlantic Book Service
University of Nebraska Press	Burns & MacEachern	University of Nebraska Press	Transatlantic Book Service
University of North Carolina Press		University of North Carolina Press	Oxford University Press (GB)
University of Notre Dame Press	Fitzhenry and Whiteside	University of Notre Dame Press	American University Publishers Group
University of Pennsylvania Press	Smithers and Bonellie	University of Pennsylvania Press	
University of Toronto Press	University of Toronto Press (CA)	University of Toronto Press (US)*	Oxford University Press
University of Victoria Press	University of Victoria Press		
University of Wisconsin Press	Burns and MacEachern	University of Wisconsin Press	American University Publishers Group
Urban Press		Urban Press	
Van Nostrand Reinhold	Van Nostrand Reinhold (CA)	Van Nostrand Reinhold (US)	Van Nostrand Reinhold (GB)
Viking Press	Macmillan of Canada	Viking Press	Transatlantic Book Service
Vintage	Random House (CA)	Random House (US)	European Book Service
Wadsworth	Wadsworth (CA)	Wadsworth (US)	Prentice-Hall (GB)
Walker	Fitzhenry and Whiteside	Walker	Transatlantic Book Service
Ives Washburn	General Publishing	McKay	
Washington Square Press	Simon and Schuster	Washington Square	
West Publishing Co.		West	
Westminster Press	McGraw Hill-Ryerson	Westminster	McGraw Hill (GB)
Weidenfeld and Nicolson	McGraw Hill-Ryerson	Humanities Press	Weidenfeld and Nicolson
John Wiley	Wiley (CA)	Wiley (US)	Wiley (GB)
Winchester Press	Nelson, Foster and Scott	Winchester	Transatlantic Book Service
Winthrop Publishers	Prentice-Hall (CA)	Winthrop	Prentice-Hall (GB)
Wright Allen Press		Wright Allen Press	Wiley (GB)
Yale University Press		Yale University Press	Yale University Press (GB)

ADDITIONAL SOURCES

PUBLISHER	CANADA	US	GREAT BRITAIN/EUROPE
Charterhouse Books Inc.	Musson	Charterhouse*	
G. T. Foulis		International Scholarly Book Service*	Foulis*
House of Anansi	Belford	Books Canada (US)	Books Canada (UK)
Jossey-Bass	Book Centre	Jossey-Bass*	Eurospan
Peter Martin Associates	Belford	Books Canada (US)	Books Canada (GB)
Charles E. Merrill	Merrill (CA)*	Merrill (US)*	
Noble and Noble	Clarke Irwin	Noble and Noble*	Transatlantic Book Service
Secker and Warburg	Collins		Secker and Warburg*
Shields Press	National	Shields	
Tilberg University Press		International Scholarly Book Service (US)*	International Scholarly Book Service (GB)
University of London Press	Musson		University of London Press*
Xerox College Publishing	Ginn (CA)	Xerox College Publishing*	Eurospan

APPENDIX TWO: Book Publishers and Distributors Address List

US	Abingdon Press	201 8th Ave. S., Nashville, Tenn. 37202
US	Academic Press, Inc.	111 5th Ave., New York, N.Y. 10003
GB	Academic Press, Ltd.	24/28 Oval Road, London, NW1
US	Ace Publishing Corp.	1120 Avenue of the Americas, New York, N.Y. 10036
US	Acropolis Books	Colortone Bldg., 2400 17th St. N.W., Washington, D.C. 20009
CA	Addison-Wesley (Canada)	36 Prince Andrew Place, Don Mills, Ont. M3C 2H4
GB	Addison-Wesley Publishers, Ltd.	West End House, 11 Hills Place, London W1R 2LR
US	Addison-Wesley Publishing Co., Inc.	Reading, Mass. 01867
EU	Aiu Sitjthofts Vitgevers	Maatschappij/n.v.
US	Aldine-Atherton	529 So. Wabash Ave., Chicago, Ill. 60615
GB	Allen Lane, The Penguin Press	74 Grosvenor St., London W1X 0AS
US	Allyn and Bacon, Inc.	Rockleigh, N.J. 07647
US	American Society of Civil Engineers	345 E. 47th St., New York, N.Y. 10017
US	American Society of Planning Officials	1313 E. 60th St., Chicago, Ill. 60637
GB	American University Publisher's Group	70 Great Russell St., London WC1B 3BY
GB	Angus and Robertson (U.K.) Ltd.	2 Fisher St., London WC1R 4QA
GB	Architectural Press, Ltd.	9-13 Queen Anne's Gate, London SW1H 9BY
GB	E. J. Arnold and Son, Ltd.	Butterley St., Hunslet Lane, Leeds 10
US	Association of American Geographers	1710 16th St., N.W. Washington, D.C. 20009
US	Atheneum Publishers	122 E. 42nd St., New York, N.Y. 10017
US	Avon Books	959 8th Ave., New York, N.Y. 10019
GB	Avon Books	20 Frances St., Truro, Cornwall
US	Ballantine Books, Inc.	101 5th Ave., New York, N.Y. 10003
CA	Ballantine Books of Canada, Ltd.	370 Alliance Ave., Toronto, Ont. M6N 2H8
US	Bantam Books, Inc.	666 5th Ave., New York, N.Y. 10019
GB	Bantam Books, Ltd.	Cavendish House, 57-59 Uxbridge Rd., Ealing, London W5
CA	Bantam Books of Canada, Ltd.	888 DuPont St., Toronto, Ont. M6G 1Z8
GB	Barmerlea Book Sales Ltd.	"Annandale" North End Rd., London NW117QY
CA	Barrdawn Sales Ltd.	1758A Victoria Park Ave., Scarborough, Ont. M1R 1R4
US	Barron's Educational Series, Inc.	113 Crossways Park Dr., Woodbury, N.Y. 11797
US	Basic Books, Inc.	404 Park Ave. S., New York, N.Y. 10016
GB	B. T. Batsford, Ltd.	4 Fitzhardinge St., London W1H 0AH
US	Beacon Press	25 Beacon St., Boston, Mass. 02108
CA	The Belford Book Distributing Co.	11 Boulton Ave., Toronto, Ont. M4M 2J4
GB	G. Bell and Sons, Ltd.	York House, 6 Portugal St., London WC2A 2HL
CA	Bellhaven House, Ltd.	1145 Bellamy Rd., Scarborough, Ont. M2L 1D4
US	Berkley Publishing Corp.	200 Madison Ave., New York, N.Y. 10016
GB	Blackie and Son, Ltd.	Bishopbriggs, Glasgow G64 2NZ
US	Bobbs Merrill Co., Inc.	4300 W. 62nd St., Indianapolis, Ind. 46268
GB	The Bodley Head	9 Bow Street, London WC2E 7AL
CA	Book Centre, Inc.	1140 Beaulac St., St. Laurent, P.Q. H4R 1R8
CA	Book Society of Canada, Ltd.	4386 Sheppard Ave. E., Agincourt, Ont. M1S 3B6
US	George Braziller, Inc.	1 Park Ave., New York, N.Y. 10016
EU	Brill N.V. Boekhandel v/h E.J.	Leiden, Oude Rijn 33a, Netherlands.
US	The Brookings Institute	1775 Massachusetts Ave. N.W., Washington, D.C. 20036
GB	Bruno Cassirer (Publ.) Ltd.	31 Portland Road, Oxford
CA	Burns and MacEachern Ltd.	62 Railside Road, Don Mills, Ont. M3A 1A6
GB	Cambridge University Press	Bentley House, P.O. Box 92, 200 Euston Rd., London NW1 2DB
US	Cambridge University Press	32 E. 57th St., New York, N.Y. 10022
GB	Frank Cass and Co. Ltd.	67 Great Russell St., London WC1B 3BT
GB	Cassell and Co., Ltd.	35 Red Lion Square, London WC1
US	Chandler Publishing Co.	Oak St. and Pawnee Ave., Scranton, Pa. 18515
GB	Chatto and Windus Ltd.	40-42 William IV St., London WC2N 4DF
US	Chilton Book Co.	401 Walnut St., Philadelphia, Pa. 19106

CA	Clarke, Irwin and Co., Ltd.	791 St. Clair Ave. W., Toronto, Ont. M6C 1B8
CA	Collier-Macmillan Canada Ltd.	539 Collier-Macmillan Dr., Cambridge, Ont. M3C 2K2
GB	CCM Publishers	35 Red Lion Sq., London WC1R 4SG
CA	William Collins Sons and Co. Canada Ltd.	100 Lesmill Rd., Don Mills, Ont. M38 2T5
GB	William Collins Sons and Co. Ltd.	14 St. James Place, London SW1
US	Columbia University Press	440 W. 110th St., New York, N.Y. 10025
GB	Columbia University Press Ltd.	70 Great Russell St., London WC1
US	Congressional Quarterly, Inc.	1735 K Street, N.W. Washington, D.C. 20006
CA	Copp Clark Publishing Co.	517 Wellington St. W., Toronto, Ont. M5V 1G1
US	Cornell University Press	124 Roberts Place, Ithaca, N.Y. 14850
US	Coward-McCann and Geoghegan, Inc.	200 Madison Ave., New York, N.Y. 10016
US	Cowles Book Corporation, Inc.	114 W. Illinois St., Chicago, Ill. 60610
US	Creative Educational Society, Inc.	515 N. Front St., Mankato, Minn. 56001
GB	C. W. Daniel Co. Ltd.	The Ashingdon, Rochford SS4 3JD
US	John Day Co.	257 Park Ave. S., New York, N.Y. 10010
CA	Dell International	156 Front St. W., Toronto, Ont. M5J 1G6
US	Dell Publishing Co., Inc.	750 3rd Ave., New York, N.Y. 10017
CA	J. M. Dent and Sons (Canada) Ltd.	100 Scarsdale Rd., Don Mills, Ont. M3B 2R8
GB	J. M. Dent and Sons, Ltd.	Aldine House, 10-13 Bedford St., London WC2E 9HG
US	Detroit Edison Company	1132 Washington Blvd., Detroit, Mich. 48226
US	Dial Press, Inc.	750 3rd Ave., New York, N.Y. 10017
US	Dodd Mead and Co.	79 Madison Ave., New York, N.Y. 10016
GB	Doubleday and Co., Inc.	100 Wigmore St., London W1H 9DR
US	Doubleday and Co., Inc.	501 Franklin Ave., Garden City, N.Y. 11530
CA	Doubleday Canada	105 Bond Street, Toronto, Ont. M5B 1V3
US	Dover Publications, Inc.	180 Varick St., New York, N.Y. 10014
US	Dow Jones Books	P.O. Box 445, Chicopee, Mass. 01020
GB	Gerald Duckworth and Co., Ltd.	43 Gloucester Crs., London N.W.1
US	Dunellen Publishing Co., Inc.	145 E. 52nd St., New York, N.Y. 10022
US	E. P. Dutton and Co., Inc.	201 Park Ave. S., New York, N.Y. 10003
US	Eckbo, Dean, Austin and Williams	7440 No. Figueroa St., Los Angeles, Calif. 90041
GB	Edinburgh University Press	22 George Square, Edinburgh, EH8 9LF
GB	Edward Arnold (Publishers) Ltd.	25 Hill St., London W1X 8LL
GB	Paul Elek Books, Ltd.	54-58 Caledonian Rd., London N1 9RN
GB	English University Press, Ltd.	St. Paul's House, Warwick Lane, London EC4P 4AH
GB	Ernest Benn Ltd.	Bouverie House, 154 Fleet St., London EC4A 2DL
EU/GB	European Book Service	Hogeweysalaan 119, P.O. Box 124 Weesp, N.V. (in G.B., available from Lyon, Grant and Green, 20-24 Uxbridge St., London W. 8)
GB	Eurospan, Ltd.	44 Hatton Gdn., London EC1
US	Exposition Press Inc.	50 Jericho Turnpike, Jericho, N.Y. 11753
GB	Faber and Faber Ltd.	3 Queens Square, London WC1B 5ED
US	Fawcett Publications, Ltd.	Fawcett Place, Greenwich, Conn. 06830
US	Fearon Publishers	6 Davis Drive, Belmont, Calif. 94002
US	Feffer and Simons, Inc.	31 Union Square, New York, N.Y. 10003
GB	Feffer and Simons	28 Norfolk St., London WC2R 2EZ
GB	Field Educational Corp.	Canterbury House, Sydenham Rd., Croydon CR9 2LR
US	Field Educational Publications, Inc.	2400 Hanover St., Palo Alto, Calif. 94304
CA	Fitzhenry and Whiteside Ltd.	150 Lesmill Rd., Don Mills, Ont. M3B 2T5
US	Follett Educational Corp.	1010 W. Washington Blvd., Chicago, Ill. 60607
CA	Gage Educational Publishing Co.	164 Commander Blvd., Agincourt, Ont. M1S 3C7
GB	Garnstone Press	50 Brampton Rd., London SW3
CA	GLC Educational Materials	115 Nugget Ave., Agincourt, Ont. M1S 3B1
US	General Learning Press	250 James St., Morristown, N.J. 07960
CA	General Publishing Co. Ltd.	30 Lesmill Rd., Don Mills, Ont. M3B 2T6
GB	George Allen and Unwin, Ltd.	40 Museum St., London WC1A 1LU
CA	Ginn and Co.	35 Mobile Dr., Toronto, Ont. M4A 1H6
US	Ginn and Co.	Statler Bldg., Back Bay, P.O. 191, Boston, Mass. 02117
GB	Ginn and Co., Ltd.	18 Bedford Row, London WC1R 4EJ
US	Globe Book Co., Ltd.	175 5th Ave., New York, N.Y. 10010

US	Greenwood Press, Inc.	51 Riverside Ave., Westport, Conn. 06880
CA	Griffin House	455 King St. W., Toronto, Ont. M5V 1K7
US	Grove Press	53 E. 11th St., New York, N.Y. 10003
CA	A.M. Hakkert Ltd.	554 Spadina Cres., Toronto, Ont. M5S 2J9
GB	Hamlyn Publishing Group, Ltd.	Hamlyn House, 42 The Centre, Feltham, Mddx.
CA	Hamlyn Publishing Group	850 York Mills Rd., Don Mills, Ont. M3B 3A7
GB	Harcourt Brace Jovanovich	24-28 Oval Rd., London NW1
US	Harcourt Brace Jovanovich, Inc.	757 3rd Ave., New York, N.Y. 10017
GB	Harper and Row, Ltd.	28 Tavistock St., London WC2E 7PN
US	Harper and Row, Publishers	10 E. 53rd St., New York, N.Y. 10022
US	Harvard University Press	79 Garden St., Cambridge, Mass. 02138
CA	Harvest House Ltd.	4795 St. Catherine St. W., Montreal, P.Q. H3Z 2B9
CA	D. C. Heath Canada Ltd.	Suite 1408, 100 Adelaide St. W., Toronto, Ont. M5H 1S9
GB	D. C. Heath (Europe) Ltd.	1 Westmead, Farnborough, Hants
US	D. C. Heath and Co.	2700 N. Richardt Ave., Indianapolis, Ind. 46219
GB	Heinemann Educational Books, Ltd.	48 Charles St., London W1X 8AH
CA	Hollinger House	25 Hollinger Road, Toronto, Ont. M4B 3G2
GB	Holt-Blond	120 Golden Lane, Barbican London EC1Y 0TU
US	Holt, Rinehart and Winston	383 Madison Avenue, New York, N.Y. 10017
CA	Holt, Rinehart and Winston of Canada, Ltd.	55 Horner Ave., Toronto, Ont. M8Z 4X6
GB	Hodder and Stoughton Ltd.	St. Paul's House, Warwick Lane, London EC4P 4AH
US	Homer Hoyt Associates	2939 Van Ness St., N.W. Washington, D.C. 20008
US	Horizon Press, Publishers	156 5th Ave., New York, N.Y. 10010
US	Houghton-Mifflin Co.	110 Tremont St., Boston, Mass. 02107
US	Humanities Press	303 Park Ave. S., New York, N.Y. 10010
GB	C. Hurst and Co. (Publishers) Ltd.	40A Royal Hill, London SE10
GB	Hutchinson Publishing Group, Ltd.	3 Fitzroy Square, London W1
US	Indiana University Press	Tenth and Morton Sts., Bloomington, Ind. 47401
GB	I.B.E.G., Ltd.	2-4 Brook St., London W1Y 1AA
CA	Information Canada	171 Slater St., Ottawa, Ont. K1A 0P7
US	International City Manager's Assoc.	1140 Connecticut Ave., NW Washington, D.C. 20036
EU	International Federation of Housing and Planning	Wassenaarseweg 43, 2018. The Hague, N.V.
US	International Scholarly Books Service, Inc.	P.O. Box 4347, Portland, Ore. 97208
GB	International Scholarly Books Service, Inc.	6 Mill Trading Estate, Acton Lane, London NW10
GB	International Textbook Co.	Intext House, Stewarts Road, London SW8
US	Intext Educational Publ.	Oak St. and Pawnee St., Scranton, Pa. 18515
US	Richard D. Irwin, Inc.	1818 Ridge Rd., Homewood, Ill. 60430
US	Johns Hopkins Press	Baltimore, Md. 21218
US	Kennikat Press, Inc.	90 S. Bayles Ave., Port Washington, N.Y. 11050
US	Alfred A. Knopf, Inc.	457 Hahn Rd., Westminster, Md. 21157
US	Kodansha International/USA, Ltd.	Box 11295, Palo Alto, Calif. 94306
	Kuwait Government Printing Press	c/o Ministry of Information, Kuwait
US	Lancer Books	1560 Broadway, New York, N.Y. 10036
GB	Lancer Books	42-44 Dock Street, London E.1
GB	Leicester Univ. Press	2 University Rd., Leicester LE1 7RB
US	J. B. Lippincott	E. Washington Square, Philadelphia, Pa. 19105
US	Little, Brown and Co.	34 Beacon St., Boston, Mass. 02106
GB	London School of Economics and Political Science	Skepper House, 13 Endsleigh St., London WC1
CA	Longman Canada Ltd.	55 Barber Greene Rd., Don Mills, Ont. M3C 2A1
GB	Longman Group Ltd.	Longman House, Burnt Mill, Harlow, Essex CM20 2JE
GB	Lund Humphries	12 Bedford Sq., London WC1
GB	MacGibbon and Kee, Ltd.	3 Upper James St., Golden Square, London W1R 4BP
CA	McGill-Queens Univ. Press	Purvis Hall, 1020 Pine Ave. West, Montreal, P.Q. H3A 1A2
GB	McGill-Queens Univ. Press	70 Great Russell St., London WC1B 3BY
US	McGraw Hill Book Co.	330 W. 42nd St., New York, N.Y. 10036
GB	McGraw Hill Book Co., Ltd.	McGraw Hill House, Shoppenhangers Rd., Maidenhead, Berks.

CA	McGraw Hill-Ryerson Ltd.	330 Progress Ave., Scarborough, Ont. M1P 2Z5
US	David McKay Co., Inc.	750 3rd Ave., New York, N.Y. 10017
US	Macmillan, Inc.	866 3rd Ave., New York, N.Y. 10022
CA	The Macmillan Co. of Canada	70 Bond St., Toronto, Ont. M5B 1X3
GB	Macmillan London, Ltd.	Little Essex St., London WC2
CA	MacLean-Hunter Learning Materials	481 University Ave., Toronto, Ont. M5W 1A7
CA	G. J. McLeod Ltd.	73 Bathurst St., Toronto, Ont. M5V 2P8
GB	Manchester Univ. Press	316-324 Oxford Rd., Manchester M13 9NR
US	Markham Publishing Co.	3322 W. Peterson Ave., Chicago, Ill. 60645
US	Matthew Bender and Co., Inc.	235 E. 45th St., New York, N.Y. 10017
US	Maudep Press	Box 480, Massapequa, N.Y. 11758
US	The Medieval Academy of America	1430 Massachusetts Ave., Cambridge, Mass. 02138
GB	Methuen and Co., Ltd.	11 New Fetter Lane, London EC4P 4EE
CA	Methuen Publications	2330 Midland Ave., Agincourt, Ont. M1S 1P7
US	The M.I.T. Press	28 Carleton St., Cambridge, Mass. 02142
US	William Morrow and Co., Inc.	105 Madison Ave., New York, N.Y. 10016
EU	Mouton	'S Gravenhage, Herderstraat 5, P.O. Box 1132, Netherlands.
CA	Musson Book Co.	30 Lesmill Rd., Don Mills, Ont. M3B 2T6
US	National Council for Geographic Education	
US	Natural History Press	501 Franklin Ave., Garden City, N.Y. 11530
CA	Nelson, Foster and Scott	299 Yorkland Ave., Willowdale, Ont. M2J 1S9
US	New American Library	P.O. Box 120, Bergenfield, N.J. 07621
GB	New English Library, Ltd.	Barnard's Inn, Holborn, London EC1N 2JR
CA	New Press	553 Richmond St. W., Toronto, Ont. M5V 1V6
US	New York University Press	Washington Square, New York, N.Y. 10003
US	W. W. Norton and Co., Inc.	55 5th Avenue, New York, N.Y. 10003
GB	Oliver and Boyd	Tweeddale Court, 14 High St., Edinburgh EH1 1YL
US	Outerbridge and Lazard	201 Park Ave. S., New York, N.Y. 10003
CA	Oxford University Press	70 Wynford Dr., Don Mills, Ont. M3C 1J9
GB	Oxford University Press	Ely House, 37 Dover St., London W1X 4AH
US	Oxford University Press, Inc.	16-00 Pollitt Dr., Fair Lawn, N.J. 07410
GB	P.A.G.E.S., Ltd.	17-21 Sunbeam Rd., London NW10
GB	Pall Mall Press Ltd.	5 Cromwell Pl., London SW7
GB	Pan Books Ltd.	33 Tothill St., London SW1
US	F. E. Peacock Publishers	401 W. Irving Park Rd., Itasca, Ill. 60143
US	Pelican/Penguin Books, Inc.	7110 Ambassador Rd., Baltimore, Md. 21207
GB	Penguin Books Ltd.	Bath Road, Hammonsworth, Mddx. UB7 ODA
US	Pergamon Press, Inc.	Maxwell House, Fairview Park, Elmsford, N.Y. 10523
GB	Pergamon Press, Ltd.	Headington Hill Hall, Oxford OX3 0BW
GB	Peter Owen Ltd.	12 Kendrick Mews, Kendrick Place, London SW7
US	Philosophical Library, Inc.	15 E. 40th St., New York, N.Y. 10016
US	Pitman Publishing Corp.	6 E. 43rd St., New York, N.Y. 10017
US	Praeger Publishers	111 4th Ave., New York, N.Y. 10003
GB	Praeger Publishing, Inc.	5 Cromwell Place, London SW7
US	Prentice Hall	Englewood Cliffs, N.J. 07632
CA	Prentice Hall of Canada, Ltd.	1870 Birchmount Rd., Scarborough, Ont. M1P 2J7
GB	Prentice Hall International, Inc.	Durrants Hill Rd., Hemel Hempstead, Herts.
US	Princeton University Press	Princeton, N.J. 08540
US	G. P. Putnam's Sons	200 Madison Ave., New York, N.Y. 10016
US	Pyramid Publications, Inc.	919 3rd Ave., New York, N.Y. 10022
US	Quadrangle Books, Inc	330 Madison Ave., New York, N.Y. 10017
US	Rand McNally	405 Park Ave., New York, N.Y. 10022
GB	Rand McNally and Co.	44 Hatton Gdn., London EC1
US	Random House, Inc.	457 Hahn Rd., Westminster, Md. 21157
CA	Random House of Canada	370 Alliance Ave., Toronto, Ont. M6N 2H8
US	Robert Speller and Sons	10 E. 23rd St., New York, N.Y. 10010
GB	Routledge and Kegan Paul Ltd.	68-74 Carter Lane, London EC4V 5EL
US	Routledge and Kegan Paul of America	9 Park St., Boston, Mass. 02108
US	Rutgers University Press	30 College Avenue, New Brunswick, N.J. 08901

US	Sage Publications	275 S. Beverly Dr., Beverly Hills, Calif. 90212
GB	Sage Publications, Ltd.	44 Hatton Gdn., London EC1
US	St. Johns University Press	Collegeville, Minn. 56321
US	St. Martin's Press, Inc.	175 5th Ave., New York, N.Y. 10010
US	San Francisco Press, Inc.	547 Howard St., San Francisco, Calif. 94105
US	Scandinavian University Books	P.O. Box 65642, Los Angeles, Calif. 90065
CA	Saunders of Toronto	1885 Leslie St., Don Mills, Ont. M3B 2M8
US	Schenkman Publishing Co., Inc.	3 Revere St., Cambridge, Mass. 02138
US	Schocken Books, Inc.	200 Madison Ave., New York, N.Y. 10016
US	Scott, Foresman and Co.	1900 E. Lake Ave., Glenview, Ill. 60025
GB	Scott, Foresman and Co. (US)	32 West Street, Brighton BN1 2RT
US	Charles Scribner's Sons	597 5th Ave., New York, N.Y. 10017
GB	Seminar Press Ltd.	24/28 Oval Rd., London NW1
US	Seminar Press	c/o Academic Press Inc. (See entry page i, App. 2)
US	Shoe String Press Inc.	955 Sherman Ave., Hamden, Conn. 06514
US	G. B. Sidgewick and Jackson, Ltd.	1 Tavistock Chambers, Bloomsbury Way, London WC1A 2SG
US	Simon and Schuster, Inc.	630 5th Ave., New York, N.Y. 10020
CA	Simon and Schuster of Canada, Ltd.	225 Yonge St. N., Richmond Hill, Ont. L4C 3C8
CA	Smithers and Bonellie	56 Esplanade St. E., Toronto, Ont.
GB	Studio Vista, Publishers	Blue Star House, Highgate Hill, London N19
US	Syracuse University Press	Box 8, University Station, Syracuse, N.Y. 13210
GB	Thames and Hudson, Ltd.	30 Bloomsbury St., London WC1
GB	Maurice Temple Smith Ltd.	37 Great Russell St., London WC1
US	Paul Theobald and Co.	5 No. Wabash Ave., Chicago, Ill. 60602
CA	Thomas Allen and Son Ltd.	850 York Mills Rd., Don Mills, Ont. M3B 3A7
US	Thomas Y. Crowell Co.	666 5th Ave., New York, N.Y. 10019
US	Thomas Nelson Inc.	Copewood and Davis Sts., Camden, N.J. 08103
CA	Thomas Nelson and Sons, Ltd.	81 Curlew Dr., Don Mills, Ont. M3A 2R1
GB	Thomas Nelson and Sons, Ltd.	36 Park St., London W1Y 4DE
US	Time Life Books, Inc.	Time and Life Bldg., Rockefeller Center, New York, N.Y. 10020
GB	Time Life International Ltd.	Time and Life Bldg., 153 New Bond St., London W1
GB	Tiptree Book Services Ltd.	Tiptree C05 0SR
GB	Trans-Atlantic Book Service, Ltd.	51 Weymouth St., London W1N 3LE
CA	Tundra Books, Inc.	1500 St. Catherine St. W., Montreal, P.Q.
US	U.S. Government Printing Office	Washington, D.C. 20402
US	Universitetsforlaget	Box 137, Boston, Mass. 02113
US	University of Alabama Press	Drawer 2877, University Alabama 35486
GB	University of California Press	2-4 Brook St., London W1Y 1AA
US	University of California Press	2223 Fulton St., Berkeley, Calif. 94720
US	University of Chicago Press	5750 Ellis Ave., Chicago, Ill. 60637
GB	University of Chicago Press	126 Buckingham Palace Road, London
US	University of Georgia Press	Waddel Hall, Athens, Ga. 30601
GB	University of Glasgow Press	The University of Glasgow G12 8QG
US	University of Illinois Press	Urbana, Ill. 61801
US	University of Kansas Press	Lawrence, Ka. 66044
US	University of Michigan Press	615 E. University, Ann Arbor, Mich. 48106
US	University of Missouri Press	107 Swallow Hall, Columbia, Mo. 65201
US	University of Nebraska Press	901 N. 17th St., Lincoln, Nebr. 68508
US	University of North Carolina Press	Box 2288 Chapel Hill, N.C. 27514
US	University of Notre Dame Press	Notre Dame, Ind. 46556
US	University of Pennsylvania Press	3933 Walnut St., Philadelphia, Pa. 19104
CA	University of Toronto Press	Front Campus, The University of Toronto, Toronto, Ont. M5S 1A6
CA	University of Victoria Press	Victoria, B.C.
US	University of Wisconsin Press	Box 1379 Madison, Wis. 33701
US	Urban Press	Box 8622, Boston, Mass. 02114
CA	Urban Educational Materials	P.O. Box 2245, Vancouver, B.C. V6B 3W2

US	Van Nostrand Reinhold Co.	450 W. 33rd St., New York, N.Y. 10001
GB	Van Nostrand Reinhold Co.	Windsor House, 46 Victoria St., London SW1H 0PB
CA	Van Nostrand Reinhold Ltd.	1410 Birchmount Rd., Scarborough, Ont. M1P 2E7
US	Viking Press	625 Madison Ave., New York, N.Y. 10022
CA	Wadsworth Publishing Co., Inc.	#808, 777 Cardero, Vancouver, B.C.
US	Wadsworth Publishing Co., Inc.	10 Davis Dr., Belmont, Calif. 94002
US	Walker and Co.	720 5th Ave., New York, N.Y. 10019
US	Washington Square Press	630 5th Ave., New York, N.Y. 10020
US	Watson-Guptill Publications, Inc.	165 W. 46th St., New York, N.Y. 10036
CA	G. R. Welch Co., Ltd.	310 Judson St., Toronto, Ont. M8Z 1J9
US	West Publishing Co.	50 W. Kellogg Blvd., St. Paul, Minn. 55102
US	Westminster Press	Witherspoon Bldg., Philadelphia, Pa. 19107
GB	Widenfeld and Nicolson	5 Winsley St., London W1N 7AQ
CA	John Wiley and Sons Canada, Ltd.	22 Worcester Rd., Rexdale, Ont. M9W 1L1
US	John Wiley and Sons, Inc.	605 3rd Ave., New York, N.Y. 10016
GB	John Wiley and Sons, Ltd.	Baffing Lane, Chichester, Sussex
US	Winthrop Publishers Inc.	17 Dunster St., Cambridge, Mass. 02138
US	Winchester Press	460 Park Ave., New York, N.Y. 10022
US	World Publishing Co.	110 E. 59th St., New York, N.Y. 10022
US	Wright Allen Press	238 Main St., Cambridge, Mass. 02142
GB	Yale University Press	20 Bloomsbury Square, London WC1A 2NP
US	Yale University Press	92A Yale Station, New Haven, Conn. 06520
GB	Visual Information Service	no address available
US	Visual Materials, Inc.	2549 Middlefield Rd., Redwood City, Calif. 94063
GB	Visual Publications, Ltd.	197 Kensington High St., London, Eng. W8
US	Warren Schloat Productions	Pleasantville, N.Y. 10570
US	Western Publishing Co., Inc.	850 Third Ave., New York, N.Y. 10022
US	Zephyrus	1201 Stanyan St., San Francisco, Calif. 94117

ADDITIONAL REPRESENTATIVES

GB	Blackwell Scientific Publications Ltd.	Osney Mead, Oxford, OX2 OEL
US	Books Canada Inc.	35 East-67th Street, New York, N.Y. 10021
GB	Books Canada, Ltd.	Ste. 600, 17 Cockspur St., London, S.W. 1Y 5BP
CA	Charles E. Merrill Publishing	115 Norfinch Drive, Downsview, Ontario M3N 1W9
US	Charles E. Merrill	1300 Alum Creek Dr., Columbus, Ohio 43216
US	Charterhouse Books, Inc.	750 Third Ave., New York, N.Y. 10017
GB	Constable and Co. Ltd.	10 Orange Street, London, WC2H 7EG
US	Cooper Square Publishers Inc.	59 Fourth Ave., New York, N.Y. 10003
GB	Dawson of Pall Mall	Cannon House, Folkestone, Kent, CT19 5EE
GB	English Universities Press	St. Paul's House, Warwick Lane, London EC4P 4AH
EU	Freal Vincent et Cie	4 Rue des Beaux-Arts, Paris 6e, France
GB	G. T. Foulis	50A Bell Street, Henley-on-Thames, Oxfordshire RG9 2BJ
CA	Har-Nal Distributors	81 Mack Avenue, Scarborough, Ont. M1L 1M8
CA	Irwin-Dorsey Ltd.	265 Guelph Street, Georgetown, Ont. L7G 4B3
US	Jossey-Bass, Inc., Publishers	615 Montgomery Street, San Francisco, Calf. 94111
GB	The M.I.T. Press	126 Buckingham Palace Road, London SW1W 9SD
CA	McClelland and Stewart Ltd.	25 Hollinger Road, Toronto, Ont. M4B 3G2
EU	Munksgaard Copenhagen	1370 Copenhagen K, 35, Norre Sogade, Denmark
CA	National Publishing Company, Inc.	690 Progress Ave., Unit 14, Scarborough, Ontario
US	Noble and Noble, Publishers Inc.	1 Dag Hammershjold Plaza, New York, N.Y. 10017
GB	Pandemic Ltd.	24a Litchfield St., London WC2H 9NJ
CA	Penguin Books Canada Ltd.	41 Steelcase Road West, Markham, Ont. L3R 1B4
CA	Renouf Publishing Co.	2182 St. Catherine St. West, Montreal 108, P.Q.
GB	Secker and Warberg	14 Carlisle St., London W1V 6NN
US	Shields Publishing Co. Inc.	155 N. College Ave., Ft. Collins, Colo. 80521
GB	Silco Books Ltd.	7 Russell Gardens, London NW11 9NJ
CA	Time Canada Ltd.	145 King Street West, Toronto, Ont.
GB	University of London Press	St. Paul's House, Warwick Lane, London EC4P 4AH
US	University of Toronto Press	33 East Tupper Street, Buffalo, N.Y. 14203
US	Xerox College Publishing	191 Spring St., Lexington, Mass. 02173

APPENDIX THREE: Non-bound and Audio-Visual Publishers and Distributors Address List

US	ABT Associates	55 Wheeler St., Cambridge, Mass. 02138
US	American Association for the Advancement of Science	1515 Massachusetts Ave., NW, Washington, D.C. 20005
US	American Heritage Publishing Co., Catalogue Dept.	P.O. Box 1776 Marion, Ohio 43302
US	Bailey Films, Inc.	6509 De Longpre Ave., Hollywood, Calif. 90028
GB	Beacon Filmstrips	no address available in Great Britain
US	Board of Cooperative Educational Services	Yorktown Heights, N.Y. 10598
US	Bobbs-Merrill Co., Inc. College Division	4300 W. 62nd St., Indianapolis, Ind. 46268
CA	Book Society of Canada	4386 Sheppard Ave. E., Agincourt, Ont. M1S 3B6
CA	British Columbia Teachers' Federation, Lesson Aids	2235 Burrard St., Vancouver, B.C. V6J 3H9
GB	BPC Publishing Ltd., Dept. D	P.O. Box 4, Radstock, Bath BA3 3RA
CA	Canfilm Screen Service, Ltd.	522-11th Ave. SW, Calgary, Alta. T2R 0C8
CA	CBC Learning Systems	Box 500, Station A, Toronto, Ont. M5W 1E6
US	Carman Educational Associates, Inc.	Box 205 Youngtown, N.Y. 14174
CA	Carman Educational Associates, Ltd.	Pine Grove, Ont. L0J 1J0
US	Center for Humanities, Inc.	2 Holland Ave., White Plains, N.Y. 10603
CA	Centre for Humanities, Ltd.	86 St. Regis Crescent N., Downsview, Ont. M3J 1Z3
US	Centre for Urban Development Research	Cornell University, 726 University Ave., Ithaca, N.Y. 14850
CA	City Films	4980 Buchan St., Montreal, P.Q.
GB	CI Audio Visual Ltd. (CIAV)	5 Rosemont Dr., London NW3 6NG
CA	Clarke, Irwin and Co., Ltd.	791 St. Clair Ave. W., Toronto, Ont. M6C 1B8
US	Classroom Dynamics Publishing Co.	231 O'Connor Dr., San Jose, Calif. 95128
CA	Collier-Macmillan Canada Ltd.	539 Collier-Macmillan Dr., Cambridge, Ont. M3C 2K2
GB	Collier-Macmillan Publishers	35 Red Lion Square WC1R 4SG
US	Commission on College Publications (AAG)	Department of Geography, Arizona State University, Tempe, Az. 85281
GB	Common Ground Filmstrips	Longman Group Ltd., Burnt Hill, Harlow, Essex CM20 2JE
US	Creative Visuals	Box 1911-7-9, Big Spring, Texas 79720
US	Curriculum Innovations, Inc.	1611 Chicago Ave., Evanston, Ill. 60201
US	DCA Educational Products	424 Valley Road, Warrington, Pa. 18976
US	Doubleday Multimedia	Box 11607, 1371 Reynolds Ave., Santa Ana, Calif. 92705
US	Denoyer Geppert Audio-Visuals	5235 Ravenswood Ave., Chicago, Ill. 60640
GB	Diana Wyllie, Ltd.	3 Park Road, Baker St., London NW1
US	Eastman Kodak Co.	Dept. 454, Rochester, N.Y. 14650
US	Educational Audio-Visual	Pleasantville, N.Y. 10570
GB	Educational Audio-Visual (UK)	30 Great Drayton Park, London N5
CA	Educational Consultants, Ltd.	Box 404, North Vancouver, B.C.
US	Educational Dimensions Corporation	P.O. Box 146, Great Neck, N.Y. 17023
CA	Educational Film Distributors	191 Eglinton Ave. E., Toronto, Ont. M4P 1K1
CA	Educational Progress Co., Ltd.	50 Galaxy Blvd., Rexdale, Ont. M9W 4V5
US	Educational Ventures, Inc.	209 Court St., Middletown, Conn. 06457
US	H. M. Elkins Co.	10031 Commerce Ave., Tujunga, Calif. 91042
CA	Encyclopedia Britannica	Offices in major cities in the U. S., Canada, and Great Britain. In Canada, all audio-visual material is handled by Visual Education Centre (address below)
US	Encyclopedia Britannica	
GB	Encyclopedia Britannica	
US	Environmetrics	1100 17th St., NW, Washington, D.C. 20036
GB	Eurospan Ltd.	St. George's House, 44 Hatton St., London, EC1
GB	Feffer and Simons	28 Norfolk St., London, Eng. WC2R 2EZ
US	Filmstrip House	432 Park Ave. S., New York, N.Y. 10010
US	W. H. Freeman and Co.	660 Market St., San Francisco, Calif. 94104
US	The Free Press	866 3rd Ave., New York, N.Y. 10022

CA	Gage Educational Publishing Ltd.	164 Commander Blvd., Agincourt, Ont. M1S 3C7
GB	Gateway Educational Films Ltd.	St. Lawrence House, 29-31 Broad St., Bristol BS1 2HF
CA	General Learning Press	115 Nugget Ave., Agincourt, Ont. M1S 3B1
CA	Ginn and Company	35 Mobile Dr., Toronto, Ont. M4A 1H6
US	Ginn and Company	Statler Bldg., Back Bay, P.O. 191, Boston, Mass. 02117
GB	Ginn and Co., Ltd.	18 Bedford Row, London WC1R 4EJ
US	Hammond, Inc.	Maplewood, N.J. 07040
CA	Harry Smith and Sons	1150 Homer St., Vancouver B.C. 520 King St. W., Toronto, Ont. M5V 1L7
US	Harwell Associates	Box 95, Convent Station, N.J. 07961
GB	Holt-Blond (HRW)	120 Golden Lane, Barbican, London EC1Y 0TU
US	Holt, Rinehart and Winston	383 Madison Ave., New York, N.Y. 10017
CA	Holt, Rinehart and Winston of Canada	55 Horner Ave., Toronto, Ont. M8Z 4X6
US	Hubbard Scientific Co.	P.O. Box 105, Northbrook, Ill. 60062
US	Imperial Film Company	Educational Development Corp. Bldg., P.O. Drawer 1007, Lakeland, Fla. 33803
US	Institute of International Studies	University of California, 2538 Channing Way, Berkeley, Calif. 94720
US	Institute of Urban and Regional Development	University of California, Berkeley, Calif. 94720
US	Instructional Simulations	2147 University Ave., St. Paul, Minn. 55114
US	Interact	P.O. Box 262, Lakeside, Calif. 92040
CA	International Telefilm Enterprises	221 Victoria St., Toronto, Ont. M5B 1V5
GB	Jackdaw Publications, Ltd.	30 Bedford Square, London, Eng. WC1
US	Kaiser Aluminum	300 Lakeside Dr., Oakland, Calif. 94604
US	Life Educational Reprint Program	Box 834, Radio City Post Office, New York, N.Y. 10019
US	McGraw Hill Book Co.	330 W. 42nd St., New York, N.Y. 10036
GB	McGraw Hill Book Co., Ltd.	Shoppenhangers Rd., Maidenhead, Berks.
CA	McGraw Hill-Ryerson, Ltd.	330 Progress Ave., Scarborough, Ont. M1P 2Z5
CA	McIntyre Educational Media, Ltd.	86 St. Regis Cres. N., Downsview, Ont. M3J 1Z3
US	The Macmillan Company	866 Third Ave., New York, N.Y. 10022
CA	Map Distribution Office	615 Booth St., Ottawa Ont.
CA	Medex	P.O. Box 32, Station B, Toronto, Ont. M5T 2T2
US	Modern Learning Aids	1212 Avenue of the Americas, New York, N.Y. 10036
US	Multi-Media Productions	P.O. Box 5097, Stanford, Calif. 94305
CA GB US	National Film Board of Canada	Offices in Canada, the U.S. and G.B. Head offices at: National Film Board, Ottawa, Ont.
US	National League of Cities	The City Bldg., 1612 K St., NW, Washington, D.C. 20006
US	New York Times Book and Educational Division	229 W. 43rd St., New York, N.Y. 10036
US	Pana-Vue Slides	c/o Sawyer's Inc., P.O. Box 444, Portland, Ore. 97207
GB	Patterson Associates	68 Copers Cope Rd., Beckenham, Kent
US	Popular Science Publishing Co., Audio-Visual Division	355 Lexington Ave., New York, N.Y. 10017
GB	Prentice Hall International, Inc.	Durrants Hill Road, Hemel Hempstead, Herts.
CA	Prentice Hall of Canada, Ltd.	1870 Birchmount Rd., Scarborough, Ont. M1P 2J7
US	Projection Arts, Inc.	20300 Ledgestone Dr., Southfield, Michigan 48076
US	Psychology Today Games	Del Mar, California 92014
GB	Rank Film Library	P.O. Box 70, Brentford, Middlesex, Eng. TW8 9HI
US	RHI Film Enterprises	4901 Main St., Kansas City, Mo. 64112
CA	School Book Fairs	55 Six Point Road, Etobicoke, Ont.
CA	School of Economic Science	2304 Islington Ave., Rexdale, Ont. M9W 3W7
US	Simile II	1150 Silverado, La Jolla, Calif. 92037
US	SVE (Society for Visual Education)	1345 Diversey Parkway, Chicago, Ill., 60614
GB	Time Life International, Ltd.	Time and Life Bldg., 153 New Bond St., London W1
CA	Urban Educational Materials	P.O. Box 2245, Vancouver, B.C. V6B 3W2
US	Urban Media Materials	212 Mineola Ave., Roslyn Heights, N.Y. 11577
EU	V-Dia Verlag Heidelberg	6900 Heidelberg 1/Postfach 1912/Heinrich-Fuchs Strasse 95-97
CA	Visual Education Centre	115 Berkeley Ave., Toronto, Ont. M5A 2W8

AUTHOR-TITLE INDEX

Abbott, B. NEW YORK IN THE THIRTIES. p 257.
Abler, R. SPATIAL ORGANIZATION. p 109.
Abrams, C. THE CITY IS THE FRONTIER. p 69.
Abrams, C. HOME OWNERSHIP FOR THE POOR. p 249.
Abrams, C. THE LANGUAGE OF CITIES. p 7.
Abrams, C. MAN'S STRUGGLE FOR SHELTER IN AN URBANIZING WORLD. p 121.
Abu-Lughod, J. L. CAIRO. p 52.
Acta Congressus Madvigiani. URBANISM AND TOWN PLANNING. p 20.
Adams, B. N. KINSHIP IN AN URBAN SETTING. p 105.
Adams, R. MacC. THE EVOLUTION OF URBAN SOCIETY. p 18.
Adamson, R. C. POLLUTION. p 115.
Adrian, C.R. GOVERNING URBAN AMERICA. 4th ed. p 99.
Africa, T.W. ROME OF THE CAESARS. p 15, 20.
Alagoa, E.J. THE SMALL BRAVE CITY STATE. p 237.
Aldred, C. EGYPT TO THE END OF THE OLD KINGDOM. p 19.
Alex, W. JAPANESE ARCHITECTURE. p 75.
Alexandersson, G. GEOGRAPHY OF MANUFACTURING. p 113.
Alford, R. BUREAUCRACY AND PARTICIPATION. p 267.
Ali, J. THE DETERMINATION OF THE COORDINATES OF CITIES. p 273.
Allen, E. STONE SHELTERS. p 78.
Almond, G.A. THE CIVIC CULTURE. p 99.
Alonso, W. LOCATION AND LAND USE. p 107.
Altshuler, A. THE CITY PLANNING PROCESS. p 99.
Ames, H.B. THE CITY BELOW THE HILL. p 25.
Anderson, N. URBANISM AND URBANIZATION. p 29.
Anderson, S. ed. PLANNING FOR DIVERSITY AND CHANGE. p 60.
Andreae. REIPUBLICAE CHRISTIANOPOLITANAE DESCRIPTIO. p 137.
Andrews, R.B. UNBAN LAND ECONOMICS AND PUBLIC POLICY. p 106.
Appleyard, D. THE VIEW FROM THE ROAD. p 83.
Arango, J. THE URBANIZATION OF THE EARTH. p 1.
Aranguren, J.L. HUMAN COMMUNICATION. p 125.
Arbital, S.L. CITIES AND METROPOLITAN AREAS. p 29.
Ardrey, R. THE TERRITORIAL IMPERATIVE. p 105.
Argan, G. C. THE RENAISSANCE CITY. p 16, 24.
Aristotle. POLITICS. p 137.
Armytage, W. H. G. HEAVENS BELOW. p 278.
Arthur, E. TORONTO. p 53.
Asbell, B. CAREERS IN URBAN AFFAIRS. p 128.
Ash, M. REGIONS OF TOMORROW. p 45.
Ashcom, B. J. STORIES OF THE INNER CITY. p 138.

Ashworth, W. THE GENESIS OF MODERN BRITISH TOWN PLANNING. p 25.
Asimov, I. THE CAVES OF STEEL. p 133.
Asimov, I. THE NAKED SUN. p 133.
Asimov, I. THE REST OF THE ROBOTS. p 134.
Augustune, H.A. CANADIAN STEROGRAMS. p 128.
Austin, A. G. URBAN GOVERNMENT FOR METROPOLITAN LIMA. p 103.
Auzelle, R. ENCYCLOPEDIA DE L'URBANISME. p 71.
Ayers, R.U. TECHNOLOGICAL FORECASTING AND LONG RANGE PLANNING. p 125.

B
Babcock, R. F. THE ZONING GAME. p 271.
Bacon, E. THE DESIGN OF CITIES. p 71, 260.
Bacon, E. DESIGN OF CITIES, 2nd ed. p 231.
Bacon, F NEW ATLANTIS. p 137.
Bagdikian, B. H. THE INFORMATION MACHINES. p 125.
Baier, K. (ed.) VALUES AND THE FUTURE. p 60.
Bailey, J. (ed.) NEW TOWNS IN AMERICA. p 232.
Baine, R.P. CALGARY. p 254.
Baine, R.P. TORONTO. p 53.
Bair, F. H. Jr. PLANNING CITIES. p 29.
Baker, T. MEDIEVAL LONDON. p 13, 22.
Baldinger, S. PLANNING AND GOVERNING THE METROPOLIS p 99.
Balfour, A. PORTSMOUTH. p 72.
Bamber, G. THE SEA IS BOILING HOT. p 133, 134.
Banfield, E. C. CITY POLITICS. p 99.
Banfield, E. C. THE UNHEAVENLY CITY. p 2.
Banfield, E. C. (ed.) URBAN GOVERNMENT. 4th ed. p 99.
Banz, G. ELEMENTS OF URBAN FORM. p 72.
Barnett, J. (ed.) OUR MISTREATED WORLD. p 115.
Bartholomew, H. LAND USES IN AMERICAN CITIES. p 30.
Bathke, W. L. (ed.) LAND MANAGEMENT IN THE '70s. p 244.
Beaujeu-Garnier, J. URBAN GEOGRAPHY. p 109.
Beckwith, B. P. THE NEXT 500 YEARS. p 60.
Bell, G. (ed.) HUMAN IDENTITY IN THE URBAN ENVIRONMENT. p 244.
Bell, G. URBAN ENVIRONMENTS AND HUMAN BEHAVIOR. p 235.
Bell, D. THE COMING OF POST-INDUSTRIAL SOCIETY. p 257.
Bell, D. (ed.) TOWARD THE YEAR 2000. p 60.
Bell, W. (ed.) THE SOCIOLOGY OF THE FUTURE. p 60.
Bellamy, E. LOOKING BACKWARD. p 137.
Bellan, R. C. THE EVOLVING CITY. p 12.
Bellush, J. (ed.) RACE AND POLITICS IN NEW YORK CITY. p 99.
Belshaw, C. S. THE GREAT VILLAGE. p 96.
Benevolo, L. THE ORIGINS OF MODERN TOWN PLANNING. p 25.

Benson, G. C. S. THE POLITICS OF URBANISM. p 267.
Benton, J. F. TOWN ORIGINS. p 22.
Bergel, E. E. URBAN SOCIOLOGY. p 85.
Bergel, E. E. SOCIAL STRATIFICATION. p 97.
Berman, B. R. PROJECTION OF A METROPOLIS. p 94.
Bernal, J. D. SCIENCE IN HISTORY. 3rd ed. p 8.
Bernard, P. AL KHANUM ON THE OXUS. p 20.
Bernari, M. L. JOURNEY THROUGH UTOPIA. p 137.
Bernheim, M. FROM BUSH TO CITY. p 48.
Berry, B. J. L. (ed.) GOALS FOR URBAN AMERICA. p 30.
Berry, B. J. L. (ed.) GEOGRAPHICAL PERSPECTIVES ON URBAN SYSTEMS. p 8.
Berry, B. J. L. THEORIES OF URBAN LOCATION. p 282.
Bertin, L. TARGET 2067. p 60.
Beshers, J. M. URBAN SOCIAL STRUCTURE. p 85.
Bestor, A. E. Jr. BACKWOODS UTOPIA. p 137.
Bestor, G. C. CITY PLANNING BIBLIOGRAPHY. 3rd ed. p 11.
Beyer, G. H. HOUSING AND SOCIETY. p 77.
Beyer, G. H. (ed.) THE URBAN EXPLOSION IN LATIN AMERICA. p 48.
Beyle, T. L. (ed.) PLANNING AND POLITICS. p 100.
Bicanic, R. PROBLEMS OF PLANNING. p 85.
Bish, R. L. THE PUBLIC ECONOMY OF METROPOLITAN AREAS. p 107.
Blackburn, P. THE CITIES. p 138.
Blair, C. L. THE CANADIAN LANSCAPE. p 128.
Blake, P. GOD'S OWN JUNKYARD. p 30.
Blecher, E. M. ADVOCACY PLANNING FOR URBAN DEVELOPMENT. p 249.
Bloomberg, W. (ed.) POWER, POVERTY, AND URBAN POLICY. p 250.
Bloomfield, P. IMAGINARY WORLDS. p 137.
Blumenfeld, H. THE MODERN METROPOLIS. p 8.
Blunden, W.R. THE LAND USE TRANSPORTATION SYSTEM. p 83.
Blunt, W. ISFAHAN. p 55.
Bock, P. K. (ed.) CULTURE SHOCK. p 86.
Bollens, J. C. COMMUNITIES AND GOVERNMENT IN A CHANGING WORLD. p 100.
Bollens, J. C. THE METROPOLIS. 2nd ed. p 30.
Bonjean, C. M. (ed.) COMMUNITY POLITICS. p 100.
Boon, G. S. TOWN LOOK, BOOK 1. p 68.
Borgstrom, G. THE HUNGRY PLANET. Rev. ed. p 119.
Boudon, P. LIVED IN ARCHITECTURE. p 261.
Bourne, L.S. THE FORM OF CITIES IN CENTRAL CANADA. p 272.
Bourne, L. S. URBAN SYSTEMS DEVELOPMENT IN CENTRAL CANADA. p 272.
Bourne, L. S. INTERNAL STRUCTURE OF THE CITY. p 109.
Boyle, T. (ed.) THE URBAN ADVENTURES. p 278.

Braidwood, R. J. (ed.) COURSES TOWARD URBAN LIFE. p 19.
Braithwaite, M. SERVANT OR MASTER. p 125.
Branch, D. P. FOLK ARCHITECTURE OF THE EASTERN MEDITERRANEAN. p 78.
Branch, M. C. CITY PLANNING AND AERIAL INFORMATION. p 128.
Branch, M. C. COMPREHENSIVE URBAN PLANNING. p 11.
Branner, R. GOTHIC ARCHITECTURE. p 75.
Branson, M. URBAN AMERICA. p 30.
Braun, H. HISTORICAL ARCHITECTURE. p 75.
Breckenfeld, G. COLUMBIA AND THE NEW CITIES. p 45.
Breese, G. (ed.) THE CITY IN NEWLY DEVELOPING COUNTRIES. p 48.
Breese, G. URBANIZATION IN NEWLY DEVELOPING COUNTRIES. p 2.
Brett, L. ARCHITECTURE IN A CROWDED WORLD. p 262.
Brewis, T. N. REGIONAL ECONOMIC POLICIES IN CANADA. p 107.
Bridenbaugh, C. CITIES IN THE WILDERNESS. p 24.
Bridenbaugh, C. CITIES IN REVOLT. p 24.
Briggs, A. VICTORIAN CITIES. p 25.
Briggs, K. FIELD WORK IN URBAN GEOGRAPHY. p 110.
Briggs, K. INTRODUCING TOWNS AND CITIES. p 273.
Brightbill, C. K. THE CHALLENGE OF LEISURE. p 122.
Brion, M. POMPEII AND HERCULANEUM. p 55.
Brion, M. VENICE. p 55.
BRITAIN TODAY SERIES. p 53.
Brody, E.B. BEHAVIOUR IN NEW ENVIRONMENTS. p 264.
Brown, F. E. ROMAN ARCHITECTURE. p 75.
Brown, H. (ed.) ARE OUR DESCENDENTS DOOMED. p 119.
Brown, H. (ed.) THE NEXT HUNDRED YEARS. p 61.
Brown, R. SOCIAL PSYCHOLOGY. p 98.
Bronwell, A. B. (ed.) SCIENCE AND TECHNOLOGY IN THE WORLD OF THE FUTURE. p 122.
Brucker, G. A. RENAISSANCE FLORENCE. p 15, 24.
Brunner, J. THE SHEEP LOOK UP. p 277.
Brunner, J. THE SQUARES OF THE CITY. p 277.
Brunner, J. STAND ON ZANZIBAR. p 277.
Brunner, J. THE WRONG END OF TIME. p 134.
Bryant, R.W.G. LAND. p 271.
Bryars, G. H. THIS BOOK IS ABOUT COMMUNICATION. BOOK I. p 125.
Buchanan Report (abr.) TRAFFIC IN TOWNS. p 83.
Buck Brothers' PANORAMA OF LONDON 1749. p 275.
Buckingham, W. AUTOMATION. p 122.
Bunge, W. FITZGERALD. p 92.
Bunker, R. TOWN AND COUNTRY OR CITY AND REGION? p 45.
Burhoe, R. W. (ed.) SCIENCE AND HUMAN VALUES IN THE 21ST CENTURY. p 61.

Burke, G. TOWNS IN THE MAKING. p 12.
Burke, J. G. (ed.) THE NEW TECHNOLOGY AND HUMAN VALUES. 2nd ed. p 61.
Burkhardt, J. THE CIVILIZATION OF THE RENAISSANCE OF ITALY p 241.
Burn, A.R. THE WARRING STATES OF GREECE. p 20.
Burns, J. ARTHROPODS: NEW DESIGN FEATURES. p 257.
Burrough, T.H.B. BRISTOL. p 72.
Bushnell, G. H. S. THE FIRST AMERICANS. p 28.

C

Cahill, S. (ed.) THE URBAN READER. p 138.
Cahn, E. S. (ed.) CITIZEN PARTICIPATION. p 92.
Calder, N. LIVING TOMORROW. p 61.
Calder, R. HOW LONG HAVE WE GOT? p 257.
Caldwell, J. C. AFRICAN RURAL-URBAN MIGRATION. p 266
Caldwell, J. C. POPULATION GROWTH AND FAMILY CHANGE IN AFRICA. p 48.
Callow, A. B. (ed.) AMERICAN URBAN HISTORY. p 12.
Calmfors, H. URBAN GOVERNMENT FOR GREATER STOCKHOLM. p 103.
Campanella, T. THE CITY OF THE SUN. p 137.
Cantacuzino, S. CANTERBURY. p 72.
Cannon, M. W. URBAN GOVERNMENT FOR VALENCIA, VENEZUELA. p 270.
Canty, D. THE NEW CITY. p 30.
Carpenter, E. FORECASTS OF THE COMING CENTURY. p 137.
Carson, R. THE SILENT SPRING. p 115.
Carter, E. THE FUTURE OF LONDON. p 53.
Carter, E. J. COUNTY OF LONDON PLAN. p 53.
Carter, F. W. DUBROVNIK. p 237.
Carter, H. THE STUDY OF URBAN GEOGRAPHY. p 273.
Carter, H. URBAN STUDIES. p 110.
Carver, H. CITIES IN THE SUBURBS. p 51.
Cary, L. J. (ed.) COMMUNITY DEVELOPMENT AS A PROCESS. p 30.
CASSELL LONDON SERIES. p 13, 235.
Castagnoli, F. ORTHOGONAL TOWN PLANNING IN ANTIQUITY. p 20.
Cattell, D. T. A CASE STUDY OF SOVIET URBAN GOVERNMENT. p 103.
Center For Policy Study. THE SOCIAL IMPACT OF URBAN DESIGN. p 69.
Chadwick, G. F. THE PARK AND THE TOWN. p 75.
Champdor, A. BABYLON. p 240.
Chandler, T. 3000 YEARS OF URBAN GROWTH. p 235, 275.
Chaoy, F. THE MODERN CITY. p 16, 26.
Chapin, F. S. URBAN LAND USE PLANNING, 2nd ed. p 245.
Chapin, F. S. (ed.) URBAN GROWTH DYNAMICS . . . p 45.
Carbonneau, L. NO PLACE ON EARTH. p 134.
Charbonneau, L. PSYCHEDELIC-40. p 134.
Chen, K. (ed.) URBAN DYNAMICS. p 245.
Chermayeff, S. COMMUNITY AND PRIVACY. p 31.

Chermayeff, S. SHAPE OF COMMUNITY. p 2.
Cherry, G. E. TOWN PLANNING IN ITS SOCIAL CONTEXT. p 31.
Cherry, G. E. URBAN CHANGE AND PLANNING. p 242.
de Chiara, J. PLANNING DESIGN CRITERIA. p 79.
Childe, V. G. MAN MAKES HIMSELF. p 13.
Childe, V. G. WHAT HAPPENED IN HISTORY. p 19.
Chinitz, B. CITY AND SUBURB. p 57.
Chinitz, B. FREIGHT AND THE METROPOLIS. p 94.
Chinoy, E. SOCIETY. p 91.
Chisholm, M. (ed.) REGIONAL FORECASTING. p 251.
Christensen, D. URBAN DEVELOPMENT. p 31.
Christopher, J. THE DEATH OF GRASS (or NO BLADE OF GRASS). p 134.
Christopher, J. THE LONG WINTER. p 134.
Churchill, H. S. THE CITY IS THE PEOPLE. p 31.
Cipolla, C. THE ECONOMIC HISTORY OF WORLD POPULATION. 4th ed. p 120.
CITIES OF THE WORLD SERIES. p 53.
CITIES SERIES. p 53.
CITY BUILDING SERIES. p 72.
THE CITY OF MAN SERIES. p 140.
Claire, W. H. HANDBOOK ON URBAN PLANNING. p 245.
Clapp, J. A. NEW TOWNS AND URBAN POLICY. p 45.
Clark, C. POPULATION GROWTH AND LAND USE. p 119.
Clark, J. I. POPULATION GEOGRAPHY AND THE DEVELOPING COUNTRIES. p 119.
Clark, P. (ed.) CRISIS AND ORDER IN ENGLISH TOWNS. p 24.
Clark, S. D. THE DEVELOPING CANADIAN COMMUNITY. 2nd ed. p 13.
Clark, S. D. THE SUBURBAN SOCIETY. p 57.
Clark, S. D. (ed.) URBANISM AND THE CHANGING CANADIAN SOCIETY. p 86.
Claster, J. N. (ed.) ATHENIAN DEMOCRACY. p 20.
Clawson, M. SUBURBAN LAND CONVERSION IN THE UNITED STATES. p 46.
Clifford, M. L. CHALLENGE OF THE CITY. p 280.
Cochrane, E. FLORENCE IN THE FORGOTTEN CENTURIES. p 241.
Cohn, N. THE PURSUIT OF THE MILLENIUM. Rev. ed. p 137.
Cole, M. ROBERT OWEN OF NEW LENARK. p 137.
Coleman, B. I. (ed.) THE IDEA OF THE CITY IN NINETEENTH CENTURY BRITAIN. p 242.
Collins, G. R. CAMILLO SITTE . . . p 26, 27.
Congressional Quarterly. THE URBAN ENVIRONMENT. p 31.
Conrad. U. THE ARCHITECTURE OF FANTASY. p 261.
Cook, P. (ed.) ARCHIGRAM. p 261, 275.
Cook, P. ARCHITECTURE. p 61, 72.
Cook, P. EXPERIMENTAL ARCHITECTURE. p 61, 72.
Cooper, J. I. MONTREAL: A BRIEF HISTORY. p 254.

Coser, R. L. (ed.) THE FAMILY. p 86.
Cottrell, L. LOST CITIES. p 13.
Couperie, P. PARIS THROUGH THE AGES. p 13, 54.
Coulborn, R. FEUDALISM IN HISTORY. p 22.
Cowan, P. (ed.) DEVELOPING PATTERNS OF URBANIZATION. p 245.
Cowan, P. (ed.) THE FUTURE OF PLANNING. p 245.
Cox, K. R. CONFLICT, POWER, AND POLITICS IN THE CITY. p 267.
Cox, F. M. (ed.) STRATEGIES OF COMMUNITY ORGANIZATION. p 86.
Crawford, K. G. CANADIAN MUNICIPAL GOVERNMENT. p 100.
Crecine, J. P. FINANCING THE METROPOLIS p 250.
Creighton, R. L. URBAN TRANSPORTATION PLANNING. p 263.
Crosby, T. ARCHITECTURE. p 72.
Cullen, G. THE CONCISE TOWNSCAPE. p 2.
Cullen, G. TOWNSCAPE. p 2, 5.
Cullingsworth, J. B. TOWN AND COUNTRY PLANNING. 3rd ed. p 31.
Curl, J. S. EUROPEAN CITIES AND SOCIETY. p 2.
Currie, A. W. CANADIAN TRANSPORTATION ECONOMICS. p 263.

D

Dahinden, J. URBAN STRUCTURES FOR THE FUTURE. p 257.
Daland, R. T. COMPARATIVE URBAN RESEARCH. p 267.
D'Antonio, W. V. INFLUENTIALS IN TWO BORDER CITIES. p 267.
D'Antonio, W. V. INFLUENTIALS IN TWO BORDER CITIES. p 249.
Dancer, W. S. GREATER LONDON. p 54.
Daniel, G. THE FIRST CIVILIZATIONS. p 13.
Danielson, M. N. (ed.) METROPOLITAN POLITICS. 2nd ed. p 100.
Dansereau, P. (ed.) CHALLENGE FOR SURVIVAL. p 116.
Darling, F.F. (ed.) FUTURE ENVIRONMENTS OF NORTH AMERICA. p 132.
David, P. URBAN LAND DEVELOPMENT. p 107.
Davidson, B. EAST 100TH ST. p 86.
Davis, M. METROPOLITAN DECISION PROCESSES. p 267.
Davies, E. TRANSPORT IN GREATER LONDON. p 56, 83.
De Camp, L. S. THE ANCIENT ENGINEERS. p 14.
De Carlo, G. URBINO. p 54.
De Jouvenal, B. THE ART OF CONJECTURE. p 61, 63.
De Volpi, C. P. OTTAWA. p 26.
De Volpi, C. P. TORONTO. p 26.
De Vos, A. (ed.) THE POLLUTION READER. p 118.
De Wofle, I. (ed.) CIVILIA. p 61, 72.
De Wofle, I. THE ITALIAN LANDSCAPE. p 73.
De la Croix, H. MILITARY CONSIDERATIONS IN CITY PLANNING. p 17, 239.

Delgado, J. M. R. PHYSICAL CONTROL OF THE MIND. p 122.
Demcyzynski, S. AUTOMATION AND THE FUTURE OF MAN. p 122.
Dentler, R. A. (ed.) AMERICAN COMMUNITY PLANNING. p 31.
Derry, T. K. A SHORT HISTORY OF TECHNOLOGY. p 14.
Detwyler, T. R. (ed.) URBANIZATION AND ENVIRONMENT. p 110.
Dickinson, R. CITY AND REGION. p 110.
Dickinson, R THE CITY REGION IN WESTERN EUROPE. p 110.
Dickinson, R. REGIONAL ECOLOGY. p 116.
Dickinson, R. THE WESTERN EUROPEAN CITY. p 110.
Diebold, J. MAN AND THE COMPUTER. p 61.
Dober, R. P. ENVIRONMENTAL DESIGN. p 79.
Dobriner, W. M. CLASS IN SUBURBIA. p 52.
Donaldson, S. THE SUBURBAN MYTH. p 52.
Donnison, D. (ed.) LONDON: URBAN PATTERNS, PROBLEMS AND POLICIES. p 254, 264.
Dore, R. P. CITY LIFE IN JAPAN. p 54.
Dosman, E. J. INDIANS. p 233.
Downes, B. T. (ed.) CITIES AND SUBURBS. p 100.
Downs, A. URBAN PROBLEMS AND PROSPECTS. p 31.
Downey, G. ANCIENT ANTIOCH. p 241.
Downey, G. A HISTORY OF ANTIOCH IN SYRIA FROM SELENCUS TO THE ARAB CONQUEST. p 241.
Doxiadis, C. A. ARCHITECTURAL SPACE IN ANCIENT GREECE. p 21.
Doxiadis, C. A. ARCHITECTURE IN TRANSITION. p 66.
Doxiadis, C. A. EKISTICS. p 1, 3.
Doxiadis, C. A. EMERGENCE AND GROWTH OF AN URBAN REGION. p 54.
Doxiadis, C.A. URBAN RENEWAL AND THE FUTURE OF THE AMERICAN CITY. p 259.
Druks, H. CITIES IN CIVILIZATION. p 14.
Duhl, L. J. (ed.) THE URBAN CONDITION. p 32.
Duncan, B. METROPOLIS AND REGION IS TRANSITION. p 110.
Dunlop, J. T. (ed.) AUTOMATION AND TECHNOLOGICAL CHANGE. p 122.
Dunstan, M. WORLDS IN THE MAKING. p 3.
Dwyer, D. J. (ed.) ASIAN URBANIZATION. p 48.
Dyos, H. J. (ed.) THE STUDY OF URBAN HISTORY. p 14.
Dyos, H. J. THE VICTORIAN CITY. p 233, 242.

E

Eckbo, G. THE LANDSCAPE WE SEE. p 116.
Eddy, E. M. (ed.) URBAN ANTHROPOLOGY. p 105.
Eden, L. CRISIS IN WATERTOWN. p 264.
Eisenstadt, S. N. BUILDING STATES AND NATIONS. p 245.
Elazar, D. J. CITIES OF THE PRAIRIE. p 245, 267.
Eldridge, H. W. (ed.) TAMING MEGALOPOLIS. p 32.

ELEK SERIES. p 55.
Elias, C. E. Jr. (ed.) METROPOLIS. p 86.
Ellul, J. THE TECHNOLOGICAL SOCIETY. p 123.
Elsner, H. THE TECHNOCRATS. p 275.
Epstein, A. L. POLITICS IN AN URBAN AFRICAN COMMUNITY. p 96.
Erber, E. URBAN PLANNING IN TRANSITION. p 32.
Ernst, M. L. UTOPIA 1976. p 61.
Esin, E. MECCA THE BLESSED, MADINAH THE RADIANT. p 55.
Esfandiary, F. M. OPTIMISM ONE. p 3.
Esfandiary, F. M. UP-WINGERS: A FUTURIST MANIFESTO. p 257.
Estall, R.C. INDUSTRIAL ACTIVITY AND ECONOMIC GEOGRAPHY. p 114.
Etzioni, A. (ed.) SOCIAL CHANGE. p 86.
Evenson, N. CHANDIGARH. p 55.
Evenson, N. LE CORBUSIER. p 16, 26, 77.
Evenson, N. TWO BRAZILIAN CAPITALS. p 254.
Everson, J. A. INSIDE THE CITY. p 245.
Everson, J. A. SETTLEMENT PATTERNS. p 100.
Ewald, W. R. Jr. (ed.) ENVIRONMENT FOR MAN. p 32.
Ewing, D. W. THE HUMAN SIDE OF PLANNING. p 32, 34.

F
Fabun, D. THE DIMENSIONS OF CHANGE. p 62.
Fabun, D. THE DYNAMICS OF CHANGE. p 62.
Fairbrother, N. NEW LIVES, NEW LANDSCAPES. p 116.
Faltermayer, E. K. REDOING AMERICA. p 32.
Fathy, H. THE ARAB HOUSE IN THE URBAN SETTING. p 252.
Fava, S. F. (ed.) URBANISM IN WORLD PERSPECTIVE. p 9.
Feldman, H. KARACHI. p 55.
Feldman, L. D. (ed.) POLITICS AND GOVERNMENT OF URBAN CANADA. p 100, 267.
Feldman, L. D. (ed.) A SURVEY OF ALTERNATIVE URBAN POLICIES. p 32.
Fenton, E. THE HUMANITIES IN THREE CITIES. p 14.
Ficker, V. B. (ed.) SOCIAL SCIENCE AND URBAN CRISIS. p 245.
Field, A. J. (ed.) CITY AND COUNTRY IN THE THIRD WORLD. p 252.
FIRST NATIONAL CITY BANK, PROFILE OF A CITY. p 251.
Firth, R. FAMILIES AND THEIR RELATIVES. p 92.
Fiser, W. S. MASTERY OF THE METROPOLIS. p 86.
Fisher, J. C. (ed.) CITY AND REGIONAL PLANNING IN POLAND. p 51.
Fogelson, R. M. THE FRAGMENTED METROPOLIS. p 55.
Foreign Policy Association. TOWARD THE YEAR 2018. p 62.
Forrester, J. W. URBAN DYNAMICS. p 62.
Forrester, J. W. WORLD DYNAMICS. p 62.
Forster, E. M. THE MACHINE STOPS. p 137.
Fortune (ed.) THE ENVIRONMENT, p 116.
Fortune (ed.) THE EXPLODING METROPOLIS. p 33.
Fourier, C. LE NOUVEAU MONDE INDUSTRIEL AND SOCIETAIRE. p 137.
Frankenberg, R. COMMUNITIES IN BRITAIN. p 33.
Fraser, D. VILLAGE PLANNING IN THE PRIMITIVE WORLD. p 16, 19.
Fraser, G. FIGHTING BACK. p 259.
Freeman, R. (ed.) POPULATION. p 120.
Freeman, T. W. GEOGRAPHY AND PLANNING. p 111.
French, R. M. (ed.) THE COMMUNITY. p 86.
Fried, J. P. HOUSING CRISIS, U.S.A. p 77.
Fried, R. C. PLANNING THE ETERNAL CITY. p 254.
Friedberg, M. P. PLAY AND INTERPLAY. p 33.
Frieden B. J. SHAPING AN URBAN FUTURE. p 246.
Frieden, B. J. (ed.) URBAN PLANNING AND SOCIAL POLICY. p 86.
Friedman, J. (ed.) REGIONAL DEVELOPMENT AND PLANNING. p 46.
Friedman, J. URBANIZATION, PLANNING AND NATIONAL DEVELOPMENT. p 251.
Frisch, M. H. TOWN INTO CITY. p 254.
Fruin, J. J. PEDESTRIAN PLANNING AND DESIGN. p 83.
Fuermann, G. HOUSTON. p 56.
Fuller, B. (ed.) APPROACHING THE BENIGN ENVIRONMENT. p 116.
Fustel de Coulanges, N. D. THE ANCIENT CITY. p 21.

G
Gabor, D. INNOVATIONS. p 123.
D. INVENTING THE FUTURE. p 62.
Gabor, D. THE MATURE SOCIETY. p 257.
Gallagher, J. E. (ed.) SOCIAL PROCESS AND INSTITUTION. p 87.
Gale, F. URBAN ABORIGINES. p 265.
Galouye, D. F. SIMULACRON-3 p 134.
Gamer, R. E. THE POLITICS OF URBAN DEVELOPMENT IN SINGAPORE. p 96.
Gans, H. THE LEVITTOWNERS. p 93.
Gans, H. (ed.) PEOPLE AND PLANS. p 33.
Gans, H. THE URBAN VILLAGERS. p 93.
Garnier, T. UN CITE INDUSTRIELLE. p 137.
Gaunt, W. FLEMISH CITIES. p 55.
Geddes, P. CITY DEVELOPMENT. p 261.
Geddes, P. CITIES IN EVOLUTION. p 67.
Gentilcore. R. L. (ed.) CANADA'S CHANGING GEOGRAPHY. p 111.
Gentilcore, R. L. GEOGRAPHICAL APPROACHES TO CANADIAN PROBLEMS. p 114.
Gerber, R. UTOPIAN FANTASY. p 137.
Gerson, W. PATTERNS OF URBAN LIVING. p 33.
Gerther, L. O. (ed.) PLANNING THE CANADIAN ENVIRONMENT. p 33.

Gertler, L. O. REGIONAL PLANNING IN CANADA. p 251.
Ghurye, G. S. CITIES AND CIVILIZATION. p 14.
Gibbs, J. P. (ed.) URBAN RESEARCH METHODS. p 68.
Gibberd, F. TOWN DESIGN. 5th ed. p 33.
Gibberd, F. TOWN DESIGN. 6th ed. p 246, 266.
Gide, C. COMMUNIST AND COOPERATIVE COLONIES. p 137.
Gideon, J. WATTER GROPIUS. p 77.
Gies, J. LIFE IN A MEDIEVAL CITY. p 22.
Gillespie, W. I. THE URBAN PUBLIC ECONOMY. p 107.
Gillie, F. B. AN APPROACH TO TOWN PLANNING. p 33.
Gillie, F. B. BASIC THINKING IN REGIONAL PLANNING. p 46.
Ginger, R. (ed.) MODERN AMERICAN CITIES. p 33.
Ginzberg, E. NEW YORK IS VERY MUCH ALIVE. p 271.
Gist, N. P. URBAN SOCIETY. 5th ed. p 87.
Glabb, C. N. A HISTORY OF URBAN AMERICA. p 14.
Glagg, D. V. (ed.) POPULATION IN HISTORY. p 120.
Glazebrook, G. P. de T. THE STORY OF TORONTO. p 254.
Glazer, N. BEYOND THE MELTING POT. 2nd ed. p 87.
Glazer, N. (ed.) CITIES IN TROUBLE. p 34.
Glikson, A. REGIONAL PLANNING AND DEVELOPMENT. p 46.
Gloag, J. A GUIDE TO WESTERN ARCHITECTURE. p 75.
Glotz, G. THE GREEK CITY AND ITS INSTITUTIONS. p 21.
Goldfinger, M. VILLAGES IN THE SUN. p 79.
Goldstein, K. K. THE WORLD OF TOMORROW. p 62.
Goldston, R. LONDON. p 254.
Goldston, R. NEW YORK. p 56.
Goldston, R. SUBURBIA. p 253.
Goldwin, R. A. (ed.) A NATION OF CITIES. p 246.
Goodall, B. THE ECONOMICS OF URBAN AREAS. p 107.
Goodman, C. LIFE FOR DEAD SPACES. p 34.
Goodman, M. CONTROLLING POLLUTION. p 116.
Goodman, P. COMMUNITAS. p 34.
Goodman, R. AFTER THE PLANNERS. p 34.
Goodman, W. I. (ed.) PRINCIPLES AND PRACTICE OF URBAN PLANNING. 4th ed. p 129.
Goracz, A. THE URBAN FUTURE. p 63.
Gordon, D. N. (ed.) SOCIAL CHANGE AND URBAN POLITICS. p 268.
Gordon, D. R. CITY LIMITS: BARRIERS TO CHANGE IN URBAN GOVERNMENT. p 268.
Gordon, M. SICK CITIES. p 34.
Gore, M. S. URBANIZATION AND SOCIAL CHANGE IN INDIA. p 96.
Gottmann, J. MEGALOPOLIS. p 93.
Gottmann, J. METROPOLIS ON THE MOVE. p 111.
Gould, J. A DICTIONARY OF THE SOCIAL SCIENCES. p 9.

Grava, S. URBAN PLANNING ASPECTS OF WATER POLLUTION. p 274.
GREAT AGES OF WORLD ARCHITECTURE. p 75.
GREAT LONDON PAPERS. p 56.
Green, C. McL. AMERICAN CITIES IN THE GROWTH OF THE NATION. p 15.
Green, C McL. THE RISE OF URBAN AMERICA. p 15.
Green, C. McL. WASHINGTON: CAPITAL CITY, 1879-1950. p 243.
Green, J. L. ECONOMIC ECOLOGY. p 203.
Greer, S. THE EMERGING CITY. p 3.
Greer, S. GOVERNING THE METROPOLIS. p 100.
Greer, S. URBAN RENEWAL AND AMERICAN CITIES. p 69.
Greer, S. THE URBANE VIEW. p 87.
Gregory, P. POLLUTED HOMES. p 116.
Griffin, P. F. GEOGRAPHY OF POPULATION. p 120.
Griffith, E. S. A HISTORY OF AMERICAN CITY GOVERNMENT. p 243, 268.
Group On Environmental Eduction (GEE). OUR MAN-MADE ENVIRONMENT, BOOK SEVEN. p 128.
Gruen, V. CENTERS FOR THE URBAN ENVIRONMENT. p 256.
Gruen, V. THE HEART OF OUR CITIES. p 3.
Gulick, J. TRIPOLI: A MODERN ARAB CITY. p 252.
Gunn, A. M. PATTERNS IN WORLD GEOGRAPHY. p 111.
Gunn, J. E. MAN AND THE FUTURE. p 63.
Gunther, J. TWELVE CITIES. p 56.
Gutkind, E. A. INTERNATIONAL HISTORY OF CITY DEVELOPMENT. p 4.
Gutkind, E. A. URBAN DEVELOPMENT IN EAST CENTRAL EUROPE. p 4.
Gutkind, E. A. URBAN DEVELOPMENT IN EASTERN EUROPE. p 4.
Gutkind, E. A. TWILIGHT OF CITIES. p 34.
Gutman, R. (ed.) NEIGHBOURHOOD, CITY AND METROPOLIS. p 87.
Gutman, R. PEOPLE AND BUILDINGS. p 246.
Gutnov, A. THE IDEAL COMMUNIST CITY. p 51.

H
Haar, C. M. (ed.) LAW AND LAND. p 245.
Hadden, J. K. (ed.) METROPOLIS IN CONFLICT. 2nd ed. p 100.
Hagman, D. G. URBAN PLANNING AND LAND DEVELOPMENT CONTROL LAW. p 105.
Hahn, H. (ed.) PEOPLE AND POLITICS IN URBAN SOCIETY. p 250.
Hahn, H. URBAN RURAL CONFLICT: THE POLITICS OF CHANGE. p 269.
Hall, E. T. THE HIDDEN DIMENSION. p 105.
Hall, P. THE CONTAINMENT OF URBAN ENGLAND. p 251.
Hall, P. LONDON 2000. p 123.
Hall, P. G. THE WORLD CITIES. p 56.
Halloran, J. D. THE EFFECTS OF MASS COMMUNICATION . . . p 126.
Halpern, J. M. THE CHANGING VILLAGE COMMUNITY. p 96.

Halprin, L. CITIES. p 35.
Halprin, L. CITIES, Rev. ed. p 246.
Halprin, L. FREEWAYS. p 80.
Halprin, L. NOTEBOOKS. p 262.
Hamblin, D. J. THE FIRST CITIES. p 240.
Hamill, R. H. PLENTY AND TROUBLE. p 123.
Hammond, J. L. THE TOWN LABOURER. p 26.
Hammond, M. THE CITY IN THE ANCIENT WORLD. p 231, 236.
Hance, W. A. POPULATION, MIGRATION & URBANIZATION IN AFRICA. p 49.
Hancock, A. MASS COMMUNICATION. p 126.
Handlin, O. THE HISTORIAN AND THE CITY. p 238.
Handlin, O. THE NEW COMERS. p 94.
Hanna, W. J. URBAN DYNAMICS IN BLACK AFRICA. p 49.
Hansen, N. M. TWELVE CITIES. p 35.
Hardoy, J. URBAN PLANNING IN PRE-COLUMBIAN AMERICA. p 16, 28.
Haring, J. E. URBAN AND REGIONAL ECONOMICS. p 271.
Harmer, R. M. UNFIT FOR HUMAN CONSUMPTION. p 116.
Harrington, J. OCEANA. p 137.
Harrington, M. THE ACCIDENTAL CENTURY. p 246.
Harris, C. C. READINGS IN KINSHIP IN URBAN SOCIETY. p 106.
Harris, C. D. CITIES IN THE SOVIET UNION. p 51.
Harris, F. THE STATE OF THE CITIES. p 246.
Harris, M. TOWN AND COUNTRY IN BRAZIL. p 96.
Harrison, H. AHEAD OF TIME. p 258.
Harrison, H. MAKE ROOM! MAKE ROOM! p 133, 135.
Harrison, H. (ed.) THE YEAR 2000. p 272.
Hartwick, J. M. URBAN ECONOMIC GROWTH. p 272.
Harvey, D. SOCIETY, THE CITY AND THE SPACE-ECONOMY OF URBANISM. p 282.
Harvey, E. B. PERSPECTIVES ON MODERNIZATION. p 246.
Harvey E. R. SYDNEY, NOVA SCOTIA. p 56.
Haskins, C. P. OF SOCIETIES AND MEN. p 87.
Hastie, T. HOME LIFE. p 87.
Hatt, P. K. (ed.) CITIES AND SOCIETY. 2nd ed. p 87.
Hauser, A. THE SOCIAL HISTORY OF ART. p 9.
Hauser, P. THE STUDY OF URBANIZATION. p 35.
Hawkins, B. W. POLITICS AND URBAN POLICIES. p 101.
Hawley, A. H. THE METROPOLITAN COMMUNITY. p 101.
Hawley, W. D. IMPROVING THE QUALITY OF URBAN MANAGEMENT. p 250.
Haworth, L. THE GOOD CITY. p 35.
Healy, S. TOWN LIFE. p 35.
Hebert, R. HIGHWAYS TO NOWHERE. p 263, 269.
Hedman, R. AND ON THE EIGHTH DAY. 2nd ed. p 35.

Heer, D. M. (ed.) READINGS ON POPULATION. p 120.
Heer, D. M. SOCIETY AND POPULATION. p 120.
Heinlein, R. VARIOUS TITLES. p 135.
Helfgott, R. B. MADE IN NEW YORK. p 94.
Hellman, H. THE CITY IN THE WORLD OF THE FUTURE. p 63.
Hellman, H. COMMUNICATIONS IN THE WORLD OF THE FUTURE. p 63.
Hellman, H. TRANSPORTATION IN THE WORLD OF THE FUTURE. p 63.
Hellwig, J. INTRODUCTION TO COMPUTERS AND PROGRAMMING. p 123.
Helmer, J. (ed.) URBAN MAN. p 233.
Helmer, O. SOCIAL TECHNOLOGY. p 63.
Hennessey, R. A. S. TRANSPORT. p 80.
Henry, E. L. (ed.) MICROPOLIS IN TRANSITION. p 93.
Henry, J. CULTURE AGAINST MAN. p 98.
Herber, L. CRISIS IN OUR CITIES. p 116.
Herbert, F. THE DRAGON IN THE SEA or 21ST CENTURY SUB. p 135.
Herbert, J. D. (ed.) URBAN PLANNING IN THE DEVELOPING COUNTRIES. p 49.
HERITAGE OF SOCIOLOGY SERIES. p 93.
Hertzler, J. O. THE HISTORY OF UTOPIAN THOUGHT. p 278.
Herzl, T. OLDNEWLAND. p 137.
Hetzler, S. A. TECHNOLOGICAL GROWTH AND SOCIAL CHANGE. p 88.
Hibbert, C. LONDON. p 238.
Hickman, D. BIRMINGHAM. p 72.
Higbee, E. A QUESTION OF PRIORITIES. p 5.
Higbee, E. THE SQUEEZE. p 35.
Highsmith, R. M. (ed.) CASE STUDIES IN WORLD GEOGRAPHY. p 111.
Hilberseimer, L. CONTEMPORARY ARCHITECTURE. p 73.
Hilberseimer, L. THE NATURE OF CITIES. p 15.
Hilberseimer, L. THE NEW REGIONAL PATTERN. p 67.
Hiller, C. E. BABYLON TO BRASILIA. p 231.
Hirsch, S. C. CITIES ARE PEOPLE. p 35.
Hirsch, W. Z. GOVERNING URBAN AMERICA IN THE 1970's. p 270.
Hirsch, W. Z. LOS ANGELES: VIABILITY AND PROSPECTS FOR METROPOLITAN LEADERSHIP. p 270.
Hirsch, W. Z. URBAN ECONOMIC ANALYSIS. p 272.
Hirsch, W. Z. (ed.) URBAN LIFE AND FORM. p 35.
HISTORICAL CITIES SERIES. p 15.
Hitchcock, H. R. THE RISE OF AMERICAN ARCHITECTURE. p 261.
Hoag, J. D. WESTERN ISLAMIC ARCHITECTURE. p 75.
Hobbes, T. LEVIATHAN. p 137.
Hobhouse, H. LOST LONDON. p 75.
Hodge, D. L. THE CHALLENGE OF AMERICA'S METROPOLITAN POPULATION OUTLOOK. p 248.
Hohauser, S. ARCHITECTURAL AND INTERIOR MODELS. p 69.

Hoiberg, O. G.   EXPLORING THE SMALL COMMUNITY.   p 269.
Hollingshead, A. B.   ELMTOWN'S YOUTH.   p 94.
Holloway, M.   HEAVENS ON EARTH.   p 137.
Holmes, E.   TOMORROW.   p 137.
Holmes, E.   WHAT IS AND WHAT MIGHT BE.   p 137.
Holmes, M.   ELIZABETHAN LONDON.   p 13, 24.
Holmes, U. T.   DAILY LIVING IN THE TWELFTH CENTURY.   p 22.
Hoover, E. M.   ANATOMY OF A METROPOLIS.   p 94.
Horton, P. B.   SOCIOLOGY. 2nd ed.   p 91.
Hoskin, F. P.   THE FUNCTIONS OF CITIES.   p 246.
Hoskin, F. P.   THE LANGUAGE OF CITIES.   p 5.
Hourani, A. H. (ed.)   THE ISLAMIC CITY.   p 49.
House, P. W.   THE URBAN ENVIRONMENTAL SYSTEM.   p 247.
Howard, E.   GARDEN CITIES OF TOMORROW.   p 67.
Hoyt, H.   ACCORDING TO HOYT.   p 36.
Hoyt, H.   THE STRUCTURE AND GROWTH OF RESIDENTIAL NEIGHBOURHOODS . . .   p 35.
Hubbard, T. K.   OUR CITIES TODAY TOMORROW.   p 36.
Hughes, H. MacG. (ed.)   CITIES AND CITY LIFE.   p 88.
Hughes, H. MacG. (ed.)   CROWD AND MASS BEHAVIOUR.   p 98.
Hughes, H. MacG. (ed.)   POPULATION GROWTH AND THE COMPLEX SOCIETY.   p 94.
Hughes, Q.   LIVERPOOL.   p 72.
Hugo-Brunt, M.   THE HISTORY OF CITY PLANNING.   p 238.
Hull, O.   FRONTIERS OF GEOGRAPHY.   p 111.
Hull, O.   LONDON.   p 56.
Hull, O.   TRANSPORT.   p 80.
Hunter, F.   COMMUNITY POWER STRUCTURE.   p 101.
Hurd, R. M.   PRINCIPLES OF CITY LAND VALUES.   p 36.
Huxley, A.   BRAVE NEW WORLD.   p 135, 137.

I
I.C.M.A.   MUNICIPAL YEARBOOK (annual)   p 129.
I.F.H.P.   URBAN RENEWAL.   p 69.
I.U.R.I.I.S.   THE WORLD'S METROPOLITAN AREAS.   p 56.
Irving, J. A.(ed.)   MASS MEDIA IN CANADA.   p 126.
Isard, W.   METHODS OF REGIONAL ANALYSIS.   p 46.

J
Jackson, J. N.   THE CANADIAN CITY.   p 247.
Jackson, J. N.   SURVEYS FOR TOWN AND COUNTRY PLANNING.   p 68.
Jackson, J. N.   THE URBAN FUTURE.   p 64, 258.
Jackson, K. T. (ed.)   CITIES IN AMERICAN HISTORY.   p 15.

Jacobs, D.   CONSTANTINOPLE.   p 22.
Jacobs, J.   THE DEATH AND LIFE OF GREAT AMERICAN CITIES.   p 36.
Jacobs, J.   THE ECONOMY OF CITIES.   p 5.
Jakobson, L. (ed.)   URBANIZATION AND NATIONAL DEVELOPMENT.   p 252.
James, E. O.   FROM CAVE TO CATHEDRAL.   p 76.
Janke, R.   ARCHITECTURAL MODELS.   p 69.
Jellicoe, G.   MOTOPIA.   p 83.
Jencks, C.   ARCHITECTURE 2000   p 64.
Johnson, E. A. J.   THE ORGANIZATION OF SPACE IN DEVELOPING COUNTRIES.   p 253.
Johnson, J. H.   URBAN GEOGRAPHY.   p 273.
Johnson, J. M.   URBAN GEOGRAPHY.   p 111.
Johnson, K. M.   URBAN GOVERNMENT FOR THE PREFECTURE OF CASABLANCA.   p 103.
Johnson-Marshall, P.   REBUILDING CITIES.   p 5.
Johnston, R. J.   URBAN RESIDENTIAL PATTERNS.   p 78.
Join-Lambert, M.   JERUSALEM.   p 238.
Jonas, G.   CITIES.   p 278.
Jones, A. H. M.   THE CITIES OF THE EASTERN ROMAN PROVINCES. 2nd ed.   p 21.
Jones, A. H. M.   THE GREEK CITY.   p 240.
Jones, E.   HUMAN GEOGRAPHY.   p 111.
Jones, E.   TOWNS AND CITIES.   p 111.
Jones F. L.   DIMENSIONS OF URBAN SOCIAL STRUCTURE.   p 265.
Jones, M. A.   HOUSING AND POVERTY IN AUSTRALIA.   p 260.
Jungk, R. (ed.)   MANKIND 2000.   p 64.

K
Kahn, H.   THINGS TO COME.   p 123.
Kahn, H.   THE YEAR 2000.   p 123.
Kammer, G. M.   THE URBAN POLITICAL COMMUNITY.   p 269.
Kaplan, H.   URBAN POLITICAL SYSTEMS.   p 101.
Kaplan, H.   URBAN RENEWAL POLITICS.   p 260.
Karp, H. M.   TOWARD EN ECOLOGICAL ANALYSIS . . .   p 46.
Keeble, L.   PRINCIPLES AND PRACTICE OF TOWN AND COUNTRY PLANNING. 4th ed.   p 36.
Keller, S.   THE URBAN NEIGHBORHOOD.   p 88.
Kennet, W.   PRESERVATION.   p 260.
Kent, T. J.   THE URBAN GENERAL PLAN.   p 36.
Kenyon, K. M.   JERUSALEM.   p 238.
Kettle, J.   FOOTNOTES ON THE FUTURE.   p 64.
Kibel, B. M.   SIMULATION OF THE URBAN ENVIRONMENT.   p 282.
Kimmich, C.M.   THE FREE CITY.   p 238.
Knelman, F. H. (ed.)   1984 AND ALL THAT.   p 64.
Koller, M. R.   MODERN SOCIOLOGY.   p 92.
Kormondy, E. J. (ed.)   READINGS IN ECOLOGY.   p 132.
Korn, A.   HISTORY BUILDS THE TOWN.   p 15.
Kornbluth, C. M.   THE SYNDIC.   p 135.
Kostelanetz, R. (ed.)   SOCIAL SPECULATIONS.   p 64.
Kotler, M.   NEIGHBORHOOD GOVERNMENT.   p 101.
Kramer, S. N.   CRADLE OF CIVILIZATION.   p 19.

Krapf-Ashari, E. YORUBA TOWNS AND CITIES. p 49.
Krueger, R. R. REGIONAL AND RESOURCE PLANNING IN CANADA. p 46.
Krueger, R. R. REGIONAL AND RESOURCE PLANNING IN CANADA. Rev. ed. p 46.
Krueger, R. R. URBAN PROBLEMS. p 36.
Kulski, J. E. LAND OF URBAN PROMISE. p 247.
Kyte, E. C. (ed.) OLD TORONTO. p 26.

L

Lagerberg, C.S.I.J. THE PROFILE OF A COMMERCIAL TOWN IN WEST-CAMERON p 273.
Lampl, P. CITIES AND PLANNING IN THE ANCIENT NEAR EAST. p 16, 19.
Landau, R. MOROCCO. p 55.
Landers, R. R. MAN'S PLACE IN THE DYBOSPHERE. p 124.
Lane, F. C. VENICE: A MARITIME REPUBLIC p 242.
Lang, J. DESIGNING FOR HUMAN BEHAVIOUR. p 262.
Lapidus, I. M. MIDDLE EASTERN CITIES. p 241.
Lapidus, I. M. MUSLIM CITIES IN THE LATE MIDDLE AGES. p 23.
Laredo, V. NEW YORK CITY. p 255.
Laumann, E. O. PRESTIGE AND ASSOCIATION IN AN URBAN SETTING. p 106.
Laurie, P. BENEATH THE CITY STREETS. p 37.
Le Corbusier (Jeanneret-Gris, C. E.) THE CITY OF TOMORROW. p 77.
Le Corbusier. CONCERNING TOWN PLANNING. p 37.
Le Corbusier. THE RADIANT CITY. p 73.
Le Corbusier. TOWARDS A NEW ARCHITECTURE. p 77.
Leach, G. THE BIOCRATS, Rev. ed. p 275.
Leahy, W. H. (ed.) URBAN ECONOMICS. p 107.
Leibbrand, K. TRANSPORTATION AND TOWN PLANNING. p 80.
Leinwald, G. THE CITY AS COMMUNITY. p 40.
Leinwald, G. CITY GOVERNMENT. p 40.
Leinwald, G. THE PEOPLE OF THE CITY. p 40.
Leinwald, G. THE SLUMS. p 40.
Leinwald, G. THE TRAFFIC JAM. p 40.
Lenz-Romeiss, F. THE CITY: NEW TOWN OR HOME TOWN. p 264.
Levin, M. R. (ed.) EXPLORING URBAN PROBLEMS. p 37.
Levine, H. J. HITLER'S FREE CITY. p 239.
Lewis, D. (ed.) THE GROWTH OF CITIES. p 232.
Lewis, D. (ed.) THE PEDESTRIAN IN THE CITY. p 37.
Lewis, D. (ed.) URBAN STRUCTURE. p 247.
Lewis, J. D. INDUSTRIAL APPROACHES TO URBAN PROBLEMS. p 249.
Lewis, O. FIVE FAMILIES. p 96.
Lewis, O. VILLAGE LIFE IN NORTHERN INDIA. p 96.
Lewis, P. F. VISUAL BLIGHT IN AMERICA. p 282.
Lin Yutang. IMPERIAL PEKING. p 55.

Lipsky, M. PROTEST IN CITY POLITICS. p 260, 269.
Lissitzky, E. RUSSIA. p 77.
Liston, R. A. DOWNTOWN. p 37, 243.
Litchenberg, R. M. ONE-TENTH OF A NATION. p 94.
Lithwick, N. H. URBAN CANADA. p 37.
Lithwick, N. H. (ed.) URBAN STUDIES. p 112.
Lithwick, N. H. URBAN POVERTY. p 107.
Little, C. E. CHALLENGE OF THE LAND. p 37.
Lobel, M. D. (ed.) HISTORIC TOWNS. p 16.
Loewenstein, L. K. (ed.) URBAN STUDIES. p 37.
Lofland, L. H. A WORLD OF STRANGERS. p 233, 267.
Logie, G. THE URBAN SCENE. p 37.
London, P. BEHAVIOUR CONTROL. p 124.
Long, N. E. THE UNWALLED CITY. p 101.
LOOK (ed.) SUBURBIA. p 52.
Lopez, R. S. MEDIEVAL TRADE IN THE MEDITERRANEAN WORLD. p 240.
Lorimer, J. A CITIZEN'S GUIDE TO CITY POLITICS. p 269.
Loveridge, R. O. CITY MANAGERS IN LEGISLATIVE POLITICS. p 101.
Lowe, J. R. CITIES IN A RACE WITH TIME. p 107.
Lowry, B. RENAISSANCE ARCHITECTURE. p 75.
Lubove, R. TWENTIETH CENTURY PITTSBURGH. p 15, 26, 57.
Lubove, R. THE URBAN COMMUNITY. p 243.
Lucas, R. A. MINETOWN, MILLTOWN, RAILTOWN. p 38.
Lynch, K. THE IMAGE OF THE CITY. p 1, 5, 68, 247.
Lynch, K. SITE PLANNING. 1st ed. p 38.
Lynch, K. SITE PLANNING. 2nd ed. p 38.
Lynch, K. WHAT TIME IS THIS PLACE? p 247.
Lynd, R. S. MIDDLETOWN. p 247.
Lynd, R. S. MIDDLETOWN IN TRANSITION. p 265.

M

MacDonald, W. EARLY CHRISTIAN AND BYZANTINE ARCHITECTURE. p 75.
MacGraw, F. M. THE RISE OF THE CITY. p 38.
Maclagan, M. THE CITY OF CONSTANTINOPLE. p 239.
MacNeill, J. W. ENVIRONMENTAL MANAGEMENT. p 117.
McDonagh, E. C. (ed.) SOCIAL PROBLEMS. p 88.
McDonagh, E. C. (ed.) SOCIAL PROBLEMS. 2nd ed. p 89.
McHale, J. THE ECOLOGICAL CONTEXT. p 117.
McHale, J. THE FUTURE OF THE FUTURE. p 64.
McHale, J. WORLD FACTS AND TRENDS, 2nd ed., p 258, 276.
McHarg, I. DESIGN WITH NATURE. p 115, 118.
McKelvey, B. THE CITY IN AMERICAN HISTORY. p 239.
McKeowen, J. E. (ed.) THE CHANGING METROPOLIS. p 248.
McLoughlin, J. B. CONTROL AND URBAN PLANNING. p 248.

McLoughlin, J. B. URBAN AND REGIONAL PLANNING. p 46.
McLuhan, M. THE GUTENBERG GALAXY. p 126.
McLuhan, M. THE MEDIUM IS THE MASSAGE. p 124.
McLuhan, M. UNDERSTANDING MEDIA. 2nd ed. p 124.
McMahon, W. SOUTH JERSEY TOWNS. p 242.
McQuade, W. (ed.) CITIES FIT TO LIVE IN. p 89.
McReynolds, D. WE HAVE BEEN INVADED BY THE 21ST CENTURY. p 258.
Machiavelli, N. DISCOURSES. p 137.
Machiavelli, N. THE PRINCE. p 137.
Maddox, J. THE DOOMSDAY SYNDROME. p 258.
Madgewick, P. J. AMERICAN CITY POLITICS. p 102.
Mahood, H. R. (ed.) URBAN POLITICS AND PROBLEMS. p 102.
Maksimovich, B. SOCIALIST PLANNING IN THE CITIES OF EASTERN EUROPE. p 17.
Mallowan, M. E. L. EARLY MESOPOTAMIA AND IRAN. p 19.
Malt, H. L. FURNISHING THE CITY. p 73.
Mandelbaum, S. J. BOSS TWEED'S NEW YORK. p 15, 26.
Mandelker, D. R. THE ZONING DILEMMA. p 70.
Mangin, W. (ed.) PEASANTS IN CITIES. p 97.
Mann, P. H. AN APPROACH TO URBAN SOCIOLOGY. p 88.
Mann, R. RIVERS OF THE CITY. p 247.
Mann, W. E. CANADA. 1st ed. p 88.
Mann, W. E. CANADA. 2nd ed. p 88.
Man, W. E. (ed.) THE UNDERSIDE OF TORONTO. p 94.
Mannheim, K. ESSAYS ON SOCIOLOGY AND SOCIAL PSYCHOLOGY. p 98.
Manuel, F. E. UTOPIAS AND UTOPIAN THOUGHT. p 278.
Margetson, S. REGENCY LONDON. p 13, 24.
Margolis, J. (ed.) THE PUBLIC ECONOMY OF URBAN COMMUNITIES. p 108.
Marsh, L. COMMUNITIES IN CANADA. p 88.
Marshall, J. U. THE LOCATION OF SERVICE TOWNS. p 112.
Martin, B. V. PRINCIPLES AND TECHNIQUES . . . URBAN AREA TRANSPORTATION. p 83.
Martin, J. THE COMPUTERED SOCIETY. p 124.
Mason, D. R. THE END BRINGERS. p 277.
Masotti, Louis H. THE URBANIZATION OF THE SUBURBS. p 250.
Mass, N. J. (ed.) READINGS IN URBAN DYNAMICS. p 248.
Masson, J. K. (ed.) EMERGING PARTY POLITICS IN URBAN CANADA. p 269.
Masters, D. C. THE RISE OF TORONTO. p 26.
Matsushita, R. (ed.) HOUSING. p 78.
Maunder, W. J. (ed.) POLLUTION. p 117.
Mayer, A. THE URGENT FUTURE. p 78.
Mayer, H. M. (ed.) A MODERN CITY. p 112.
Mayer, H. M. (ed.) READINGS IN URBAN GEOGRAPHY. p 88.
Mayer, H. M. THE SPATIAL EXPRESSION OF URBAN GROWTH. p 282.
Mayer, P. TOWNSMEN OR TRIBESMEN. p 106.
Mayerovitch, H. OVERSTREET. p 248.
Meadow, C. T. MAN-MADE COMMUNICATION. p 126.
Meadows, D. H. THE LIMITS TO GROWTH. p 9, 65.
Meadows, P. (ed.) URBANISM, URBANIZATION, AND CHANGE. p 38.
Medhurst, D. F. URBAN DECAY. p 70.
Meier, R. L. A COMMUNICATIONS THEORY OF URBAN GROWTH. p 126.
Mellaart, J. CATAL HUYUK. p 240.
Mellaart, J. EARLIEST CIVILIZATIONS IN THE ANCIENT NEAR EAST. p 19.
Mercier, L. S. MEMOIRS OF THE YEAR 2500. p 137.
Merlin, P. NEW TOWNS. p 47.
Merrfield, R. ROMAN LONDON. p 13, 21.
Mesthene, E. TECHNOLOGICAL CHANGE. p 124.
Mesthene, E. TECHNOLOGICAL AND SOCIAL CHANGE. p 124.
Metcalf, P. VICTORIAN LONDON. p 238, 243.
Meyer, J. R. THE URBAN TRANSPORTATION PROBLEM. p 80.
Meyerson, M. BOSTON. p 57.
Meyerson, M. FACE OF THE METROPOLIS. p 39.
Meyerson, M. (ed.) HOUSING, PEOPLE, AND CITIES. p 38.
Michael, D. N. THE UNPREPARED SOCIETY. p 65.
Michel, J. CITY OF RELEVATION. p 248.
Michelson, W. MAN AND HIS URBAN ENVIRONMENT. p 89.
Midura, E. M. (ed.) WHY AREN'T WE GETTING THROUGH. p 125.
Miles, S. METROPOLITAN PROBLEMS. p 39.
Mill, J. S. ON LIBERTY. p 126.
Miller, A. R. THE ASSAULT ON PRIVACY. p 126.
Miller, D. A. IMPERIAL CONSTANTINOPLE. p 15, 24.
Millon, H. A. BAROQUE AND ROCOCO ARCHITECTURE. p 75.
Mills, C. W. THE POWER ELITE. p 89.
Mills, T. M. THE SOCIOLOGY OF SMALL GROUPS. p 98.
Milner, J. B. (ed.) COMMUNITY PLANNING. p 102.
Minar, D. THE CONCEPT OF COMMUNITY. p 6.
Minar, H. (ed.) THE CITY IN MODERN AFRICA. p 97.
Miner, R. W. CONSERVATION OF HISTORICAL AND CULTURAL RESOURCES. p 70.
Minshull, R. SETTLEMENTS FROM THE AIR. p 128.
Mitchell, J. C. (ed.) SOCIAL NETWORKS IN URBAN SITUATIONS. p 97.
Mitchell, J. G. (ed.) ECOTACTICS. p 117.
Mitchell, J. G. HISTORICAL GEOGRAPHY. p 113.
Mohl, R. A. THE URBAN EXPERIENCE. p 239.
Moholy-Nagy, S. MATRIX OF MAN. p 9.
Monter, W. CALVIN'S GENEVA. p 15, 24.

Moore, E. RESIDENTIAL MOBILITY IN THE CITY. p 282.
Moore, W. E. SOCIAL CHANGE. p 89.
More, T. UTOPIA. p 137.
Morgan, F. POLLUTION. p 117.
Morgan, W. T. W. NAIROBI. p 57, 114.
Morrill, R. L. THE SPATIAL ORGANIZATION OF SOCIETY. p 112.
Morris, D. THE HUMAN ZOO. p 106.
Morris, J. CITIES. p 57.
Morris, R. N. THE SOCIOLOGY OF HOUSING. p 89.
Morris, R. N. URBAN SOCIOLOGY. p 89.
Morris, W. A DREAM OF JOHN BALL. p 137.
Morris, W. NEWS FROM NOWHERE. p 137.
Moscow, A. CITY AT SEA. p 39.
Moss, R. THE WAR FOR THE CITIES. p 234.
Moynihan, D. (ed.) TOWARD A NATIONAL URBAN POLICY. p 39.
Mulvihill, D. F. GEOGRAPHY, MARKETING, AND URBAN GROWTH. p 114.
Mumford, L. ARTS AND TECHNIQUES. p 67.
Mumford, L. THE CITY IN HISTORY. p 1, 7, 12.
Mumford, L. THE HIGHWAY AND THE CITY. p 80.
Mumford, L. STICKS AND STONES. 2nd rev. ed. p 73.
Mumford, L. THE URBAN PROSPECT. p 39.
Mundy, J. H. THE MEDIEVAL TOWN. p 22.
Murin, W. J. MASS TRANSIT POLICY PLANNING. p 81.
Murphy, R. E. THA AMERICAN CITY. p 9.
Murphy, R. E. THE CENTRAL BUSINESS DISTRICT. p 257.

N
N.C.D.C. THE FUTURE CANBARRA. p 57.
N.C.G.E. STATISTICS FOR GEOGRAPHY TEACHERS. p 129.
N.C.G.E. URBAN GEOGRAPHY. p 112.
Negley, P. THE QUEST FOR UTOPIA. p 137.
Negroponte, N. THE ARCHITECTURAL MACHINE. p 258, 261.
Neil, E. M. CRAWLEY. p 53.
Neil, E. M. NEWCASTLE. p 53.
Neil, E. M. TEESIDE. p 53.
Neutra, R. SURVIVAL THROUGH DESIGN. p 73.
Neutze, M. THE SUBURBAN APARTMENT BOOM. p 52.
Newman, O. DEFENSIBLE SPACE. p 234.
New York City Planning Commission. PLAN FOR NEW YORK CITY. p 57, 243.
New York City Planning Commission. CRITICAL ISSUES. p 57.
NEW YORK METROPOLITAN REGION STUDY SERIES. p 94.
Niebanck, P. L. RELOCATION IN URBAN PLANNING. p 94.
Nims, C. F. THEBES OF THE PHAROAHS. p 55.
Nisbet, R. A. QUEST FOR COMMUNITY. p 102.
Nixon, G. P. FOUR CITIES. p 39.

Norberg-Schulz, C. EXISTENCE, SPACE AND ARCHITECTURE. p 79.
Nuttgens, P. THE LANDSCAPE OF IDEAS. p 261.
Nuttgens, P. YORK. p 72.

O
Oakley, D. THE PHENOMENON OF ARCHITECTURE IN CULTURES OF CHANGE. p 49.
O'Connor, J. R. EXPLORING THE URBAN WORLD. p 249.
Odum, E. P. ECOLOGY. p 133.
Ofshe, R. (ed.) THE SOCIOLOGY OF THE POSSIBLE. p 65.
Okin, T. A. THE URBANIZED NIGERIAN. p 49.
Oram, N. TOWNS IN AFRICA. p 49.
Orleans, P. (ed.) RACE, CHANGE, AND URBAN SOCIETY. p 250.
Orr, S. C. REGIONAL AND URBAN STUDIES. p 47.
Orwell, G. ANIMAL FARM. p 135.
Orwell, G. 1948. p 135, 137.
Osborn, F. J. GREEN BELT CITIES. New ed. p 47.
Osborn, F. J. THE NEW TOWNS. 2nd ed. p 47.
Ostrowski, W. CONTEMPORARY TOWN PLANNING . . . p 67.
Owen, R. A NEW VIEW OF SOCIETY. p 137.
Owen, W. THE ACCESSIBLE CITY. p 40.
Owen, W. CITIES IN THE MOTOR AGE. p 81.
Owen, W. METROPOLITAN TRANSPORTATION PROBLEMS. rev. ed. p 81.

P
Pahl, R. E. PATTERNS OF URBAN LIFE. p 89.
Pahl, R. E. (ed.) READINGS IN URBAN SOCIOLOGY. p 89.
Pahl, R. E. WHOSE CITY? p 90.
Palen, J. J. (ed.) URBAN AMERICA. p 90.
Palladio, A. THE FOUR BOOKS OF ARCHITECTURE. p 261.
Palmer, M. CITIES. p 40.
Papageorgiou, A. CONTINUITY AND CHANGE. p 40.
Park, R. E. THE CITY. p 93.
Parker, R. S. (ed.) THE POLITICS OF URBAN GROWTH. p 269.
Parker, S. THE FUTURE OF WORK AND LEISURE. p 65, 94.
Parkin, H. (ed.) THE SOCIAL ANIMAL. p 10.
Parsons, T. SOCIAL STRUCTURE AND PERSONALITY. p 98.
Pass, D. VALLINGBY AND FARSTA. p 252.
Passonneau, J. R. URBAN ATLAS: 20 AMERICAN CITIES. p 275.
Patrick, J. H. MONTREAL. p 57.
Pauw, E. A. THE SECOND GENERATION. p 106.
Pawley, M. ARCHITECTURE VERSUS HOUSING. p 78.

Peccei, A. THE CHASM AHEAD. p 258.
Pell, C. MEGALOPOLIS UNBOUND. p 81.
PEOPLE AND THE CITY SERIES. p 143.
Perin, C. WITH MAN IN MIND. p 98.
Perloff, H. S. (ed.) THE FUTURE OF THE U.S. GOVERNMENT. p 65.
Perloff, H. S. ISSUES IN URBAN ECONOMICS. p 108.
Perloff, H. S. (ed.) THE QUALITY OF THE URBAN ENVIRONMENT. p 117.
Pevsner, N. AN OUTLINE OF EUROPEAN ARCHITECTURE. 7th ed. p 76.
Pfautz, H. W. (ed.) CHARLES BOOTH ON THE CITY. p 93.
Philipson, M. AUTOMATION. p 125.
Phillips, B. S. WORLD OF THE FUTURE. p 258.
Phillips, J. C. MUNICIPAL GOVERNMENT AND ADMINISTRATION IN AMERICA. p 102.
Piggott, S. PRE-HISTORIC INDIA. p 19.
Pirenne, H. MEDIEVAL CITIES. p 22.
PLANNING AND CITIES SERIES. p 12, 16-17.
Plato. REPUBLIC. p 137.
Plunkett, T. J. URBAN CANADA AND ITS GOVERNMENT. p 102.
Pohl, F. GLADIATOR AT LAW. p 135.
Pohl, F. NIGHTMARE AGE. p 135.
Pohl, F. SPACE MERCHANTS. p 135.
Porter, J. CANADIAN SOCIAL STRUCTURE. p 95.
Potter, J. M. (ed.) PEASANT SOCIETY. p 106.
Powell, A. (ed.) THE CITY. p 255.
Power, J., (ed.) POLITICS IN A SUBURBAN COMMUNITY. p 270.
Powicke, M. R. THE COMMUNITY OF THE REALM. p 241.
PRAEGER SPECIAL STUDIES IN INTERNATIONAL POLITICS AND PUBLIC AFFAIRS. p 102.
Prak, N. L. THE LANGUAGE OF CITIES. p 261.
Pred, A. R. URBAN GROWTH AND CIRCULATION OF INFORMATION. p 242.
Prehoda, R. W. DESIGNING THE FUTURE. p 126.
Price, J. A. TIJUANA. p 255, 266.
Price, R. YELLOWKNIFE. p 255.
Pritchard, J. M. TOWNS AND CITIES. p 112.
PROBLEMS OF AMERICAN SOCIETY SERIES. p 40.
Procopiou, A. ATHENS. p 55.
Pundt, H. G. SCHINKEL'S BERLIN. p 262.
Purdom, C. B. THE BUILDING OF SATELLITE TOWNS. new ed. p 47.
Pusic, E. URBAN GOVERNMENT FOR ZAGREB. p 103.
Putnam, R. G. (ed.) A GEOGRAPHY OF URBAN PLACES. p 112.
Rabinovitz, F. F. (ed.) LATIN AMERICAN URBAN RESEARCH. p 253.
Radford, E. THE NEW VILLAGERS. p 265.
Radinowitz, F. F. CITY POLITICS AND PLANNING. p 103.
Rand, C. LOS ANGELES. p 58.
Ranney, G. LANDLORD AND TENANT. p 278.
Ranum, O. PARIS IN THE AGE OF ABSOLUTISM. p 15, 25.
Raphael, R. CODE THERE. p 136.
Rapoport, A. HOUSE FORM AND CULTURE. p 262.

Rasmussen, S. E. EXPERIENCING ARCHITECTURE. p 73.
Rasmussen, S. E. TOWNS AND BUILDINGS. p 76.
Read, B. HEALTHY CITIES. p 117.
Rechy, J. CITY OF NIGHT. p 249.
Regional Plan Association. URBAN DESIGN MANHATTAN. p 58, 243.
Reich, C. A. THE GREENING OF AMERICA. p 65.
Reid, C. 21ST CENTURY MAN EMERGING. p 65.
Reid, T. E. CONTEMPORARY CANADA. p 108.
Reiner, T. A. THE PLACE OF THE IDEAL COMMUNITY . . . p 67.
Reisman, D. THE LONELY CROWD. p 98.
Reiss, A. J. LOUIS WIRTH ON CITIES AND SOCIAL LIFE. p 93.
Reissman, L. THE URBAN PROCESS. p 40.
Reps, J. W. TOWN PLANNING IN FRONTIER AMERICA. p 25.
Reps, J. W. THE MAKING OF URBAN AMERICA. p 243.
Reynolds, D. J. THE URBAN TRANSPORTATION PROBLEM. p 81.
Rice, D. T. CONSTANTINOPLE. p 55.
Rice, M. J. CHICAGO. p 58.
Richards, B. NEW MOVEMENT IN CITIES. 2nd ed. p 81.
Richards, F. HOMONOVUS: THE NEW MAN. p 258.
Richardson, B. THE FUTURE OF CANADIAN CITIES. p 234.
Richardson, H. W. URBAN ECONOMICS. p 108.
Richardson, I. L. URBAN GOVERNMENT FOR RIO DE JANEIRO. p 270.
Richardson, J. F. THE AMERICAN CITY. p 239.
Richardson, M. SAN PEDRO, COLUMBIA. p 266.
Richardson, R. E. BUILDING FOR PEOPLE. p 40.
Richardson, R. E. (ed.) DEVELOPING WATER RESOURCES. p 132.
Ritter, P. PLANNING FOR MAN AND MOTOR. p 81.
Rivet, A. L. F. TOWN AND COUNTRY IN ROMAN BRITAIN. 2nd ed. p 21.
Robbins, S. M. MONEY METROPOLIS. p 94.
Roberts, E. T. LAND USE PLANNING. p 105.
Robertson, D. PRE-COLUMBIAN ARCHITECTURE. p 75.
Robertson, D. W. CHAUCER'S LONDON. p 15, 23.
Robinson, J. HIGHWAYS AND OUR ENVIRONMENT. p 263.
Robson, W. A. GREAT CITIES OF THE WORLD. 1st ed. p 58.
Robson, W. A. (ed.) GREAT CITIES OF THE WORLD. 3rd ed. p 10.
Robson, W. A. THE HEART OF GREATER LONDON. p 56.
Robson, W. A. LOCAL GOVERNMENT IN CRISIS, 2nd rev. ed. p 103.
Rodwin, L. (ed.) THE FUTURE METROPOLIS. p 65.
Rodwin, L. NATIONS AND CITIES. p 50.
Rodwin, L. PLANNING URBAN GROWTH . . . p 50.
Rogers, D. 110 LIVINGSTON STREET. p 270.

Rogers, D. THE MANAGEMENT OF BIG CITIES. p 103.
Rorig, F. THE MEDIEVAL TOWN. p. 23.
Rose, A. J. PATTERNS OF CITIES. p 112.
Rose, H. M. SOCIAL PROCESSES IN THE CITY. p 282.
Rose, J. AUTOMATION. p 126.
Rose, S. M. THE BETRAYAL OF THE POOR. p 95.
Rosenau, H. THE IDEAL CITY IN ITS ARCHITECTURAL EVOLUTION. p 76.
Rosenau, H. SOCIAL PURPOSE IN ARCHITECTURE. p 76.
Rosenfeld, A. THE SECOND GENESIS. p 10.
Rosenbloom, R. S. (ed.) SOCIAL INNOVATION IN THE CITY. p 90.
Rosenwaike, I. POPULATION HISTORY OF NEW YORK CITY. p 274.
Roshwald, M. LEVEL 7. p 136.
Rosman, G. URBAN NETWORK IN CH'ING CHINA AND TOKUGAWA JAPAN. p 244.
Ross, A. D. THE HINDU FAMILY IN ITS URBAN SETTING. p 97.
Roth, G. PAYING FOR ROADS. p 84.
Rousseau, J. J. THE SOCIAL CONTRACT. p 137.
Rowat, D. C. THE CANADIAN MUNICIPAL SYSTEM. p 103.
Rowland, K. THE SHAPE OF TOWNS. p 17.
Ruchelman, L. I. (ed.) BIG CITY MAYORS. p 103.
Rudnick, R. IN THE HEART OF OUR CITY. p 249.
Rudofsky, B. ARCHITECTURE WITHOUT ARCHITECTS. p 79.
Rudofsky, B. STREETS FOR PEOPLE. p 74.
Russell, J. C. MEDIEVAL REGIONS AND THEIR CITIES. p 23.
Ruste, R. G. AMERICAN HERITAGE. p 66.
Rutledge, A. J. ANATOMY OF A PARK. p 274.

S
Saalman, H. MEDIEVAL ARCHITECTURE. p 75.
Saalman, H. MEDIEVAL CITIES. p 16, 23.
Saalman, H. HAUSSMANN. p 17, 27.
Saarinen, E. THE CITY. p 7.
Safdie, M. BEYOND HABITAT. p 74.
Sandstrom, G. E. MAN THE BUILDER. p 76.
S.C.E.P. MAN'S IMPACT ON THE GLOBAL ENVIRONMENT. p 118.
Schaffer, A. WOODRUFF. p 95.
Schaller, L. E. IMPACT OF THE FUTURE. p 66.
Schlesinger, A. M. THE RISE OF THE CITY. p 27.
Schlivek, L. B. MAN IN METROPOLIS. p 90.
Schmandt, H. J. (ed.) THE QUALITY OF URBAN LIFE. p 43.
Schmid, A. A. CONVERTING LAND FROM RURAL TO URBAN USES. p 108.
Schneider, K. R. AUTOKIND VS. MANKIND. p 81.
Schneider, W. BABYLON IS EVERYWHERE. p 10.
Schnore, L. F. (ed.) SOCIAL SCIENCE AND THE CITY. p 249.
Schnore, L. F. (ed.) URBAN RESEARCH AND URBAN PLANNING. p 43.
Schnore, L. F. THE URBAN SCENE. p 90.
Schonfeld, O. (ed.) CITY LIFE. p 138.
Schreiber, A. F. ECONOMICS OF URBAN PROBLEMS.: AN INTRODUCTION. p 27.
Schreiber, A. F. ECONOMICS OF URBAN PROBLEMS: SELECTED READINGS. p 272.
Schreiner, J. TRANSPORTATION: THE EVOLUTION OF CANADA'S NETWORKS. p 263.
Schwartz, A. OLD CITIES AND NEW TOWNS. p 58.
Schwarz, H. PAINTING IN TOWNS AND CITIES. p 278.
Scientific American (ed.) CITIES. p 10.
Scobie, J. R. ARGENTINA. 2nd ed. p 253.
Scott, M. AMERICAN CITY PLANNING SINCE 1890. p 27.
Scranton, R. L. GREEK ARCHITECTURE. p 75.
Scullard, H. H. THE ETRUSCAN CITIES AND ROME. p 21.
Scully, V. AMERICAN ARCHITECTURE AND URBANISM. p 74.
Scully, V. MODERN ARCHITECTURE. p 75.
Seabrook, J. CITY CLOSE-UP. p 90.
Seashore, S. E. (ed.) MANAGEMENT OF THE URBAN CRISIS. p 104.
Seeley, J. R. CRESTWOOD HEIGHTS. p 95.
Segal, J. B. EDESSA. p 17.
Segal, M. WAGES IN THE METROPOLIS. p 94.
Self, P. METROPOLITAN PLANNING. p 58.
Self, P. TOWN PLANNING IN GREATER LONDON. p 56.
Senior, D. (ed.) THE REGIONAL CITY. p 58.
Sert, J. L. CAN OUR CITIES SURVIVE? p 41.
Severino, R. EQUIPOTENTIAL SPACE. p 74.
Sewell, J. UP AGAINST CITY HALL. p 270.
Seymour, W. N. Jr. (ed.) SMALL URBAN SPACES. p 41.
Shannon, L. MINORITY MIGRANTS IN THE URBAN COMMUNITY. p 265.
Sharp, D. (ed.) MANCHESTER. p 72.
Sheckley, R. THE STATUS CIVILIZATION. p 136.
Sherif, M. SOCIAL JUDGEMENT. p 90.
Sherrard, P. BYZANTIUM. p 24.
Shibir, S. G. RECENT ARAB CITY GROWTH. p 50.
Shillaber, C. A LIBRARY CLASSIFICATION FOR CITY AND REGIONAL PLANNING. p 236.
Shipman, G. A. DESIGNING PROGRAM ACTION. p 90.
Shomon, J. J. OPEN LAND FOR URBAN AMERICA. p 41.
Showers, V. THE WORLD OF FIGURES. p 236, 276.
Shvidkovsky, O. A., (ed.) BUILDING IN THE USSR, 1917-1932. p 262.
Siegan, B. H. LAND USE WITHOUT ZONING. p 249.
Silverberg, R. THE WORLD INSIDE. p 133, 136.
Simic, A. THE PEASANT URBANITIES. p 266.
Simmons, J. URBAN CANADA. p 41.
Simon, A. FACE OF POVERTY. p 108.
Sirjamaki, J. THE SOCIOLOGY OF CITIES. p 90.
Sitte, C. CITY PLANNING ACCORDING TO ARTISTIC PRINCIPLES. p 27.

Sjoberg, G.   THE PRE-INDUSTRIAL CITY.   p 17.
Skinner, B. F.   BEYOND FREEDOM AND DIGNITY.   p 232.
Smailes, A. E.   THE GEOGRAPHY OF TOWNS. 5th ed.   p 113.
Smallwood, F.   GREATER LONDON.   p 104.
Smerk, G. O. (ed.)   READINGS IN URBAN TRANSPORTATION.   p 82.
S.M.I.C.   INADVERTENT CLIMATE MODIFICATION.   p 118.
Smith, C. M.   CURIOSITIES OF LONDON LIFE.   p 243.
Smith, D. A.   ROCKY MOUNTAIN MINING CAMPS.   p 243.
Smith, D. C.   CHANGING VALUES.   p 11.
Smithson, A.   URBAN STRUCTURING.   p 74.
Sobin, D. P.   THE FUTURE OF THE AMERICAN SUBURBS.   p 52.
SOCIOLOGICAL RESOURCES FOR THE SOCIAL SCIENCES SERIES.   p 142.
Soja, E. W.   THE POLITICAL ORGANIZATION OF SPACE.   p 282.
Soleri, P.   ARCOLOGY.   p 7.
Soleri, P.   THE SKETCHBOOKS OF PAOLO SOLERI.   p 7.
Sollers, A.   OURS IS THE EARTH.   p 133.
Sommer, R.   DESIGN AWARENESS.   p 267.
Sommer, R.   PERSONAL SPACE.   p 85, 98.
Sordo, E.   MOORISH SPAIN.   p 55.
Spatt, B. M.   A PROPOSAL TO CHANGE THE STRUCTURE OF CITY PLANNING.   p 248.
Speizman, M. D. (ed.)   URBAN AMERICA IN THE TWENTIETH CENTURY.   p 27.
Spelt, J.   TORONTO.   p 255.
Spelt, J.   URBAN DEVELOPMENT IN SOUTH CENTRAL ONTARIO.   p 249.
Spiegel, E.   NEW TOWNS IN ISRAEL.   p 47.
Spinrad, N.   BUGJACK BARRON.   p 133, 136.
Spreiregen, P. A. (ed.)   ON THE ART OF DESIGNING CITIES.   p 58.
Spreiregen, P. A.   URBAN DESIGN.   p 41, 74.
Spyer, G.   ARCHITECT AND COMMUNITY.   p 74.
Stamp, L. D.   APPLIED GEOGRAPHY.   p 113.
Stanbeck, T. M.   THE METROPOLITAN ECONOMY.   p 108.
Starr, R.   URBAN CHOICES. (also titled THE LIVING END.)   p 41.
Stedman, M. S. Jr.   URBAN POLITICS.   p 270.
Stein C. S.   TOWARD NEW TOWNS FOR AMERICA.   p 47.
Stein, D. L.   TORONTO FOR SALE.   p 270.
Stein, M.   THE ECLIPSE OF COMMUNITY.   p 95.
Steinitz, C.   A SYSTEMS ANALYSIS MODEL OF URBANIZATION AND CHANGE . . .   p 127.
Stephenson, C.   BOROUGH AND TOWN.   p 23.
Stevens, L. C.   EST: THE STEERSMAN HANDBOOK.   p 66.
Stewart, M. (ed.)   THE CITY.   p 249.
Stone, L. O.   URBAN DEVELOPMENT IN CANADA.   p 121.
Stone, T. R.   BEYOND THE AUTOMOBILE.   p 82.
Storm, M.   URBAN GROWTH IN BRITAIN.   p 41.
Strauss, A. L. (ed.)   THE AMERICAN CITY.   p 27.
Strauss, E.   NUREMBERG IN THE 16TH CENTURY.   p 15, 25.
Strauss, L.   THE CITY AND MAN.   p 17, 138.
Strong, A. L.   PLANNING URBAN ENVIRONMENTS.   p 47.
Stulman, J.   EVOLVING MANKIND'S FUTURE.   p 66.
Stycos, J. M.   CHILDREN OF THE BARRIADA.   p 97.
Summerson, J.   THE LONDON BUILDING WORLD OF THE EIGHTEEN-SIXTIES.   p 244.
Sutcliffe, A.   THE AUTUMN OF CENTRAL PARIS.   p 244.
Suttles, G.   THE SOCIAL CONSTRUCTION OF COMMUNITIES.   p 248.
Suttles, G.   THE SOCIAL ORDER OF THE SLUM.   p 265.
Sutter, R. E.   THE NEXT PLACE YOU COME TO.   p 235.
Swann, W.   LOST CITIES OF ASIA.   p 55.
Swanson, B. E.   THE CONCERN FOR COMMUNITY.   p 90.
Swanson, G. E.   SOCIAL CHANGE.   p 91.
Swartz, R. D. (ed.)   METROPOLITAN AMERICA.   p 273, 276.
Swatridge, L. A.   THE BOSNYWASH MEGALOPOLIS.   p 41.
Swatridge, L. A.   PROBLEMS OF THE BOSNYWASH MEGALOPOLIS.   p 42.
Sweet, L. E. (ed.)   PEOPLE AND CULTURES OF THE MIDDLE EAST, VOLUME 2.   p 97.
Sweetser, F. L.   STUDIES IN AMERICAN URBAN SOCIETY.   p 91.

T

Taylor, N.   THE VILLAGE IN THE CITY.   p 250.
Taylor, G.   URBAN GEOGRAPHY.   p 113.
Taylor, J. L. (ed.)   PLANNING FOR URBAN GROWTH.   p 248.
Tetlow, J.   HOMES, TOWNS AND TRAFFIC. 2nd ed.   p 42.
Theobald, R.   HABIT AND HABITAT.   p 275.
Theobald, R.   FUTURES CONDITIONAL.   p 258.
Thernstrom, S., (ed.)   19TH CENTURY CITIES.   p 244.
THIS BEAUTIFUL WORLD SERIES.   p 59.
Thomas, B.   MIGRATION AND URBAN DEVELOPMENT.   p 244.
Thomas, D.   LONDON'S GREEN BELT.   p 59.
Thomas, D. St. J.   THE RURAL TRANSPORTATION PROBLEM.   p 84.
Thomas, S.   COMPUTERS.   p 127.
Thomlinson, R.   URBAN STRUCTURE.   p 7.
Thompson, W. R.   A PREFACE TO URBAN ECONOMICS.   p 108.
Thoreau, H. D.   WALDEN.   p 137.
Tietze, F. J. (ed.)   THE CHANGING METROPOLIS.   p 42.
Tinbergen, J.   DEVELOPMENT PLANNING   p 47.
Toffler, A.   FUTURE SHOCK.   p 66.
Toffler, A., (ed.)   THE FUTURISTS.   p 259.
Toynbee, A. (ed.)   CITIES OF DESTINY.   p 59.
Toynbee, A.   CITIES ON THE MOVE.   p 17.
Trachtenberg, A. (ed.)   THE CITY.   p 139.

Tretten, R. W. (ed.) CITIES IN CRISIS. p 42.
Troedsson, C. B. ARCHITECTURE, URBANISM AND SOCIO-POLITICAL DEVELOPMENTS... p 18.
Troedsson, C. B. THE GROWTH OF THE WESTERN CITY . . . p 23.
Tunnard, C. AMERICAN SKYLINE. p 18.
Tunnard, C. THE CITY OF MAN. p 42.
Tunnard, C. MAN MADE AMERICA. p 42, 82.
Tunnard, C. THE MODERN AMERICAN CITY. p 18.
Turner, J. F. C. (ed.) FREEDOM TO BUILD. p 260.
Turner, P. M. TOWNS. p 113.
Turner, R. (ed.) ROBERT E. PARK . . . p 93.
Tyrwhitt, J. (ed.) THE HEART OF THE CITY. p 42, 243.

U
U.S.G.P.O. THE FREEWAY IN THE CITY. p 82.
University of Amsterdam. URBAN CORE AND INNER CITY. p 59, 243.
URBAN AFFAIRS ANNUAL REVIEW. p 42.
Urban, G. R. (ed.) CAN WE SURVIVE OUR FUTURE. p 259.
Urban Studies Project. THE TEACHER AND THE CITY. p 7.

V
Vallentine, H. R. WATER IN THE SERVICE OF MAN. p 118.
Van Cleef, E. CITIES IN ACTION. p 43.
Vass, B. TORONTO. p 59.
Venetoulis. I. (ed.) UP AGAINST THE URBAN WALL. p 43.
Vermilye, D. (ed.) THE FUTURE IN THE MAKING. p 259.
Vernon, R. METROPOLIS 1985. p 94.
Vernon, R. THE MYTH AND REALITY OF OUR URBAN PROBLEMS. p 43.
Vidich, A. J. SMALL TOWN IN MASS SOCIETY. p 95.
Visscher, Hollar and de Witt's LONDON BEFORE THE FIRE. p 242, 276.
Vitruvius. THE TEN BOOKS OF ARCHITECTURE. p 76.
Von Eckardt, W. THE CHALLENGE OF MEGALOPOLIS. p 95.
Von Eckardt, W. A PLACE TO LIVE. p 74.
Von Hertzen, H. BUILDING A NEW TOWN. p 47.

W
Wade, M. (ed.) THE INTERNATIONAL MEGALOPOLIS. p 43.
Wade, R. C. THE URBAN FRONTIER. p 27.
Wager, W. W. BUILDING THE CITY OF MAN. p 250.

Wager, W. W. THE CITY OF MAN. p 91.
Wakstein, A. M. (ed.) THE URBANIZATION OF AMERICA. p 18.
Waley, D. THE ITALIAN CITY REPUBLICS. p 23.
Walker, C. R. (ed.) TECHNOLOGY, INDUSTRY, AND MAN. p 125.
Wall, D. VISIONARY CITIES. p 64.
Wall Street Journal. HERE COMES TOMORROW. p 66.
Wallace, D. A. METROPOLITAN OPEN SPACE AND NATURAL PROCESS. p 43.
Wallia, C. S. (ed.) TOWARD CENTURY 21. p 66.
Walsh, A. H. THE URBAN CHALLENGE TO GOVERNMENT. p 104.
Walsh, A. H. URBAN GOVERNMENT IN THE PARIS REGION. p 103.
Ward, D. CITIES AND IMMIGRANTS. p 113.
Walsh, C. FROM UTOPIA TO NIGHTMARE. p 137.
Ward, S. A. URBAN PLANNING AND ARCHITECTURE. p 43.
Ward Perkins, J. B. CITIES OF ANCIENT GREECE AND ITALY. p 239, 240.
Warmington, B. H. CARTHAGE. p 21.
Warner, S. B. (ed.) PLANNING FOR A NATION OF CITIES. p 91.
Warner, W. L. YANKEE CITY. p 95.
Warren, R. L. THE COMMUNITY IN AMERICA 2nd ed. p 271.
Warren, R. L. (ed.) PERSPECTIVES ON THE AMERICAN COMMUNITY. p 44.
Warren, R. L. STUDYING YOUR COMMUNITY. p 68.
Watson, E. W. COURSE IN PENCIL SKETCHING, BOOK 1 AND 2. p 139.
Watson, E. W. PERSPECTIVE FOR SKETCHES. p 139.
Watson, W. EARLY CIVILIZATION IN CHINA. p 19.
Weaver, R. C. DILEMMAS OF URBAN AMERICA. p 44.
Weaver, R. C. THE URBAN COMPLEX. p 91.
Webber, E. ESCAPE TO UTOPIA. p 137.
Webber, M. L. EXPLORATIONS INTO URBAN STRUCTURE. p 250.
Weber, A. GROWTH OF CITIES IN THE NINETEENTH CENTURY. p 28.
Webber, M. THE CITY. p 18.
Wechsberg, J. PRAGUE. p 60.
Weidner, C. H. WATER FOR A CITY. p 274.
Weinberg, S. K. SOCIAL PROBLEMS IN MODERN URBAN SOCIETY. p 264.
Weiner, M. (ed.) MODERNIZATION. p 44.
Wells, H. G. A MODERN UTOPIA. p 137.
Wells, H. G. THE SHAPE OF THINGS TO COME. p 136.
Westoff, C. F. FAMILY GROWTH IN METROPOLITAN AMERICA. p 274.
Whalen, R. J. A CITY DESTROYING ITSELF. p 256.
Wheaton, W. L. C. (ed.) URBAN HOUSING. p 78.
Wheeler, Michael (ed.) THE RIGHT TO HOUSING. p 78.
Wheeler, Mortimer. CIVILIZATIONS OF THE INDUS VALLEY AND BEYOND. p 19.

Whiffen, M. (ed.)   THE ARCHITECT AND THE CITY.   p 74.
Whitaker, B.   PARKS FOR PEOPLE.   p 44.
White, B.   SOURCE BOOK OF PLANNING INFORMATION.   p 236.
White, M.   THE INTELLECTUAL VERSUS THE CITY.   p 138.
Whitehall, W. M.   BOSTON.   p 28.
Whittick, A. (ed.)   ENCYCLOPEDIA OF URBAN PLANNING.   p 237.
Whyte, W. H.   THE LAST LANDSCAPE.   p 44.
Whyte, W. H.   THE ORGANIZATION MAN.   p 91.
Wiebenson, D.   TONY GARNIER.   p 17, 28, 77.
Wiener, N.   CYBERNETICS.   p 125.
Wilhelm, S. M.   URBAN ZONING AND LAND USE THEORY.   p 44.
Willbern, Y.   THE WITHERING AWAY OF THE CITY.   p 104.
Williams, B.   URBAN GOVERNMENT FOR METROPOLITAN LAGOS.   p 103.
Williams, E. A.   OPEN SPACE.   p 68.
Williams, E. W. Jr. (ed.)   THE FUTURE OF AMERICAN TRANSPORTATION.   p 82.
Williams, M.   NEW TOWNS.   p 48.
Williams, O. P. (ed.)   DEMOCRACY IN URBAN AMERICA. 2nd ed.   p 104.
Williams, O. P.   FOUR CITIES.   p 104.
Williams, O.P.   METROPOLITAN POLITICAL ANALYSIS.   p 104.
Williams, O. P.   SUBURBAN DIFFERENCES . . .   p 60.
Wilson, F.   ARCHITECTURE.   p 69.
Wilson, J. Q. (ed.)   CITY POLITICS AND PUBLIC POLICY.   p 104.
Wilson, J. Q.   THE METROPOLITAN ENIGMA.   p 251.
Wilson, J. Q. (ed.)   URBAN RENEWAL.   p 70.
Wilson, W. H.   LIFE ON PARADISE ISLAND.   p 129.
Wingo, L. (ed.)   CITIES AND SPACE.   p 44.
Winter, E.   URBAN AREAS.   p 44.
Winter, E.   URBAN LANDSCAPES.   p 44.
Wisniewski, R. (ed.)   TEACHING ABOUT THE CITY.   p 276.
Wolfe, R.   TRANSPORTATION AND POLITICS.   p 73.
Wolforth, J.   URBAN PROSPECTS.   p 45.
Wolpert, J.   METROPOLITAN NEIGHBOURHOODS.   p 282.
Wood, R. C.   1400 GOVERNMENTS.   p 94.
Wooley, L.   DIGGING UP THE PAST.   p 20.
Wooley, L.   UR OF THE CHALDEES.   p 20.
Worskett, R.   THE CHARACTER OF TOWNS.   p 70.
Wright, F. L.   THE LIVING CITY.   p 67.
Wright, W. D. C.   THE EXPLODING CITY.   p 251.
Wu, N. I.   CHINESE AND INDIAN ARCHITECTURE.   p 75.
Wurman, R. S.   MAN MADE PHILADELPHIA.   p 256.
Wycherley, R. E.   HOW THE GREEKS BUILT CITIES.   p 22.
Wylie, P.   THE END OF THE DREAM.   p 277.

Y
Yeates, M. H.   THE NORTH AMERICAN CITY.   p 11.
Young, M.   THE RISE OF THE MERITOCRACY.   p 136.
Yin, R. N. (ed.)   THE CITY IN THE SEVENTIES.   p 91.

Z
Zamiatin, E.   WE.   p 137.
Zevin, J.   LAW AND THE CITY.   p 279.
Zucker, P.   TOWN AND SQUARE . . .   p 18.
n.a.   THE ARCHITECTURE OF PAUL RUDOLPH.   p 246.
n.a.   THE GRAND PANORAMA OF LONDON FROM THE THAMES.   p 238, 253.

Ref
Z
7164
U7
B75

DEC 19 1979